THE INCONSPICUOUS GOD

INDIANA SERIES IN THE PHILOSOPHY OF RELIGION

Merold Westphal, Editor

THE INCONSPICUOUS GOD

Heidegger, French Phenomenology, and the Theological Turn

Jason W. Alvis

Indiana University Press

This book is a publication of

Indiana University Press
Office of Scholarly Publishing
Herman B Wells Library 350
1320 East 10th Street
Bloomington, Indiana 47405 USA

iupress.indiana.edu

Manufactured in the United States of America

Library of Congress Cataloging-in-Publication Data

Names: Alvis, Jason W., author.
Title: The inconspicuous God : Heidegger, French phenomenology, and the theological turn / Jason W. Alvis.
Description: Bloomington : Indiana University Press, 2018. | Series: Indiana series in the philosophy of religion | Includes bibliographical references and index.
Identifiers: LCCN 2018011094 (print) | LCCN 2018003891 (ebook) | ISBN 9780253033338 (ebook) | ISBN 9780253033321 (hc : alk. paper)
Subjects: LCSH: Philosophy and religion—France. | God. | Phenomenology. | Philosophy, French. | Phenomenological theology. | Heidegger, Martin, 1889–1976.
Classification: LCC BL51 (print) | LCC BL51 .A53 2018 (ebook) | DDC 211—dc23 LC record available at https://lccn.loc.gov/2018011094

1 2 3 4 5 23 22 21 20 19 18

Contents

Acknowledgments

Many individuals and institutions have contributed to bringing this book about. First to be acknowledged is the outstanding editorial team at Indiana University Press, namely Dee Mortensen, Merold Westphal, and Paige Rasmussen, who have continuously supported the project from start to finish. Next, there are a number of research institutes that hosted me during my time of writing selections of this work, and they each provided substantive resources to complete such a task: the Philosophy Faculty at the University of Vienna, the Philosophy/Religious Studies Departments at Stanford University, and the Institut für die Wissenschaften vom Menschen (The Institute for Human Sciences). Further, the generous support of the Austrian Science Fund (FWF) has provided financial assistance through three research grants: "Religion beyond Myth and Enlightenment," the EU bilateral FWF-SRA project "The Return of Religion as a Challenge to Thought," and more recently, "Secularism and Its Discontents: Toward a Phenomenology of Religious Violence."

There also are a number of individuals who have encouraged me in my work over the years. I would like to thank Jean-Luc Marion, whose work in phenomenology has furnished a means of seeing more clearly a way through the problems that here are introduced, and whose support as a teacher has been a lasting source of inspiration. A number of other colleagues deserve significant recognition for helping me work through earlier drafts of the manuscript: Frank Seeburger, Thomas Sheehan, Michael Staudigl, Carl Raschke, J. Aaron Simmons, and Ludger Hagedorn. Finally, I would like to thank my wife, Julia Alvis-Seidel, not only for her patience and support during the long process of writing this book, but also for her corrections of my occasionally sloppy German grammar.

THE INCONSPICUOUS GOD

Inconspicuous Turns: Heidegger and the "Inapparent" Theological Turn

When they [the French] think, they speak in German.

—Heidegger[1]

I wish I had not written my "Zarathustra" in German . . .
I wish I had written it in French.

—Nietzsche[2]

God is not a spectacle. While at first this proposition may seem easy enough to accept, its basic tendency is taken for granted far too often, as it goes presumed that the phenomenality, givenness, or revelation of God necessarily is (or would be) spectacular. Recent postmodern theory reflects this pseudo-Christian characterization of revelation, that life is staked on almighty events that must shock and awe us with entertained assuredness and splendor. The greater degree the spectacle, we are implicit to believe, the more sacred an event becomes and the closer to divinity it presents itself. Yet an insistence on the seemingly opposite of the spectacle of God, *in nuce*, that God is hidden and enigmatically inconceivable, presents more problems than it does solutions to this concern. The proposition that God is inconceivable runs the risk of leaving God unthinkable and—despite all well-meaning hopes to the opposite—therefore reducible to a static idol that conjures only a liminal or provisionary sense of wonder. Reference to such an unthinkable God unfortunately can instill an even greater degree of passivity, inadvertently circling-back to an even more vicious spectacularity. Both the spectacle of God and the pure inconceivability of God could be reduced to the same basic generative belief and anticipation: the phenomenality of God must operate according to a spectacular and bedazzling clarity.

Instead, Divine phenomenality is counterspectacular, revolts against the many spectacles of our present social imaginaries by integrating within them as marginal to the point of even conjuring an attitude of ambivalence. Such givenness is not univocally mysterious or hidden, but is shrouded uniquely in the measure according to that which or who it intends to present and characterize. This God may be found where a spectacular phenomenality is suspended in favor of banality and ordinariness. Such a character trait could be seen as a corrective and shift from the dominant paradigms of understanding God (e.g., invisible and visible, supernatural and natural, present and absent) and toward one that experiences divinity as that which actively destabilizes any presumptions that there is but one, univocal form of phenomenality or presentation.

Whatever slips conscious grasping as marginal and ordinary, and is integrated within the hustle and grind of everyday life is inconspicuous—thus, in following the root *conspicere* is *counter-specere*. Inconspicuousness characterizes what is like a wallflower, fully present yet quickly overlooked by merit of not immediately seeming illustrious. As the German *Unscheinbarkeit* indicates, inconspicuousness is irreducible to visibility or invisibility (*Unsichtbarkeit*). It alludes the grasp of consciousness while still presenting an intelligibility and draws from the privation of its root *schein*, a license, ticket, or warrant (e.g., *Der Fahrschein*, "travel ticket") that references a thing's status as candor or trustworthy.[3] It is not simply—as many have rendered it in French—*l'inapparent*, but is instead *un peu frappant* or *peu en évidence* by merit of not being striking or presenting its evidence on command, and by operating in the peripheries of consciousness. It is in these senses that God can be thought as inconspicuous.

This book seeks to accomplish four primary aims through a phenomenological approach. One involves the constructive development of what Heidegger briefly and somewhat ambiguously referred to as a "phenomenology of the inconspicuous," which, if successful, would be a means of experiencing more deeply that which does not attract attention, yet counteracts the privileged *form* of presentation today in an era of social phantasm, illusion, and spectacle.[4] The book takes seriously Feuerbach's claim that "anthropology is the secret of theology," and attempts to get beyond how our Debordian "society of the spectacle" has helped fashion also a spectacle of God's phenomenality.[5] It of course is common knowledge that today's Western societies are commodity and spectacle driven. From Hollywood to Wall Street, spectacles seek to command our attention, and we therefore remain aware of the need to limit our intake of them. However, it largely has gone unrecognized that phenomenological and theological thinking also may suffer from their implicit reliance on forms of givenness that are *in nuce* spectacular, operating with an unrecognizable formation and totalizing education as to what is of value by merit of privileging and relying on matrixes of opposition germane to spectacularity. This kind of formation, which throughout the book is referred to as a "spectacular phenomenality," disguises its operations, relies on its own secret theological devices, and feeds the habitual privileging of what is distinct, branded, and obvious, thereby entailing the autorejection of what is common, insignificant, or marginal.

A second aim is to describe in greater detail the generative relation between Heidegger and those phenomenologists in France associated with the "Theological

Turn." The book does so by describing and contextualizing Heidegger's—at times ambiguous—development of inconspicuousness alongside investigations into Henry's autoaffective life, Lacoste's liturgy, Marion's revelation, Nancy's adoration, Levinas's Other, and Chrétien's hope—some fundamental concepts unique to this movement. It was Janicaud's harsh critique in 1991 that Heidegger's approach to the inapparent or inconspicuous (which is not a central concept in Heidegger's works) was precisely the corrupt core on which these thinkers relied for warrant to use phenomenology for theological agendas.[6] Since then, secondary scholarship only has continued to reiterate uncritically Janicaud's claim without a careful treatment of this concept, and whether or not Janicaud was right. Here, inconspicuousness is employed as an investigative lever for probing more deeply into some of the essential concepts each of the prominent figures in this movement have contributed to phenomenological theology. In this sense, the book seeks to understand better Heidegger's phenomenology, and how aspects of inconspicuousness are imbedded implicitly within the work of those associated with the Theological Turn.

A third aim, which often is less explicit, is to employ inconspicuousness to issue a challenge within phenomenology to retrieve evidences unique to the description of religious experiences, and to do so in a way that resists a number of matrixes of opposition inherent within it, such as the twin extremes of: (a) an autodilution of phenomenology into epistemology (which abandons entirely Husserl's calls for phenomenology to be first philosophy); and (b) the entrapment of a subjective fideism beholden to a solipsistic, warrantless, and private theatre of consciousness. This dichotomy furnishes an index of questionability as to whether or not phenomenology, the method that prides itself on presuppositionless descriptions of what appears clearly, is to autoreject whatever does not present itself as obvious in this world. *Phainesthai*, from which phenomenology's namesake is derived, concerns what is made-to-open or is open-able (*öffen-bar*) in this world, and what shines or burns (*Phaeithein*, IPE root *bhā*) in its being obvious and illuminated (related to the Greek *phōs*). If phenomenology cannot provide some way of at least paying closer attention to the phenomenality of theological life, then this method is diminished from adding anything new to what the ontic sciences of theology already are capable of providing with their own hermeneutic devices. To offer something new for theological thinking, a phenomenology of the inconspicuous would hope to provide a means of being more closely attuned to how things dynamically alter their state in the vicissitudes of consciousness neither as present, nor absent, but as present-absent, oftentimes making the world itself a phenomenon up for description. This could be a path to thinking religious experiences, and while it is no new development to discuss the unique evidence inherent within such experiences, in this case inconspicuousness is employed to furnish more specificity as to how such a type of evidence could overcome dogmatic dichotomies and prejudices held between what does and what does not get illuminated or "shine" in the way most other phenomena do.

The fourth, and most constructive aim of the book is to use this developed notion of inconspicuousness to take the work of each of these thinkers one small step further toward describing the phenomenality of God, which is claimed here to be just as important as the content or character traits of God. One of the most relied on half-truths of phenomenology (the insistence on which amounts to a falsehood) is that it seeks to provide only pedantic and painstakingly detailed descriptions of an experienced phenomenon. Perhaps more fundamentally, it concerns also "the how" of that phenomenon's appearance, as the suspension (*epoché*) suspends also one's running thesis about a thing's givenness or coming-into-appearance. The book ultimately arrives at the argument that one of the forms of the phenomenality of God can be described as inconspicuous, or put otherwise, that inconspicuousness is an essential means by which God "gives Godself." It of course is nothing new, and indeed *au courant* to insist that extremities within religious thought are to be torn down, unraveled, or mediated in the name of good, hermeneutically honest thinking. While this book does not run antithetical to this tendency, there are only a few exceptions today in which the how or form of such alternative paradigms are described, not to mention some practical tactics by which it is possible to arrive at an experience of them. Although the notion of the inconspicuous God seeks to negotiate some of the aforementioned matrices of opposition that entrap theological thinking today, it seeks to do so in a way that goes beyond mere mediation.

Each chapter demonstrates how inconspicuousness can provide another tool or means by which the many dichotomies that polarize and entrap theological thinking and cloud our vision of Divine phenomenality today might be rethought. Since the hoped-for result of this book is not only a hermeneutic interpretation of inconspicuousness, but also a constructive development of it after Heidegger, such an approach may be of use, not only for phenomenologists of religion, but for anyone in search of a new topography to describe religious experience beyond the many, half-true oppositions on which we so easily rely. While the topic of inconspicuousness bears a conceptual unity throughout the book, each of the following chapters furnishes a different axis or angle of inconspicuousness. Each chapter also contributes another means by which Heidegger's usages of, and allusions to inconspicuousness (found throughout the *Gesamtausgabe* in lectures, seminars, and implicitly in *Sein und Zeit*) might be understood more closely according to Heidegger's overall interests, even though this concept is not central to his work. The aim is not to conflate this concept to being a central one for Heidegger, but to use it heuristically to engage more deeply certain aspects of his thought that point the way to a phenomenological theology.

Chapters

Chapter 1 introduces an inconspicuous revelation that is paraglorious by building out and extending Heidegger's actively counterconceptual, mysterious, and self-concealing nature of Being alongside Marion's notion that revelation is a phenomenon that phenomenalizes by countering other modes of givenness. How do the mysteries of revelation phenomenalize paradoxically in this counter movement? Despite Marion's attendance to revelation as an inherently paradoxical phenomenon that phenomenalizes, the phenomenality of revelation as a paradox remains in need of development beyond a spectacular nature. If no means is only a means (as Anders repeatedly insisted), and if revelation is the paradox of paradoxes as Marion remains convinced, then revelation also is in need of description as a *counterphenomenality*.[7] The status of revelation being only eventful, shocking, and bedazzling runs the risk of contradicting revelation's paradoxical quality. Although Saul was knocked to the ground and spoken audibly to by Christ, most revelations occur to ordinary people in everyday life.

Heidegger understood that eventhood itself usually is inconspicuous and therefore nonspectacular. For most religious individuals, religious moments are presented less through shock and awe, and more through the mundane pots and pans as St. Teresa of Avila knew. This points to how revelation must provide a countershock that disrupts the preference for spectacular phenomenality, to which any dismissal of poor or common law phenomena would seem to auto-justify. If it is to be paradoxical, being-given in a way that one least expects, then must not revelation's phenomenality be understood also as running counter to the shiny brilliance of a spectacular phenomenality?

In chapter 2, a step is taken back from religious reflection to investigate more closely Heidegger's inconspicuous phenomenology. After turning to references to the *Phänomenologie des Unscheinbaren* in his last seminar in Zähringen in 1973, it is argued that there are three possible (though not necessarily conflicting) interpretations of such an approach. It could be that whatever is inconspicuous is interwoven within all forms of appearing (*scheinbar*) as an active characteristic or form of hiddenness (Λήθη, *lethe*), especially because for Heidegger the a priori of appearance never can be brought fully to light or manifestation. It also is possible to treat this approach as a particular step or reduction that involves one's becoming attuned to the various modes of potential hiddenness (*Verborgenheit* and its cognates), of which inconspicuousness is a particular form. Or it may be that there are particular, unique, and specific phenomena that give themselves inconspicuously, which entails also a corresponding, particular phenomenology in which one must engage to gain access to these specific things' phenomenal strata.

Is it possible for phenomenology (which often is conceived either to command phenomena into illuminative presentation or to disregard those that cannot do so) to be employed in studying phenomena that present themselves as unshiny, dull, or nonobvious, and does Heidegger supply us with a type of phenomenological experiencing that is irreducible to apprehension and totalizing comprehension? The chapter brings these interpretations into the context of Heidegger's generally understood interests as developed throughout his career, puts forward a proposal for how this somewhat precarious term of inconspicuousness might be handled, and then sets the stage for the remainder of the book's more theologically oriented reflections.

Is there a horizon of givenness irreducible to the glory of the world, and could it be understood without reverting to the totalizing notions of invisibility and incomprehensibility? Chapter 3 aims to demonstrate an inconspicuous religious lifeworld, and does so in three steps. First, after an articulation of how Heidegger radicalizes Husserl's lifeworld and world view as the possibility of bringing the world itself into view, it is shown how Henry's conception of life can be characterized as inconspicuous, as the common and obvious give rise to immanent, autoaffective life. For Henry, living Christianly entails that life and its power of revealing is protected from being reduced to the world's horizon of illumination. Second, it is articulated how, after Heidegger and Henry, the lifeworld itself is infused with inconspicuous life, which furnishes access points to the phenomenality of the world.

These first two steps lead to the third, more constructive demonstration that there is a religious world of life, in which one might actively engage to set a kind of condition for the experience of the Inconspicuous God. This world of life is brought about through a turn to various conflictive tensions between life and world, the response to which is inherently religious, or the core of religious experiencing. The inherent challenge, to which inconspicuousness hopefully provides some solutions, consists of deprivileging the world's Godlike neutrality, which allows ontotheology to return with an even greater vengeance through relying on pure incomprehensibility, which seems to be but the backside of what Henry pejoratively thought to be the reign of the visible. A central task of living religiously is a carburetion of the tensions between seemingly invisible life and a purportedly obvious and neutral world in a—nondichotomous—way so the pragmatic clarity and totalizing effects of the world are distorted.

Chapter 4 develops an inconspicuous liturgy in response to the question: how can the dwelling of the inconspicuous God be characterized? Here a relatively late figure on the scene of the "French Theological Turn," Jean-Yves Lacoste, is turned to for his unique development of a liturgical reduction, which can suspend and bracket the horizon of the world's forms of experiencing, thereby lending to something *before* a conscious grasping. Lacoste realizes both that perception can grasp simultaneously the visible and the invisible and that there is a necessity of conceiving (without mastering) the place of the Absolute beyond such conscious grasping. Liturgy (*esse coram deo*, being before God), is an intranscendental experience that puts the being-in-the-world of humanity at risk and exacerbates our sense of the uncanny or not-being-at-home.

Yet there are a few problematic interpretations of Heidegger within Lacoste's work (the reduction of *Dasein* to "being-there," the straw man of an atheistic Heidegger, and the simplification of the staticity of Heidegger's being-in-the-world), and these interpretations are employed here as thematic springboards to apply a deeper analysis of Heidegger's work to Lacoste's liturgy, ultimately arriving at an inconspicuous liturgical reduction. Lacoste helps disorient the totality of place through his unique reduction, and Heidegger's domain of the inconspicuous points to a dwelling that is paradoxically the most familiar to us. It then becomes a matter of synthesizing these notions toward an investigation into the dwelling (as being-in, subsistence, living) or space of Godhood as it relates to the humanity of man. As Heidegger knew, whatever is closest to us always and naturally becomes the furthest away, and an inconspicuous liturgical reduction can help us turn to that which always already is *there-in* in its overfamiliarity.

Attempting to access the overly familiar does not entail bringing it to clarity, for clarity is never a character trait that makes something worthy of adoration. Chapter 5 develops an inconspicuous adoration, reframing the *what* of Augustine's question "What do I adore when I adore my God?" to consider the *how* or formation of God. This is accomplished through placing Nancy's notions of adoration and differentiation alongside Heidegger's developments of disclosure and truth. Nancy lays out some necessary conditions for what makes something worthy of adoration, which is not accomplished via appropriation but rather truth as dis-en-closure (an update on Heidegger's "disclosure," *Entbergen*), an expression of being-appropriated-by, namely by what he calls a divinity of pure differentiation (*Adoration: The Deconstruction of Christianity II*). God is capable of differentiating by passing into withdrawal and thereby drawing attention to a productive void. Such an abyss-creating differentiation helps us set apart, adore, and become actively enraptured by what one knows is inaccessible (*sans accès*) and absent, yet with which one seeks relation nonetheless.

Yet it seems to go unnoticed by Nancy that there also exists a nightmarish kind of differentiation today that drives, through diversity, a society of spectacles and simulacra, ultimately destining subjects through enframement (Heidegger). What is necessary then is a differentiation that has the ability to hold back these simulations of infinite production and their "substitute Images of the divine" (Adorno), which create passivity. Because it is not merely a God of content or attributes that one worships, but also a *God of formation*, then adoration is directed toward what—by merit of being a framing or forming—hides in the margins and lattices of experience. Forms have the tendency to withdraw and go undetected, yet still remain effective in ordinary life. An inconspicuous adoration is developed to offer a proper address to a God that operates with such an extraordinary ordinariness.

Chapter 6 conceives of an inconspicuous evidence that might demonstrate the unique forms of legitimacy of the intelligibility of religious experiences without their being reduced to either the oversight of modern epistemology, or the gravity of a fideistic and solipsistic subjectivity that tends to characterize phenomenologies of religion. Do religious experiences furnish a presentative *Evidenz* without allowing consciousness an exacting and totalizing control over them? The root *Schein* in *Un-schein-bar* (inconspicuous) refers to "warrant," and an inconspicuous evidence operates by delegitimizing what is obvious. This chapter works out this idea in a threefold manner, beginning with the work of Dominique Janicaud, who has helped push the cautions of a phenomenology of religious experience to their necessary limit. Second, it introduces these concerns into some recent phenomenological approaches to religious experience in the works of Alston, Westphal, and Steinbock. And third, after locating within their works a red thread that helps address Janicaud's concerns, the chapter puts forward a proposal as to what such evidence could look like in the context of inconspicuousness.

Without prima facie barring miraculous or spectacularly supernatural events, religious experiences, more often than not, take place in mundane, everyday life, and this calls for a type of evidence that honors the range of finesse and subtlety of such experiences. Such evidence is a resource of privation, attests to experiences of a dynamic *potentia* (an omnipotence), is not isolatable from that or who the religious experience is intended to represent or characterize, and actively frustrates any wish to bring the experience into full clarity. Evidence usually is achieved by isolating external information relevant to the phenomenon, then applying it back to the whole context to learn something new about it. Yet an inconspicuous evidence of religious experience is achieved by locating what actively resists such isolation, precisely because the experience is substantiated by what/who operates with a uniquely effective reign and potence.

Chapter 7 addresses the potential of an inconspicuous faith and demonstrates means by which it can be understood through a lens of forgetting, which is essential to faith in its *how*. The root of truth (*a-letheia*) is *lethe*, a "forgetting" that also relates to what is latent, escapes notice (Greek *lanthanein*), or inconspicuous. There is a positive dimension of forgetting, and truth must go through the trial of loss instantiated by dememorialization. This chapter develops—out of a synthesis of the work of Heidegger and Chrétien—three ways forgetting is essential to the experience of faith. Under Chrétien's development, forgetting is a kind of active giving-up and bringing-to-truth whereby what is confidently taken to be the case is surrendered for one to be rendered open to what is absent, yet effective.

It becomes necessary to see, then, that to forget is to overcome—even positive—memories that yearn for attention. Such forgetting fuels the faith act, which is an act unlike any other, and it is achieved indirectly. As inherently interpersonal, faith cannot be coaxed through directly willing faithfulness, yet it also is not possible to have faith through nonwilling. Instead, there can be a middle voice of faith—faith faiths—via this active forgetting. Truth can actively and dynamically subsist and sustain faith through its partial veiling of the object of faith. Heidegger's reflections on forgetting and testimony, and Chrétien's notion of the unhoped for (as the French *l'inespéré* refers to a hope for what is impossible to ever dream of hoping) helps to develop this notion of faith. Such unhoping is the content of forgetting, and concerns attributing potential to what is always, already here yet latent. Forgetting supports an inconspicuous faith through instantiating the active attempt to overlook something, not in favor of something else new, but rather more radically, an interpersonal potential that has been there all along. Because faithfulness is not able to be the product of an iron will, how does it bring an unseen reality to life?

Chapter 8, inconspicuous God employs the works of Levinas and Heidegger to cut against the grains of the traditional notions of God as the luminous one (as the Proto Indo-European [PIE] *Deiwos* and *Dyeus* indicate). Such theologies have contributed to the preferred associations of manifestation with enlightenment and apparent clarity rather than with obscurity and marginality. For Descartes, the idea of infinity is a kind of appearance, and the Greek *idea* (from *idein*) originates in *opan* (to see). As Marion's well-known claim in *God without Being* sustains, this idea of Being has consequences for God's becoming an idol, *ideal, eidolon*, or *eidos*. Yet the seemingly opposite approach, to remove God from phenomenalization all together may entail equally damning effects. A reversion to a total incomprehensibility may be an inherently agnostic one that would result in the numbing of theological thinking.

Gaining inspiration from Levinas and Marion, this chapter seeks to think more carefully about the givenness of God as inconspicuous in efforts to avoid these two extremes. As Levinas knew, irrespective of whether or not one thinks there is a God, the thought of God is given [*es gibt*] in particular ways. The enigmatic character of Levinas's Other is marked by a riddle and paradox: The Other that one "cannot think" becomes experienced as the unthought. This is Levinas's God "who comes to mind" by still being able to avoid becoming a phenomenon among other phenomena.[8] The givenness of God here is thought according to two formulations (inconspicuous phenomena and inconspicuous givenness), which are developed by returning to some of the premonitions of inconspicuousness nascent in *Being and Time*. Might inconspicuousness provide one avenue on which the enigmatic phenomenality of God can be understood without reverting to the cause and effect structure that has entrapped the thought of God as *causa sui*?

Reading Heidegger in French

The remainder of this introduction lays the historical groundwork and conceptual apparatus for understanding what led-up to Heidegger's influence on those associated with the Theological Turn in French Phenomenology, and provides a general structure of what a "phenomenology of the inconspicuous" entails. These thinkers faced a variety of historical challenges: the political and social upheaval of May 1968, the demands to rethink the human condition after the holocaust, the interdisciplinary recognition of the conflict between a variety of affective and cognitive forces, and the hermeneutic challenges of an ever-increasing, technological, and modern society that separates social bonds as quickly as it forms them. In these regards, Heidegger played fundamental roles, from his anti-Cartesian and antisubjectivist challenges to Catholicism, to his seemingly humanist rhetoric. How could it be that someone such as the young, Jewish Levinas could claim that Heidegger was initiating "a new phase, and one of the high points, of the phenomenological movement"?

The extracting of an individual's ideas from the life they conduct indeed at times can be bewildering. French thinkers amassed a unique following of Heidegger despite (or perhaps even in some cases due to) Heidegger's temporary associations with the Nazi regime and his arguably anti-Semitic past; a past that has been at the center of fiery quarrels to which the recently released and controversial *Schwarze Hefte* (his little "black books") has added only more fuel. Nevertheless, Heidegger became a sort of omnipotent master figure for French philosophers, especially after World War II. France is not simply one among many lands to have developed an interest in his work, for its thinkers' engagements with and developments of his philosophical legacy have uniquely exceeded that of other countries. This is quite astonishing given the *Zeitgeist* of the twentieth century French intellectuals' *opponere* to everything that stood for the Nazi regime with its totalitarian ideologies that sought to cripple the democratic liberties of *Le grand public*. It also is odd that Heidegger achieved this status in a country that he did not visit until he was 65 in 1955, despite living only a few miles from the French border. Given such oddities, how did Heidegger come to prominence in France?[9]

First, in the midst of World War II between the 1930s and 1950s there were ongoing discussions in France concerning philosophical contextualism, and how far it is possible to dissociate ideas from their real, lived experiences.[10] This is exemplified in the engagements between the Existentialist Sartre and the Structuralist Lévi-Strauss, both of whom debated the possibilities of human freedom in the face of the political structures in which freedoms should develop and thrive. Sartre was committed to the idea that the powerful elite actively oppresses and limits the freedoms of the lower classes, while Lévi-Strauss believed the historical and social undertones of a society commit the lower class to passively surrender their freedoms. Sartre held to an atomistic understanding of the human condition that undergirded how human possibilities can at any point transform and exceed one's societal and structural limitations. Therefore, his humanism touted the freedom-instituting *potentia* of knowledge as possibly independent from the structures within which it appears so often to be problematically bound. This is one reason why Sartre, not ignorant of Heidegger's political ties, would pen *Being and Nothingness* as a humanistic development of Heidegger's *Being and Time* (although before 1939 Sartre introduces Heidegger as only "another phenomenologist").[11] Contrary to Lévi-Strauss, many like Sartre maintained an interpretation of knowledge (at points paradoxically and controversially anti-Heideggerian) as "absolute" insofar as it is not entirely tempered by historical concepts and contextual limits. For those who agreed with Sartre, knowledge was, as Rockmore put it, "in time but not of time," and Heidegger, the brilliant "wizard of thinking," was to be distinguished from Heidegger, the Nazi-rector of the University of Freiburg.[12]

Secondly, Heidegger may have been accepted into the deepest of inner-circles of French thought due to his explicit attempt to provide a new theory of the human; a never-ending French project engrained in the country's *la devise nationale* of *liberté, égalité, fraternité* since 1848. Yet after the great irrational wars (which eventually climaxed in the unfathomable Holocaust), a frenzy of rethinking even the means of the *studia humanitatis* was underwent, often undercutting the more cognitivist approaches to philosophy. Attractive about Heidegger was his conception of the human as a holistic, intersubjective being who responds to his basic nature, yet at the same time, one marked by a fundamental anxiety over that nature and being in the world. This led to a mistaken interpretation of Heidegger as the new darling of humanism.

Such a misinterpretation stems from a recognition of two successive waves of reception of Heidegger scholarship in France, the first of which began in the late 1920s, and grew strongly from Alexandre Kojève's Hegel lectures and seminars in the 1930s, which he took over from Koyré (who wrote the preface in 1931 to the French translation of "What Is Metaphysics?"). Kojève, who studied in Heidelberg under Karl Jaspers and completed his thesis in 1931, taught his seminars on Hegel from 1933–1939 at L'Ecole Pratique des Hautes Études, and along with Jean Hyppolite, initiated a new revival of Hegel studies into France. This background likely contributed to Kojève's proposal that Heidegger took up the mantle initiated by Hegel's philosophical anthropology, and in this regard Kojève was highly influential on Lévinas, Sartre, and Henry.

The second wave, however, was initiated by Heidegger himself, who wished to set the record straight that his theoretical project was not a philosophical anthropology, for it did not address in any typical fashion the sciences of being human. In his "Letter on Humanism" Heidegger called his approach a "post-metaphysical humanism" that embraces the double bind of understanding the human subject and fundamental ontology in its inconspicuous and paradoxical character: "Being is the nearest. Yet the near remains farthest from the human being."[13] This letter, written to Jean Beaufret, and in a critical response to Sartre's "L'existentialisme est un humanisme" led to the second wave's beginning to crest, especially due to the committed efforts of Beaufret to return thinkers to the phenomenological import of Heidegger's work; efforts that ultimately would influence Derrida, Lacoue-Labarthe, and the next generation of poststructuralists.

A third reason for Heidegger's reception in France is that he acted, in a way distinct from Husserl, as the *provocateur extraordinaire* of at least two of the most beloved imaginaries held by French intellectuals: the eminence of Descartes and the intelligible meaning of organized Catholic religion. Both of which, to some degree, the French were committed to more out of obligation, than of principle, and Heidegger provided occasion to stir these deep-seated commitments from their respective dogmatic slumbers. From Heidegger's view, Descartes's *solus ipse* represented the inhibition of our "access to the problem of Being," and in *Sein und Zeit* as well as the later essay "The Age of the World Picture" Descartes's subject was the object of attack, namely for its ignorance of the Greek philosophical understanding of "Being" in all its dynamic and active strata of influence. One positive relation Heidegger had with Descartes (whom he simultaneously subtlety critiqued and explicitly praised in a way that his French colleagues could embrace in the "Letter on Humanism") of course was the way in which he saw Descartes's provision of a basis for phenomenological thinking, which Husserl built upon and subsequently developed for his transcendental phenomenology.

In many respects the whipping boy of the Cartesian tradition ultimately became Husserl. Heidegger's relationship with him is well known, and the early French engagements with Husserl's work are well documented.[14] Although the early years of phenomenological reception in France began primarily with Husserl, they often developed and grew out of Heidegger's (often-implicit) engagements with Husserl in *Sein und Zeit*. Where Husserl focused on the deepening of an ego-oriented engagement with transcendental idealism, Heidegger wanted to root phenomenology in a realist yet dynamic ontology that sought an explication of the *how* of appearance for embodied, involved human beings who cannot become worldless. The blacksmith, carpenter, and shoemaker can each teach us something about what it means to relate with Being.

Despite *Sein und Zeit*'s thoroughgoing provocation and criticisms of Husserlian thought (which also contributed to Heidegger's mystique), the earliest French engagements with Heidegger still situated him in continuity with Husserl to an important degree. The first published study of Heidegger's work in France was from a lesser-known figure, Georges Gurvitch, who (although first referencing Heidegger's work in 1928) in 1930 investigated the appeal of knowledge and that appeal's role in conscious experience.[15] The second study of Heidegger's work in France came from Levinas in his 1932 article "Martin Heidegger et l'ontologie," in which Heidegger's unique innovations were praised.[16] Levinas, once a student of Husserl's in Freiburg, was beginning to recognize that phenomenology, in order to remain as such, must not be reduced to epistemology. Yet he also intuited that the turn to transcendence could be equally damning for the description of the experience of cognition due in part to a solipsistic tendency. Thus, Levinas became convinced by Heidegger's approach for its contestation of the hegemony of a Cartesian solipsistic ego, and Levinas attempted to further displace its centrality by expanding the web of a self-world relation toward an intersubjectivity that drew heavily on Heidegger's ontological turn of disclosure (*dévoilement*).[17] Reappropriating the claim of Husserl's, this culminates in Ethics as first philosophy.

As for religion, Heidegger provided the perfect engagement for whetting the appetites of the French, especially those reared on Catholic, Thomistic theology, and therefore already primed for a turn from the neoscholasticism and heady rationalism that was often seen to entrench Catholic thought in early twentieth century France. Major figures associated with the *ressourcement* (returning to the sources) of *Nouvelle Théologie* (a pejorative coined by Garrigou-Lagrange to show the inconsistences in their approaches) were some of the first in France to critically engage the work of Heidegger, who is known to have wrestled with his Roman Catholic origins until the end of his life. *Nouvelle Théologie* was influential especially between the 1930s and 1960s, and thinkers such as de Lubac, Congar, Daniélou, and Chenu (with von Balthasar and Rahner to the north in Switzerland and Germany) employed a number of critical engagements with neoscholasticism that ultimately exerted influence on the second Vatican Council.[18] Heidegger's reception among this group was mixed, ranging from enthusiastic (e.g., Rahner) to somewhat critical (Von Balthasar), yet it was becoming clear that anyone hoping to do rigorous theology would need to grapple with Heidegger's subtle yet broad philosophical engagements, which were deeply influenced by his own complicated Roman Catholic background.[19]

There was a dramatic theological shift that took place in Heidegger's thinking, even in his late 20s and before the writing of *Being and Time*, and this provided further challenge to the French intellectual scene that held to the intertwining of theology and philosophy, faith and reason. Hegel's "protestant principle" of such a separation led some to believe that Heidegger's approach had become fundamentally atheistic and one might surmise that this is likely what led Kojève (a Hegelian specialist) to consider Heidegger's work to offer the most important atheistic philosophy since Hegel.[20] It was likely this influence that contributed to Heidegger's being cast as an atheist, and thus feeding the paradox of French Philosophy that, as Rockmore put it, "predisposes it to Heidegger's antireligious philosophical theory."[21]

The idea that Heidegger was atheistic was not entirely fabricated however, and Heidegger's 1927/28 essay on philosophy and theology marks a more formal abandonment of Theology as the queen of the sciences. Yet the investigation then involves what kind of atheist Heidegger might have been. Of course, Heidegger understood that becoming an atheist likely would, as Hemming put it "decide in advance and ... foreclose any question of God."[22] A footnote tucked away in Heidegger's 1928 lecture course, *The Metaphysical Foundations of Logic*, is instructive, for in the midst of arguing against the "enormously phony religiosity" of the current intellectual climate, he claimed: "It is preferable to put up with the cheap accusation of atheism, which, if it is intended ontically, is in fact completely correct. But might not the presumably ontic faith in God be at bottom godlessness? And might the genuine metaphysician be more religious than the usual faithful, than the members of a 'church' or even the 'theologians' of every confession?"

Irrespective of Heidegger's own theology at the time, his work elicited responses that went in every direction. Sartre was inspired to reject faith while Gilson and other Thomists sought room for compromise between Heidegger and Christianity. Thinkers like Merleau-Ponty, who despite leaving faith, is often thought to have cherished aspects of a certain "Christian framework." Then in the early 1970s, Mikel Dufrenne's *Le poétique: Précédé de Pour une philosophie non théologique* embodied one of the first criticisms of those beginning to plumb phenomenology for its theological potential.[23] Amidst this swirl of confusion, however, one thing remained certain: Heidegger's often-implicit engagements with the themes germane to religious experience would shake the intellectual foundations of multiple generations of French thinkers in a way that would test the limits of both phenomenology and theology.[24]

Janicaud and the "Inconspicuous" Theological Turn in French Phenomenology

The next generation of phenomenologists in France would face a variety of historical, social, and political challenges, such as those in Paris in May 1968. Ultimately, these thinkers would do something different with Heidegger's work than previous generations: They would invert the existing paradigm by employing religious experience and conceptuality to influence and feedback into phenomenology in toto. That, at least, is a significant result of the work of the group of thinkers Dominique Janicaud pejoratively accused of initiating *Le tournant théologique de la phénomenénologie Français*. Janicaud's 1991 critique of this nascent movement is by now well documented, yet his basic claim was that the work of these thinkers involved the abuse of phenomenological language to do the science of theology, and that they were fundamentally out of the bounds Husserl had set into motion for this method in § 58 of *Ideen*. Phenomenology, concluded Janicaud, must remain a field of studying pure consciousness, otherwise the overarching goal of achieving presuppositionlessness in our descriptive enterprises is abandoned. These thinkers ignored Husserl's enterprise of constitution, operated from out of an idealist *metaphysica specialis*, and rigged the game of phenomenology by presuming an invisible hinterland that does *not* appear clearly and *obviously* to the senses.[25] Of course, the same critique can be leveled back to Janicaud, whose approach entailed, from the opposite end of the spectrum, a different kind of methodological requirement by claiming that theological concepts putatively *cannot* appear for investigation, thereby limiting phenomenology's wide-open horizon, which is supposed to remain entirely unsuspecting to thoughts as they are given.

Yet at the same time Janicaud raised reasonable caution, for it should not be taken for granted so easily that the phenomenology Husserl developed for understanding the conscious experience of things as they come in and out of one's sensual worlds can be used to justify the existence of any invisible phenomena. For Husserl, immanent reality is essenceless without a transcendental and intersubjective connection to the outside world achieved through impressions. And this leads to the golden rule of phenomenology, which is not to claim anything that we "*cannot make essentially transparent to ourselves by reference to consciousness* and on purely immanental lines."[26] The immanent, "really real" is the place and means according to which things are reduced to their most basic data. It was Heidegger who rendered the so-called limitation of immanence in Husserl's thought to be problematic, inadvertently setting the conditions for those of the so-called Theological Turn. Indeed, what is perhaps most interesting about this movement is that it was *not* generally reliant on Heidegger's religious or theological work, but rather, a certain kernel of thought within his overall phenomenological approach. Why would that be, especially because Heidegger was one of the most engaged of early phenomenological thinkers in theological thinking? What was it about Heidegger's overall approach that inspired this entire generation of thinkers to demonstrate phenomenology's viability of exfoliating anew religious and theological topoi?

Despite the defeasibility of some of Janicaud's claims, he recognized one essential aspect concerning this movement, which many have passed over: these thinkers relied on Heidegger's "phenomenology of the inapparent" or inconspicuous, which Janicaud claimed to be the topic that "places us at the crux of the matter where everything is decided: at the point of rupture" for if "the 'phenomenology of the unapparent' finally makes all rule-based presentation of the phenomena vacillate in favor of a hearkening to a world . . . a line (is) extended toward the originary, the nonvisible, the reserved." This is why if "the 'phenomenology of the unapparent' is to be interpreted not as a regression, but as full of promise, then the most audacious soundings stand permitted."[27] Despite Heidegger's keeping phenomenology and theology separate, he alone is thought to have provided warrant for these thinkers to import theology into phenomenology, and to questioning the intentionality of Husserl's approach in favor of a Dasein of windows and doors and the givenness of intuition.

Yet Janicaud never carefully explained this approach of Heidegger's, which did not formally appear until (still ambiguously) his last seminar in Zähringen in 1973. Janicaud nevertheless returned to the question of *das Unscheinbare* in 1997 in *Chronos*, claiming it complicates Husserlian time-consciousness, is irreducible to eidetic intention, and "reserves the most problematic of 'phenomenalities' in the temporal dimension."[28] Then in *Phenomenology Wide Open* (2005) he claimed that a "'phenomenology of the inapparent' is not reducible to a mere appendix to the thought of the later Heidegger" but instead inaugurates "a new meditative form of thought."[29] Although Janicaud recognized how the concept raises essential stakes and is either "an oxymoron, a supreme paradox, or a disconcerting impossibility," some serious ambiguities remain.[30]

Secondary Sources on Heidegger's "Inconspicuous"

Despite Janicaud's naming the genesis of the theological turn to be Heidegger's *Phänomenologie des Unscheinbaren*, it strangely has gone underinvestigated and glossed over for nearly 30 years, thus lending to several fast and loose interpretations. The number of ambiguous references to the concept combined with a lack of attention to Janicaud's claims (not to mention the lack of consensus on how *unscheinbar* should be translated into English) has led to a plurality of interpretations.[31] Does this sparsely referenced approach concern phenomena that are have-not-yet-appeared, have-appeared-yet-are-obscured, never-are-to-appear, or always-already-remaining-in-the-blind-spots-of-appearance? Nearly without fail, most commentators in the philosophy of religion reiterate Janicaud's claim concerning Heidegger's "inapparent" as a central point of corruption for the young phenomenologists, yet do so without careful analysis. The editors of the recent *Retreating Religion* (2012) follow Janicaud in interpreting the theological turn's engagement in the inapparent as attempts to "reintroduce absence into presence, bringing the nonapparent toward a new state of appearing."[32] Yates interprets Janicaud's view on Heidegger's "inapparent" as clearing a path for a "rendering of the other-worldly invisible."[33] Bornemark and Ruin reiterate that Janicaud's critique of this movement concerned how "its move toward the phenomenon of the inapparent was about to abandon the methodological atheism" of phenomenology.[34] Benson and Simmons endorse the view that "phenomenology, at its root, is for Heidegger an inquiry into appearance in such a radical way that it begins with a receptivity to the inapparent insofar as it allows for the apparent to then be considered according to the categories of being."[35] Gondek and the late Tengelyi recognize that Janicaud "borrowed this term from the later Heidegger" and interpret *unscheinbar* as a "non-appearing" (*Nicht-Erscheinendes*). [36]

Overall, when scholars of religion address a "phenomenology of the inconspicuous," their works raise the questions: is such an approach truly congenial to a more accurate hermeneutic of theological phenomena? Does inconspicuousness provide a basis for those of the "Theological Turn" to alter the possibilities of phenomenology *in toto*?[37] Despite recognizing the importance of this topic, scholars of religion and specialists in the theological turn often conflate (as Janicaud at points himself does) the invisible with the inconspicuous. This likely is due to the usage of the French "inapparent," which can be translated as "invisible," and therefore is far afield from the intended meaning of Heidegger's *unscheinbar* as it certainly must be distinguished from *unsichtbar* (invisible). Heidegger makes this as clear as possible: "The inconspicuous is by no means to be confused with 'the invisible' as ... philological translations incorrectly render it."[38] Heidegger's overall approach, however, concerned a much deeper, systemic rooting-out of the entrenched oppositions between the visible and invisible, and therefore references to the inconspicuous must be considered otherwise. Marion recognized this recently in 2012: "the unapparent and the invisible do not mean the same thing, despite the fact that they challenge the privilege given to the visible." This lack of clarification calls for how, as Marion continues, "this difference must be measured."[39]

From the side of Heidegger scholars, the broad consensus is that this notion can be integrated into the already existent scaffolding of Heidegger's phenomenology, and indeed goes beyond the "invisible." Peter Trawny suggests of *das Unscheinbare* that "because of its unobtrusiveness [*Unauffälligkeit*], it is overlooked [*übersehen*]," as "we walk past it without it striking our attention [*Aufmerksamkeit erregen*]. That does not mean, however, that we are not still dealing with it [*mit ihm umgehen*]."[40] Most recently (2015) Günter Figal constructively applies the notion to space, which "does not appear and is therefore inconspicuous," thereby challenging phenomenology *in toto*.[41] Although a stunning study of space, Figal's treatment of Heidegger's concept is limited to but a few pages.[42] Figal does recognize that Heidegger was the one who initiated inconspicuousness into phenomenological thinking, and that phenomena can "only be adequately understood in their unison with the inconspicuous," yet he ultimately questions if Heidegger's tautological thinking is "really a phenomenology of the inconspicuous."[43]

Other Heidegger scholars over the years have engaged only briefly the inconspicuous or inapparent. As Françoise Dastur interprets, Heidegger's "inapparent" is "the nonappearance that resides in all appearing, the event itself of apparition and the giving of being."[44] Jacques Taminiaux, who played a decisive role in the early reception of the Zähringen seminar, concludes that the coming-into-appearance of things is inconspicuous insofar as it always is transfixed with an inaccessible "excessiveness at the very heart of seeing."[45] Gonzalez conceives the inapparent to be everimbued within the experience of Being, and can "never be brought into view."[46] Jean-François Courtine argued that even within

Sein und Zeit there is already an operative inapparent that characterizes the various strata of covering and uncovering (*désocculation*). Then like Courtine, Polt recently insisted that the being of beings is not to be conceived simply as a "not yet appearing" but more specifically (especially for the later Heidegger) as "intrinsically unapparent."[47]

Overall, the majority of Heidegger scholars who have (albeit briefly) engaged this topic generally subscribe that all phenomena can be characterized according to the paradox of inconspicuousness, namely because the radical *potentia* of Being cannot be expressed directly, despite its deep relation with ordinary phenomena. Their work sparks a host of questions: Is the being (the coming-to-be or giving of the being of beings) of *Sein und Zeit* to be characterized as inconspicuous? Is such an approach to the inconspicuous a threat and radical provocation to phenomenology's investigations into only what or how things appear? Further, does this concept play any impactful role in the (especially late) thought of Heidegger, and if so how might one negotiate the somewhat ambiguous usages of the phrase "phenomenology of the inconspicuous," which was used in only one seminar, Heidegger's last, no less?

What Is Heidegger's Phenomenology of the Inconspicuous?

In general terms, throughout this work Heidegger's phenomenology of the inconspicuous will be treated as a particular way and means of experiencing phenomena as their intelligibilities oscillate over the breaches between presence and withdrawal. Whatever is inconspicuous has a distinctly unique "ability" (*barkeit*) and understood in its "paradoxical" (as "contrary to appearances") provenance, seeks to get beyond dichotomies that often hinder phenomenological thinking. It refers to what is integrated within, yet holistically impacting the everyday, and as the German adjective *unscheinbar* (traceable to the fifteenth century) refers, it does not signify by being bright (*leuchtend*), manifested (*offenbar*), brilliant (*glänzend*), or clear (*klar*). Yet it is distinguishable from what is nonvisible and is not the opposite of what *does* shine. The root *scheinbar* refers not to what is obvious, but rather what seems or appears to be the case, and when the privative *un* is paired up with this root, reference is made to how a thing's features are so obscured that even a conjecture concerning its status is not made easily. As far as any phenomenological exercise of the inconspicuous goes, it is taken for granted here that some phenomenal experiences actively evade any attempt to grasp them directly, and they indeed require a holistic vision for them to be experienced.

Some practical, visual examples can help illustrate this point. I am looking down a long path at a distant runner, and wish to know if she is running toward me or away from me. By focusing in on the runner, all I am permitted to detect are flapping legs and arms. Yet if I take a broader view, and do not look directly at the runner, but also the field of space in which she is running, then I can determine quite easily if the runner's size is increasing or decreasing, indicating to me the runner's direction. Or, let's say I am in the woods hunting birds, seeking their movement along the forest floor and trying to detect motion from multiple places at once. This is not possible through a focusing foveal vision that privileges clarity. I need a broad awareness of the field of vision, and only when I peripherate my vision am I afforded a sense of the general movement of multiple birds. Or finally, to use a more urban example, if I am trying to walk through a congested crowd as quickly as possible, I must defocus on what stands in front of me by using my cone vision to detect the regioning of the crowd and therefore negative space that constitutes the open path before me. Otherwise, I see only what is directly in front of me, and remain constantly overwhelmed by the bombardment of the stream of faces and details.

These examples merely serve to illustrate at least one of the paradoxes of inconspicuousness. An inconspicuous phenomenon furnishes enough data for the experience of it, yet in a way that eludes direct comprehension. As such, what is attributed the status of being *Un-scheinbar* also counteracts one's prevailing sense of phenomenality itself and the conditions of experience on which one relies. Although "inapparent" will be used on occasion throughout the book (especially in the context of secondary literature), *unscheinbar* generally will be translated as "inconspicuous" for it indicates this positive ability and remains freer from being immediately reduced to invisibility, an association the present study hopes to overcome.

Inconspicuousness in the 1973 Zähringen Seminar

The ambiguities of translation and lack of clear consensus concerning this concept, however, are justifiable. Heidegger's elusive description of his phenomenology of the inconspicuous did not even appear (though the word occasionally was employed) until Heidegger's last seminar, which was in Zähringen in 1973.[48] Yet when this description is contextualized in Heidegger's overall approach it becomes less obscure. It is by now well known that Heidegger often laid emphasis on the value and power of ordinary things, namely, those that resist technological efficiency and machination.[49] Shoes, hammers, tools—these seemingly insignificant things often tell us infinitely more about the mysteries of Being than do those things that are spectacular. These things are not lacking in intelligibility, but rather, precisely by merit of their easily being overlooked, retain an integrated value and worth. This remains consistent with his description of the concept in 1973: "Phenomenology is a path that leads away to come before . . . and it lets that before which it is led show itself. This phenomenology is a phenomenology of the inapparent [*Unscheinbar*]." . . . Indeed, "in conceiving [*Be-greifen*], there is the gesture of taking possession. The Greek [perspective] . . . on the contrary surrounds firmly and delicately [that] that which sight takes into view, it does not conceive."[50]

Such a phenomenology is tautological, paradoxical, and seemingly sophistical. One must follow in a "way" (*Weg*) of thinking whereby one seeks to understand, in a particular instance, one's relation with how distance creates nearness (*der hinführt vor . . . und sich das zeigen läßt*), and how this distance is the means whereby something shows or bears its intelligibility. This (*diese*, i.e., something *particular*) phenomenology is "a phenomenology of the inconspicuous."[51] The interplay between "away" (distance) and "before" (closeness) is a basic and formative mode that fundamentally influences how we experience things, and Heidegger employs it here to reveal a certain truth about presence.

The meaning of presence (or "meaningful presence") plays an indicative role in understanding that something *is*, or in phenomenological terms, taking something *as*. The present itself is given, manifested, or presences itself. How? One answer: There are modalities or laminates of presence that can be indicated without their being consciously grasped in any straightforward way. For example, despite the clear fact that one's experience of a horse is technically with the "sense data" or *hyle* of sensual intuition, one instead engages a categorial intuition to make that data intelligible. The *hyle* of hair, teeth, and hooves are all in a sense overlooked in preference of the categorial intuition of "horse" that one wishes to see. Although Heidegger first engaged the question of categorial intuition vis-à-vis sensual intuition in his 1925 lecture course *History of the Concept of Time*, it takes on a distinctly "inconspicuous" tone in 1973.

In a letter written to Roger Munier shortly after the seminar at Zähringen, Heidegger reiterated how his approach to categorial intuition is distinguishable from Husserl's (in § 2 "sense and understanding" of the 4th of *the Logical Investigations*) then claimed that "actually performing an exercise in a phenomenology of the inconspicuous [*unscheinbar*]" allows one to arrive at a unique kind of phenomenological "seeing." The use of the word "exercise" here necessitates an investigation into the "how structure" of appearance. Then, in this letter Heidegger claimed that "you can easily link this text to what particularly concerned you [Munier] in my lecture 'What is Called Thinking?'."[52] Within "What Is Called Thinking?" is a careful attendance to how one relates with the interplay between the withdrawal and arrival of phenomenal intelligibilities. How might withdrawal be give description? For Heidegger "Whatever withdraws refuses arrival. But—withdrawing is not nothing. Withdrawal is event [appropriation, *ereignis*]. In fact, what withdraws may even concern and claim man more essentially than anything present that strikes and touches him."[53] In the mid-1950s, he showed how the event (which some postmodern literature has commandeered as a spectacularly shocking experience) or "appropriation is the most inconspicuous of the inconspicuous [*Das Ereignis ist das Unscheinbarste des Unscheinbaren*]."[54] Not only are the most significant events not glamorous, but also enact their greatest power when they go undetected.

This leads back to the Zähringen seminar in which Heidegger claims that inconspicuousness marks a presencing of presence that is clearly a tautology: "We are here [at the aforementioned tautology] in the domain [*Bereich*] of the inconspicuous: presencing itself presences. The name for what is addressed in this state of affairs is: *to eon*, which neither beings, nor simply being, but *to eon*: presencing: presencing itself."[55] Tautology here might better be thought as a kind of involution, a process whereby an operation or proposition is inverted only to determine that its inverse claim or operation is equal to it, although stated or arrived at differently.[56] Things in their provenance are sought in order to arrive at *how* those appearances come and go in a way that they are yet to be polarized with other phenomena, and "in this regard we must thoroughly recognize that tautology is the only possibility for thinking what dialectic can only veil."[57] Phenomenology must trade in its namesake of studying only shiny appearances or spectacular givens for an attendance to a more primordial point of conception that hopes to get beyond even the distinction between appearance and nonappearance.

Broadly interpreted (and returned to in detail in chapter 2), this Seminar points to a class of phenomenology trained on the modes of paradoxical givenness that does not automatically discard what is obscure or seemingly insignificant from having any doxastic merit. Heidegger calls for a revision of the pretensions of how consciousness constitutes its world and engages in the reflective pure inwardness of intentionality—an active basis of Husserl's transcendental-phenomenology as distinguished from epistemology.

Inconspicuousness beyond Heidegger's Turn from Ontotheology

It may be that a phenomenology of the inconspicuous provides a tonic correction to the polarizing receptions of Heidegger's own pejorative conclusions concerning the ontotheological constitution of metaphysics; critiques that often are misunderstood and subsequently employed to utterly reject Being as a name of God. What began in the Hegel Seminars of the 1930/31 winter semester in terms of the "speculatively conceived" nature of Being, was neither some atheistic endeavor, nor a theistic one, but one that sought to undermine the distinction altogether, as both often put an end to the task of theological thinking. Ontotheology later is named a means whereby philosophy "requires how the deity enters into it."[58] As Westphal demonstrated, ontotheology "consists in the pride that refuses to accept the limits of human knowledge" and is the attempt to render "the whole of being intelligible to human understanding," and therefore can be overcome by faith itself.[59] As Marion concluded in *God without Being*, ontotheology amounts to a science of the idol and a metaphysics of presence via reversion to the *causa sui* as a first name of God, and as such eliminates the possible variations of mystery and produce an irrelevant God before whom "we cannot fall on our knees in awe or sing and dance."[60] And as Schrijvers argued recently, ontotheology should take us all the way back to a deconstruction and decentering of our inherited modern self-certainty.[61]

Despite Heidegger's own, seemingly religious turns or conversions, such as the turn from Roman Catholicism around 1915, to his provocative turn from Protestantism in 1921, and his seemingly mystical and spiritual turns with Hölderlin from 1930 to 1935, he recognized in 1937/38 that within him Christianity all along had been doing a certain turning; Christianity had "affected the whole path of [his] questioning like subterranean, seismic shocks" and that his "entire path so far has been accompanied by a silent engagement with Christianity."[62] Max Müller, Heidegger's friend once reflected on Heidegger's relationship with Christianity in 1947: "Heidegger is an immensely deep, but torn and tormented man who cannot tear the fishhook of God . . . from his flesh, though this hook is often a torment to him. This may explain why he hates the church as often and as passionately as he loves it."[63] It may not, in the final analysis, be fruitful any longer to lay claim to Heidegger's remaining Christian even though shortly before his death and subsequent burial in Meßkirch, he entrusted to a close confidant that "*Ich bin niemals aus der Kirche ausgetreten*" ("I never left the church").[64] Instead, it remains an unanswered question as to how and to what degree those associated with the Theological Turn can truly follow the grand, Heideggerian commission to being radically "in the world." It will be from within a world—one whereby its citizens unflinchingly are enraptured by glorious spectacles, and remain under threat of a Nihilistic escapism modern technological advancement uniquely poses—that a saving power might arise. Perhaps it is in such a context today, to renarrate Heidegger's famously ambiguous claim, that "only an [inconspicuous] God can save us now."[65]

Notes

1. Heidegger remarked that the German language has a special relationship with the Greek, and therefore is more suited for philosophical thinking than French. Martin Heidegger, "Only a God Can Save Us: Der Spiegel's Interview with Martin Heidegger," *Philosophy Today* 20 (1976): 282.

2. Nietzsche continues "so that it might not appear to be a confirmation of the aspirations of the German Reich." Friedrich Nietzsche, "Unpublished Notes," in *Beyond Good and Evil*, ed. Marion Faber (New York: Oxford University Press, 1998), 246.

3. All German language etymologies throughout the work are influenced highly by Kathrin Kunkel-Razum, ed., *Duden: Das Bedeutungswörterbuch, Band 10* (Mannheim: Duden Verlag, 2002), 764, 946.

4. Martin Heidegger, "Seminar in Zähringen 1973," in *Four Seminars*, trans. Andrew J. Mitchell and François Raffoul (Bloomington: Indiana University Press, 2003), 80.

5. Or "The true sense of Theology is Anthropology." Ludwig Feuerbach, "Preface to the Second Edition," in *The Essence of Christianity*, trans. George Eliot (New York: Harper Row,

1957), xxxvii. Guy Debord, *Society of the Spectacle*, trans. Ken Knabb (London: Rebel Press, 2005).

6. Dominique Janicaud, *Phenomenology and the "Theological Turn": The French Debate* (New York: Fordham University Press, 2000).

7. Günther Anders, *Die Antiquiertheit des Menschen, Ausgabe in einem Band, vol. 1* (Munich: Beck Verlag, 1980), chapter 1, part 2.

8. Emmanuel Levinas, *Of God Who Comes to Mind*, trans. Bettina Bergo (Stanford, CA: Stanford University Press, 1998).

9. See here Dominique Janicaud, *Heidegger en France Tome 1* (Paris: Hachette, 2001) and *Tome 2* (Paris: Hachette, 2005). There, Janicaud studies how Heidegger took up the privileged position of being a master thinker for French philosophy. Aspects of this work have been translated recently as *Heidegger in France*, trans. François Raffoul and David Pettigrew (Bloomington: Indiana University Press, 2015).

10. Foucault also described the rupture in French thought as having begun after the introduction of Edmund Husserl's *Cartesian Meditations* in 1929, and as "the line that separates a philosophy of experience, of sense, and of subject, and a philosophy of knowledge, of rationality and of concept. On the one hand, one network is that of Sartre and Merleau-Ponty; and then another is that of Cavaillès, Bachelard, and Canguilhem. In other words, we are dealing with two modalities according to which phenomenology was taken up in France, when quite late—around 1930—it finally came to be if not known, at least recognized." Michel Foucault, "Introduction," in *On the Normal and the Pathological*, ed. George Canguilhem and trans. Carolyn R. Fawcett (Dordrecht: Reidel, 1978), x.

11. As Dupont notes, in his 1939 *Esquisse d'une théorie des emotions* Jean-Paul Sartre "introduces Heidegger in this essay as 'another phenomenologist'—not yet as an existentialist, as he will do after 1945" and indeed "Simone de Beauvoir reports that Sartre only began a serious study of Heidegger after Corbin's volume of translations appeared." Christian Dupont, *Phenomenology in French Philosophy: Early Encounters* (Dordrecht: Springer, 2013), 150–51.

12. Rockmore for example, perhaps controversially associates anticontextualism with Husserl, Descartes, Kant, and Derrida, while among the contextualists he includes Hegel, Marx, and Merleau-Ponty. Rockmore finds the anticontextualist thesis entirely problematic especially because Heidegger himself held to a contextualist view, for in "*Being and Time*, he proposes a theory of Dasein, understood as existence, in order to study being and time . . . assertions of all kinds are based in interpretation; and interpretation is grounded in understanding that, with state of mind and discourse, is one of the fundamental ways in which human being is in the world." Tom Rockmore, *Heidegger and French Philosophy: Humanism, Antihumanism, and Being* (New York: Routledge, 1995), xiii.

13. For Heidegger, Being *is* in itself. Martin Heidegger, "Letter on Humanism," in *Pathmarks*, trans. William McNeill (Cambridge: Cambridge University Press, 1998), 252.

14. See Dupont, *Phenomenology in French Philosophy*, 4. Dupont offers an examination of the historical and intellectual lineage developed in France especially due to Husserl's influence as well as a "background for understanding contemporary engagements of phenomenology and theology." See also Herbert Spiegelberg, *The Phenomenological Movement: A Historical Introduction* (The Hague: Martinus Nijhoff, 1960), 426. Spiegelberg charts the "reception" and subsequent "production" of phenomenology according to "two overlapping phases: a mainly receptive period, during which phenomenology remained

almost completely an exotic plant, represented by German-trained scholars . . . and a predominantly productive phase, when phenomenology became an active tool in the hands of native Frenchmen." In the German language there was also Bernhard Waldenfels's *Phänomenologie in Frankreich* in 1983, which focused on the earlier development of French phenomenology, although he introduces the *Umbruchphase* in the 1960s that saw the turn from structuralism to semiotics, to an initiation of postmodern thought. For engagements with Heidegger's work from this period. See also Jean-François Courtine, *Heidegger et la phénoménologie* (Paris: Vrin, 1990).

15. Georges Gurvitch, *Les tendances actuelles de la philosophie allemande, E. Husserl, M. Scheler, E. Lask, M. Hartmann, M. Heidegger* (Paris: Vrin, 1930).

16. Emmanuel Levinas, "Martin Heidegger et l'ontologie," *Revue philosophiques de la France et de l'étranger*, CXIII, 57e, Vol année 5–6 (May–June 1932): 395–31.

17. See also Levinas, *Le temps et l'autre'* (1947).

18. See here Conor Sweeney, *Sacramental Presence after Heidegger: Onto-Theology, Sacraments, and the Mother's Smile* (Eugene, OR: Cascade Books, 2015), 42. For Sweeney, Heidegger represented a rumbling "of discontent in the Catholic tradition regarding questions related to the relationship between metaphysics and theology, nature and grace, and history and ontology." Sweeney continues, "Twenty-first-century Catholic theology needs to first be understood against the twin poles of neoscholasticism and the theme of *aggiornamento* and 'openness to the world.'" See also David Grumett, "Nouvelle Théologie," in *The Cambridge Dictionary of Christian Theology*, eds. Ian A. McFarland, David A. S. Fergusson, Karen Kilby, and Iain R. Torrance (Cambridge: Cambridge University Press, 2011), 347–50.

19. See here Jack Arthur Bonsor, *Rahner, Heidegger, and Truth: Karl Rahner's Notion of Christian Truth, the Influence of Heidegger* (Lanham, MD: University Press of America, 1987). In his *Love Alone Is Credible*, Rahner casts some blame on a Heideggerian way of thinking "being" for contributing to the decline of Christianity, while at the same time Rahner's notion of truth was to some degree influenced by Heidegger.

20. Rockmore, *Heidegger and French Philosophy*, 13.

21. Ibid., 10.

22. Laurence Paul Hemming, *Heidegger's Atheism: The Refusal of a Theological Voice* (South Bend, IN: University of Notre Dame Press, 2002), 180, cf. 69.

23. This particular criticism began with Heidegger, but was extended to Lévinas, Blanchot, and Derrida for allowing religion and the sacred to enter philosophical discourse once again in a mystical way. For Dufrenne, what was developed by "Heidegger, sous les espéces du divin. Et chez Derrida? Reprenant un mot de Lévinas: nous sommes dans la trace de Dieu, Derrida ajoute: 'Et si Dieu était *un effet de trace*?' Nous voice à nouveau apparemment délivrés de Dieu, mais à quell prix? Il faut que la trace, au d'être un effet, produise un effet." Mikel Dufrenne, *Le poétique: Précédé de Pour une philosophie non théologique* (Paris: Presses Universitaires de France, 1973), 20. See also 18 for Dufrenne's assessment of Derrida's distinction from Lévinas on the grounds of the infinity of the other, and the other to come. Derrida's criticisms of Levinas's ethics, found in "Violence and Metaphysics" are by now well known.

24. Dupont also appears to support this view, but holds to a more sharply bifurcated position that some French philosophers took interest in phenomenology as a continuation of the Cartesian tradition, while others interested in religion wanted to "break from the strict rationalism that Cartesianism represented." Dupont, *Phenomenology in French Philosophy*, 5.

25. Janicaud, *Phenomenology and the "Theological Turn,"* 30.

26. Edmund Husserl, *Ideas: General Introduction to Pure Phenomenology, vol. I.*, trans. W. R. Boyce Gibson (New York: MacMillan Company, 1931), 154, 176.

27. Janicaud, *Phenomenology and the "Theological Turn,"* 30–31, cf. 28–29.

28. Dominique Janicaud, *Chronos: Pour l'intelligence du partage temporal* (Paris: Bernard Grasset, 1997), 159. See also Janicaud, *Phenomenology and the "Theological Turn,"* 28–31. And Dominique Janicaud, *Phenomenology "Wide Open": After the French Debate* (New York: Fordham University Press, 2005), 100, footnote 14.

29. Janicaud, *Phenomenology "Wide Open,"* 75.

30. Dominique Janicaud, *La phénoménologie eclatée* (Paris: Editions de l'Eclat, 1998), 106. On this point see also Janicaud's earlier work before his critique of the theological turn, namely, *La puissance du rationnel* (Paris: Editions Gallimard, 1985); Dominique Janicaud, *Powers of the Rational: Science, Technology, and the Future of Thought*, trans. Peg Birmingham and Elizabeth Birmingham (Bloomington: Indiana University Press, 1994).

31. There is little consensus on how *unscheinbar* is to be translated into English. Figal recently shares a similar sensitivity to my own, and translates it as "inconspicuous." Most of the French choose "inapparent" likely because it at first appears to be metonymic of the French "l'inapparent." Then, there is William McNeill's strange reference to *unscheinbar* as "improbable" (though it does not get translated as such in *Pathmarks*): "We are held enraptured by something 'improbable' (*unscheinbar*), by something that, in its shining forth, also does not shine, or does not yet shine—by the approach of an event that could not have been foreseen." William McNeill, *The Glance of the Eye: Heidegger, Aristotle, and The Ends of Theory* (New York: SUNY Press, 1999), 291.

32. Ignaas Devisch, Laurens ten Kate, and Aukje van Rooden, *Retreating Religion: Deconstructing Christianity with Jean-Luc Nancy* ed. Alena Alexandrova (New York: Fordham University Press, 2012).

33. Christopher Yates, "Checking Janicaud's Arithmetic: How Phenomenology and Theology 'Make Two,'" in *Words of Life*, eds. Bruce Ellis Benson and Norman Wirzba (New York: Fordham University Press, 2010), 78.

34. Jonna Bornemark and Hans Ruin, eds., *Phenomenology and Religion: New Frontiers* (Södertörn Sweden: Södertörn University Library, 2010), 9.

35. For Heidegger "Phenomenology is not merely about phenomena, but ultimately about phenomenality itself." J. Aaron Simmons and Bruce Ellis Benson, *The New Phenomenology* (London: Bloomsbury Press, 2013), 41.

36. "Er entlehnt beim späten Heidegger einen Ausdruck um diese sachliche Notwendigkeit deutlicher zu erfassen: Er spricht von verschiedenen Anstzen zu einer 'Phnomenologie des Unscheinbaren' [phenomenologie de l'inapparent]." László Tengelyi and Hans-Dieter Gondek, *Neue Phänomenologie in Frankreich* (Berlin: Suhrkamp, 2011), 14, see also 16–17. This 650-page work assesses recent phenomenology in France. Another influential figure at this time was Rudolf Bernet, who as president of the German Society for Phenomenological Research, organized a confererence to study the distinction between the visible and the invisible in 1998 in Leuven. Among those to have given presentations were Janicaud, Marion, and Richir, and the papers were collected in 2009. Rudolf Bernet and Antje Kapust, eds., *Die Sichtbarkeit des Unsichtbaren* (Munich: Wilhelm Fink, 2009).

37. The late Tengelyi might agree with this hypothesis, and he notes that "What he [Janicaud] misses in these attempts is solely a methodological reflection upon the possibility of transcending the limits of what appears and shows itself, i.e., the limits of

the phenomenon—and this not in a metaphysics, but in a phenomenology." L. Tengelyi, *Phenomenology and Religion: New Frontiers*, ed. Jonna Bornemark and Hans Ruin (Södertörn Sweden: Södertörn University Library, 2010), 20.

38. This remark is made in the context of *phusis*, and it could be translated as such: "φύσις does not come within the ever-rising and withdrawing, in a kind of appearing, but rather it is in every case of its appearance, the inconspicuous. But by no means is this [inconspicuousness] to be confused with 'the unseen,' as the already mentioned philological translations incorrectly render it. The φύσις is not 'invisible,' it is on the contrary just the initially visible, which although initially detected, yes, although initially and mostly often and in general, is never specifically seen." Martin Heidegger, GA 55, *Heraklit. 1. Der Anfang des abendländischen Denkens (Heraklit)* (Frankfurt am Main: Vittorio Klostermann, 1943). And 2. *Logik. Heraklits Lehre vom Logos* (Frankfurt am Main: Vittorio Klostermann, 1944), 142, 143.

39. Jean-Luc Marion, "The Invisible and the Phenomenon," in *Michel Henry: The Affects of Thought*, ed. Jeffrey Hanson and Michael R. Kelly (New York: Continuum, 2012), 20.

40. For Trawny "Das 'Unscheinbare' ist das Unauffällige und wird wegen seiner Unauffälligkeit meistens übersehen. Wir gehen daran vorbei, ohne dass es unsere Aufmerksamkeit erregt. Das bedeutet jedoch nicht, dass wir nicht ständig mit ihm umgehen." Peter Trawny, "Die unscheinbare Differenz. Heideggers Grundlegung einer Ethik der Sprache," in *Phénoménologie française et phénoménologie allemande*, ed. Eliane Escoubas and Bernhard Waldenfels (Paris: L'Harmattan, 2000), 88. Coincidentally, it was at the aforementioned conference organized by Bernet that Trawney initiated thinking on the inconspicuousness of Heidegger's *Differenz*.

41. Given the recent publication of Heidegger's anti-Semitic *Notebooks*, being distanced from Heidegger at the moment is in some cases justifiable. This book follows Figal's recent resignation from the role of President of the German Heidegger Society. For Figal, "Raum, so läßt diese Überlegung sich zusammenfassen, erscheint nicht, sondern ist *unscheinbar*, sodass eine *Phänomenologie der Äußerlichkeit*, eine realistische Phänomenologie, also eine *Phänomenologie der Unscheinbarkeit* ist." Or "Space, to sum it all up, does not appear, but is inconspicuous, thus the *phenomenology of externality*, which is a realistic phenomenology, is a *phenomenology of the inconspicuous*." Günter Figal, *Unscheinbarkeit: Der Raum der Phänomenologie* (Tübingen: Mohr Siebeck, 2015), 4.

42. Ibid., 11. "Dass es Phänomenologie, die von Unscheinbaren her denkt, bisher noch nicht gab, könnte eine voreilige Behauptung sein, denn in jedem Fall gibt es einen auf sie hindeutenden Titel. Heidegger hat ihn geprägt; die spätesten Zeugnisse seines Denkens dokumentieren ihn." "the claim that there has not yet been any thinking of a phenomenology of the inconspicuous would be a hasty assertion, because the title has definitely been already suggested. Heidegger has crafted it; the latest testimony of his thinking documents it." And Figal continues, Or "is Heidegger tautological thinking, as outlined and explained in its developmental history, truly a phenomenology of the inconspicuous? If his tautological thinking is to be understood in its presentation, the question may merit the answer 'no.'" Ibid., 15.

43. Ibid., 11.

44. Françoise Dastur, "La pensée à venir: une pheénoménologie de l'inapparent?" in *L'avenir de la philosophie est-il grec?*, ed. Catherine Collobert (Saint-Laurent, QC: Fides, 2002), 146. See also Miguel de Beistegui, *Truth and Genesis: Philosophy as Differential Ontology* (Bloomington: Indiana University Press, 2004), 115–16, cf. 127.

45. For Taminiaux, this seeing "grasps things in their coming-into-appearance, intentionality, is itself transfixed with excessiveness; seeing must be beyond the given in order for things to be and to be what they are." Jacques Taminiaux, "Heidegger and Husserl's Logical Investigations in Remembrance of Heidegger's Last Seminar (Zähringen, 1973)," *Research in Phenomenology* 7, no. 1 (1977): 79.

46. For Gonzalez, such inapparency entails "a continually self-deconstructing attempt to bring into view what can never be brought into view but where the always inapparent could nevertheless be indicated in the very process of self-deconstruction." Perhaps this concept is left ambiguous "precisely in order to be able to practice dialectic while insisting on and aspiring to something else which this very practice undermines." Francisco J. Gonzalez, *Plato and Heidegger: A Question of Dialogue* (College Station, PA: Penn State Press, 2011), 308. In *Being and Time* Heidegger states the aims of phenomenology as clearly as possible: "And precisely because phenomena are initially and for the most part *not* given phenomenology is needed. Being covered up is the counter concept to 'phenomenon.'" Martin Heidegger, *Being and Time*, trans. John Macquarrie and Edward Robinson (New York: Harper & Row, 1962), 31. Martin Heidegger, *Sein und Zeit*, ed. Friedrich-Wilhelm von Herrmann (Frankfurt am Main: Vittorio Klostermann, 1977), 36.

47. For Polt, it seems, the later Heidegger does have a "being" that is more inconspicuous than the earlier Heidegger, suggesting that the Heidegger of *Being and Time* "claims that the being of beings is simply not-yet-appearing (being can be thematized as a phenomenon, even though it can never appear as ontically present (Heidegger, *Sein und Zeit*, 35); in contrast, the *Contributions* focus on be-ing (the giving of the being of beings) and claim that it is, at least in some ways, intrinsically unapparent." Richard F. H. Polt, *The Emergency of Being on Heidegger's Contributions to Philosophy* (Ithaca, NY: Cornell University Press, 2006), note 38.

48. Martin Heidegger, "Seminar in Zähringen," in GA 15, *Vier Seminare*, ed. Curd Ochwadt (Frankfurt am Main: Vittorio Klostermann, 1986), 372–407.

49. As Dreyfus straightforwardly put it, "Heidegger holds that we must learn to appreciate marginal practices—what Heidegger calls the saving power of insignificant things—practices such as friendship, backpacking in the wilderness, and drinking the local wine with friends. All these practices remain marginal precisely because they resist efficiency." Hubert L. Dreyfus, "Nihilism, Art, Technology, and Politics," in *Cambridge Companion to Heidegger*, ed. Charles B Guignon (Cambridge: Cambridge University Press, 1993), 310.

50. Heidegger, "Seminar in Zähringen 1973," 80. "So verstanden ist die Phänomenologie ein Weg, der hinführt vor . . . und sich das zeigen läßt, wovor er geführt wird. Diese Phänomenologie ist eine Phänomenologie des Unscheinbaren." Heidegger, "Seminar in Zähringen," 397.

51. Ibid., 80/377.

52. This kind of "seeing" cannot be attained through the "reading of books," says Heidegger. Martin Heidegger, "German Translator's Afterword," in *Four Seminars*, ed. Curd Ochwadt (Bloomington: Indiana University Press, 2003), 89.

53. For Heidegger "that which is to be thought turns away from us. It withdraws from us. But how can we have the least knowledge of something that is withdrawn from the outset? How can we even give it a name?" Martin Heidegger, *What Is Called Thinking?*, trans. Fred D. Wieck and J. Glenn Gray (New York: Harper & Row, 1968), 9. (GA 8, 1951–1952, 10), see also 19 (GA 8, 21) where Heidegger refers to the nature of the beauty artwork gaining its source from the truth of being *Unscheinbar*: "Beauty is a fateful gift of the essence of truth, whereby truth

means the unconcealment of the self-concealing. The beautiful is not what pleases, but what falls within that fateful gift of truth which comes into its own when that which is eternally unapparent [*Unscheinbare*, i.e., inconspicuous] and therefore invisible attains its most radiantly apparent appearance."

54. Martin Heidegger, GA 12, *Unterwegs zur Sprache* (Frankfurt am Main: Vittorio Klostermann, 1985), 247.

55. Heidegger, "Seminar in Zähringen 1973."

56. What Heidegger names a tautology, however, is not void of conflict. The "truthing" of truth engages the truth-beyond in a way that a deep tension is created, and out of which "differentiation" might be given to the experience of reason.

57. Heidegger, "Seminar in Zähringen 1973," 81.

58. Martin Heidegger, GA 11, *Identity and Difference*, trans. John Stambaugh (Chicago: University of Chicago Press, 2002), 56.

59. Merold Westphal, *Overcoming Ontotheology: Toward a Postmodern Christian Faith* (New York: Fordham University Press, 2001), 6–7.

60. Heidegger, *Identity and Difference*, 72.

61. Joeri Schrijvers, *Ontotheological Turnings?: The Decentering of the Modern Subject in Recent French Phenomenology* (Albany, NY: SUNY Press, 2011), 24.

62. Heidegger continues, informing that it is "an engagement that has never taken the form of an explicitly raised 'problem,' but was rather at once the preservation of my ownmost provenance—the childhood house, home, and youth—and a painful emancipation from it." Martin Heidegger, "Mein bisheriger Weg" in GA 66, Frankfurt am Main: Vittorio Klostermann, 1939 (1937/1938), 411–28, 415. Cited by Judith Wolfe, *Heidegger and Theology* (London: Bloomsbury, 2014), 136. Wolfe argues Heidegger's relationship with theology constantly informs his engagements of provocatively rethinking the chronological constitution of the human.

63. Max Müller quoted by Wolfe, *Heidegger and Theology*, 135. Müller was a "friend" because Heidegger once in 1938 prevented him from getting an important academic position in Freiburg due to Müller's being supposedly "unfavorably disposed" to the Nazi regime. See here Bernd Martin and Gottfried Schramm, "Ein Gespräch mit Max Müller," *Freiburger Universitätsblätter* 92 (June 1986): 13–31, 27–29.

64. This is common nomenclature today for those who claim to not "cancel" their membership in the church in the more bureaucratic sense (like living abroad but still keeping the passport of one's nationality). The original quote appeared in Thomas Sheehan, "Reading a Life: Heidegger in Hard Times," in *Cambridge Companion to Heidegger*, ed. Charles Guignon (Cambridge: Cambridge Press, 1993), 72.

65. "Nur noch ein Gott kann uns retten," that is "Only a God Can Save Us" claimed Heidegger in an interview conducted on September 23, 1966, and later printed in *Der Spiegel* May 31, 1976. Martin Heidegger, "'Only a God Can Save Us Now': An Interview with Martin Heidegger," trans. David Schendler, *Graduate Faculty Philosophy Journal* 6, no. 1 (1977): 5–27.

1 Inconspicuous Revelation: Marion, Heidegger, and an Antinomic Phenomenality

The aspects of things that are most important for us are hidden because of their simplicity and familiarity.... And this means: we fail to be struck by what, once seen, is most striking and most powerful.

—*Wittgenstein*[1]

Ontically, Dasein is not only close to us—even that which is closest. In spite of this, or rather for just this reason, it is ontologically that which is furthest away.

—*Heidegger*[2]

Those things that are the clearest and the most common are the very things that are most obscure, and understanding them is a novelty.

—*Augustine*[3]

When taking on a religious attitude, words are truthful insofar as they are instantiated through an experience with revelation. And for Marion revelation inherently is paradoxical. One of the questions to which his concept of revelation is an answer is this: What does it mean for a thing to appear paradoxically? The answer is paradoxical in its formulation, for a paradox is what attests to the subtle inconsistencies harbored by the world of which we make sense by reference to what disturbs the "how structure" of the world's shining "glory" (*doxa*). *Doxa* refers not only to what is right, decent (Proto-Indo-European [PIE] *deke, dike*, δικαιος, or righteous), expected, or appropriate, but also (in following the Greek *doxastikos*) to a kind of right reasoning about beliefs or conjectures. In a more phenomenological context, *doxa* also refers to what appears or seems (*dokein*), and after the 1600s came to refer to praise (e.g., the dox-ology) or giving glory.[4] Appearing and seeming (*Scheinbar*) also have—in their PIE roots—connotations of shining or burning. Thus this relation with glory, which generally is used to describe what wondrously shines in its self-luminescence, is not without some etymological basis. The New Testament Scriptures often refer to *doxa* in terms of expectation, especially in the context of the Christ figure, and thus any *para* of this particular *doxa*, would entail something unknown, unexpected, or, to employ the language of Chrétien, "unhoped for." The *paradoxos* refers to the incredible, unbelievable, the contrary-to-expectation, and the taken-for-granted. To think at the limit of paradoxicality, then, is to turn to what is the most non-glorious or marginal, which in a kind of paraglory would admit of the glorious to shine in its own characteristic ways, precisely and importantly aside from what and counter to how one anticipates.

In perhaps more phenomenological terms, a paradox is what obtains within consciousness the status of two seemingly contradictory things simultaneously. This double-status is at the heart of truth's being presenced (and therefore in its being presenced, contradicting itself) and its pregiven (*Vorgegebenheit*) ontological status. Not unlike the well-known duck-rabbit Gestalt shift, this marks the inherent power of a thing in its transformability from one status to another, from one intelligibility to an entirely different one. Phenomenology would demand attention to how the meaningful presence of a thing has changed, is in the process of changing, or is changing back to a previous intelligibility.

The seemingly slippery nature of things that the idea of paradoxes produces tends to make philosophers and even phenomenologists uneasy and skeptical. Do not paradoxes lead, as Dan Zahavi wonders, to the abandonment of phenomenology's privileging of "the precision and clarity of vision"?[5] Often claimed the more elusive, deceptive, and unruly version of contradictions, paradoxes are what logic aggressively seeks to dissolve. Yet the suturing of logical clarity and doxastic right should not immediately be presumed, nor does it always bring about human flourishing. Fulfilling the expected right can become a trenchant form of bad faith that blindly follows the voice of public opinion and consensus.[6] This points to a perhaps irresolvable paradox within any attempt to respond to a paradox: to do faithfully what is right by interpreting the intelligibility of phenomena correctly, while simultaneously touting a correct interpretation of a thing that threatens persistently with the potential conformity of bad faith. This may be why Kierkegaard privileged a different kind of faith, one that acts as a kind of dedoxifier that promotes a particular kind of leap into the acceptance of and faith in the various paradoxes inherent to both religious life and everyday life. One is to overcome the jaundiced prejudices for calculative reason and its inherently dichotomous paradigms, and to embrace the uncalculated at its most radical points of origination, despite the potential anxieties this creates. While some philosophers celebrate this knight of faith, others deride his fideism.

One could interpret Heidegger's work as an attempt to integrate Kierkegaard's insights regarding the paradox and its resultant anxieties and moods into a phenomenological approach. In *Sein und Zeit* Heidegger counters any claims to the dichotomies or "contradictions" between appearance and nonappearance and—contrary to Husserl—declares "Covered-up-ness is the counter-concept to 'phenomenon'" (*Verdecktheit ist der Gegenbegriff zu 'Phänomenon'*).[7] The various forms of covering—such as disguising, burying, and so on—generally are understood to be para (counter) to the shining and appearing of *phainesthai*, which phenomenology thus far had prided itself on exclusively focusing. Yet Heidegger risks injecting these various forms of the counterconcept of covering-over into what it means for a thing to appear. Thus, redefining phenomenon as what "does *not* show itself at all: it is something that lies hidden, in contrast to that which proximally and for the most part does show itself; but at the same time it is something that belongs to what thus shows itself, and it belongs to it so essentially as to constitute its meaning and ground."[8] It is the nonshowing of things in their hiddenness and the veiled-unveiling of truth that drives one's interest in phenomena and their subsequent unfolding. Yet still phenomena are not banally invisible; this is not a redux version of the platonic *eidos*, for such nonshowing belongs to the shown, the immanent, the constituted, and the meaningfully present.

This paradox of phenomenality reaches its highest potential in Being; the primal aspect of phenomenology, and the truth of Being (*Wahrheit des Seins*) always paradoxically remains hidden, even in its giving itself.[9] The "closest and most" (*zunächst und zumeist*) present-yet-hidden from view is Being, which for Heidegger is not to be understood as a substance or essence, but rather a certain *woher* or whence of occurence.[10] Given the many words Heidegger used to refer to Being, perhaps even the concept and definition of Being is meant to be covered up.[11] Being does not come into presence like other entities or phenomena, yet in keeping with the paradox of phenomenology, Being is a phenomenon despite not appearing ontically.[12] Its operations seek to challenge the purity of phenomenology. Thus, one aim of *Sein und Zeit* became to show how Being itself must be addressed in its paradoxicality (not as the being of entities): "Being can be covered up so extensively that it becomes forgotten and no question arises about it or about its meaning."[13] These early engagements with Being, which often appear in conjunction with a turn from the traditional understanding of *Schein* (appearance) results in a reformulation of phenomenology as no longer a tool that allows us to usher the intelligibility of something into clear appearance, but rather one of deformalization of that which is already here. Surely at times, such deformalization occurs through bringing to clarity. Yet perhaps the most fecund of experiences may involve the active darkening or obfuscation of the phenomenon, to allow it to invoke wonder at its self-disclosure.[14] Without this paradoxical element of phenomenology, we would remain stuck in the ontic realm of the everyday and its straightforward (and banally mundane) efforts of clarification. The hiddenness of the phenomenon marks the most fundamental value of phenomenology: It is "precisely because phenomena are proximally and for the most part not given that there is need for phenomenology."[15] Indeed the masking of Being by some other kind of being, the nature of truth as both uncovering and covering, and the deformalization of a straightforward or ordinary means of coming into presence, all point to the antinomies of the making-manifest.

In major ways, Marion might be seen as a phenomenological heir to these antinomies. For him phenomenology's legitimacy consists precisely in its efforts to dislodge the crystalized experience of the hidden, or that which would otherwise remain "invisible without it [phenomenology] and its effort."[16] Yet is there a way to seriously bridge the gaps between the invisible and the visible?[17] Marion addresses such a question, and without hesitation wishes to "also call saturated phenomena 'paradoxes.'"[18] Their operations indeed can be described phenomenologically: "The fundamental characteristic of the paradox lies in the fact that intuition sets forth a surplus that the concept cannot organize, therefore that the intention cannot foresee" and such "intuition subverts, therefore precedes, every intention, which it exceeds and decenters" by way of a paradoxical counterappearance.[19] In a way that is strikingly similar to Heidegger's counterconcept, Marion's paradox receives its force of thought from its being counterappearance and counterexpectation. As counterexpectation, it is also ipso facto counterintentionality, a directedness that gains its force from a subject-oriented volition. Ultimately "the paradox therefore belongs, indisputably, to the domain of truth."[20] It is such a paradoxicality that is employed throughout the entirety of Marion's project of liberating and unbinding the excessive possibilities that phenomena hold.

In a more theological key, Marion's work has been marked by daring to "take interest in the meaning" of transcendence, as Levinas once put it.[21] Although some have considered the differences between phenomenology and theology to be based on differently accepted forms of warrant and evidence, Marion conceives of these disciplines differently according to how the presence of each is based on their own version of warrant for how things announce, appear, "are given," or "reveal" themselves.[22] By ushering phenomenology into theological reflection, we naturally arrive at the question of revelation, a phenomenon that reveals in its being revealed. This is because revelation is the paradox par excellence as it marks the appearing of appearing itself, givenness. And in his by now famous engagements with "saturated phenomena," which the "reduction to givenness"—"so much reduction, so much givenness"[23]—practically helps to exfoliate, revelation is conceived as that which revels in the revelation of the inexhaustibility of phenomena. It is in the originary antinomies of saturation (that some are more saturated or ripe with possibility than others) that what appear to be lacking in phenomenal data, in fact shine all the more by their absence, and therefore are exfoliated according to the possibility of excess.

This chapter develops a notion of inconspicuous revelation by building out and extending Heidegger's notion of a mysterious (*Das Geheimnis*), self-concealing, and counterconceptual Being alongside Marion's conclusion that revelation is a phenomenon that phenomenalizes by countering its own modes of givenness. The central question the chapter seeks to address is to what degree do the mysteries of revelation phenomenalize paradoxically in this counter movement? Despite Marion's attendance to revelation as a paradoxical phenomenon, and his development of counterphenomena, the means by which revelation phenomenalizes often are overlooked, and we are left to presume instead that they operate not according to paradoxicality as a form of phenomenality, but rather another kind of phenomenality, one not unlike that of a spectacularity. If Günther Anders was right to repeatedly insist that "no means is only a means," and if Marion is correct to claim that revelation is the paradox of paradoxes then, to go one small yet consequential step further, revelation also must be a counter-phenomenality that goes against the conditioning of other means.[24]

Indeed, if the content of a revelation is supposed to come as a paradoxical shock to an unsuspecting subject, then should not the form also operate as such, as a paradox? Christ knocking Saul to the ground and speaking audibly to him notwithstanding, the majority of today's revelations or religious experiences are not bedazzling, and occur to ordinary people in the hustle and grind of everyday life. Heidegger was aware that eventhood is usually nonspectacular, and that being appropriated in an experience indeed generally is inconspicuous. Like Gregory of Nyssa's *epektasis*, the sanctification of the soul is a long and eternal journey, and as St. Teresa of Avila knew, divine revelation for the saint is less shock and awe and more "among the pots and pans."[25] If revelation is a paradox, then it phenomenalizes through the provision of a countershock that disrupts the preference for spectacular phenomenality and its tyrannical numbing of thought. It becomes necessary to provide more explanatory power to Marion's claim that revelation is a "paradox—a phenomenology of the unapparent [inconspicuous] *as such*, and not simply of the not-yet-appearing"[26] It also is of paramount importance not to disqualify automatically poor or common law phenomena from having any uncanny potential. Revelation must be understood also as coming from within the marginal and poor, and as obscuring itself as a counterspectacle—as an inconspicuous phenomenality.

The Paradox of *Reduction and Givenness*

In what sense is Heidegger's Being (like Marion's revelation) a specific phenomenon that is to be experienced on terms of a primordial deformalizing of phenomenality? When reflecting in 1973 on the singular contributions of *Sein und Zeit*, Heidegger arrived at how "Being in the world" or *Dasein* (existence, being-open) is a more originary experience to phenomenological life than is a Husserlian "being-conscious" (*Bewußt-sein*, consciousness). Especially pertinent to this reflection is how one can access somehow this dynamic state through what is taken for granted: the ever-hiding and concealed work of Being. Husserl overlooked Being and thought of it only in terms of the constant and steadfastly present (*Anwesenheit und Beständigkeit*), whereas for Heidegger, Being (and its experience in or as the clearing) enacts a distinctly hidden and withdrawn nature all of its own.[27] Being is the basic means, an according-to-which whereby intelligibility is revealed. It is in one's fundamental involvement in or with the world's horizon that Being is truthed or disclosed (ἀλήθεια); the activities of which are self-evident and prephilosophical.[28] In *Being and Time* Dasein becomes the transcendentally and ek-statically outside and dynamically *made-to-open* (appropriated, *ereignet*, thrown-open) toward being-in-the-clearing of Being in a way that proves how immanence always remains broken through and through.[29] Inconspicuousness plays an active role here. As Dastur interprets, the appropriation of appearing, the active "giving of Being," and "the nonappearance that resides in all appearing" provides the fundamental make-up of Heidegger's "inapparent."[30] And to reiterate Polt's claims, perhaps more extremely, Being itself, as the coming to be or giving of the being of beings, may be "intrinsically unapparent."[31]

In *Reduction and Givenness*, Marion's interpretation of Heidegger at points provides detailed attention to how *Sein und Zeit* appropriates the aforementioned "Being-covered-up" (*Verdecktsein*) and its simultaneous counterconcept of Being-opened. Marion of course recognizes that Heidegger initiates an inversion of phenomenology, turning its interests from studying things that appear clearly to things that do not. Heidegger held to how Being-covered-up enacts a more static phenomenal state. Concealments, which are enacted through the practice of "covering up" (*Verdeckung*) become "really the immediate theme of phenomenological reflection" in part because it is the aforementioned presencing of things to which our attentions are to be directed.[32] Marion seems to realize that this paradoxical counterconcept (*Gegenbegriff*) is *not* a dichotomous opposite of a phenomenon that appears or shines, but instead that which counters the phenomenon by (perhaps distractingly) firing back and thus drawing the potential for the dynamic intelligibility of things:

> [What fires back] inscribes manifestation in the very orbit of concealment, such that in arriving at its own manifestation, the phenomenon only covers up the covered, takes up again in the mode of the manifest that which remained concealed in the mode of the covered-up. The phenomenon manifests only inasmuch as it manifests that which remained nonmanifest before [prior to] that very manifestation, and which still obscurely governs its brilliance.[33]

This points to an oscillatory movement between manifestations and covering up, between not only the visible and the invisible, but between what will come to be the title of Marion's later, 2008 book, the *Visible and the Revealed*—the title that gestures to how revelation operates according to its own horizon, which disturbs the dominant paradigm of visibility and invisibility.

In a phenomenon's giving itself to presence, it also effectively is covering over (which we already know to take on many potential modes of enactment such as disguising, treasuring, etc.) the nonmanifest. A phenomenon makes manifest what was previously never manifested before. Yet what is perhaps most fascinating in this recognition of Marion's is that a phenomenon is a manifesting phenomenon only in so far as it "obscurely governs its brilliance." What could this obscure governing mean? The manifestation of the phenomenon manifests only in its still obscuring the potential luminescence or brilliance of this non-manifesting *potentia* of the phenomenon. It safeguards through obscurity; that is, via the active rendering obscure or obfuscating of the phenomenon itself. This resituating of the phenomenon subsequently alters the course of how phenomenology in its newly minted paradoxical character after Heidegger is to be understood. The approach now "renders manifest not simply the manifest, but indeed the nonmanifest."[34]

Similarly, Heidegger argues for "the necessity of thinking (φύσις) on the essential ground of ἀλήθεια," which points to emergence-as-disclosedness, that is, the becoming-available of something in and from its concealment.[35] Such an intertwining of emergence and unfolding comes from the phenomenon itself, which steadfastly remains still-in-relation with the closedness of *Un-wahrheit* and *Verborgenheit*. For Heidegger, there must be something that allows for the phenomenon to appear to us (and for us to subsequently accept it) as correct (*adaequatio*); there must be the appearance or manifestation of meaningful-*ness* for something to appear and be accepted as meaning-*ful*. Something must be disclosed from its "inaccessibility."[36] Therefore ἀλήθεια (especially when understood in conjunction with φύσις) is first of all a kind of truthiness that still retains the nonmanifest.

It precisely is in this sort of context that the theme of the visible and invisible arises, and that Marion first begins to reflect on the unapparent, inapparent, or inconspicuous. All three references to the inconspicuous in *Reduction and Givenness* deserve attention here:

> the Heideggerian phenomenon, originating in the rise to visibility of the not-yet visible, implies by right and in principle what is unapparent in apparition. In one case evidence reduces apparition to presence (and thus to objectivity for consciousness), and in the other case apparition reveals *as such* the unapparent whose contrast haloes the apparent. Instead of offering the certain evidence of an object for consciousness, the phenomenon offers itself as the enigma of the forever unobjectifiable play of the apparent with the unapparent. Phenomenon no longer signifies the certain object, but a certain play of the apparent in its

> apparition. Consequently, the work of phenomenology is to render apparent not only the unapparent, but even the play between the apparent and the unapparent within apparition: "'Behind' the phenomena of phenomenology there is essentially nothing else; on the other hand, what is to become a phenomenon can be hidden."[37]

Heidegger's understanding of the oscillatory movement between the visible and not-yet visible implies that in the manifestation of phenomena there is something obscurely inconspicuous. It is not merely that an apparition should be reduced immediately to a cognate of presence or objectivity in its capability of being grasped in a concept (*Begriff*), but perhaps more importantly, that it reveals *as such* the inconspicuous. Inconspicuousness itself should be thought essential to the experience. Marion here refers to the inconspicuous as an "as such," which implies it has a phenomenal character beyond an approach, method, or reduction, and is perhaps to be thought of precisely as this counterconcept to apparency or apparition. Relatedly, although at first it seems Marion will reduce the inapparent to being the dichotomous opposite of apparition, he then wisely notes, and therefore colors his prior reflection, in the claim that phenomenology does not merely lure or coax the inapparent into presence, but also, and importantly, attends to the play or open space that reveals in its own phenomenality, its location in presence and absence.

There is a second reference to the inconspicuous. Because Heidegger's rhyming reduction "*Soviel Schein—Soviel Sein*" ("So much appearance, so much Being") should be taken as a recognition that Being always and already eludes direct or objective appearance, it therefore harbors a paradoxical inconspicuousness. Under Marion's watch this reduction of Heidegger's "covers over an unapparentness that, if it appeared, would offer a completely different appearance; thus, the appearance of the *Schein* attests to the enigma of the phenomenon as a play of the apparent and the unapparent."[38] This is not some kind of illusory, always hidden mystery, or mystical conjecture of things that cannot be experienced. Instead, the appearing of the inapparent would do so in its own unique form of presencing that corresponds to its inconspicuousness, not according to the straightforward presencing of what Marion will much later name "poor" or "common law" phenomena, but in the enigma of what Marion here calls the play within phenomena that is marked by both the inapparent and the visible. This unfolds how Marion recognizes that perhaps *all* phenomena bear the marks of such play. Yet could this treatment imply the possibility that inconspicuousness is referential to specific and particular phenomena that could be thought of as privileged in their singular forms of presentation? Marion's reference to *the* inapparent "as such" could mean that it is in and of itself a phenomenon that colors, characterizes, or imbues other phenomena. If so, it would mark a paradoxical relation with apparition on the grounds that it is given (via the active force of givenness to or in intuition), yet that it takes on the status of and mirages itself as not-given. Inconspicuousness could be thought as one primary point of origination for what will become Marion's particular saturated, and saturating phenomena. These phenomena are particularized instantiations of what Heidegger centralized in Being.

Marion is well aware that Heidegger's phenomenological task is to develop a paradox that should avoid falling into contradiction: to think "Being as Being" in its inaccessibility, although simultaneously conceiving of it as a phenomenon. To achieve this, Heidegger had to fashion a concept of space, instantiated in *Spielraum* (a buffer, margin, or free-play-between), *Erschlossenheit* (an opening or unlockingness), or *Lichtung*, (a clearing). This play of space is what Marion theorizes:

> The phenomenon had to pass from evident presence to the enigma of the play within it between the unapparent and the apparent only in order to be able to give rise to the phenomenality of Being, which, par excellence, is covered over in the very uncovering of beings—since it brings about that uncovering.[39]

Can the phenomenon and the Being that inherently imbues it not fall prey to Heidegger's own concerns for the metaphysics of presence? Yes, but only on the grounds that (a) it is not illusory or mystical, (b) it is rooted in the immanent presence of the world, and (c) it retains in itself a concept that can offer space, distance, or elbow room between visibility and invisibility.

Although Marion at first seems to play a bit loose with this term "inapparent," and never fully to articulate the overall potential of what a phenomenology of the inconspicuous could mean, he does clarify some of its general potential in a third, perhaps most explicit reflection on the inconspicuous:

> We have therefore come to the situation where, as the Zähringen seminar will put it in 1973, "this phenomenology is a phenomenology of the unapparent."' Before retorting a bit too quickly that one must choose between, on the one hand, a phenomenology, and therefore the apparent, and, on the other hand, the unapparent and therefore an impossibility for phenomenology, let us ask why this paradox—a phenomenology of the unapparent *as such*, and not simply of the not-yet appearing—is here fully required by the necessity of thought.... Phenomenology must bear on the unapparent because Being does not appear, "is not perceivable"; being is never perceived within the horizon of presence as a perfectly obedient and lawful phenomenon. Why? Because the presence uncovered in evident permanence receives, and is suitable to, beings alone; only a being can remain here and now in order to respond "present!" to the command of evidence.[40]

Heidegger's assertion in *Sein und Zeit* that "The Being of beings 'is' not itself a being"[41] entails the necessity of moving from the static onticity of beings to Being.

Marion recognizes that the inapparent, which culminates in a particular phenomenology in 1973, is not to be thought of as dichotomous ("one must not choose between.") with what directly appears or is brought into presence, but actually is referential to an originary paradox. The inconspicuous may be more than Marion realizes, however, not only as a paradox, but even as a means of furnishing the very conditions for paradoxicality. In which case, the inconspicuous is not fueled by paradoxicality, but rather, the paradox is given its force of up-ending intentionality by inconspicuousness. In paradoxical phenomena's challenging the *doxa*, some kind of inner-operative machinery is revealed to be at work.

Yet in a significant way Marion does recognize that this inapparent is not simply a cognate of invisibility, and once again refers to the inconspicuous as the inconspicuous *as such*; simultaneously distinguishing inconspicuousness from invisibility and from the not-yet-present or yet-to-be-disclosed. And this inapparency describes (perhaps at points even represents) Being, whose *Horizont* exceeds the world itself, while its *es gibt* gives the "most present," especially *Dasein*: the being-open and being-out. This indeed initiates a new means of thinking presencing itself. These engagements in *Reduction and Givenness* can be interpreted as an implicit staging and signaling of things to come in Marion's development of the saturating character of the phenomenon of revelation. One goal and question has made up a significant portion of Marion's career: "To render phenomenal not that which, being invisible, could become visible, and therefore become a being, but, paradoxically, to render phenomenal that which, invisible as such, could not in any way become visible in the mode of a present being—can this task be taken on, or even formulated?"[42] Marion takes up this task and develops an answer in terms of "saturation."

A Phenomenon that Phenomenalizes Uniquely: Revelation

The topic of saturation can be thought of in the context of Heidegger's reference to truth as an overabundance that goes beyond the present. The *Übermaß* (surplus) or *Überfülle* (over-full) personify ἐπέκεινα in its *excessus*. Indeed "higher than actuality [*Wirklichkeit*, reality] stands possibility,"[43] which, in its unpredictability, stands for the coming-into-appearance of things. Heidegger's things are transfixed with "excessiveness."[44] Technology attempts to veil and refuse the enowing of Being, as the 1936–1938 *Contributions to Philosophy (from Enowing)* show. The world is not a machine, and even the attempt to incorporate everything economically into standing-reserves, as he again put it in 1969, cannot hold back the powers of excess, and philosophy's rising up from within it: "the dimension of the entirely excessive is that in which philosophy arises." We, as humanity, therefore are to respond to being struck by excess, namely, "the excess of presence" via philosophy "which is itself excessive."[45] For something to be excessive is for it to house a latent and dormant force of something otherwise covered over from conscious experience. Such latency is to be thought of in terms of an intertwining of seeing and the seen. It is a phenomenon that phenomenalizes, and makes something stand out and beyond that which is given to sight. This is a mystery.

It was especially in Heidegger's later work that the coming-to-be of Being took on a *more* mysteriously copresent concealing as one is thrown into, or appropriated within the world.[46] In "On the Essence of Truth" *das Geheimnis* (mystery) is claimed to be the self-concealing nature of Being and truth.[47] Then, in the *Introduction to Metaphysics*, it is argued that the origin and structure of language "remains a mystery" on the grounds that language "could have begun only from the overwhelming and the uncanny, in the breakaway of humanity into being."[48] And finally, the essence of humanity (*Das Wesen des Menschseins*) itself is given in a shrouded mystery whose absence can be "glimpsed into" (*das Ausblick in das Geheimnis*).[49] As I investigate in the following chapters, his *Parmenides Seminars* and writings in the early 1930s name *Unscheinbarkeit* the primary characteristic of the mysterious, and thus that it should be considered alongside these aforementioned particular phenomena that house the mysterious, which is *Dasein*'s being thrown-open in the present-yet-absent-clearing.[50] This mysteriousness, as mentioned in chapter 1, is not a complete "unknown" that Humans cannot attain, but rather is right there in the most ordinary of things, even in the human itself, which marks *das Geheimnis des Daseins*. The inconspicuous, the primary "characteristic trait" (*Zug*) of mysteriousness, is inherently ordinary and unsuspected to bear the uncanny.

Marion's Intuiting Excess

Yet *how* does the mysterious phenomenalize? In *Sein und Zeit* Heidegger references *Phainesthai* in its doubling character of showing and the shown; the phenomenalizing (*Phainein*) that—in following the root *phaino*—brings things (mostly itself) into light. Already in *Sein und Zeit* there is a recognized need to think of phenomenality as the intertwining of this how and what, and to conceive of ways (perhaps even specific *phenomena*) that provide for the eventhood of phenomenality to occur. It is precisely this wedding between manifestation and the manifested that Marion seamlessly interweaves into his version of "revelation," at which he seeks to arrive via the inversion of relations established by Husserl between intention and intuition.

Marion's conception of intuition often is reflective of how Husserl, in *Ideas I*, redevelops Kant's *Anschauung* to refer to impressions or, more broadly, awareness in and through which a conscious subject attributes meaningfulness to things. Yet in ascribing this meaningfulness, there often is an overlooked assigning to things particular modes of presentation, and sense perception can alter these meanings, which at first are intuited.[51] Husserl had hoped to conceive of how things do not change fundamentally as a result of experience, yet at the same time, originate in and derive from the subject absolutely. It is in this context that Marion's "saturated phenomena" are established, as they help furnish the conclusion that the subject itself must be bracketed in order for the multifarious meanings of things to give themselves independent from any meaning-giving subject. Marion arrives at Husserl's minimally described notion of how intuition is qualified by the givenness or arrival of "sensuous content," and seeks to show how there are phenomena that hold manifold possibilities for us via our intuitions of them, which for Marion are the inner-conscious acts that unfold our particular hows.

Of course, Marion has deeper interests in phenomenology than for only reconstructing Husserlian intuition, and a number of commentators, including myself, have addressed these concerns elsewhere.[52] Yet in general, he aims to test phenomenology as a ground for thinking what theology otherwise traditionally has been incapable of thinking on its own, and to do so without contradicting phenomenology's most essential character traits. In chapter 1 of *The Visible and the Revealed* phenomenality is broadened to include the *phenomena* of revelation, not as an exception to phenomenality *per se*, but as another paradigm developed from out of phenomenology.[53] In "The Banality if Saturation," Marion later reflects on the merit of such an approach: "What is at stake here is offering legitimacy to nonobjectifiable, even nonbeing phenomena" which could provide a tonic correction to how we interpret and have religious experiences.[54] Before closer reflection on the particularly paradoxical and even inconspicuous nature of Marion's saturated phenomenon of revelation, it is necessary to understand his theory of saturation more generally, and the four phenomena according to which such revelation ultimately are exfoliated and experienced fundamentally.

Saturated phenomena appear in and out of the generosity of givenness in the double movement both of freeing phenomena from their otherwise understood stativity, and by saturating intuition in a way that imbues it with certain attunements and dispositions given in accord with that thing as it is given. His hypothesis of saturated phenomena was built around the hope that they could be inscribed within an experience and simultaneously go beyond how phenomenology often has limited and foreclosed the possibility of experience itself. What these phenomena saturate therefore is intuition, thereby obfuscating phenomenology's ideal norms of evidence via their excessiveness.[55] "The Given" (*l'adonné*) "who" receives these saturating experiences and phenomena can never grasp, predict, or control them in their entirety. They are therefore unconditioned phenomena in that there is no subject whose horizons of possibility stand in their way from giving and saturating the experience.[56] Saturated phenomena provide for a counterexperience, yet not all phenomena are saturated or offer the "same degrees of givenness" although "there can and must be indefinite degrees of givenness, but no exception."[57] These nonsaturated phenomena are named "poor" and "common law" phenomena, which lack in intuition (e.g., a geometrical shape) or the potential for any paradoxical relation. Marion's reference to these phenomena frequently have been critiqued and called on for more careful clarification (e.g., Steinbock, 2010; Gschwandtner, 2014).[58]

In leading up to revelation as a fifth type of saturated phenomena, Marion describes four others that—in directly corresponding to Kant's four classes of his twelve categories—synthesize intuition and the concepts received, and then are developed in accord with them: the event, the idol, the icon, and the flesh.[59] The classes of Kant's (quantity, quality, modality, and relation) are the backpacks brought by a cognizer prior to experience, and Marion employs these categories to demonstrate how intuition is saturated in his four types. The event, which saturates a horizontal field of vision, is a phenomenon that represents the quantity of possible significations and interpretations that historically appropriated data can embody and entail.[60] The idol is often a visible thing that saturates the field of visibility according to its quality and fineness, such as a work of art at which one gazes and through which one realizes one utterly lacks total understanding.[61] Its phenomenality consists in both its being the most immanent of saturated phenomena, and its acting as a conduit between the visible and the invisible in unique ways (as demonstrated recently by Gschwandtner).[62] The icon (or face of the other) saturates according to modality, or the manifold of possibilities in which a thing could be, in part because the face's expressions are always changing and therefore altering the (often difficult to interpret) demands implicitly placed on me.[63] Then the flesh saturates relation between myself and the other, who is necessary in order for the phenomenon to phenomenalize; an action that leaves me surprised that I am here as I am "in touch" with another via affection.[64]

These four types culminate and confound in revelation, a saturated and saturating phenomenon par excellence. Marion names Revelation a *Phenomenon* (which already says much regarding phenomenology's role in studying it) that amounts to an "ultimate variation on saturation, the *paradoxotaton*, the paradox to the second degree and par excellence, which encompasses all types of paradox"; even assuming "the figure of the paradox of paradoxes." Such revelation can be exemplified by the Christ figure, whose quality, quantity, modality, and relation each culminate in a paradigm of unforseeability for the gaze and horizon, thereby deconstituting the subject's sense of primacy, its confidence in totalizing the visible field, and its abilities to take account of all that appears.[65] Revelation is unique in that it is a phenomenon that is also a "mode of appearance," whereby experience itself is saturated. This does not entail a presupposition or a priori acceptance of certain information (e.g., a doctrinal theological system) arrived at via the linking-up between the content and form. Revelation is integrated and intertwined not according to only its what or how, but rather to the space that embodies the formness and contentness between the two, thus simultaneously linking-up and transgressing the tendencies of both.

The question then becomes: How does revelation give itself? One answer: As a phenomenon that overfills the field of experience in its appearing, and therefore laminating phenomenology itself, one's means of accessing its intelligibility. Marion's revelation is the "letting appear" of the paradox that defines the inner logics of religious experience, which marks the inconspicuous experience of absence. And for Marion, it is telling that because "religion attains its highest figure only when it becomes established by and as a revelation, where an authority that is transcendent to experience nevertheless manifests itself experientially," religion itself is made up of the paradoxical experiencing that is beyond or transcends experience while being within the possibilities of appearance: "Revelation takes its strength of provocation from what it speaks universally, yet without this word being able to ground itself in reason within the limits of the world. As long as this paradox is not admitted, or at least thought of honestly, the phenomenon of religion remains misunderstood."[66]

This revelation is what composes the basis of the particular set of paradoxes that religion itself entails. To refer to things in their universality and seemingly-natural coordinates of thought indeed is to step from the boundaries of calculative reason. Yet such a reference is inherent within the nature of revelation, which is by definition that which is superimposed or laminated on nature as supernatural. The supernatural is also the supernatal, in that it seeks the ultimate point of origin for determining and charting the possibilities of all that could appear. Yet with revelation the *causa* (and the imaginaries it creates) cannot account for their activities, which is one reason why religion often has been expelled from rationality and into various versions of fideism.

This leads back to the question of the inconspicuous or inapparent, especially as it might relate with Heidegger's Being. Revelation marks or implies a certain experienced transition from the unseen to the visible, which takes place "on the stage of *this* world," and this stands as a reminder that we are to attend not only to what appears "most easily and most rapidly."[67] Revelation concerns possibility (in Marion's case, an impossible possibility for it thwarts expectations) and therefore is not dependent on the intentionality of the subject. Yet as Marion's dictum "So much reduction, so much givenness" indicates, the reduction allows one to see what could be possible and to wait for what could be announced or given.[68] Heidegger's understanding that Being is the most immanent yet inaccessible of phenomena, is certainly at play in Marion's engagement with the inconspicuous in *The Visible and Revealed*: "From the ontic point of view, Being as such strictly amounts to nothing. Hence it gives itself inasmuch as it gives nothing.... This paradox of a givenness without given is repeated for visibility... and... just as easily, Heidegger will later speak of a 'phenomenology of the unapparent.' Being can therefore only reach phenomenality if phenomenology also concerns what, at first glance, precisely does not manifest itself."[69]

This paradox of the givenness of a thing without a given reiterates in a different context Marion's already referenced reflections on the inconspicuous in *Reduction and Givenness*. Yet in this case the question of what is allowed to have warrant to appear is brought to a greater intensity. Marion employs the case of Being's having no ontic value, but then suggests it to be a phenomenon that is a nonphenomenon that nevertheless gives—then employs this as warrant to turn to revelation as a phenomenon! Revelation is a phenomenon that is not given, yet via phenomenology, nevertheless can allow for a kind of (what Heidegger calls) seeing without conceiving via an indication and announcing (*anmelden*) that subtly modifies the present without negating it. Marion recognizes that the distinction between Being and beings is an important one, and that the absence of what is called "Being" is experienceable despite "remaining invisible" precisely because Heidegger's phenomenology provides for a deformalization intention. In this limited sense, Being is a privileged phenomenon, and Marion's revelation also receives a certain kind of privileging in its challenging of phenomenality, its giving in its absence, and its saturation of intuition despite not being "given" to appearances in the ways that we tend to prefer in an ontic attitude.

The similarities between revelation and Being underscored here are rather obvious, yet at the same time, Marion does not simply wish to conceive revelation on the terms of Being but in the place of it. Phenomenology exists only by merit of its abilities to interrogate the not directly visible and to allow its phenomenality to appear in new ways, and thus phenomenology would be the method par excellence for the manifestation of the invisible through the phenomena that indicate it—hence also the method for theology. However, phenomenology and theology are two distinct approaches in the sense that the former lays conditions of manifestation while the latter furnishes the free possibility of revelation in its active nonrestriction of horizons. It is in this context that Marion wonders, "Can revelation retain any meaning without the horizon of Being?"[70]

One might answer in the affirmative because revelation can take place without a limited or restricted horizon, and in no way needs the word "Being" to accomplish this. This is due to givenness, which is the register of all that is given, without exception, and Marion's replacement concept for Heidegger's Being (although in *On Time and Being*, Being is conceived according to a dynamic sending or fundamental giving). Marion then turns to found his revelation on givenness, which in its dynamic activities cannot be limited to a static horizon of what is given. Yet still, like Heidegger's Being, Marion's revelation is not a transcendent *eidos*-oriented metaphysical supplement superimposed onto the illuminating screen of the immanent. Revelation is fully immanent. Yet nor is revelation bound to the rules of visibility, which demand that phenomena accord to a particular theater or staging of presentation. In Marion's view, this leads to an important problem that is not easy to solve regarding revelation's relation with phenomenology's horizon of possibility: On the one hand "If revelation admits of a horizon, it acknowledges the horizon a priori and therefore renounces possibility [and] regresses to the rank of a simple constituted manifestation." Yet on the other hand, "if revelation excludes any horizon on principle, it can no longer present itself anywhere, to no gaze nor as any phenomenon: thus, it would lose any relation with phenomenology and its presentation."[71] Thus can there be a relation between horizon and revelation that does not allow the horizon to prohibit a priori the appearing or appearance of this phenomenon?

One solution: return to the founding paradoxicality on which Heidegger based phenomenology and the intelligibility of Being, and claim that without restriction to the horizon of visibility, revelation can nevertheless (exactly like Heidegger's Being!) lower itself to the status of a horizon while simultaneously challenging any conditions that such a horizon might impose on it. It is right to conclude that any horizon "that determines the scene of incoming phenomena" limits, perhaps even forbids revelation.[72] Marion arrives at the claim that if revelation presents something, and if in every revelation there is content revealed (which could be claimed to in turn feed back into the intuition and awareness of what could come or be presented), then therefore revelation can challenge from within "any a priori condition imposed on its possibility."[73] Yet because this being-given to a horizon takes place in a paradoxical saturation of the horizon, it thereby disrupts and confuses the horizon, ultimately interfering with phenomenality. At the risk of sounding sophistical: although revelation clearly gives, it does not give clearly. Thus, "revelation does not enter phenomenality except under the figure of a paradox—as saturated phenomena that saturate the entire horizon of phenomenality."[74]

It is a certain paradoxicality that holds Marion's phenomenology of religious experience together, and like Heidegger's Being, the presentation of its truth (ἀλήθεια) is not to be thought of as beginning in correctness (*adaequatio*), but in what it first of all does to the one on whom truth ultimately arrives as intelligible. Yet to remain still phenomenological, naming anything that does not appear a paradox does not submit the truth to a trope of contradiction. To be truly phenomenological, revelation still must be taken as coming purely from itself without any preliminary determinations.[75] This is the infinite openness to which one must remain committed if one is to do a phenomenology of revelation. And given its paradoxical nature, revelation, in its alternation between revealing and being a phenomenon that reveals, is inherently a particular, inconspicuous phenomenon that operates in an excessive way, saturating all that it touches.

Inconspicuousness of the Sensual

There is one last way in which we might observe Marion engaging the inconspicuous. When explaining the work of saturation, he interestingly turns to the categorial or sensual distinction (without directly naming it) to which Heidegger devoted attention in the Zähringen seminar in the explanation of *Unscheinbarkeit* as a phenomenology. There Heidegger reiterates phenomenology's most primal aims according to the *transcendens* of Being and the *Seinsfrage*: Being is able to transcend the distinction between the sensual and categorial intuitions of things—and our preferences for past memorialized experiences that we subsequently project on those things—over the sensual *hyle* that an experience gives or presents objectively. Chapter 6 of Husserl's *Logical Investigations*, "Sensuous and Categorial Intuition," opened-up the possibilities of a new means of thinking about the meaning of the being of things.[76] It is to this chapter that Heidegger refers, then alters the conclusions of which to include the possibilities for how the categorial is not "added to the sense data" but is laminated over it and actually intuited or "sensed" in a surplus (one cannot help but think here of Marion's "excess").[77]

Heidegger then refashions this surplus into a means of describing the possibilities of an inconspicuous "seeing" that provides an intelligibility of an otherwise inaccessible Being. In a particular, yet limited sense, phenomenology under Heidegger's watch becomes also an approach to uniquely look-past-things in their ontic presence by way of one's becoming or being Dasein, which is accomplished by being the open-being that fashions creatively a space (*Raumlichkeit*) of play for these appearances. The sense data or *hyle* (ὕλη) are paradoxically the most immanently present, yet they become inconspicuous in one's preference for what is putatively not given in any ontic way, those categorial intuitions.[78] One effectively can be situated, however, (or bring one's thinking to this place) in a way that allows a variation of access to the seemingly invisible movement from sensual to categorial intuitions. This is called the "domain" or "the clearing of the appearing of the unapparent" in which one performs "an exercise in a phenomenology of the inapparent."[79] As I have considered it in closer detail elsewhere, it is in the Zähringen seminar that Heidegger sums up this aspect of his career that demonstrated how the nonappearing and nonmanifesting of phenomena make it possible for one to be tuned-in to the fundamental concealments of things as they appear. He indeed showed that the thing itself does not appear on the grounds of the objectivity of consciousness but rather according to the disclosedness and hiddenness of things.

Marion reflects in his own way on such an oscillation between categorial and sensual intuition, especially as it sets the stage for thinking about saturation:

> Suppose that I perceive, or rather that I undergo, the sensation of three colors arranged one on top of the other—for example, green, orange, and red.... This intuition ... opens onto two radically different types of

> phenomena.... When I assign these three colors to the flag of a nation or a signal that regulates traffic at an intersection ... the concept ... grasps intuition without remainder, and the intuition literally disappears in it—to the point that it becomes insignificant, pointless, and even dangerous to concentrate one's attention on the exact form of the colored spots, their intensity, or their nuances. If one does so, one is distracted from the significant, which alone is important to practical knowledge and therefore to the use of this phenomenon.[80]

The sensuous intuitions of these three colors are overlooked in favor of what one is *doing* at a particular moment, what one's present situation demands of them. When driving, one never takes it that these colors refer to the flag of the country of Ghana. This is already an inherent paradox interwoven within intuition itself. Objectivity is laminated by categorial intuitions that hide the sensual in order for one to deal with real life, what is *really there*, namely, the practical goals one has when driving. We overlook this overlooking all of the time. The nearness of my interests in things constantly wins-out attention over the sensuous givings or objective appearances of those things. This is likely one more reason why Marion privileges intuition (over intention) as the place of saturation; as the conscious locale of intelligibility in which one's *intelligibility* itself can be deformalized as the gift from the outside of any subject, ego, or "*l'adonné*."

An analogy is used to elucidate this problem more vividly. When one is fumbling about in the darkness perhaps in the middle of the night, one is not seeking intuition so much as a signification, comprehended even without anything being seen. In such a case, one does not intend so much as feelabout in order to meet some objective, for example of getting through the room to the kitchen. In this going through the room "I would like to know whether I have run up against a wall or a door to open ... the corner of a table ... or the back of a chair."[81] This example illustrates how my groping about is not for the purpose of gaining sensual impressions, but first, with eyes shut, touching significations without mediation: a table, a chair, a door, broken glass. I want to know what they are because their meanings are profoundly pertinent to me in that moment. Each of these categorial laminates tell me something significant about where I am.[82] Ultimately, this brings to manifestation a very particular, shifting gap in which "saturated phenomena become visible" in a way that saturates the field of vision itself.[83]

Inconspicuousness and the Paradox of the Banal

Although present and scattered throughout the different phases of his work, Marion's engagements with Heidegger's inconspicuousness are subtle and lacking in specificity for what it can mean as a concept. As recently as 2012, either he or his translator makes the mistake in translating the unapparent not as *unscheinbar* (inconspicuous) but *unsichtbar* (invisible) as Marion asks: "how should we understand the enigmatic but unavoidable expression 'phenomenology of the unapparent' (*Phänomenologie des Unsichtbaren*)?" Confusing, however, is that in the following sentence the opposite is indicated, that "the unapparent and the invisible do not mean the same thing, despite the fact that they challenge the privilege given to the visible."[84] At the very least, this discrepancy demonstrates the need for closer attention to this concept.

Yet Marion's work on occasion reflects the objective affinity to a phenomenology of the inconspicuous given his concerted efforts to conceive the—far too often contrasted—spaces between the invisible and the visible (as his 2016 *Givenness and Revelation* again demonstrates). Saturated phenomena oscillate between the visible and invisible in ways that thwart an intending expectation and controlling horizon, which usually shroud the possibilities of intuition's reception. In these regards Marion seems to be not far from Heidegger, who claims that the visible and invisible dialectic, especially when used to conceive the mysterious as purely unknown or unthinkable, can have a totalizing and mind-numbing effect. In a brief remark on inconspicuousness in "Aufzeichnung aus Der Werkstatt," Heidegger notes that it is precisely in wanting "to control everything" that one prohibits oneself from experiencing the "inconspicuous givens" (*unscheinbar gegebenen*).[85] Totalization insists and fundamentally thrives on this invisible and visible distinction without compromise, and Marion's understanding of revelation as a phenomenon attests to overcoming this fact.

However, revelation also phenomenalizes, and etymologically is referential to an *unveiling* of what is present, yet hitherto concealed. The Greek *apokálypsis* (*apo*, from; *kalyptein*, to conceal) refers to an impactful uncovering (not unlike *a-letheia*) and striking disclosure according to which one's life is altered through becoming aware of its unique phenomenalization. This awareness however, need not bring the revelation into full view, as it provides but a unique surplus for cutting against the grains of totality, which is exacted most powerfully from within the ordinariness of ontic life. This surplus can disrupt the tendency to a revelation-blindness, which is personified in a blind abstraction whereby the banalities of the everyday are thought to be meaningless. The impact of this uncovering rarely is straightforward, and often runs counter to clairvoyance.

Marion's work seems to be in need of a supplement to conceive of revelation's phenomenality beyond the spectacular terms that emphasize and auto-privilege what is superlative by merit of a bedazzling quality. This is because preferences for the glorious and spectacular seem to run contrary to the basic notion of what counts as counterintentional. Marion does not develop how it is in the inconspicuous and ordinary that revelation also can occur, and he instead focuses on an underlying saturation of phenomena, which can at any point overwhelm our pregiven conceptions because they have been overlooked or become banal. It is especially in the present cultural context of the mechanization of social life that Marion rightfully develops his notion of overlooked, saturated phenomena.

Marion wants to do justice to these phenomena, and then refers to how there are "poor phenomena" that are lacking in intuition because they are in fact surface diversions commodified in our societal context of industrialization that distract us from seeing properly what has become banal. Most of the time, these poor phenomena "assume the status of technically produced objects," which can be reproduced in "limitless quantity" and the cycle of consumption and production (*Vorhandenheit*, present-to-handed) authorizes their reproduction (*Zuhandenheit*, readiness-to-hand). These produced objects point to a negative sociality that inherently "covers over" and therefore makes more intuition-rich phenomena banal. As he puts it quite directly, "it could even be said that the world is covered with an invasive and highly visible layer of poor phenomena . . . which ends up eclipsing what it covers over"; that is, these saturated phenomena, which are ever-present yet overlooked.[86] It is in this context of the social criticisms of industrialized and technical life that Marion remains an ally to—the especially later—Heidegger, and an implicit critic of our society of spectacles.

Although Marion's "poor" or "common-law" phenomena have not gone uncritiqued, Marion does suggest that "the majority of phenomena, if not all, can undergo saturation by the excess of intuition over the concept" and that "the majority of phenomena that appear at first glance to be poor in intuition could be . . . phenomena that intuition saturates and therefore exceed any univocal concept."[87] Even the most simple can indeed entail a double interpretation, pending on how I relate with them at a given moment. Yet still, it seems Marion does not articular how the most common or marginalized could be a means by which revelation might phenomenalize. Despite the potential any and all phenomena hold for experience, the examples employed by Marion overwhelmingly point to a bedazzling spectacularity available to connoisseurs of high culture. The artwork of Rothko, an alto singing the Bach cantata, the fine tastes of a wine sommelier, and the saturating perfumes of Chanel or Guerlain are all cultural examples that point far beyond ordinary and common life. Although these examples suffice perfectly to illustrate his forms of saturation, truly common experience, it seems, is overlooked in favor of valued celebrity phenomena such as the "artistic genius."[88]

Inconspicuous Revelation

This opens onto the necessity of developing the ordinariness of Revelation as a paraphenomenon that operates with a counterness that is itself paradoxical even in its phenomenalization. If, as Marion thinks, Revelation is a paradox or counter experience, then it needs also to counter the predominant forms of phenomenality by "striking back" (para, counter) in an inconspicuous way that vandalizes and unravels the privileged forms of phenomenalization. It can be understood to do so in two ways. First, revelation's phenomenality generally is limited to altering reality through the shock and awe of an *Ereignis* that once and for all changes and leaves an eternal imprint, setting the experience apart from the everyday. Yet it is precisely such spectacular shock, glory, and setting apart (which in part is responsible for the compartmentalizing of modern life) that are in need of being bracketed in order for most experiences of revelation to occur. The hope of attaining the experience of anysuch glory even can inhibit the experience of revelation. In all practicality, many of the most fervent religious believers and theologians have not experienced firsthand these kinds of supernatural revelations. Thus, should it be claimed that these individuals do not experience Revelation?

Answering in the negative, it is possible to suggest that most revelations do not have this dazzling, event-like character. They more seamlessly phenomenalize by interweaving revelatory phenomena into the fabrics of the everyday. Seeking a revelation that entails a more spectacular shock still runs the risk of abiding by the generally preferred paradigm of phenomenality inherent within our present society of the spectacle. It thus cannot be taken for granted (1) that revelation must come as a surprise through creating an event uncommanded by intention, yet also (2) that what it furnishes is a spectacular, fantastic, and glorious bedazzlement. Instead, it seems more consistent to suggest that revelation, if it truly is to be shocking, must take place in the most unexpected of places and ways: in the marginal, inconspicuous, and banal. In equal parts, revelation shrouds just as much as it reveals, and operates according to its own inconspicuous horizon that prevents the experience of paradoxicality from crystalizing into a universalizable phenomenon readily available under the exacting control of an intending I.

A second way of understanding revelation as counterspectacular is that most revelations occur (and make their impact) incrementally and in varying degrees. This incrementality also allows revelation to operate in a nondetectable and inconspicuous way by subtly countering the dominant modes and rules of presentation through its own unique subversions. Its operation distills the preference for what presents itself clearly and spectacularly, altering not only through the presentation of information, but through uniquely reformatting the entire frame of presentation. This occurs through revelation taking on the character of a unique surplus. As Heidegger knew, a surplus of a thing furnishes other possibilities and potentialities in a way that ultimately might prevent us from becoming standing reserves (Le Thor Seminar, 1969) in the totality of machination.

Overall, Marion is right to suggest that revelation operates according to a saturation and excess that overwhelms the field of experience, yet it cannot be presumed that this excess is universally spectacular or bedazzling. Instead, some forms of revelation have small beginnings that operate incrementally, slowly, and therefore often inconspicuously. Such revelation incrementally deformalizes intention through excess, or a surplus. Revelation is not added to the sense data of an experience or introduced as a label or compartment of experience, but rather is integrated into the whole of the life of the one who experiences it. Revelation then is incarnate, and becomes a unique laminate placed over the *hyle* or sense data, ultimately influencing not just what appears, but how things appear. Such a deformalization usually is inconspicuous, and "as long as this paradox is not admitted, or at least thought honestly," to commandeer Marion's formulation, "the phenomenon of religion remains misunderstood."[89] Only as inconspicuous can the phenomenality or givenness of revelation escape the spectacle, and this marks a particular *whence* of the inconspicuous God.

Notes

1. Ludwig Wittgenstein, *Philosophical Investigations*, ed. G. E. M. Anscombe (Oxford: Basil Blackwell, 1994), 129.

2. Martin Heidegger, *Being and Time*, trans. John Macquarrie and Edward Robinson (New York: Harper & Row, 1962), 15.

3. St. Augustine, *Confessions*, trans. Rex Warner (New York: Signet Press, 2001), 270–71, § 11.22, 28. Jean-Luc Marion, *The Visible and the Revealed*, trans. Christina Gschwandtner (New York: Fordham University Press, 2008), 126.

4. *Doxa* may even have some relation with what "gives," for the Proto-Indo European root *dek* refers to "taking" or "accepting."

5. Zahavi refers to Janicaud's claim concerning the theological turn as a turn to the "invisible," and away from precision and clarity: "Janicaud asks whether this movement still deserves to be called phenomenological, or whether it should not rather be called metaphysical or theological. Is it not paradoxical to characterize a thinking that abandons the precision and clarity of vision and delves into the dark and mystical regions of invisibility, phenomenological? In short, is it not simply an absurdity to speak of a phenomenology of the invisible?" Dan Zahavi, "Michel Henry and the Phenomenology of the Invisible," *Continental Philosophy Review* 32 (1999): 235.

6. This is a debate internal to contemporary religious epistemology. Pollock sums up what is referred to as the "doxastic assumption" to be erroneous for all the theory can do is "tell us how our overall doxastic state determines which of our beliefs can be justified." John L. Pollock, *Contemporary Theories of Knowledge* (Totowa, NJ: Rowman & Littlefield, 1986), 19.

7. Heidegger, *Being and Time*, 60.

8. See here Martin Heidegger, *Sein und Zeit*, ed. Friedrich-Wilhelm von Herrmann (Frankfurt am Main: Vittorio Klostermann, 1977), 7, 35. Ibid., 59.

9. See here also Heidegger, *Sein und Zeit*, 47.

10. Zahavi confirms this position: "If we turn to Heidegger, he already in *Sein und Zeit* remarks that the specific task of phenomenology is to disclose that which 'zunächst und zumeist' remains hidden from view, namely Being. It is exactly because there are phenomena which do not reveal themselves immediately that we are in need of a phenomenology." Zahavi, "Michel Henry and the Phenomenology of the Invisible," 235. Zahavi then references Jean-Luc Marion, *Reduction and Givenness: Investigations of Husserl, Heidegger, and Phenomenology*, trans. Evanston Carlson (Evanston, IL: Northwestern University Press, 1998), 90–97.

11. For example, Seinder, Seindste, das Sein, die Seindheit, das Sein selbst, and Seyn.

12. Marion, *Reduction and Givenness*, 60. See also Jean-Luc Marion, *Réduction et donation: Recherches sur Husserl, Heidegger et la phénoménologie* (Paris: Presses Universitaires de France, 1989).

13. Heidegger, *Being and Time*, 59, § 7.

14. It is on this point in particular that Heraclitus "the obscure" becomes a formidable source of inspiration for Heidegger in the early 1940s.

15. Heidegger, *Being and Time*, 60. Being is a masking some other kind of being. See also 54, § 7.

16. Jean-Luc Marion, "The Invisible and the Phenomenon," in *Michel Henry: The Affects of Thought*, ed. Jeffrey Hanson and Michael R. Kelly (New York: Continuum Press, 2012), 19.

17. Most recently, Gschwandtner has made the argument that the answer should be "yes," at least for Marion and Henry: "Art bridges the gap between the realms of the invisible and the visible. That is both Henry's and Marion's most central claim about art. Exactly how it does so and why this matters differs in the two thinkers, yet for both the realm of the invisible is central and privileged." She continues to suggest that Marion's "analysis of art is also concerned with the interplay between visible and invisible realms" and that his "focus is more clearly on how the invisible becomes visible. Art does not remain invisible ... but, rather, crosses from the invisible into the visible." Christina M. Gschwandtner, "Revealing the Invisible: Henry and Marion on Aesthetic Experience," *The Journal of Speculative Philosophy* 28 no. 3 (2014): 306

18. Jean-Luc Marion, *Being Given: Toward a Phenomenology of Givenness*, trans. Jeffrey Kosky (Stanford, CA: Stanford University Press, 2002), 225.

19. Ibid.

20. And Marion continues "with this minor qualification: that its givenness contravenes, in its intuition, what previous experience should reasonably permit us to foresee." Ibid., 226.

21. In his essay "Transcendence and Evil" Levinas referred to two thinkers "daring to take interest in the meaning of transcendence;" The first was the lesser-known Philippe Nemo, whose work *Job and the Excess of Evil* attended to the matter of transcendence by starting with evil, which "interrupts" the flow of the world. The second was Marion, and for both thinkers, "the *ontological difference* seems ... to have been the chief encouragement to thinking anew and critically vis-à-vis a metaphysical tradition defined through ontology the meaning of transcendence." Emmanuel Lévinas, "Transcendence and Evil," in *Of God who comes to Mind*, (Stanford, CA: Stanford University Press, 1998), 126.

22. For Marion, we can "not rule out that one might have the right or even the duty to limit the field of phenomenology." However, "one must take the time and the trouble to justify this exclusion and to what about possible types of phenomena and degrees of phenomenality. One would certainly have to wonder whether this repression does not do more wrong to phenomenology itself (which would thus contradict its principal intention) than to the phenomena that it censures and that, despite this rejection, do not cease to manifest themselves." Marion, *Visible and Revealed*, xii.

23. Jean-Luc Marion, *Being Given: Toward a Phenomenology of Givenness*, trans. Jeffrey L. Kosky (Stanford: Stanford University Press, 2002), 16.

24. Günther Anders, *Die Antiquiertheit des Menschen. Ausgabe in einem Band, vol. 1* (Munich: Beck Verlag, 1980), 2.

25. Peter Grego, *The Collected Works of St. Teresa of Avila, vol. 3*, trans. Kieran Kavanaugh and Otilio Rodriguez (Washington, DC: ICS Publications, 1985), 121.

26. Marion, *Visible and Revealed*, 60.

27. See here Martin Heidegger, *Poetry, Language, Thought*, trans. Albert Hofstadter (New York, Harper & Row, 1971), 51. For Heidegger: "And yet—beyond what is, not away from it but before it, there is still something else that happens. In the midst of beings as a whole an open place occurs. There is a clearing, a lighting (*Lichtung*). Thought of in reference to what is, to beings, this clearing is in a greater degree than are beings."

28. Heidegger, *Being and Time*, 219 and Heidegger, *Sein und Zeit*, 262.

29. Martin Heidegger, "The Seminar in Zähringen 1973," in *Four Seminars*, trans. Andrew J. Mitchell and François Raffoul (Bloomington: Indiana University Press, 2003), 70. From ex-sistence, "*sistere*" is a verb that, as Sheehan notes, means "to *make* someone or something stand out and beyond." And "Thus the term *Existenz* is already a pre-indication of what gets expressed in Heidegger's early work as *Geworfenheit* and *der geworfene Entwurf*." Thomas Sheehan, *Making Sense of Heidegger: A Paradigm Shift* (London: Rowman & Littlefield International, 2014), xvii.

30. Françoise Dastur, "La pensée àvenir: une pheénoménologie de l'inapparent?," in *L'avenir de la philosophie est-il grec?*, ed. Catherine Collobert (Saint-Laurent, QC: Fides, 2002), 146.

31. Polt critiques that the Heidegger of *Being and Time* "claims that the being of beings is simply not-yet-appearing (being can be thematized as a phenomenon, even though it can never appear as ontically present (Heidegger, *Sein und Zeit*, 35); in contrast, the *Contributions* focus on be-ing (the giving of the being of beings) and claim that it is, at least in some ways, intrinsically unapparent." Richard F. H. Polt, *The Emergency of Being: On Heidegger's Contributions to Philosophy* (Ithaca, NY: Cornell University Press, 2006), note 38.

32. For Heidegger, "Being-covered-up (*Verdecktsein*) is the counter concept to phenomenon, and such concealments through covering up (*Verdeckungen*) are really the immediate theme of phenomenological reflection." Heidegger, *Sein und Zeit*, 35, § 7. Heidegger, *Being and Time*, 59.

33. Marion, *Reduction and Givenness*, 57. There are grounds for caution to claim Marion realizes how this paradoxical counterconcept isn't the opposite of "phenomenon" because Marion interprets Heidegger's counterconcept a bit differently in 2012. When speaking of Henry's differences from Heidegger, Marion suggests that for Henry the invisible is not an "antithetical concept" of the visible. Yet this seems to be precisely what Heidegger was

claiming in *Sein und Zeit* when referencing hiddenness within phenomena. Marion, "The Invisible and the Phenomenon," 33

34. Marion, *Reduction and Givenness*, 58.

35. Martin Heidegger, *The Event*, trans. Richard Rojcewicz (Bloomington: Indiana University Press, 2013), 8.

36. Heidegger's "truth" is different from Aristotle's *adaequatio*, which concerned "correctness." Ibid., 8–9.

37. Marion, *Reduction and Givenness*, 59.

38. Ibid.

39. Ibid., 60. And Marion interprets "For Heidegger the repetition and radicalization of the Husserlian watchword (*das Ding*) had no other goal than to succeed in formulating this incomparably ambitious and paradoxical task—to return to Being as Being and, in the same movement, to return to it as to a phenomenon."

40. Ibid. The phenomenological conceptuality of the gift entails that it is a phenomenon that cannot be brought into full presence because it would then be economized. Elsewhere, Marion once somewhat enigmatically suggested that "Derrida therefore recovers 'the phenomenology of the unapparent', without any theological turn, simply by criticizing the supposed evidence of the gift." Marion, *Visible and Revealed*, 84.

41. Heidegger, *Being and Time*, 5.

42. Marion, *Reduction and Givenness*, 61.

43. Heidegger, *Sein und Zeit*, 63: "Höher als die Wirklichkeit steht die *Möglichkeit*." In another context, as Sheehan notes, Heidegger refers to saturation that is referential to *Dasein*: "I a priori 'exceed' things insofar as I am always already 'beyond them,' related to their significance. The different and constantly changing worlds I live in—as student, worker, parent—are saturated with meaning, as is everything that shows up within those meaning-giving worlds. Everything I attend to—everything I can 'mind'—turns out to make sense, whether actually or potentially." Sheehan, *Making Sense of Heidegger*, 112.

44. For Taminiaux, "Heidegger's fascinated gaze found in the Logical Investigations the emergence of a group of themes which incite the *Seinsfrage* in *Sein und Zeit*: namely that being transcends the entity, that being is the *transcendens* par excellence, that being is in a special sense *the* phenomenon of phenomenology, that the entity's coming-into-appearance requires a prior understanding of being, that this understanding, to the extent to which it is beyond, is nonetheless inseparable from an exposition of an entity, that the excessiveness of being is the cradle of truth." This seeing is one that "grasps things in their coming-into-appearance, intentionality, is itself transfixed with excessiveness; seeing must be beyond the given in order for things to be and to be what they are." Jacques Taminiaux, "Heidegger and Husserl's Logical Investigations in Remembrance of Heidegger's Last Seminar (Zähringen, 1973)," *Research in Phenomenology* 7 no. 1 (1977): 79

45. Martin Heidegger, "Seminar in Le Thor 1969," in *Four Seminars*, trans. Andrew J. Mitchell and François Raffoul (Bloomington: Indiana University Press, 2003), 62, cf. 38. On this point, see here Carl Raschke, *Force of God: Political Theology and the Crisis of Liberal Democracy* (New York: Columbia University Press, 2015).

46. As Heidegger insists, "that which frees—the mystery—is concealed and always concealing itself." Further, "Freedom is that which conceals in a way that opens to light, in whose clearing shimmers the veil that hides the essential occurrence of all truth (i.e.,

a-lethia) and lets the veil appear as what veils." Martin Heidegger, *The Question Concerning Technology, and Other Essays* (New York: Harper & Row, 1977), 330.

47. Mystery is essential to truth, as Heidegger claims in "On the Essence of Truth." There, Heidegger uses *das Geheimnis*, according to Withy, "to refer to being as self-concealing, and he identifies this self-concealing as the nonessence of truth." Katherine Withy, *Heidegger on Being Uncanny* (Cambridge: Harvard University Press, 2015), 133. Withy's recent work takes this thesis one step further and argues that for Heidegger the human *is* such an uncanny being; that is, *Dasein* is *called* to be not-at-home.

48. Martin Heidegger, *Introduction to Metaphysics*, 2nd ed., trans. Gregory Fried and Richard Polt (New Haven, CT: Yale University Press, 2014), 182. Cf. Martin Heidegger, GA 40, *Einführung in die Metaphysik* (Frankfurt am Main: Vittorio Klostermann, 1966), 131.

49. Ibid., 175. Cf. Martin Heidegger, GA 9, *Wegmarken* (Frankfurt am Main: Vittorio Klostermann, 1967), 198.

50. Heidegger, *Wegmarken*, 197.

51. Edmund Husserl, *The Idea of Phenomenology*, trans. William Alston and Georege Nakhnikian (The Hague: Martinus Nijhoff, 1964), 169, cf. 148.

52. Of particular note is the work of Christina M. Gschwandtner, *Degrees of Givenness: On Saturation in Jean-Luc Marion* (Bloomington: Indiana University Press, 2014). I also have addressed and described Marion's conception of givenness, especially as it relates to the ever-prescient conception of love and desire in his work. See Jason W. Alvis, *Marion and Derrida on the Gift and Desire: Debating the Generosity of Things*. Contributions to Phenomenology Series (Switzerland: Springer Press, 2016).

53. This chapter was published first in German. Jean-Luc Marion, "Aspekte der Religionsphänomenologie: Grund, Horizont und Offenbarung," in *Religionsphilosophie heute*, ed. Alois Halder, Klaus Kinzler, and Joseph Möller (Düsseldorf: Patmos Press, 1988), 84–103 This essay marked the first attempt to articulate saturated phenomena, and ambitiously sets "revelation" out as one among them.

54. Marion, *Visible and Revealed*, 121.

55. Ibid., 122, cf. 120. Marion continues, "the ideal norm of evidence (equality between intuition and the concept) is no longer threatened only and as usual by a shortage of intuition, but by its excess. I named and explained this phenomenon by excess as the (intuitively) saturated phenomenon."

56. Regarding this unconditionality, see Marion, *Being Given*, 212.

57. Jean-Luc Marion, "The Other First Philosophy and the Question of Givenness," trans. Jeffrey L. Kosky, *Critical Inquiry* 25 no. 4 (1999): 794.

58. For example, Gschwandtner contends that if all phenomena are "given" via the powers of givenness, as Marion himself claims, then even these "poor" phenomena also have at least some level or "degree" of saturation. Marion opens this interpretation in concluding that phenomena give in variation. From my perspective, given Marion's often stated interests in delineating the differences between gift and economy, it would be inconsistent for Marion to hold too strictly to a dyad between excess and nonexcess or saturation and nonsaturation, for this would raise the question of "purity," which involves an economical assessment and appropriation of things. See Marion, *Being Given*, 234.

59. For Marion, "in order to introduce the concept of the saturated phenomenon in phenomenology, I have just described it as *invisible* (unforeseeable) according to quantity, unbearable according to quality, but also *unconditioned* (absolved from any horizon)

according to relation, and *irreducible* to the *I* (incapable of being looked at) according to modality. These four characteristics imply the term-for-term reversal of all the rubrics under which Kant classifies the principles and thus the phenomena that these determine." Marion, *Visible and Revealed*, 45. See also Marion, *Being Given*, 233.

60. See again Gschwandtner, who questions to what extent givenness already implies excess and saturation. The infinite variation "of degrees of givenness from poorer to richer phenomenality, the notion of the paradox and Marion's descriptions of the saturated phenomenon instead indicate far more absolute distinctions: a phenomenon is *either* 'poor' *or* 'saturated,' intuition is *either* 'empty' *or* 'full,' consciousness *either* controls and constitutes the phenomenon *or* it is overwhelmed by what is given and utterly unable to constitute it or impose its own parameters on it." Gschwandtner, *Degrees of Givenness*, 5.

61. Jean-Luc Marion, *The Crossing of the Visible*, trans. James K. A. Smith (Stanford, CA: Stanford University Press, 2004), 63, 82. See also 33 where he suggests of paintings that they thwart expectations.

62. Marion's "idol" is a saturated phenomenon that embodies art and its unique saturation of visibility itself. See also Marion's *The Crossing of the Visible* where he contends that art produces "new visibles" via the painter who acts as "the porter who filters the unseen's access to the visible, the master of every entrée onto the scene, [and as] the guardian of the limits of appearance … grants visibility to the unseen, delivering the unseen from its anterior invisibility." Marion, *Crossing of the Visible*, 26. Then in a most recent reflection on the idol, Marion reflects on how art provides access to the invisible precisely through its making vision "dazzling" with radiance. Jean-Luc Marion, "What We See and What Appears," in *Idol Anxiety*, ed. J. Ellenbogen and A. Tugendhaft (Stanford CA: Stanford University Press, 2011), 161–162. See also Peter Joseph Fritz, "Black Holes and Revelations: Michel Henry and Jean-Luc Marion on the Aesthetics of the Invisible," *Modern Theology* 25 no. 3 (2009): 415–40.

63. The icon saturates in the other's "burdening" my gaze. Marion, *Being Given*, 233.

64. Ibid.

65. Ibid., 235–37. Marion also attends to this matter in the preface to *The Visible and the Revealed*. The Biblical references Marion uses to color this visibility tellingly emphasize a correlation between lighting, God, and revelation: "Christ's Revelation is given as an event that *appears* within history and in the present; it appears rightfully and even as a phenomenon par excellence. Not only is 'God [himself] revealed' (Romans 1:19) in the light of this visibility, but anything else also becomes fully visible, as it never would otherwise. Revelation reveals any phenomenon to itself." This statement of Revelation resonates as if it suggested a phenomenology of the revealed. The difference between the two spellings (uppercase and lowercase) marks the difficulty exactly here: "If 'the light appears in the darkness' (John 1:5), then what light is at stake? That of a revealing phenomenology or a completely different one, that of Revelation revealing itself?" Marion, *Visible and Revealed*, xi.

66. Ibid., 2. The paradoxical character of Christianity is a topic most recently taken up by Felix Ó. Murchadha, *Phenomenology of Christian Life: Glory and Night* (Bloomington: Indiana University Press, 2013).

67. Marion, *Visible and Revealed*, 2.

68. "What appears is as and according to how it gives itself." Marion, *Visible and Revealed*, 6.

69. Ibid.

70. Ibid., 7–8, 13, 15. On page 13 he continues, "Phenomenology cannot give its status to theology, because the conditions of manifestation contradict or at least are different from the free possibility of revelation. Yet the result is not necessarily a divorce."

71. Ibid., 15.

72. Ibid. Further, "In any case, possibility actually submits straightaway to the restriction of a horizon. Any horizon that determines the scene of incoming phenomena in a priori fashion delimits the possible, hence limits (or forbids) revelation."

73. This is why the way to "do justice to the possibility of revelation" in a phenomenological key, Marion concludes, is for the "I" to admit that it is not the basis of all things, and for one to see how the horizon does not necessarily *determine* that which is given, but when thought of as saturated, truth's evidence is converted from "doxa to the paradoxon of the revealed." Ibid., 16.

74. Ibid. "In this situation, truth no longer comes for doxa (true or false) appearance, but from paradoxon, an appearance that contradicts opinion or appearance, and above all saturates the horizon."

75. This all should be taken in conjunction with later claims concerning revelation: "Let me repeat that by 'revelation' I here intend a strictly phenomenological concept: an appearance that is purely of itself and starting from itself, that does not subject its possibility to any preliminary determination." Ibid., 47. This is all also compounded by the fact that, as Marion claims in a later chapter of this book "The Banality of Saturation" (Ibid., 122): "no Revelation, with a capital R, can be given within phenomenality." This is because there is no "'pure experience' of 'full transcendence.'"

76. For closer engagements with Heidegger's interest in Husserl's categorial/sensical intuitions, see Daniel Dahlstrom, *Heidegger's Concept of Truth* (New York: Cambridge University Press, 2001), 80.

77. See here the Heidegger, "Seminar in Zähringen 1973," 77–80.

78. Ibid., 67. "In this sense, one can even say that it is more apparent than what itself appears."

79. Martin Heidegger, "Letters to Roger Munier (dated Feb 22, 1974)," in *Martin Heidegger*, ed. Michel Haar (Paris: Editions de l'Herne, 1983), 115. Prior to that, on April 16, 1973, he writes "for me it is a matter of actually performing an exercise in a phenomenology of the inapparent; by the reading of books, no one ever arrives at phenomenological 'seeing.'" Martin Heidegger, *Four Seminars* (Bloomington: Indiana University Press, 2003), 89.

80. Jean-Luc Marion, "The Banality of Saturation," in *The Visible and the Revealed*, trans. Jeffrey Koskey (New York: Fordham University Press, 2008), 127.

81. Ibid., 130.

82. Ibid. "In this darkness I therefore do not first touch surfaces or materials; rather I recognize objects, which is to say that I touch significations directly."

83. Ibid., 133. Marion continues to suggest that there is a "gap between the phenomenon as object and the phenomenon that 'fills the soul beyond its capacity.'"

84. Marion, "The Invisible and the Phenomenon," 20. This mistake is strange, especially because in note 2 (ibid., 35) Marion refers to the unapparent correctly as "*unscheinbar.*"

85. Martin Heidegger, "Aufzeichnung aus Der Werkstatt" in GA 13, *Aus der Erfahrung des Denkens*. "Doch man will alles steuern, möchte keine Spur mehr spüren, das heißt einer schon unscheinbar gegebenen Weisung nachgehen, um sie erblickend zu hören."

86. Marion, "The Banality of Saturation," 125.

87. Ibid.

88. Does Marion conceive of how the paradox must appear in the "ordinary?" He does not appear to do so, and instead lays emphasis on the opposite, that sacredness comes through more glorious forms, such as those of high culture, for example, that "since our times seem to have lost the aesthetic means to build churches and even to construct palaces, let's not joke too much about the museum, this unavowed avatar of the sanctuary of pilgrimage" Jean-Luc Marion, *In Excess: Studies of Saturated Phenomena*, trans. Robyn Horner and Vincent Berraud (New York: Fordham University Press, 2002), 70. Then, most recently he focuses on a very particular, spectacularly skilled person: the artistic genius, who is required in order to bring to visibility the invisible. Marion, "What We See and What Appears," 167.

89. Marion, *Visible and Revealed*, 2.

2 Inconspicuous Phenomenology: On Heidegger's *Unscheinbarkeit* or Inapparent

The art of being wise is the art of knowing what to overlook.
—William James[1]

Sic transit Gloria *mundi*. Fleeting is the glory of the world. Yet it is in the world that religious life and its intricate manifold of phenomena are experienced. The glory of religiously experienced phenomena, as experienced in the world, may then share the same fate as the world in which they appear, as fleeting. This illustrates a perplexing double bind that a phenomenology of religious experience would entail: To be phenomenological, its descriptive approaches as experiences must be limited to how they appear in and of this world as the theater in which they present themselves to an unsuspecting horizon of thought. Yet as religious, one is called to abandon precisely such a justificatory and calculative process, whose glory is limited to this world and its seemingly natural and thereby intersocial proceedings.

Of course, neither extreme offers good options. On the one hand, a phenomenology that overbearingly demands a methodological atheism can be reduced quickly to epistemology, thus abandoning any primacy of phenomenology and its descriptive apparatus. Yet on the other, a phenomenology that presumes religious experience immediately to shun the power of explanatory and justificatory approaches runs the risk of being a kind of autofideism (perhaps even delusion) that allows any and all phenomena (even flying spaghetti monsters) warrant to appear without any justification, and therefore, as solipsistic, lacking in explanatory, intersocial power. Can phenomenologies of religious experience actually ever be more than fundamentally solipsistic endeavors, and at the same time escape from being trapped under what Rorty once called the "collapsed circus tent of epistemology?"[2] More pointedly, can phenomenology say anything putatively new about religion and God that is not reducible to previously held beliefs, or perhaps worse, mere speculation?

It is on these accounts and matrixes of opposition that a phenomenology of the inconspicuous might make an intervention. Before continuing in the following chapters to consider the potential inconspicuousness might have for theological thinking, this chapter makes three more phenomenologically oriented steps in understanding Heidegger's "Phänomenologie des Unscheinbaren." It provides a contextualization of the concept in the framework of the Zähringen seminar, seminar an interpretation of his usages of the term in the Parmenides seminars, and then a determination as to what Heidegger likely intends when he refers to it given his overall interests (which never are without some controversy). I argue there are three different lenses by which these references might be interpreted, all of which point to a particular approach:

1. Following Heidegger's reformation of Husserlian phenomenology according to how the *a priori* of appearance can never be brought to light, the *unscheinbar* is interwoven with the *scheinbar* as a form of "hiddenness" (Λήθη, *lethe*) that lets things be brought into presence; it is germane to the "clearing" (*Lichtung*) and intertwined within every aspect of appropriated human existence (*ereignete Dasein*) in which and to whom the intelligibility of things appear. This would make *unscheinbar* inherently applicable to *all* of Heidegger's phenomenology.
2. Another option is that Heidegger is introducing into phenomenology a particular step that involves the attuning of oneself to the many strata of various modes of potential hiddenness (*Verborgenheit* and its cognates) that all phenomena are capable of enacting, and inconspicuousness is now to be included as a form, characteristic, or mode among them.
3. Alternatively there may be particular, unique, and specific phenomena that have the tendency to give themselves inconspicuously, and, if so, it likely also is true that there is a corresponding, particular phenomenology in which one must engage in order to have access to the phenomenal strata of their paradoxical intelligibility.

Overall, it is hoped that this chapter can present at least some core aspects of what Heidegger's "phenomenology of the inconspicuous" entails and what it does not. Such a concept, if it could be formalizable into an approach, might allow further access to the site of interaction between the multivalent forms of withdrawal and presence (*Präsenz* or *Anwesenheit*), which take place in presencing or the-becoming-essential (*An-wesen*), language on which Heidegger came to rely more strongly in the mid-1940s.[3] Although there is a level of ambiguity (even to the point of seeming sophistical) in Heidegger's references to *das Unscheinbare* in the Zähringen seminar, I would suggest that they can play a role (and be contextualized) in Heidegger's broader interests concerning the status of *Dasein*, the "how" of appearance, and the grounding of phenomenology in truth and the clearing that to some degree is metonymic with Being.[4] Further, his occasional uses of the word *unscheinbar* in his engagements with Parmenides's work helps illuminate a red thread that runs throughout these works, thus offering a greater degree of precision in an interpretation of the concept.

Inconspicuousness in the 1973 Zähringen Seminar

Often inspired by an interest in synthesizing Heraclitus's focus on becoming with Parmenides's "it is" of Being, Heidegger lays emphasis on the power of insignificant things in an embrace of the ordinary, marginal, and bare, namely, those things that resist technological efficiency and machination. Things that hold strata of ordinariness are not necessarily insignificant (as some have translated *unscheinbar*) in the sense of their lacking in signification or meaningfulness, but they are on the contrary meaning-*full* despite their not drawing immediate attention within conscious experience. For something to be insignificant in these specific terms is for such a thing to bear paradoxically great significance, despite its having certain tendencies or traits of being easily overlooked (e.g., tools at hand). The most explicit attention paid by Heidegger to such inconspicuousness (at least, as a concept) was in his seminar on the outskirts of Freiburg in Zähringen, in 1973:

> Thus understood, phenomenology is a path that leads away to come before . . ., and it lets that before which it is led show itself. This phenomenology is a phenomenology of the inapparent [*unscheinbar*]. Only now can one understand that there were no concepts for the Greeks. Indeed, in conceiving [*be-greifen*], there is the gesture of taking possession. The Greek . . . on the contrary surrounds firmly and delicately that which sight takes into view; it does not conceive.[5]

It first must be understood that such a phenomenology is tautological and paradoxical. One must follow in a "way" (*Weg*) of thinking whereby one engages in how distance creates nearness (*der hinführt vor . . . und sich das zeigen läßt*), and this distance, this awayness is the only way in which one can experience the thing as it shows or bears its intelligibility. *This* (*diese*, that is, something *particular*) phenomenology is "a phenomenology of the inapparent."[6] Away and before, modes of distance and closeness that are basic conditioners of relation, play a formative role in the experiencing of the inconspicuousness of phenomena.

Throughout the Zähringen seminar Heidegger reflects back, nearly forty-five years later, to what he thinks was the original merit of *Sein und Zeit*. The seminar is propelled by a question posed by Jean Beufret that leads Heidegger to describe how his own work might be distinguished from Husserl's. How and why did Heidegger find it necessary to turn from Husserl's method? Such a turn was on the basis of Husserl's negligence of the important, nonmetaphysical meaning or truth of Being. Being in the world, Dasein (Ex-sistence, being-open) is a more originary experience to thinking than a being-conscious (*be-greifen*, conceiving), and one can somehow access it through what we constantly take for granted: the ever-hiding and concealed clearing work of Being. Although Husserl references "Being" as one of the facets of relation in consciousness, he never addresses or inquires into its meaning in and of itself, and simply follows the philosophical tradition with an understanding of Being as a constant, steadfast presence (*Anwesenheit und Beständigkeit*), thus overlooking the appropriation of ex-sistence. Yet at the same time, Being (and our experience of it in as the clearing) is fundamentally hidden and withdrawn.[7] Being is the basic way in which things reveal themselves and their intelligibility. The truthing or disclosure (or discovery) of Being (which also entails various laminates of concealment), as Heidegger interprets *Sein*, holds the keys to one's most fundamental experience with things. Such a truth is always already both temporally and spatially before. As he refers to ἀλήθεια in *Sein und Zeit*, unconcealment has a self-evident and prephilosophical basis.[8] Thus, the worldhood of the world is but a means to raise anew the question of Being (and the clearing of Being), which in its preconscious and prephilosophical truth is to be understood or grasped uniquely.

In beginning to answer Beaufret's question, Heidegger references, in an obvious nod to Husserl's *Logical Investigations*, the differences between sensuous intuition and categorial intuition, and the ways in which one's initial experience with objects, for example, is not with their sensual data, but actually their categorial projections. Despite my material experience with brown wood and four posts, I only see the table because I am involved with it in particular ways, and therefore treat it as such because it is pertinent to my present involvement in the world. I take it as a table to toss my house keys on. Thus the object's coming into appearance is not first the result of sense data, but rather my particular representations of what it does for me in that moment. This leads to a perplexing paradox: Sense data and substantiality are what truly bring things to appearance, yet they generally do not manifest themselves to us. The *hyle* or building blocks of sensuous perception (color, taste, and shape) make objects' appearance possible, yet their data elusively disappear and slide into the shadows of consciousness in preference for the thing we wish to see—so much so that they often could change in drastic ways without our even being aware. In short, *hyle* become marginalized and inconspicuous insofar as they are effective on the changing structure of consciousness as well as the object itself. Yet their sense data operate in such a way that they go overlooked. The fact that we overlook the *hyle* in favor of the categorial is not to be criticized as a result of fallenness, but is further proof that we are situated beings whose interests in things are brought to bear upon the experience. This furnishes us with an evident fact that consciousness seems to prefer that which one has experienced before and is not necessarily visible, over actually seeing the sense data that appears. This allows for one understanding of how a thing can be inconspicuousness.

Yet there is another aspect of the categorial and sensuous relation on which Heidegger calls us to reflect: Our relation with the categorial is indeed mediated, and this points to how the appearance of things has a tendency to make semi-permanent impressions that fix phenomena into place without the movement of taking things as. Taking things as entails the knowledge that there is a certain unfixed relation one has with things and their various meanings, which one must think of discursively (*discurrere*) by traversing back and forth between one's thoughts about the matter at hand, and how one thinks the things happen to be showing themselves.[9] As Sheehan recently has conceived, this is the important process of "making sense" in Heidegger's work. Yet Husserl (and his conception of consciousness, *Bewußt-sein*) follows much of the rest of the philosophical tradition of metaphysics and makes the faulty preference for fixation, and therefore for that which appears clearly, over that which does not seem or appear.

There are many relations one has with the nonappearing. Yet one typically relates with that which does not appear according to the hope and interest in actively making its data come into appearance, and thus, such a relation is still centered around or motivated by an interest in appearance. Thus, the preference for that which appears or is revealed over that which is inconspicuously hidden or obscure remains intact. Husserlian being-conscious is a matter of regarding, preserving, and safekeeping that which one has seen or known, beginning with a presuming *ego cogito* that not only prefers appearance and presence, but initially operates according to a number of preunderstood distinctions, such as appearing/nonappearing, inside/outside (though Husserl often explicitly rejects this distinction), and covered/uncovered. These distinctions may effectively undermine the phenomenological project and its status as *Erste Philosophie*, for they hinder its interests (and therefore thinking) by resorting to a thinking by way of dichotomies.

Instead, Heideggerian Being is the lever that allows for one to go beyond both conceiving of the objecthood of the object, and the distinction between the sensuous and categorial. Such Being helps deformalize what we take to be seemingly ideal preferences for that which straightforwardly appears to us as obvious, and comes to be regarded by us as clear. There is a sense in which phenomenology also must become the study of how one looks past things on both the sensual and categorial levels, and toward Dasein, ex-sistence or open-being, which gives "space" (*Räumlichkeit*) for both the sensual and categorial to appear. In *Sein und Zeit*, the thing is in the world, which is not immanent to consciousness; Dasein becomes the ek-statically outside and made-to-open (as *Ereignet*, or event of being-appropriated) beyond the stationary and immobile.[10] It is here *in* Being and on this level that immanence is broken through and through. Yet there is still a sense in which one relates with things instantaneously via a going out of oneself. One can be attuned (again, as thrown-open and as appropriated) to such a state of ex-sistence, as one is always already in this state of being-in-the-clearing outside of oneself. Such an attunement or relation is instantaneous, for one is in relation not with the thing in its mere presence, but in its presencing itself (*Anwesen-heit*).[11] The here and now and the sensual are brought into presence, into a giving of sense in the distant reach of what appears to be given immediately. Even instantaneousness, the "immediate" (*sofort*) that lacks a medium or go between, is subject to the temporal and spatial dimensions of being-open. This is the necessary distance or space that makes up one's comportment or ex-sistence as Dasein.

This initiates a turn to the meaning of presence (or "meaningful presence"), which plays an indicative role in understanding that something is, or in taking something as, namely in this case as inconspicuous. The present is given or is brought into manifestation or presence. How, though, might the present presence itself? Could there be differing modalities or laminates of presence? Such modalities could be indicated, despite their not giving themselves in and of themselves in any straightforward way. The key, perhaps, is that one is to hold, for as long as possible, presencing itself into view by engaging the truthing disclosure and inherent closure of presencing, as they both simultaneously form presencing itself; an inherently creative act. The present is essentially truth-being, and to access it one must follow a certain paradoxical path (the "path that leads away to come before") of going away in order to truly relate with that which is at home or before oneself.[12] No such kind of paradoxical away-presence was thought of by Husserl, yet for Heidegger absence or awayness is essential to attaining a phenomenology that is befitting of the *conditio humana*, which is marked by projections beyond the subject.

These general interpretations of Heidegger's "inconspicuous" in relation to categorial intuition and presencing are further confirmed in a letter written to Roger Munier shortly after the seminar at Zähringen concerning how Heidegger differentiates his view on "categorial intuition" from Husserl's in section 2, "Sense and Understanding," of the fourth of *the Logical Investigations.* An approach to the inconspicuous allows one to arrive at a phenomenological "seeing," according to which one performs an exercise, which would involve an investigation (that is to say a study of the how structure of the appearance) of that which is present-absent or inconspicuous. Heidegger then suggests to Munier that "you can easily link this text to what particularly concerned you in my lecture 'What Is Called Thinking?'"[13] In "What Is Called Thinking" the interplay between withdrawal (away) and arrival (before) figures prominently. One's responding to the call of thinking, leads this to happen:

> That which is to be thought turns away from us. It withdraws from us. But how can we have the least knowledge of something that is withdrawn from the outset? How can we even give it a name? Whatever withdraws refuses arrival. But—withdrawing is not nothing. Withdrawal is event [appropriation, *ereignis*]. In fact, what withdraws may even concern and claim man more essentially than anything present that strikes and touches him.[14]

This also intimately is related to withdrawal and inconspicuousness in *Poetry, Language, Thought*: "The inconspicuous [*unscheinbare*] thing withdraws itself from thought most stubbornly. Or can it be that this self-refusal of the mere thing, this self-contained refusal to be pushed around, belongs precisely to the essential nature of things?"[15]

And finally, of note in *Unterwegs zur Sprache* is reference to the kind of relations we have with this withdrawal, which is appropriation: "Das Ereignis ist das Unscheinbarste des Unscheinbaren"—(appropriation is the most inconspicuous of the inconspicuous).[16]

As *unscheinbar*, things are inherently elusive and evade our attempts to keep them from withdrawing. Withdrawal (*Entzug*) is equated with the appropriated or mine-made appropriation (*Ereignis*), which operate in such an impressively inconspicuous manner. That is, the retreat of that which mobilized into the shadows of thought has a form (perhaps its very own) of impressing itself on us, most especially as we appropriate its movement as withdrawn. This is not withdrawal merely as invisibility (*unsichtbar*) or even a form of hiddenness or obscurity (*Dunkelheit*), but a withdrawal that "gives" (i.e., giving one the experience of its withdrawal and thereby being of concern to us) even in its achieving the status of moving away, and retreating from being before us in visibility (*Sichtbarkeit*). Inconspicuousness must exceed the *a priori* distinction between the visible and invisible, and even though events generally are referred to as shocking (e.g. St. Paul being knocked to the ground by God in a radical darkening of his vision), the greatest forms of eventhood or being-appropriated may in fact be inconspicuous, incarnate, and integrated.

Concealment and Unconcealment in the Early *Parmenides Seminar*

Before turning back to the Zähringen seminar, it is helpful to contextualize these interpretations of *unscheinbar* alongside other references to the word in Heidegger's work. The earliest meaningful references to *unscheinbar* (though no explicit exercise in experiencing it) is found in the Parmenides seminar in the winter semester of 1942/1943 (GA 54), and it appears in the context of Heidegger reiterating the false dialectic between unconcealedness and concealment, the relation of which should instead be thought about according to more specific, distinct modes (*Weisen*). Our understandings of truth and concealedness far too often lead us to quarantine the sphere of mystery to the "merely not yet known."[17] We thus need a return to the various cognates or intelligible meanings of concealment, which are essential to truth (ἀλήθεια), the Greek meanings of which are uniquely rethought by Heidegger.[18] In order to experience the truth of truth (the active "ἀ" of "λήθεια" so to speak), we must be led, according to Parmenides in *Fragment 8* "to the 'that it is'" which is such an unusual path that leads one out there to the open—a "lighting" (*Lichtung*) that does not fully present or give itself in any straightforward sense.[19] For Parmenides, Being in its most fundamental sense is ἀλήθεια. In Heidegger's seminars, then, the dimension of *lethe* (Λήθη), is conceived as an *a priori* aspect of unconcealment, and thus truth already contains within itself, as part and parcel of its essence, laden aspects of concealment (e.g., withdrawal). Heidegger makes this explicit: "the essential form of unconcealedness, [the active *Unverborgenheit*] . . . in a certain way retains within itself concealedness [*Verborgenheit*] and concealment [the more passive *Verbergung*] and even must do so."[20] That is, some modes of concealment are always already at work in unconcealment in order for unconcealment to be properly unconcealment *as such*. Concealment is essential to the make-up of unconcealment (alternatively "disclosure" or *entbergen*).

How does this work and how might one experience it? Overall, there are two general ways in which we might understand the operative functions of such concealment: first, there is concealment as such, which for "the Greeks the essence of concealment [*Verbergung*] and unconcealedness [*Unverborgenheit*] was experienced so essentially as the basic feature of Being itself." It is this concealment and unconcealment that operates as a primordial essence that goes beyond any interpretation of concealment as simply being a form of partially hiding (*Pseudos*), disguising, and dissembling. Heidegger calls this the "one mode of concealment that for the Greeks . . . has codetermined the truth, the unconcealedness and unhiddenness, of all beings."[21] This might be thought of as one overarching concealment (perhaps as *concealedness 1*) within truth itself.

Yet, there is another way of thinking about concealment (*concealedness 2*) namely, in its various "modes" (*Weisen*) and kinds (*Arten*). This second form breaks up and distinguishes the many faces of concealment, which Heidegger appears to classify under two overall sorts: those that displace and those that shelter or save. Under the former, such concealing can be in the form of "putting away" (*weg*), setting aside, making disappear, making absent, destroying, or withdrawing. Under the latter, shattering form of concealment falls preserving, safeguarding, and rarifying, namely, of that which is of worth and to be treasured. There are forms of concealment that specifically pertain more to the domain of presence than of absence, and can be given to phenomenological description. Yet their being described can take place only through various forms of renouncement (e.g., resistance, ignorance). Further, there is never a full unconcealment of concealment, and the thing itself reveals its strata inconspicuously. Intuition (*Anschauung*) does not bring such phenomena to full appearance.

It is thus these forms (esp., preserving and treasuring) that are closer to the heart of mysteriousness, which essentially is far more than its misunderstood nature as the unexplained or unknown. Un-knowing occurs in various forms of concealment and their many possible combinations. For example, in the experience of mystery one encounters its active concealing movement (*Verborgenheit*).

And there are various kinds of concealment at work within the mysterious, which points to an "open secret" (*offenes Geheimnis*) that is characterized by the fact that one knows that there is a secret, and one is familiar with it as a secret, yet one does not know the secret-as-told, as its most essential features are not revealed. This points to one of the paradoxes of how concealment is the productive and operative element within unconcealment: Its various indications immediately give the general fact that something is concealed and not-revealed. One is given a kind of intuition or awareness of such mysteries, yet accessing their multivalent features remains unthinkable, though the mystery prods one to attempt to do so.

The mysterious plays a formative role in Heidegger's thinking, and he names inconspicuousness to be essential to its dynamic activities. It is this latter subclassification of concealedness under which is referenced the mysterious, which is an inherent movement within ἀλήθεια. Not unlike the former, *concealedness one*, the concealment at work within or as mystery should not be taken merely as a form of partially hiding (*pseudos*) or deception. In the Parmenides seminars, *Unscheinbarkeit* appears as one of the *characterizations* of concealment. It is a way in which marginal, simple things can and do paradoxically give or bestow themselves mysteriously.[22] Yet instead of merely a form of hiddenness, the features of the mysterious or clandestine remain inherently foreign to us, as they exceed both calculability and inexplicability, and are thereby characterized by their own nondialectical category, *Unscheinbarkeit*:

> The mystery thus becomes a "residue" still remaining to be explained. But since technical explaining and explicability provide the criterion for what can claim to be real, the inexplicable residue left over becomes the superfluous [i.e., the mysterious must exceed the explicable]. In this way the mysterious is only what is left over, what is not yet accounted for and incorporated within the circuit of explicative procedures. It would surely be simplistic and not thoughtful at all if we were saying that the little ego of some individual man were capable of elevating calculability to the rank of the measure of the reality of the real. Instead, the modern age corresponds to the metaphysical depth of the course of its history, when, in accordance with its will toward the unconditional "residuelessness" [*Restlosigkeit*] of all procedure and all organizing, it builds broad avenues through all continents and so no longer has a place free from that residue in which the mystery would still glimmer in the form of mere inexplicability. The secret in the mystery [*Das Geheime des Geheimnisvollen*] is a kind of concealment [*Verbergung*], characterized by its insignificance [*Unscheinbarkeit*, i.e., *inconspicuousness*] in virtue of which the mystery is an open one.[23]

How optimistic the claim that man's little ego is capable of calculating the full measure of the real and attaining a level of residuelessness wherein nothing is overlooked or inconspicuous! The "secret" (*Geheime*), which is a kind or sort of "covering over" (*Verbergung, lethe*) is *in* the mysterious. Of interest here is that the nature of a secret is most characterized by *Unscheinbarkeit*. Further, inconspicuousness is the definitive reason or ground for mystery holding and keeping the status of remaining open and not congealing into either the visible or the invisible. This version of *Verbergung* is the more passive version of covering in the sense of something having already secured the status of being covered-over. The root of which relates intimately with the more active concealing of *Verborgenheit*. It is in this sense that inconspicuousness plays the active role of both opening (which is essential to *Dasein*'s status as a being-open) and keeping open the mysterious. The secret within mystery (which is the closest we get to any opposite of un-covering) is that, in some inconspicuous way, it remains open:

> Another kind of concealment [the passive *Verbergung*] within the mysterious is displayed by the clandestine, under the cover of which, e.g., a conspiracy simmers [*Verschwörung bewegt*]. There the concealment has the character of an extended yet at the same time tightly knit ambush, lying in wait for the moment of the sudden outburst. The inconspicuous [*das Unscheinbare*] is here too. But now it [i.e., the inconspicuous] takes the form of camouflage and deception. Therefore this inconspicuousness [*Unscheinbare*] must explicitly protrude [or trespass] everywhere and must always be concerned with safeguarding its outward appearance [or "shininess," *Scheins*].[24]

Although deception alone does not characterize mysteriousness, there is also a kind of concealment within the mysterious that functions deceptively, and the inconspicuous also plays an active role by allowing it to take the form of a camouflage. That is not to say that it gives itself with or via another appearance, but only that it blends in with what is easily seen. When the inconspicuous takes this form, it trespasses (as it "protrudes" or *hervortreten*) into the field of visibility, yet it actively safeguards itself from being located. It can draw notice to its nature as enclosed. Once again we see the inconspicuous taking on a form that is distinct from the merely not-yet-known.[25]

Therefore, another operative role played by inconspicuousness within the mysterious is that inconspicuousness characterizes (without "shining," *Scheins*) the protrusion of mystery outward. Once again, it is open beyond the visible and invisible. The inconspicuous can work within the forms of both concealment and deception, without being reducible to either. Inconspicuousness is in the mysterious, which is the opposite of truth as the never-to-be-enlightened or brought into the light. Also, inconspicuousness is distinct from merely the hidden (which is capable of being uncovered or unconcealed), and is here subtly different from the unnoticed and overlooked (which can be perceived if one chooses to make the effort), which are more properly visible, like the forms of hiding and deceit. One reason for these somewhat tedious clarifications of concealment and mysteriousness in general, is to draw some distinction between inconspicuousness and hiddenness, which operates still according to the dichotomy between visible and invisible. The inconspicuous is incapable of being exhausted, is never fully revealed, and is yet an entirely immanent character trait. This is more than a paradoxical nonshowing–showing, however. Inconspicuousness operates within mystery and represents a certain oscillation between types of presence and presencing.

There is another sort of mystery to which Heidegger refers in the Parmenides seminars—the uncanny (*Unheimlich*), which is an eerie and un-homely mystery that operates according to an astounding inconspicuousness. The uncanny is that which is revealed and concealed in its inconspicuousness, and indeed "the uncanny in the ordinary, the normal, the everyday" was the basic means of the "Divine for the Greeks." The uncanny is always "there" (*Es gibt*) giving itself, yet without being merely subjected to a stable presence. The uncanny belongs at the heart of concealment and unconcealment, and is therefore essential to the truth of Being. Like mysteriousness, the uncanny is characterized by its *Unscheinbarkeit:*

> The uncanny is also not what has never yet been present; it is what comes into presence always already and in advance prior to all "uncanniness." The uncanny, as the being that shines into everything ordinary, i.e., into beings, and that in its shining often grazes beings like the shadow of a cloud silently passing, has nothing in common with the monstrous or the alarming. The uncanny is the simple, the insignificant [*unscheinbar*], ungraspable by the fangs of the will, withdrawing itself from all artifices of calculation, because it surpasses all planning. The astounding for the Greeks is the simple, the insignificant [*unscheinbar*], Being itself. The astounding, visible in the astonishing, is the uncanny, and it pertains so immediately to the ordinary that it can never be explained on the basis of the ordinary.[26]

And similarly, in *Poetry, Language, Thought*:

> We believe we are at home in the immediate circle of beings. That which is, is familiar, reliable, ordinary. Nevertheless, the clearing is pervaded by a constant concealment in the double form of refusal and dissembling. At bottom, the ordinary is not ordinary; it is extra-ordinary, uncanny. The nature of truth, that is, of unconcealedness, is dominated throughout by a denial. Yet this denial is not a defect or a fault, as though truth were an unalloyed unconcealedness that has rid itself of everything concealed. If truth could accomplish this, it would no longer be itself. This denial in the form of a double concealment belongs to the nature of truth as unconcealedness. Truth, in its nature, is un-truth.[27]

Both the ordinary (which simply and immediately *is*) and the uncanny (which does the work of astonishing) are primordially sutured to, yet capable of suspending, one another's activities in, the untruth–truth oscillation. This is one reason why the simple and everyday take on such prominent roles—they mark the *ways* in which the Greek gods present themselves without doing so straightforwardly. For our purposes, it is helpful to highlight how the inconspicuous *is* such a kind of uncanniness. The uncanny is given and taken away, appears and then withdraws in a way that subverts our understanding of visibility: The uncanny "itself in its essence is the inconspicuous, the simple, the insignificant, which nevertheless shines in all beings."[28] However surprising, the inconspicuous nevertheless, despite its having the tendency (*Zug*) to not shine, gives itself in all things. It is this peculiar shining in and of the *unshining* (*Un-schein-bar*), of giving familiarity and dullness in such an impressive manner that initiates phenomena to appear in somewhat strange ways. When in the astounding presencing of the inconspicuous uncanny, the entire world appears out of sorts.

The uncanny gives itself according to its own terms, and does so *in all beings* (this lends support to the thesis that Heidegger's "phenomenology of the inconspicuous" should be applicable to his entire philosophical approach).[29] And as an inconspicuous sort of concealedness, its givenness is not explicable in the domain of the ordinary, for it is by no means "obvious" (*selbstverständlich*). It is likely that the ordinary, by merit of its simplicity, is best at concealing the mysterious precisely because it so easily is overlooked. This ability is what, in part, makes ordinariness so full of potential. It is the best at inconspicuously concealing, and the form of concealment that Heidegger accords the highest honor. Much like the *hyle* of sense perception, one overlooks that which appears to be ordinary by merit of its lacking any profound ability to draw attention to itself. The ordinary appears banal and therefore one actively sets the intelligibility of its phenomena aside in preference for seeing something else (categorial). The memory, overfamiliarity, and experience with particular phenomena as ordinary contribute to the active setting-aside of their data from investigation, no matter the astonishing *potentia* they may hold. Meaningful presence congeals into stativity, and this marks the territory of our ontological laziness born in passivity—our not thinking Being. This is also the territory of a totality that reinforces such passivity.

Forms of Presence and the Zähringen Seminar

It now becomes possible to turn back to the Zähringen seminar, wherein Heidegger argues that "presence presences" or presence gets presented (*anwest nämlich anwesen*) in a way that its active presencing can be bracketed momentarily and long enough for one to think beyond the dialectic between presence and absence. In part, this is because (as gestured in the introduction) the inconspicuous is capable of being indicated (as it protrudes into the visible, *hervortreten*) or sketched (in distinction from indication as a straightforward signaling or pointing). And this necessarily leads one, through an experience of what presences itself as distant and what presences itself as proximal, to a deeply radicalization of presence itself. The point of tautological thinking is reached when awayness and beforeness both are given or sent simultaneously. This is indeed an extension of Heidegger's understanding of temporality. The verb "to presence" effectively brings about or presences the present in both its temporal and spatial dimensions, which indicates that Heidegger has a certain place or space in mind. In the appendix to the *Four Seminars*, Heidegger adds that the location in which presencing presences is "right 'at' and in unconcealment" in the crevices of ἀλήθεια, which is not simply some "rigid openness" but one of vacillation, or of "encircling" that allows for such presencing in what he calls a "fitting, encircling revelation."[30] Such a revelation (again, which is characterized by the oscillatory movement between presence and absence) of presence-tautologically-presencing-itself operates in an inconspicuous way. The present as it is given is experienced, although its givenness is only of that which is always already there.

Is all of this tautology-speak mere sophistry, or is it indeed a helpful means to fulfill the tasks of phenomenology to get beyond the dialectic between appearance and nonappearance? For Heidegger claims that this presencing of presence is "clearly a tautology," and it is at this point that we arrive at something inconspicuous: "We are here (at the aforementioned tautology) in the domain of the inconspicuous (*Bereich des Unscheinbaren*): presencing itself presences. The name for what is addressed in this state of affairs is: *to eon*, which neither beings, nor simply being, but *to eon*: presencing: presencing itself. In this domain of the inapparent, however, 'along this path there are a great number of indications.'"[31]

Presencing is to be understood as a breaking into presence, which gets at the very untrembling heart of *aletheia*. Thus Being is synonymous with truth, which reveals or gives itself in indications. As for these indications, which for Heidegger "must be understood in the domain of the inconspicuous," they are neither mere signs (for indication "is not something which stands as a sign for something else"), nor are they gestures to always accessible and unconcealed meanings. In these regards, one might be aligned with the Greek understanding of truth: "Indication is what shows and lets be seen, in that it depicts what is to be seen."[32] This kind of indication works in two senses. First, it actively depicts something in such a way that it is *meaningfully* present for the one to whom that which is given is depicted (e.g., a police officer sketching the image of a perpetrator of a crime for a victim). The depiction says something about one's presently given context, as such an indication is not meant to last. And second, indication is that which gives something permission simply to *be itself*, that is, to be what it already is as it is unconcealed from its laden status. In the thing's being indicated, it comes forth or is partially unconcealed to the degree that its being indicated suffices to describe it.

This leads back to Heidegger's reflections on his phenomenological project, as he distinguishes it from Husserl's in the Zähringen seminar. Although the tautology of presence getting presenced appears to be perhaps mere sophistry, tautology is the necessary tool for phenomenology to employ to get beyond dialectical thinking. This tautology here is an involution insofar as it initiates a thought process whereby the operation is inverted only to determine that its inverse claim or operation is equal to it, though stated or arrived at differently. For Heidegger, it was "Heraclitus [who] signified the first step towards" such a tautology, yet it was Parmenides who championed it, allowing for the most "primordial sense of phenomenology."[33] Things in their provenance are sought to understand truly in the phenomenological sense not simply *that* there are appearances (*phainesthai*), but *how* those appearances come and go in such a way that they are yet to be polarized with other phenomena. This indeed marks the most extreme of phenomenologies for it trades its namesake of studying shiny appearances for the most simple and ordinary to arrive at a more primordial point of conception, even prior to the dialectic of appearance/nonappearance. Therefore, "in this regard we must thoroughly recognize that tautology is the only possibility for thinking what dialectic can only veil."[34] The tautology of presencing being given to presence is at the primordial core of how phenomenal experience is composed of a constant oscillation between presence and absence. Therefore, what is necessary is a new attunement to the unconcealment of concealment (concealedness 1) and the various modes and forms of concealment (concealedness 2). we should direct our attention not to presence itself, but to the breach between presence and absence, which sets the conditions for a thing's being inconspicuous.

Further, the nonappearing of phenomena makes for the possibilities of their appearing, and vice versa; it is the appearing of phenomena that attune one to their concealment. This is exemplified in the multi-laminated experiences of the categorial/sensual. For example, when one has a fundamental experience with a particular dog, the *hyle* of that dog withdraws from experience. The *hyle*, which is indeed the most physically or materially present in an entity, becomes inconspicuous and is overlooked: "It is the substantiality [i.e., the *hyle*] that, in its nonappearance, enables what appears to appear. In this sense, one can even say that it is more apparent than what itself appears."[35] This indeed takes us beyond paradoxical thinking. The fact that what is overlooked is "more apparent" says something about the place, role, and means of thinking. To *perform* "an exercise in a phenomenology of the inapparent," one must make the effort of thinking in a particular way, namely, by bringing though *itself* "into the clearing of the appearing of the unapparent."[36] This is that domain of inconspicuousness that Heidegger references in the Zähringen seminar. At the very least, there is a form of thinking in which inconspicuousness can, to a limited degree, be given. Yet as inconspicuous or inapparent, such a form of thinking is, of course, not easily corralled into a method for further determining its features. One enters into a realm or space (*Raum*) of nonexperience (which is distinct, e.g., from blind *a priori* conjecture) that is beyond one's will or grasp.[37] When inconspicuousness is given, it gives, along with it, a level of disorienting confusion at its lack of clarity.

Thus, when thought reaches the clearing (*Lichtung*) in which the inconspicuous appears, one thinks at that place of *slippage* between unconcealment/concealment, withdrawal/forward-coming, and awayness/beforeness. These, at least, are what I take to be some of the broader features of Heidegger's "phenomenology of the inconspicuous."

Three Interpretations

This chapter has engaged directly Heidegger's works on the topic of inconspicuousness hopefully to dispel some common misunderstandings, such as Janicaud's seeming conflation between invisibility and inconspicuousness. It also has set the groundwork for distinguishing his approach to *Unscheinbarkeit* from other recent, creative elaborations on the topic in contemporary phenomenology, such as Figal's *Unscheinbarkeit: Der Raum der Phänomenologie* (2015), in which this concept is applied to space. There are at least three possible interpretations as to what Heidegger could mean by "eine Phänomenologie des Unscheinbaren" and among those treatments still different possible paths and points of overlap, which the following chapters will address and further apply in more constructive ways.

The first possibility is the most likely to be accepted, in part because of its generality: *Unscheinbarkeit* is germane to the becoming-intelligible of any and all phenomena, and therefore fundamentally applicable to all of Heidegger's phenomenology. After all, for Heidegger the phenomenological process is an interminable one as the appearing and not-yet-appearing of Being takes place *in* and *through* the various strata of phenomenal intelligibility. Under such a thesis, the employment of phenomenology is for the sake of uncovering the hidden (Λήθη) in its many forms (*Arten*) by performing the *epoché* that effectively reveals such interminability and *how* its always-more-to-be-disclosed is disclosed. Appropriation (*Ereignis*) is the moment at which the inconspicuousness of phenomena becomes ever present to Dasein as he/she is appropriated (*ereignete Dasein*). One is aware *that* things are coming into appearance, yet the intricacies of the possible combinations of their phenomenal data inevitably are obscure (though they shine in the ordinary). Inconspicuousness resides within *any phenomenal appearance*, and the task is to respond to the uncovering of that which is covered by attempting to bring Being into intelligibility. Of course, Heidegger is not so much interested in reiterating that phenomena reveal themselves in new and important ways each time we perform the reduction (in the not-yet-appearing of phenomena), but rather in showing how the clearing is a fundamental concealment that hides and is itself hidden, just as much as the clearing is an unconcealment. The clearing is a clearing away that is comparable to hitting the reset button on consciousness.

Most who have proffered some interpretation of this concept of Heidegger's more or less seem to support this position. As mentioned in the introduction,

Dastur interprets the inapparent as a nonappearance that is in all appearing in which Being is given.[38] With the appropriation by Being comes an existential shock saturated with this sense of the inapparent. For Taminiaux, the coming-into-appearance of things is always already transfixed with a certain excessiveness that alters phenomenality in toto.[39] To see is to observe what stands-out and beyond that which is given to sight, and this excessiveness is somehow unable to be accessed. As Gonzalez interprets, the inconspicuous is never capable of being seen, otherwise it forfeits its status as such.[40] Under Benson and Simmons's assessment, Heidegger's entire phenomenology radicalizes appearance to the point that what is inconspicuous is found imbued within it.[41] Phenomenology, at its root, begins with an openness to the inconspicuous, which forms a primordial basis of that which shines. These views all seem consistent with Merleau-Ponty's broader claims about Heidegger's project, which "seeks out a direct expression of Being while at the same time suggesting that it does not give itself through any direct expression."[42] Indeed seeking the clarity of Being should not be confused with uncovering Being and unfolding it as a concept. The most recent engagement with inconspicuousness comes from Figal, who develops this concept grounded by Heidegger, and claims that ultimately phenomena can "only be adequately understood in their unison with the inconspicuous" ("*wären Phänomene im skizzierten phänomenologischen Sinner also nur angemessen in ihrer Zusammengehörigkeit mit dem Unscheinbaren zu verstehen.*")[43]

This first interpretation holds that all phenomena have within them the paradox of inconspicuousness and the radical *potentia* of revealing Being, which cannot be directly expressed despite its relationship with ordinary beings. It is likely that many would accept this view because it fits quite nicely into the already existent Heideggerian scaffolding of phenomenal experience. It is surely the case that the *a priori* of appearance can never be fully brought to light, and there is something *unscheinbar* about the essence of the inner oscillation at work in *a-letheia* between unconcealment and concealment. Being transcends the entities of that which it shines in and through. After all, the Zähringen seminar was inspired by Jean Beaufret's question concerning the *Seinsfrage* and the way in which the *transcendens* of Being is phenomenology's most primal quest.[44]

Yet one complication with this view concerns how phenomenology therefore is to be reconstructed. If all of phenomenology contains some element of inconspicuousness, then it appears as if one therefore is obliged to find ways of being attuned to the specific features and activities of inconspicuousness when doing phenomenology. Heidegger indeed references exercises in a phenomenology *of* the inconspicuous, and this "of" indicates that there is some way in which inconspicuousness demarcates this study of the appearance/nonappearance of things. If we take it that such inconspicuousness is to be integrated into Heidegger's overall, already existent scaffolding for studying the intelligibility of things and the ways in which they are appropriated, then ways must be found to account for (and consequently attune to) such inconspicuousness. This would demand at least a cursory reassessment of Heidegger's entire approach: To what degree is Being itself, as a nonmetaphysical, yet mystery-laden and operative aspect of the worlding of the world, expected to enact inconspicuousness? How far might it be said that Dasein maintains laminates of inapparency, and to what degree is being (the coming to be or giving of the being of beings, intrinsically inapparent (as Polt suggests to be especially true of the later Heidegger)?[45] It is indeed in Heidegger's later work that the coming-to-be of Being takes on a more mysteriously copresent concealing as one is thrown into or appropriated within the world. Though concealing is inherent within this approach to thinking, is this *the mysteriousness* in and of itself, and how are we not back in the quagmire of the ontotheological constitution of metaphysics about which Heidegger repeatedly warns? Despite the potential saliency of these concerns, it is likely that this interpretation of inconspicuousness can be integrated into Heidegger's work. As chapter 3 of the present study considers closely, inconspicuousness is indeed a character trait of Being. Nevertheless, this view appears to not account for why he references in the Zähringen seminar a phenomenology "of" the inconspicuous, which is engaged through the performance of exercises.

A second interpretation of Heidegger's phenomenology of the inconspicuous seems to have less demanding consequences. It is not so much that all of phenomenology is to be rethought as a "phenomenology of the inconspicuous" per se, but that only an aspect of phenomenology *involves* the study of the stratification of the inapparent within the apparent. Heidegger is indeed introducing something new into phenomenology, what Janicaud wagered to be a "new form of thought."[46] Thus, a new *step* is being introduced into *all* of phenomenology that involves the attuning of oneself to the various modes of potential hiddenness (*Verborgenheit* and its cognates) within *all* phenomena, and inconspicuousness is now to be included as a form, trait, or mode among them. In which case, one can only get at these particularly dark or unshiny corners of experience within intuition through actually performing the exercises of such a phenomenology. How might one access inconspicuousness in and of itself, and is this even possible?

It may be that such exercises are the means of becoming attuned more closely to the aforementioned oscillation between the present and absent. The effort that one would make in such an exercise would be not unlike a reduction to the inconspicuous. There are many things that are inconspicuous to me right now, for example, such as the feeling on the tips of my fingers of the computer keyboard on which I type, or the sensation of an ache in my back to which I have grown so accustomed in the last hour. I exercise my ability to experience things and be affected by them, despite their ordinary status of being accepted into my meaning-given experience within the world. They still can affect me significantly. By turning attention to the pain in my back, I might come into a profound experience with my contingency. By relaying to the physical experience of typing, I would operate with an inhibition that keeps attention away from the present task of thinking and writing.

The profound experience with the uncanny is in the most ordinary of things. As I engage the inconspicuous (the phenomenology of which Heidegger says cannot occur "through the reading of books") in my surroundings, like a rack and pinion, the most profound *potentia* of phenomena are given warrant (*scheinen*) to make an appearance, despite the fact they may give themselves only contingently. It cannot be overstated: *Unscheinbar* is not a cognate of *Unsichtbar*, or invisible, and it is capable of being given, yet in a way that its mode of detection has a mysterious characteristic of withdrawal within the present. Under this interpretation, all phenomena, no matter how ordinary, are capable of bearing such inconspicuousness, yet one engages it only at a particular step or time within phenomenological reflection.

The third interpretation of Heidegger's *Unscheinbar* would hold that it is a direct reference to specific and *distinct phenomena* that paradoxically exceed this visible/invisible (*Sichtbar/Unsichtbar*) polarity, yet still somehow are present and affective. If this is the case, then there also should be a corresponding *approach* to accessing the very special means of phenomenality such things hold, which might be studied only when one is trained on the modalities of inconspicuousness (e.g., forms of hiding, which can be thought as the unconcealedness or manifestation of inconspicuousness). They are very particular sorts of phenomena, which require a unique kind of phenomenology that corresponds with their unique modes of givenness. They are phenomena that forfeit their phenomenality, yet remain qualified as phenomena with which one might relate, for they are fully present-at-hand.

There are intrinsically inconspicuous phenomena that do not reach presence in the same way that ordinary object-beings can. Although they may appear in the ordinary, or at least, present themselves *as if* they are ordinary (*a'la* the Parmenides seminars), it may be that not all ordinary phenomena have the potential for such *Unscheinbarkeit*. In which case, such phenomena would follow Heidegger's amendment of the ground rules of phenomenology, Husserl's "principle of principles," which trains us on the making-present of that which is hidden, or the direct description of that which clearly appears to consciousness.[47] Inconspicuous phenomena, which would be in the margins or residue of what gets bracketed in Husserl's reductions, call for an inconspicuous phenomenology for thinking about them and making them intelligible, despite never attaining a level of "residuelessness." In some cases, as intelligible data of these phenomena are overlooked by conscious awareness, it is likely that other sensations of human experience are indeed, simultaneously fully undergoing a thorough experience with or of them. These phenomena would not be accessible in any traditional sense, yet their unshininess is not to be reduced to being one of the cognates of hiddenness. Through thinking tautologically, namely by thinking the presencing (*das Anwesen*) of presence (*die Anwesenheit*), one can be attuned to the multivalent forms of withdrawal.

Two thinkers who seem to hold this view are Janicaud and Marion. First, for Marion, there are specific phenomena capable of enacting excess or saturation (saturated phenomena) more than others (poor or common law phenomena). For Janicaud, who holds that "this 'phenomenology of the inapparent' is not reducible to a mere appendix to the thought of the later Heidegger" thinks that this approach is meant "to train sight and hearing to get as close as possible to phenomenality. [And therefore] the 'phenomenology of the inapparent' is a phenomenology of proximity." An approach to proximity, in this case, concerns the presencing of presence and the closeness/farness withdrawal/presence that is always taking place in the grand experience of Being. This tautology is about returning to "the first self-evident insight of phenomenal appearing: time temporalizes, saying speaks, the world worlds." One engaged in such a phenomenology actively attends to "the withdrawal of things."[48] Yet most importantly, Janicaud's interpretation of this concept becomes clearer in his earlier book *Chronos*, in which he characterizes "the inapparent, in the most essential sense, as that 'phenomenality par excellence,' which, while neither immediate nor ontic, also cannot be reduced to an eidetic intention."[49] Such phenomena have the unique quality or *state* of being inconspicuous and of not attracting attention. Thus, these are *specific* phenomena that effectively do not appear.

Despite Janicaud's appearing to conflate the terms inapparent/invisible, he nevertheless on occasion refers to them as quite specific phenomena in Heidegger's approach. After all, he was the prime accuser of the thinkers associated with the theological turn in French Phenomenology on the grounds that they relied on Heidegger's approach to inapparent phenomena. There are indeed phenomena that might carry traits of inconspicuousness more than others, such as those that Heidegger claims to house the mysterious. In "On the Essence of Truth" mysteriousness (*das Geheimnis*) is claimed to have the privileged role of enacting the self-concealing nature of Being and truth.[50] Then, in the *Introduction to Metaphysics*, Heidegger argues that the origin of language and its structure remain a mystery for language "can have begun only from the overwhelming and the uncanny, in the breakaway of humanity into being."[51] And finally, the essence of humanity (*Das Wesen des Menschseins*) is or gives itself in mysteries or secrets.[52] Because we already know from the Parmenides seminars that *Unscheinbarkeit* is the prime characteristic of the mysterious, then this interpretation should be brought to bear on these aforementioned particular phenomena.

This latter interpretation of Heidegger's phenomenology of the inconspicuous is not without concern, however: If these phenomena are to remain inconspicuous and inapparent, then how might they be accessed or described at all? Would not a direct explanation of them exhaust them of their inconspicuousness? Is an aspect of inconspicuousness sufficient for one to have had an experience with that which is presented to experience as inconspicuous?[53] One wonders if there could be an approach to such inconspicuousness without it ultimately undermining itself. One would also need to take care not to describe such an approach as a new point of access to a metaphysical *eidos*; again, one that Heidegger already banished in his critique of ontotheology. A phenomenology of the inconspicuous must be a study of Being in *this world*. Such questions and concerns may depend on the preunderstanding held by many that the inconspicuous is merely a cognate of the inaccessible. Inconspicuousness, however, is the character trait of/within that which is or is not presented, and undermines any dialectic or contradiction, not by resolving its own inner tensions, but by *indicating* them through making the outlines of their movements more intelligible. This is still a far cry from exhaustively understanding such movements.

Being, Overlooked: The Inconspicuousness of Heidegger

There are reasons why Heidegger, after his last seminar in 1973, left his treatment of inconspicuousness slightly ambiguous. Each of the interpretations reflects some general interest of Heidegger's, and the following chapters will experiment more constructively with a number of them. Yet a version of this third interpretation may be the most convincing as well as the most fecund for initiating something new for phenomenological thinking (namely, on religion). Aside from the later thesis's reflecting a slightly more radical and daring attempt for phenomenology (which I find to be most likely, given that the approach was introduced in his last seminar), it might at least be suggested in general that there are phenomena bearing a greater *tendency* to inconspicuousness than others; certain phenomena that are more likely to maintain *traits* of inconspicuousness. There could be varying degrees or shades of inconspicuousness that phenomena can bear, likely telling us more about ourselves—what we care about, how we ignore, disguise, and select data—than they do about the phenomena or what is hidden in/by them. It is not about their *being* inconspicuous per se, but what their status as inconspicuous says about the one experiencing them.

This can be thought in terms of mystery. There are indeed various "always hiddens" within phenomenal experience (even Being-toward-death indicates how we are sutured to a hidden mysteriousness) that always-remain-concealed within Being through an unintelligible excess. There are things that are mysteriously inconceivable in the colloquial sense of their not being intelligible or knowable to/by us. Yet there is also a sense of *the* mysterious in which inconspicuousness is a primary characteristic, as Heidegger put it in the Parmenides seminars. Even if all ordinary phenomena are capable of bearing, sending, or presenting such an uncanny mysteriousness, some phenomena will take on more profound layers of intelligibility as they are made-meaningful by me as I relate with the world and its constant stream of intelligible data. Thus understood, inconspicuous phenomena (and their ensuing phenomenologies or steps) lead one to a particular path: One that "leads away to come before" a phenomenon.

One nearly inarguable and consistent thread that runs throughout Heidegger's references to the inconspicuous is the theme of ordinariness. Yet this does not mean that only ordinary things are inconspicuous, for—and this is a fundamental insight phenomenology teaches—anything can become ordinary. The unique paradox of inconspicuousness is that what one thinks and presumes to be clear is precisely, in that moment, the most unclear of things, for its intelligibility no longer is deemed worthy of attention. It is to this matter of clarity and obviousness that the next chapter will turn. Yet overall, an approach that allows for the experience of something inconspicuous involves the active being-caught-up in the ordinary in such a way that mysteriousness can shine through it.

Whatever is inconspicuous is in the margins of what typically gets reduced to being present, and therefore resides in the breach between presence and absence, between withdrawal and approach. It is the absence that is a remainder of the appearance (*scheinbar*) and the leftovers of the reduction. Therefore, one element of the functioning of truth, and one's realization of the inconspicuous is a part of the very nature of the act of unconcealment. This is the phenomenological seeing (as stated in the Zähringen seminar) at which one might arrive, which is a contested presencing that goes beyond what the fangs of the will could ever apprehend. The inconspicuous way of things can be taken as the most basic transgression of phenomenal appearance, and to see things *inconspicuously* could refer to modes of apprehension without conceiving, for example, according to darkness (as nonshining, nonreflecting), hiddenness (as seemingly unknown), intentional overlooking, or even underlooking (downplaying something to have little value).

Ultimately, the overlooking of things at-hand and in direct proximity in favor of shinier things whose celebrity or spectacle (*conspicere* relates to *specere*) steal away our attention, is a way of actively making such phenomena insignificant through disrecognition. Yet phenomenology, as one of the methods trained on sharpening the ability to study the relation between *lethe* and *aletheia*, between the concealment of oblivion (λήθη), and the "un-forgetfulness" (ἀλήθεια) of that which is given over to experience, indeed is of use today, namely for its ushering one into an unhomeliness with the most basic and banal of things in a way that such things might become wondrous without being fully revealed. The inconspicuousness within the ordinary lends to wonder, as the uncanny (*unheimlich*) "itself in its essence is the inconspicuous, the simple, the insignificant, which nevertheless shines in all beings."[54]

In Heidegger's 1932 lectures on *The Beginning of Western Philosophy: Interpretation of Anaximander and Parmenides* (recently translated into English in 2015), he addresses how time is an all-powerful and incalculable essence that "lets emerge everything not manifest and conceals everything standing in appearance."[55] It is the framework of time that permits the emerging-concealing of things and even ourselves, who are perhaps the most hidden or covered-over. Withdrawal and closeness are matters of temporal and spatial distance and proximity accessed by Dasein by involving ourselves in ourselves. As the pre-Socratics understood, we become the ordinary out of which the uncanny or *to deinon* of Being is to be experienced most deeply. As chapter 4 will address more closely, an engagement with inconspicuousness may permit one to find oneself as always already estranged from oneself and one's world; only able to retrieve it through being-appropriated in a way that calls for a *kenotic* self-emptying whereby one is lowered to the status of insignificance.

One question then becomes whether it is possible to overlook one's subjectivity long enough to engage that with which is always already at hand. Relationships are what phenomenology always beckons us to concern ourselves with, and thus they should be deformalized.[56] Despite phenomenology's reputation for the—at times painstaking—descriptions of abstract details, it also could be employed as a tool for intentionally overlooking the clarity of details, namely those that grab the attention with an almost unavoidable immediacy. Such spectacles can be overlooked intentionally in favor of the simplicity of ordinary things. To State the dictum falsely attributed to Freud, sometimes a cigar is simply a cigar, and it may very well be such seemingly insignificant things like cigars that mark, following Heidegger, a "saving power" today. Indeed, there is a wisdom to the ordinary; a wisdom to be distinguished from the skillful bringing of things into spectacular clarity. This makes wisdom, as William James once put it, "the art of knowing what to overlook."[57]

Notes

1. William James, *The Principles of Psychology, vol. 2* (New York: Cosimo Classics, 2007), 369.

2. Richard Rorty, *Truth and Progress: Philosophical Papers* (Cambridge: Cambridge University Press, 1998), 93.

3. It also is of note that the term "away," correlates to *Weg*, which also refers to "path." The *Holzweg*, or hiking trail has no clear or apparent path, mostly because of the needles or leaves that cover the forest floor. One German colloquialism is telling: To be "*schwer auf dem Holzweg*" or "heavy on the woodway," is to be out, lost, and in need of finding one's path again. One might only follow such an inconspicuous path if one is aware of the many other factors that go along in the environment of the path (such as light, markers, scents, etc.). For someone like Pöggeler, *Der Denkweg* was the best way to summarize Heidegger's

approach to thinking, as it is a meandering to and fro within thoughts, within a vision of thinking Being. See Otto Pöggeler, *Martin Heidegger's Path of Thinking* (Amherst, NY: Humanity Books, 1991).

4. See Martin Heidegger, GA 9, 248, 325 and *Zollikoner Seminare: Protokolle, Gespräche, Briefe*, ed. Merdard Boss (Frankfurt am Main: Vittorio Klostermann, 1987), 351. Martin Heidegger, *Zollikon Seminars: Protocols, Conversations, Letters*, ed. Medard Boss and trans. Franz Mayr and Richard Askay (Evanston, IL: Northwestern University Press, 2001). Sheehan interprets the "da" of Dasein to suggest that the human occurs as the "da," that is to say the "out thereness" or clearing of being. For Sheehan, "Heidegger would have us hear the Latin *ex + sistere*, where the "ex-" or "out-and-beyond" dimension of human being forms an openness or clearing that he called "the *Da*." Thomas Sheehan, *Making Sense of Heidegger: A Paradigm Shift* (London: Rowman & Littlefield International, 2014), xvi.

5. Martin Heidegger, "Seminar in Zähringen 1973," in *Four Seminars*, trans. Andrew J. Mitchell and François Raffoul (Bloomington: Indiana University Press, 2003), 80–81. "So verstanden ist die Phänomenologie ein Weg, der hinführt vor . . . und sich das zeigen läßt, wovor er geführt wird. Diese Phänomenologie ist eine Phänomenologie des Unscheinbaren." Martin Heidegger, "Seminar in Zähringen," in GA 15, *Seminare*, ed. Curd Ochwadt (Frankfurt am Main: Vittorio Klostermann, 1986), 397.

6. Ibid., 80/397.

7. In *Poetry, Language, Thought*: "And yet—beyond what is, not away from it but before it, there is still something else that happens. In the midst of beings as a whole an open place occurs. There is a clearing, a lighting (*Lichtung*). Thought of in reference to what is, to beings, this clearing is in a greater degree than are beings. This open center is therefore not surrounded by what is; rather, the lighting center itself encircles all that is, like the Nothing which we scarcely know. That which is can only be, as a being, if it stands within and stands out within what is lighted in this clearing. Only this clearing grants and guarantees to us humans a passage to those beings that we ourselves are not, and access to the being that we ourselves are. Thanks to this clearing, beings are unconcealed in certain changing degrees. And yet a being can be concealed, too, only within the sphere of what is lighted. Each being we encounter and which encounters us keeps to this curious opposition of presence in that it always withholds itself at the same time in a concealedness. The clearing in which beings' stand is in itself at the same time concealment. Concealment prevails in the midst of beings in a twofold way." Martin Heidegger, *Poetry, Language, Thought*, trans. Albert Hofstadter (New York: Harper & Row, 1971), 51. See also GA 31, 113.

8. Martin Heidegger, *Being and Time*, trans. John Macquarrie and Edward Robinson (New York: Harper & Row, 1962), 219. Martin Heidegger, *GA 2*, *Sein und Zeit*, ed. Friedrich-Wilhelm von Herrmann (Frankfurt am Main: Vittorio Klostermann, 1977; first edition 1927), 262.

9. Sheehan interprets that "[f]or us, the *Sein* of something shows up only in discursive thinking and acting—that is, only when we take a thing as such-and-so, or in terms of this or that possibility. When I take something as, whether in theory or praxis, I understand the *Sein* of the thing, whether correctly or incorrectly." Further, from exsistence, "*sistere*" is a verb that means "to *make* someone or something stand out and beyond." Thus, the term "*Existenz* is already a pre-indication of what gets expressed in Heidegger's early work as *Geworfenheit* and *der geworfene Entwurf*." Sheehan, *Making Sense of Heidegger*, xvii, 21.

10. Heidegger, "Seminar in Zähringen 1973," 70.

11. Heidegger makes reference to *Abwesenheit*, which is associable with das *Nichts*. Heidegger refers to a "mögliche *Abwesenheit*" or dynamic "possible absence" in GA 18, *Grundbegriffe der Aristotelischen Philosophie*, 376.

12. A number of questions remain for whether or not this paradigm is tenable beyond how we are to think of "static structures" in the more traditional, metaphysical sense. Steinbock would hold that "in many if not most cases, static structures are surpassed through 'deeper' genetic analyses, and genetic matters and methods are 'rattled' or 'ruined' by generative ones." The home and away, the "homeworld and alienworld" structure is articulated according to Steinbock's provisional/transcendental relation in the life world. Anthony J. Steinbock, *Home and Beyond: Generative Phenomenology after Husserl* (Evanston, IL: Northwestern University Press, 1995), 265.

13. This kind of "seeing" cannot be attained through the "reading of books," says Heidegger here. Martin Heidegger, "German Translator's Afterword," in *Four Seminars*, ed. Curd Ochwadt (Bloomington: Indiana University Press, 2003), 89.

14. Martin Heidegger, *What Is Called Thinking?*, trans. Fred D. Wieck and J. Glenn Gray (New York: Harper & Row, 1968), 9. GA 8 (1951–1952), 10. See also 19 (GA 9, 21) where Heidegger refers to the nature of the beauty of artwork gaining its source from its Inconspicuousness: "Beauty is a fateful gift of the essence of truth, whereby truth means the unconcealment of the self-concealing. The beautiful is not what pleases, but what falls within that fateful gift of truth which comes into its own when that which is eternally unapparent (*unscheinbar*, i.e., inconspicuous) and therefore invisible attains its most radiantly apparent appearance."

15. Heidegger, *Poetry, Language, Thought*, 31. (GA 5, 17).

16. Martin Heidegger, GA 12, *Unterwegs zur Sprache* (Frankfurt am Main: Vittorio Klostermann, 1985), 247.

17. It is to this sort of concealedness that Heidegger begins to gesture in his meditations on technology. Such concealedness operates "in the horizon of scientific and technical discoveries" and "when the concealed in this sense is brought into unconcealedness, there arise 'the miracles of technology' and what is specifically 'American.'" Martin Heidegger, *Parmenides*, trans. André Schuwer and Richard Rojcewicz (Bloomington: Indiana University Press, 1992), 64.

18. See here John Caputo's claim that *A-lethia* is no longer a Greek word for Heidegger. John Caputo, *Demythologizing Heidegger* (Bloomington: Indiana University Press, 1993), 21.

19. Heidegger, "Seminar in Zähringen 1973," 79.

20. Heidegger, *Parmenides*, 64–65, cf. 14. There are different types of closure, and different ways of interpreting unconcealedness. Unconcealedness "can mean concealedness is taken away, cancelled, evicted, or banned, where taking away, cancelling evicting, and banning are essentially distinct."

21. Ibid., 62. GA 54, 91.

22. For Rudolf Bernet, such phenomena would include those "of oblivion, anamnesis, the rare, the gift and the secret." As for the secret, "it can only be saved if one renounces using the mysterious thing for one's personal profit. To keep the secret of this thing, one must, Heidegger says, keep silent. Only silence preserves the secret, only silence respects the simplicity and the *Unscheinbarkeit* with which the secret offers a glimpse of itself through a thing which, by withdrawing for the sake of its mystery, runs the risk of going unnoticed." Bernet employs Heidegger's *Unscheinbarkeit* to better understand the secret: "The unconcealment of the

concealment which is typical of the true secret, the coming into presence of what stays necessarily unapparent in the secret can only be realized under the form of an appearance that goes almost unnoticed or, as Heidegger says, that is characterized by its 'insignificance' (*Unscheinbarkeit*). The same holds true for the mysterious thing and the given thing: it is given as the carrier of a secret it does not deliver to us. The welcoming of this givenness by someone consists, here again, in letting the mysterious thing accomplish the unconcealment of the concealment of its secret." Rudolf Bernet, "The Secret According to Heidegger and 'The Purloined Letter' by Poe," *Continental Philosophy Review* 47 no. 3–4 (2014): 353–71.

23. Heidegger, *Parmenides*, 63. GA 54, 93. "Das Geheime des Geheimnisvollen ist eine Art, die sich durch ihre auszeichnet, kraft deren das Geheimnis ein offenes ist."

24. Ibid., 63.

25. "Far away from these modes of concealment, and yet within the sphere of the same essence, resides the concealed in the sense of the merely not yet known." Ibid., 26.

26. Ibid., x, cf. 101.

27. Heidegger, *Poetry, Language, Thought*, 53.

28. Heidegger, *Parmenides*, 105. The uncanny shows itself in the ordinary: "the uncanny, or the extraordinary, shines throughout the familiar ambit of the being we deal with and known, beings we call ordinary."

29. Ibid., 106: "Yet what we are calling the 'uncanny' we still grasp on the basis of the ordinary. What the so-called uncanny is in itself and what first admits of the character of the uncanny as its consequence, that is based on the shining into beings, on self-presentation, in Greek: *daio*." Further, on 130: "And this original belonging together of both, precisely as primordial must also possess the inconspicuous character of what, like a source, comes to presence out of itself in its essence."

30. Heidegger, "Seminar in Zähringen 1973," 96.

31. Ibid., 79.

32. Ibid.

33. Ibid., 80. This is one more reason as to why Heidegger here prefers Parmenides, for "Parmenides is more profound and essential (if it is the case that dialectic, as is said in *Being and Time*, is 'a genuine philosophic embarrassment')." For Raffoul and Mitchell, the translators of this seminar, Heidegger's naming phenomenology that of the "inapparent" is an adaptation of the "methodology in its most extreme possibility and formulation." Raffoul and Mitchell, "Translator's Foreword," in *Four Seminars*, trans. Andrew J. Mitchell and François Raffoul (Bloomington: Indiana University Press, 2003), xvi.

34. Heidegger, "Seminar in Zähringen 1973," 81.

35. Ibid., 67.

36. Martin Heidegger, "Letters to Roger Munier (dated Feb 22, 1974)," in *Martin Heidegger*, ed. Michel Haar (Paris: Editions de l'Herne, 1983), 115.

37. Heidegger, *Parmenides*, 64. When it comes to matters of unconcealment, "We are here only broaching a realm whose fullness of essence we hardly surmise and certainly do not fathom, for we are outside the mode of experience proper to it."

38. Françoise Dastur, "La pensée à venir: une pheénoménologie de l'inapparent?" in *L'avenir de la philosophie est-il grec?*, ed. Catherine Collobert (Saint-Laurent, Quebec: Fides, 2002), 146.

39. Jacques Taminiaux, "Heidegger and Husserl's Logical Investigations in Remembrance of Heidegger's last Seminar (Zähringen, 1973)," *Research in Phenomenology* 7 no. 1 (1977): 79.

40. Francisco J. Gonzalez, *Plato and Heidegger: A Question of Dialogue* (College Station, PA: Penn State Press, 2011), 308.

41. J. Aaron Simmons and Bruce Ellis Benson, *The New Phenomenology* (London: Bloomsbury Press, 2013), 41.

42. For Martin Heidegger "cherche une expression directe de l'être dont il montre par ailleurs qu'il n'est pas susceptible d'expression direct," in *Notes de cours, 1959–1961*, ed. Maurice Merleau-Ponty (Paris: Gallimard, 1996), 148.

43. Günter Figal, *Unscheinbarkeit: Der Raum der Phänomenologie* (Tübingen: Mohr Siebeck, 2015), 11.

44. Taminiaux, "Heidegger and Husserl's Logical Investigations in Remembrance," 79.

45. Richard F. H. Polt, *The Emergency of Being on Heidegger's Contributions to Philosophy* (Ithaca, NY: Cornell University Press, 2006), note 38.

46. Dominique Janicaud, *Phenomenology "Wide Open": After the French Debate* (New York: Fordham University Press, 2005), 75.

47. One concern is that under this phenomenology of the inconspicuous one is dealing strictly with possible phenomena for the "I." The subjective grounding of the appearing of things, as they appeal to my own intentionality, insinuates that I am the one constituting the phenomenon. Manoussakis is concerned that "the world becomes a private spectacle for consciousness, a consciousness that is also the absolute director and the exclusive audience of this performance. Husserl himself was aware of the 'grave objection' that already arises here." John P. Manoussakis, "The Phenomenon of God: From Husserl to Marion," *American Catholic Quarterly* 78 no. 1 (2004): 56.

48. Janicaud, *Phenomenology "Wide Open,"* 75. cf. 73. Continuing on 75: "The 'phenomenologist of the inapparent' is no longer an ideal spectator of the truth of the world and of its essences: he learns to inhabit the world 'at arm's length' from the withdrawal of things."

49. In *Chronos* Janicaud refers to how "the inapparent is that which does not appear at first glance and escapes even the most common experiences ("l'inapparent comme ce qui échappe à l'expérience la plus courante, ce qui n'apparaît pas de soi-même au premier regard.")." After briefly offering his own ways of interpreting this concept (that which can never be brought to light, that which disturbs phenomenology, and that which is the inherent nature of temporality) Janicaud seems to suggest that all three carry some weight, "but what is the phenomenality par excellence which is neither immediate nor ontic . . .? It is precisely the one that reserves the most problematic of 'phenomenalities' in the temporal dimension" (Or quelle est la phenomenalite par excellene qui, ni immediate ni ontique, ne se laisse pas non plus réduire à une vise eidétique? C'est precisement celle qui reserve la plus problématique des "phenomenalities": la dimension temporelle.). See Dominique Janicaud, *Chronos: Pour l'intelligence du partage temporel* (Paris: Bernard Grasset, 1997), 159. See here also Dominique Janicaud, *Phenomenology and the Theological Turn* (New York: Fordham University Press, 2000), 28–31. As well as Janicaud, *Phenomenology "Wide Open,"* 100, footnote 14.

50. Mystery is essential to truth, as Heidegger suggests in "On the Essence of Truth." There, Heidegger uses *das Geheimnis* "to refer to being as self-concealing, and he identifies this self-concealing as the non-essence of truth."

51. Martin Heidegger, *Introduction to Metaphysics*, trans. Gregory Fried and Richard Polt (New Haven, CT: Yale University Press, 2014), 182. (GA 40, 131).

52. Ibid., 175.

53. Gonzales wonders if such an approach is left ambiguous "precisely in order to be able to practice dialectic while insisting on and aspiring to something else which this very practice undermines." Gonzales, *Plato and Heidegger*, 308.

54. Heidegger, *Parmenides*, 105. Again, it is the uncanny that reveals itself from *within* the ordinary: "the uncanny, or the extraordinary, shines throughout the familiar ambit of the being we deal with and known, beings we call ordinary."

55. This collection displays his sustained effort to find just that, the *beginning* of Western philosophy. Martin Heidegger, *The Beginning of Western Philosophy: Interpretation of Anaximander and Parmenides*, trans. Richard Rojcewicz (Bloomington: Indiana University Press, 2015).

56. For Steinbock, "Phenomenology has shown . . . that what is primary is the relation itself." Anthony J. Steinbock, *Phenomenology and Mysticism: The Verticality of Religious Experience* (Bloomington: Indiana University Press, 2007), 225.

57. James, *Principles of Psychology*, 369.

3 Inconspicuous Lifeworld of Religion: Henry's "Life," Heidegger's "World"

Is there anything that can appear that is not subject to doing so in the supposed neutrality of this world? This question may presuppose already a dichotomy between what appears clearly to the senses, and what is deemed nonvisible; a dualism that underwrites the social imaginaries nourishing the distinctions between the sacred and profane. Were phenomenology to provide a means of getting beyond this intricate dichotomy, it would need to address the interrelated concepts of obviousness, neutrality, and commonality—all of which are integral to a cosmological phenomenality of the world itself, which so often is granted carte blanche the privileged status of having an indescribable and uninvestigable neutrality. The world is thought to be the theatre in which things appear clearly, obviously, and therefore knowable in this space and time in which we live. We generally think that the world or *Kosmos* is the provisional backdrop of the order of things in a public space, and that whatever appears there shines with spectacular radiance in a way that it must go unquestioned.

Our contemporary understandings of world also are rooted in the Latin *saecularis*, which associates such an order of things in space with an age or period of time in this, our present world (to which the Greek *aion* refers).[1] This concurrence between what is temporally and spatially present allows for a rooted attention to what seems obvious as things become meaningfully present. This is perhaps why student and colleague of Heidegger, Eugen Fink, referred to *aion* as the *Weltlauf* or the course, run, and continuation of the world as it operates in conjunction with time.[2] To some degree obviousness is necessary for this operation for the world to function as a shared space. A presupposition of neutral space or what Taylor calls an "immanent frame" entails the preferential option for clarity.[3] And as Barbieri recently noted, our contemporary orientation in the world champions "the obvious" and "attempts to capture the meaning of the mundane."[4] This harbors some necessarily phenomenological problems, namely, *how* preference is given to things-as-ordinary, mundane, and clear—putatively limiting apprehensions that come from other, perhaps more inconspicuous forms of appearance. Phenomenology prides itself on studying the experiences of what appears in the world, yet to what degree might the world itself appear, and how is it something with which it is possible to enter a genuine "relation?"

It was Descartes who first demonstrated how all real things in the world come about through an originary relation one has with oneself; a claim that is constituent of how the *ego cogito* is distinguished from the *res corporea* (with *res extensa* as the ontological definition of "world").[5] This separation between subject and world furnished a new confidence in describing neutrally that which is in the world, and it was in Kant's *Critique of Pure Reason* that, for the first time, a cosmological phenomenology was risked via the a priori intuitions (those "ways of showing") of space and time, which when combined with the categories of understanding, provide for the meaningful constitution of one's world. These intuitions and forms were described as *vor-stellen* or "placing in front" of oneself as representations, which, like a view finder, function by sliding in and out new affective images for experience to grasp and process. Unique to Kant's analysis is that the fundamental, transcendental access to the concrete content of the world itself does not first come through a decidedly cognitive and conscious apprehension, but rather sensation, a more affective relation as *sensum* (perception). This was a unique twist on what Aristotle argued for in *On the Soul* as a *sensus communis* (sense in "common") by turning to the various imprints on us that furnish the mind with its needed evidences.

Hume called these imprints "impressions," which inexplicably arise from the senses of perception, and perhaps this influenced Husserl's eventually admitting that "the consciousness which judges [even] a mathematical 'state of things' is an impression,"[6] which can be taken as the after-affects that things uniquely have on us. Yet instead of the neoskepticism of Hume, Husserl took these impressions to have cognitive potential for describing realities that build-up the fundaments of the "lifeworld" (*Lebenswelt*), which after 1917 became the shared "world for us all." This is our "experience world" (*Erfahrungswelt*), which is unmediated, "taken-for-granted," immediate, obvious (*selbstverständlich*), pregiven (*Vorgegebenheit*), and always already there in its "enigmatic" and "prescientific objectivity." It is precisely this taken-for-grantedness of the world that must be overcome, and in his 1937 "Philosophy and the Crisis of European Man" (the "Vienna Lecture" of 1935), Husserl bemoans how the privileging of "worlds" visible to objective scrutiny, succumbed to "a mistaken rationalism," and presumed the "pregiven" world to be the *only* world. "We must see that objectivism" claims Husserl, is strictly and naively "based on a naturalistic focusing on the environing world."[7] Only phenomenology can save us now, for its epoché can suspend those worldly presumptions of ordinary consciousness, even of the world itself and its infinitely being taken for granted.[8]

The World itself so often goes unthought, and its forms of appearance must be brought under investigation. About eight years before Husserl's Vienna

Lecture, Heidegger had posed that phenomenology's sole task is to question "the world-hood of the world as such" and to study the appearing of the world, for any presumption of the nature of things (which he subtlety claimed Husserl had made) has already "tacitly anticipated their ontological structure."[9] For him it was not only appearances in this world that are to be studied, but how this world in and of itself gets worlded by us. On the one hand, the world is not subjectively construed, yet on the other, phenomenology does not take as its sole objective to discern and describe neutrally what is really in the world or not. Any possibility of neutrality would require one to be transcendentally standing outside of that which one claims to be neutral, and to be distant from ones concerns. This points to a more specific problem within phenomenology itself: it is supposed to be a method that studies both what visibly manifests itself, and how it comes into light, yet "world" is the supposed space in which that light is cast. Thus, how can the world be given phenomenological description?

First, Heidegger challenges the simple dichotomy between visibility and invisibility.[10] What appears or announces itself very well may not be given. He employs the example of the tool-as-used: the hammer disappears or is far from my consciousness when I am, for example, at work building a table. In a limited sense, it becomes "inconspicuous" in its being entirely immanent and wholly experienceable, yet absent to a meaning-giving and conscious grasping. Because an important task of *Sein und Zeit* was to give expression to "the world itself" beyond its traditional understanding as the only space of manifestation, Heidegger turns to the affective strands (e.g., Kant's sensations, Husserl's impressions) of how experience of the world could take place. Without attempting to get beyond the world, he refers to them as "moods," which are symptoms of our construed relations with the world. By "tuning in" (*Befindlichkeit*) to the world through various forms of comportment primordial to a conceptual grasping, knowing, or conceiving, we experience the disclosure or construal of the world: "ontologically mood is a primordial kind of Being for Dasein, in which Dasein is disclosed to itself *prior to* all cognition and volition, and *beyond* their range of disclosure."[11] These moods concern not simply those "things" to which Husserl commanded us to "get back," but also how we relate with the phenomenality of the world.

There are a number of essential figures who followed Heidegger and Husserl in the extension and further elaboration of the lifeworld in cosmological terms, such as Jan Patocka and Eugen Fink. Yet in many ways, Michel Henry takes up a unique strand of thought left by Heidegger, especially in regards to how the affects of "world" effectively conceal things in their obviousness. Henry demonstrates that our modern western thinking has incorrectly limited man to only one type of seeing; a seeing that concerns the ordinary appearing of things in clarity. This gets reduced to the problem of "the Greek *phainomenon* which reserves manifestation to the light of exteriority, [and thus] modernity proves incapable of grasping the invisible in its proper phenomenological positivity."[12] Although often reliant on Heidegger, Henry eventually claims that Heidegger's cosmology mistakenly took for granted that "'to show oneself' means 'to show oneself in the world,'" in an ek-static "outside," thus reducing "truth" to the "horizon of visibility." The privileging of obviousness and the seemingly self-evident is marked by a fundamental paradox: in privileging the obvious, one overlooks the most obvious.

Henry recognizes that a phenomenology of the visible (and perhaps also by proxy the invisible) may be a "contradiction in terms," and thus seeks out the most overlooked, yet constantly experienced, of phenomena precisely due to its obviousness in this world: life. Privileging the visible strips "life" of its "power of revealing" and limits the forms of its potentially appearing.[13] Following Heidegger's "moods," life is experienced foremost though the *pathos* or affective dimension of experience that provides the very key internal to accessing the appearing of the "outside" transcendental world—the world on which Henry claims our Modern enchantments to rely on so deeply.[14] Thus, life can be understood as what challenges any unchecked privileging of what one takes to be manifested as obvious. Henry calls this the "reign of the visible" for it misses the most obvious of experiences and in fact rational thought itself is given in "the pathetic auto-revelation of life," which is essential to how we describe the phenomenal appearances of the world itself.[15]

Is there a horizon of givenness that is irreducible to the spectacular glory of the world's presentation and could it be investigated without a reversion to metaphysical paradigms that already presuppose the world? This chapter aims to demonstrate three things. First, after an articulation of how Heidegger teaches the possibility of bringing the world itself into view, it is shown how Henry's conception of "life" can be characterized as inconspicuous, as it is "the common" and "obvious" that give rise to immanent life. Second, it articulates how, after Heidegger and Henry, the world itself can become "inconspicuous," namely, due to these thinkers' provisions of access points to the phenomenality of the world via affective life. These first two steps lead to the third, more constructive demonstration that it is possible to interpret religiously the lifeworld/world of life as one in which it becomes possible to engage actively in order to set a nonintentional condition for the experience of the Inconspicuous God.

This world of life is brought about through a turn to various conflictive tensions between life and world, the response to which is religious, or the core of religious experiencing. The inherent challenge, to which a development of the concept of "inconspicuousness" hopefully provides some solutions here, consists in how the understanding of the world as the neutral, yet invisible theatre in which all experience takes place, can be thought otherwise. Bereft of such a cosmological phenomenology, the ontotheological structures of thought would come back with a vengeance through the resorting to a pure incomprehensibility of the world, which could be argued to be merely the backside of the reign of the visible. A central task of living religiously is to carburate the tensions between seemingly invisible life and a purportedly obvious and neutral world, and inconspicuousness provides one means of articulating how such a task might be achieved in a nondichotomous way.

Heidegger's World

First to be addressed is Heidegger's cosmological phenomenology. It was Merleau-Ponty who first observed that despite Heidegger's turn from Husserl's principle of principles, Heidegger importantly took-up and prolonged Husserl's concept of the lifeworld (*Lebenswelt*) by offering a radical description of being-in-the-world that questions the "cares" of "living."[16] It was indeed the investigation of *Dasein*'s relation with the world that Heidegger claimed to be a fundamental goal of *Being and Time*. As he puts it in another essay around the time of its publication: "What is the mode of being of the entity in which 'world' is constituted? That is *Being and Time*'s central problem—namely, a fundamental ontology of Dasein. It has to be shown that the mode of being of human Dasein is totally different from that of all other entities and that, as the mode of being that it is, it harbors right within itself the possibility of transcendental constitution."[17]

World is constituted in Dasein. Transcendental constitution is a central possibility for Dasein as ek-sisting, as Dasein is never a "worldly real fact" as present-at-hand. To a limited extent, Heidegger treats world as if it is intertwined with Dasein itself, whose cares in the world help fashion Dasein. Caring involves both enduring (that is, continuing in time) and "living:" "To live means to care. What we care for and about, what care adheres to, is equivalent to what is meaningful. Meaningfulness is a categorial determination of the world; the objects of a world—'worldly' or 'world-some' objects—are lived inasmuch as they embody the character of meaningfulness."[18]

Living is caring, caring is meaning-making, and meaning-making constitutes the world. When one actively ascribes meaningfulness to the world in a determinate manner one is "living out" those forms of meaningfulness through "worldly" (*weltlich*) objects. Such objects, even the most banal, tell me about my involvement with things, and *how* I am *in* the world. The keys are keys to my house, where I enjoy time with family. The stop sign on the street not only communicates information to me, but draws me into how I care and how it is pertinent to my involvement in the world in that present space and moment; my duration, enduring, and living. "Life" is indeed an important means by which "world" is to be understood.

This widens the view on Heidegger's most formative phenomenological analysis of the world in part 1, section 3 of *Sein und Zeit* in which the question is posed: is it dubious to attempt to conceive of "the world-hood of the world as such" which would by necessity "show itself in 'entities' within the world"? In order to arrive at a satisfactory answer, he demonstrates two ways "world" has been conceived thus far falsely according to false dialectics that need to be overcome. On the one hand the "materialist" preunderstandings of the world leave it as the total "sum" of data, the many parts of which it is composed or in which it is contained. This amounts to the denial of the world *as such*, leaving it only the sum of its parts. On the other hand, our religious traditions and myths have described the world as something to be overcome, and that instead the more true "world of things" (*cosmos*) are inaccessible, and invisibly held together. Heidegger thus responds to this problematic, and claims that "*neither the ontical depiction of entitles within-the-world nor the ontological Interpretation of Being is such as to reach the phenomenon of the 'world.'* In both of these ways … the 'world' has already been 'presupposed.'"[19] These two depictions are flawed for a number of reasons, and the latter is more closely addressed in the winter semester of 1930–1931 Hegel Seminars in terms of the "speculatively conceived" nature of Being, which is pejoratively named there, for the first time "ontotheology" (a topic to which he returns twenty years later).[20] *Being and Time* demonstrates how both of these depictions of "world" rely on flawed ontologies that are but two sides of the same coin: seeking to conceive things in their clear or nonvisible states of intelligibility in a supposed objectivity amounts to being tautological with its exact opposite, ultimate unintelligibility or incomprehensibility.

He eventually suggests in *Poetry, Language, Thought* that "the clearing" or opening maintains precedence over the world: "This Open happens in the midst of beings … [and] to the Open there belong a world and the earth. But the world is not simply the Open that corresponds to clearing, and the earth is not simply the Closed that corresponds to concealment."[21] The world must not be mistaken for the clearing. The world is not the *Lichtung*, nor is it a neutral "open" space. The more ontic "earth" should not be understood as the straightforward or objective appearance. This view of "world" is consistent with claims made in the 1927 Encyclopedia Britannica entry on phenomenology, which was written in response to a disagreement he had with Husserl's ontology:

> Each and every entity, the whole world that we talk about straightforwardly and that is the constant field (pre-given as self-evidently real) of all our theoretical and practical activities—all of that suddenly becomes unintelligible. Every sense it has for us, whether unconditionally universal or applicable case by case to individuals, is, as we then see, a meaning that occurs in the immanence of our own perceiving, representing, thinking, evaluating (and so on) lives and that takes shape in subjective genesis.… This applies to the world in each of the determinations [we make about it], including the taken-for-granted determination that what belongs to the world is "in and for itself" just the way it is, regardless of whether or not I or anyone else happen to take cognizance of it.[22]

Heidegger already questions the way of straightforwardly taking the world as this "constant" and pregiven actuality, concluding that we in fact make faulty determinations about the world that do not include the careful consideration of ourselves, its constitutors and experiencers. Yet at the same time, Heidegger (perhaps unlike Henry) does not want Dasein to get *away* from the world or stand outside it: "All 'pure' mental phenomena have the ontological sense of worldly real facts, even when they are treated eidetically as possible facts of a world . . ." and, Heidegger continues, "thus, as a transcendental phenomenologist, what I have now is not my ego as a mind—for the very meaning of the word 'mind' presupposes an actual or possible world."[23] There is no getting away from "the world" for Heidegger, and "world-as-such" is indeed still the meaning-giving context that cannot be bracketed-out or suspended. However, the world, as possible and actual, is precisely in, how, and through which meaningful descriptions of the world as a phenomenon can be given. It is precisely by being in the world that description of its intelligibility is possible, from the inside. How? This leads to the enigma of the phenomenality of things.

There is a stunning and fecund quality that the world maintains beyond the aforementioned interdicts, namely, in things which also must be understood beyond their seemingly "natural," clear, and objectively ontic conceptions. The *Sachheit* or "material content" of things is effectively the glue that holds the descriptions of encounters with phenomena together.[24] As Husserl once put it, the world is somehow simultaneously "subjectively" constituted by us and constituting us, and this enigma of constitution allows for some objective, shared, and public means of understanding world; otherwise all appearances would be reduced to a private theater for consciousness. Heidegger takes up this insight and describes its inner relation in ontological terms, claiming that *Dasein* operates with a preontological, preunderstanding of the world. The "world" is essential to the very essence of Dasein, who is fundamentally described as "being-open" in the clearing of the world. Thus, it first is necessary to understand that things are in the world, and being in the world is Dasein's fundamental means to unfolding the meaning-giving activities of Being itself. This runs contrary to any Modern, Western, ontically-oriented paradigm of understanding the world as either a blank canvas or a frame on which phenomenality is stretched for display. In part, this is because the world needs *Dasein* to perceive and understand it, and therefore world (not simply entities within it, or the data of things germane to it) is an aspect of the core of Dasein as an "*Ich bin*" whose *amness* is a being-alongside-the-world. This is Dasein's "essential state."[25] The world is not pregiven to our intuition as a *Vorgegebenheit* (as Husserl might have put it in his earlier writings) but is disclosed in and through the ontological attunements or moods of Dasein as it lives, endures, and has its being.

Thus, phenomena are construed as those things that reveal Being, and therefore say something meaningful *to* Dasein *about* Dasein in a given space and time. The red stop sign does not communicate simply information *to* me, but also information *about* me, what I am interested in at that moment, my present mood-as-lived, which ultimately indicates what I care about in toto. Things tell me something about me. Thus, to experience *a* phenomenon is to undergo the potentially transformative and excessive dynamic out of which Being might operate. The being of an entity "present at hand" signifies the meaningfulness and intelligibility of my being out in the open "clearing." Even the most banal phenomena, like the stop sign, bear overwhelming, excessive, constituting, and existentially meaningful intelligibility for me. In fact, it is precisely such "simple" or "ordinary" phenomena that uniquely retain a certain "quiet gleam" of mysteriousness. Our world is as such that it is charged with a mysterious character and potential meaningfulness, and it is up to Dasein to "reveal" Being, which is found in entities in the world.

This leads back to the question of *how* the world itself can be a phenomenon. There is one essential aspect of the aforementioned "traditional" conception of the world that is of value, and it concerns how we relate with ontic meanings of the world, things whose "worldly character" (*Weltmäßigkeit*) or "worldhood" (*Weltlichkeit*) bring about the worlding of the world as such. Worldhood designates what is taken, a priori, to be one's world, and can therefore be investigated in its phenomenal character. How does one provide or describe the phenomena of worldhood? One answer: By appropriately synthesizing the frames of reference between the world of the ontic, and that of the ontological. In doing so, we get the temporally and spatially contingent worldhood that is proper to these experiences, and the way the world itself appears and communicates to me at that moment. Heidegger still follows Kant in one important regard: space and time are essential to worldhood, and there is no way to get "outside the world" per se, for we are still immanent beings whose cares and concerns are sutured to the various aspects of "the world." And for Heidegger, it is through a synthetic unity between: (a) the appearing of the world as the blank "neutral" canvas on which phenomena in the world are projected; and (b) the meaning-giving constitution of that which I *give* to the world as I am in the world (as I care, take up interests, etc.), that provides me with the possibility of seeing the world as "a phenomenon." Dasein is indeed "worldly."[26]

These "things-in" (which have character according to their being "in" the world) indicate that the world in which they are given retains a unique role in their being understood. In the end, it is still "things" (to which Husserl always claimed we are to "go back to") that usher us into the confrontation with the worldhood of the world, for their present-at-handedness allow for new discoveries about the world beyond their ontic status.[27] This inconspicuous character of Being's operation in the world is one reason why "when we investigate the phenomenon of the 'world' we must do so by the avenue of entities within-the-world and the Being which they possess." Yet this does not mean, ultimately, that things have primacy over world, for in phenomenological description, things disappear and withdraw. This marks the paradox of Being, and worldhood is an *existentiale* revealed only by Dasein. The way Dasein relates with the appearances of things (especially in the Greek sense of "things" defined according to their pragmatic use as equipment such as the ready-to-handedness of tools) is paradoxically in their withdrawal (*zurückziehen*) from consciousness in favor of the focused work one undertakes with such equipment.[28] It is in this shifting between a thing-as-such and a thing-as-indicative-of-involvement-in-the-world that an engagement with "inconspicuousness" might provide further clarification.

Heidegger, Heraclitus, and the Inconspicuous World

Although Heidegger's "phenomenology of the inconspicuous" goes unformulated until 1973, his seminars on Heraclitus (which Eugen Fink became essential to developing) foreshadow inconspicuousness as it relates to "world." In his 1966 "Seminar in Le Thor," Heraclitus' κόσμος is interpreted not simply as referential to the "order" of things, but also as a structure of appearing for things as radiating, burning, and shining (*phanesthai*). There, a threefold sense of *cosmos* is presented as: (1) a bringing-into-order; (2) a gleaming radiance and adornment; and (3) a decoration that reveals the decorated in a new light and brilliance. For Heidegger "this threefold sense constitutes the Heraclitean sense of 'world.'"[29] This sense of world seemingly is opposite from the aforementioned descriptions of how "world" is understood by us today. Heraclitus' world was the space that, contrary to an "impure" or profane banality, inconspicuously held not simply a stage for radiant things to be displayed, but a radiating potential that emanated from its own presentative quality. This entailed that world itself becomes a phenomenon. The senses and meanings of appearances in such a Heraclitean world, although radiant, therefore are not to be understood as shining spectacles that stand out, but as inconspicuously integrated in ways we remain unready to notice as they are intertwined with what is common. The mysteries of the world do not shine in a "clearly visible" (*conspicuus*) manner, yet the world is active in its profusion of obviousness that actively obfuscates itself.

Roughly thirty years prior to the Le Thor seminars, Heidegger referred to Heraclitus' quip that "Asses choose hay rather than gold" to demonstrate that it is in the "quiet gleam" of simplicity that the mysterious and uncanny appear from within the world.[30] It is a matter of being-in-the-open, which is an open-here that speaks to the nature of the world as not only the space of revealing or visibility, but also, according to the very nature of truth, as concealing. One can be trained on this oscillation between concealing and revealing through a "wonder at what is simple," a wonder that begins with the question: "What does all this mean and how could it happen?"[31] Mortality and temporality paradoxically usher in the task of pondering possible relations with the never-setting of truth. Dasein relates with this truth not by performing the activities of unconcealing or revealing, but by submitting oneself to the never-setting of things and their mysterious nature within the world. This quasi eternality of things is discomfiting, and operates according to a mysteriousness that is not incomprehensible but one whose givenness is manifested inconspicuously. This marks a kind of relation with the world.[32] As developed in Eugen Fink's cosmological phenomenology, which relies heavily on both Heidegger and Heraclitus, there is something alive that provides the essence or *phusis* to the world's play and operation.[33]

Heidegger then risks to invert Heraclitus' adjectival use of the negative "never-setting" in reference to the essence of the world into a positive affirmation, as "the always rising" or "the ever and always-enduring disclosure"[34] The not-setting-ever holds to Heraclitus' theory of eternal motion, and Heidegger interprets this on phenomenological terms: to not-ever-set is not a reference to time as stillborn, but precisely the opposite: time is the profusion and continuous giving of things within the world. It is not that the never-setting and the always-rising are "two different occurrences merely jammed together, but[,] as one and the same" a representation of the double helix of the world's operation.[35] Dasein is tasked with attending to the at times banal correspondence between the "whatnesses" of man and world, in which this subtle gleam of mystery appears. Heidegger turns to Heraclitus' fragments for the sake of reinterpreting the fundamental nature of the world, not as a place for revelation or manifestation, but rather as the temporal and spatial instance at/in which the suturing of both revealing and concealing actively take place. The world is not *phusis* as the ontological "essence of things" but rather, *phusis* as "the essential unfolding" (the German *Wesen* here is used as a verb).[36] Essence, in other words, as the "essential" basis of how the world is worlded, is composed of this melding of revealing and concealing.

Importantly for our purposes here, Heidegger develops a concept of the inconspicuous in his other (untranslated) seminars on Heraclitus in GA 55 precisely in the context of how the world gains this essence. There, he names *Phusis* "inconspicuous" in its mode of appearance:

> "φύσις is the Inconspicuous. As such, the ever-rising in general is the lit clearing that waits for an appearance, brings itself into all appearances, brings every appearance back to itself, and is not an appearance that can be categorized under others ... φύσις does not come within the ever-rising and withdrawing, in a kind of appearing, but rather it is in every case of its appearance, the inconspicuous. Yet by no means is this to be confused with 'the unseen,' as the before mentioned philological translations incorrectly render it. The φύσις is

> not 'invisible,' [das Unsichtbare] it is on the contrary just the initially visible, which although initially detected, most often and in general never is seen in its specificity."[37]

The ever-rising to which he refers in the other seminar has its own horizon that is present, yet not easily detectable. It is barely visible by merit of its inconspicuousness. Heidegger makes it clear here that this ever-rising is not to be confused with the invisible or unseen, for its active presence demands a different kind of description in order to make sense of it. What he calls here *the* inconspicuous is ascribed the important role of operating on behalf of *phusis* in its unique hiding from within appearances and appearing itself.

It is in these contexts that we must understand that "World is enduring fire, enduring rising in the full sense of *phusis*." Building from Heidegger's insight, the way to be attuned properly to the world is to dwell in it by seeking the enduring (i.e., living), rising, and falling of phenomenal data within its spatial and temporal parameters. This observation of the worlding of the world redefines presence not according to what is or is not here, but according to the paradoxical notion of what we can observe in the inconspicuous nature of *phusis*, which in this rising and falling creates a breach between the given and the not given.[38] In this world, presence, as "the presencing of what is present," concerns "the revealing-concealing lighting." The straightforward and traditional understanding of "appearing" no longer can operate according to the bifurcation between presence and absence, as Dasein becomes the entertainer or coconstitutor of the revealing-concealing of phenomenality within the world, which ultimately births a reenchanted world. Dasein is charged with the unique privilege to find the uncanny and mysterious on the surface of the ordinarily simple and near-by. The inconspicuous lighting that lights everything present in its presencing has been forgotten, and instead we become accustomed to attuning our vision toward what is present, clear, and spectacular. A conception of world that reduces its conditions to the totalizing dyad between the visible and invisible only can end with a preference for spectacular novelties, as what is the most familiar has become the most foreign.[39] To sum up, for Heidegger one gains attention to the phenomenality of the world by seeking what endures, as that acts as a signal to the world's conditions via affective moods. Through living and dwelling (which are essentially inconspicuous), these moods tell us something about the world's phenomenality and given intelligibility.

Henry's Autoaffection of Life beyond the World

It is on the points of moods and affects of the world that Henry picks up where Heidegger left off. One somewhat lengthy passage in *I Am the Truth* encapsulates

Henry's position in relation to Heidegger, inconspicuousness, and Henry's own means to interpreting "world:"

> "Despite his repeated criticism of the history of western metaphysics and his own efforts to put an end to it, Heidegger's phenomenology recognized (thought through and took to the limit) only the phenomenological presuppositions that had guided, or rather misguided, this thought from the start. By inexorably and ingeniously unveiling the implications of the Greek concept of phenomenon, these presuppositions led to the truth of the world being laid bare. This phenomenology was not about things but rather about nothingness, not about what is shown, but rather the 'unapparent' [i.e., inconspicuous]. Far from turning us away from the world and its 'insight,' this phenomenology concerns itself with nothing other than the original event in which this insight is produced. With respect to the question of life, the immediate consequences of these presuppositions are overwhelming. The first is the fact that we know nothing about a mode of revelation other than that in which the illumination of the world occurs. Life has no phenomenological existence if we understand it as a specific mode of the phenomenologization of pure phenomenality."[40]

When reduced to the paltry role of a medium of phenomenology, life is ignored from having any actual value. Throughout his works, Henry seeks to demonstrate how it is not the case that "the world is the environment of all possible manifestation," and that the visible world is not the only existing world. Manifestation manifests itself, and life, as one experiences it as one's own life, is a *revelation that*; namely that affectivity *is* revelation, especially of both the world and the self.[41] Because Henry on occasion employs the word "invisible" it easily can be mistaken that his work seeks to disclose phenomenology to new intimacies with the "not here," which is reducible to the kinds of speculation Heidegger critiqued. However, this could not be any further from the truth for Henry, for he seeks to turn phenomenology to its most originary and immanent of experiences via a genealogy of that which exceeds infinitely the visible/invisible paradigm. The autorevelation of life is what enacts this movement.

What has perhaps led some to think of Henry's approach as a turn to the putatively not-given is a misrecognition of the paradox that, for Henry, the most originary immanence is not experienced objectively: "nothing of ourselves is explained in the end by objectivity. We are not worldly beings because in the world there is no life."[42] Although life is not reduced to visibility in any traditional sense of the word, it can be experienced uniquely. This is because the true horizon of the world is not in the world as it generally gets understood. "Life" provides a point of access to transcending the world itself, and therefore describing the world's phenomenality. The immediate obviousness with which the world generally is taken to present itself is obfuscated or estranged from out of its own logics of revelation. There is no objective grasping of a phenomenology of life, for life-as-lived is the first point of arrival that the affective dimension opens on, and does not give itself to worldly experience.[43] Affectivity is Henry's replacement concept for a nonaffected "perception." Affectivity is to experience oneself as perceiving with *pathos*, and being "moved" by and toward certain things.

This can be given further expression in etymological terms. *Pathos* refers to anything that "might befall me" or enter into my experience. It is what one undergoes. The Greek *Pathetik* does not refer necessarily to sympathy, but rather to living-through an emotion or being subject to "feeling something." To feel some-thing (which is also a perceiving) is to experience oneself as alive: Life is affected and moved (*pathétique*), and to follow Spinoza is the "striving to persevere" (*in suo esse perseverare*) that seeks to dwell, maintain, and adhere in a kind of "stayability" (*suo esse*).[44] Life is the experience of feeling-remaining that is also a being moved, or remaining moved. This kind of life also is found in the Greek *liaprein* (to persist), and this is perhaps why Heidegger comes to see perseverance not a "permanence," but as a presencing beyond the moment (*jetz vuv nunc*) that points to the basic form of human life—dwelling.

To dwell is to be a life-lived in particularity and in accord with the contingency of experience in a particular moment; to dwell is to belong somewhere and, for *Dasein*, to be (alive) in the world. It is in fact on the grounds of this most originary of experiences through the affective dimension (Heideggerian mood, Husserlian expression, Kantian sensation) that we come to relate with, and find ourselves transcendentally affected by the surrounding world. It is in this precise context that Henry believes he might go one step further than Heidegger: "It is solely because we have first come into life that we are then able to come into the world."[45] Life is experienced before the world is. In order to defend this claim, Henry unfolds three basic traits that characterize how the world (as a phenomenon) appears.

Henry's Three Traits of "World"

These traits cannot contain the appearing of life itself, and therefore no life can appear in the appearing of the world of objectivity. The inherent paradox of life is that it is the most originary and obvious, yet modern interpretations of world (which champion the presentation of things neutrally in their obviousness) cannot account for this originary experience of life. The first trait is that the appearing of the world is a matter of being outside of self; as exterior, other, and at a distance. This exteriority is predicated on difference, which marks a division of distance. It is this setting at a distance of things that allows things to appear to me "in the horizon of the world."[46] The second trait of "the how" of the world's appearance follows from the first in that its appearing (in this case, "seeming") is not only on the basis of difference, but also of indifference. The world's appearance is indifferent in its neutrality: "the appearing which unveils in the difference of the world . . .

is in principle indifferent to it" and therefore "the appearing of the world illuminates everything . . . in a terrifying neutrality." Such neutrality and indifference to what is unveiled leads to the third trait of the appearing of the world: "it is incapable of conferring existence on it [that which is unveiled]." Due to the appearing of the world as indifferent to things, it must therefore be powerless to make things appear, or cause them to exist. What remains unique about the unveiling or manifestation of the world-as-given is that it is a phenomenon that presents, but one that cannot take account of the data it presents or what appears in it; the world's "unveiling unveils . . . but does not create (*macht nicht, öffnet*)."[47] All three of these traits of the world tell us about how the world operates.

Henry believes himself able to establish these traits of the phenomenality or "bracketability" of the world, in part due to the self-affection of life, which is interior to these exterior activities of the world. Not all affects are attached to the world, and only sometimes can the world account for affections. Affections act as the binding material between ourselves and the world, yet without losing their independence from the world. Yet this raises a concern in this context, for any state of being-affected is the being-affected-by-some-thing. There are no empty content-less affects. Henry's proposed solution to this problem is to suggest that life "experiences itself" (*s'é prouve soi-même*) and is passive vis-á-vis itself. Life is phenomenality as a welding of the phenomenon and its unique *how* of showing. In a more Heideggerian middle voice, "life lives" as simultaneously passive and active, and affirmative on an autorevelatory basis. This is why Henry turns Husserl's lifeworld inside-out by recasting it as an interior "world of life," which constitutes "the world's content."[48] The Lifeworld construction privileges the world, yet it is life that initially sets the world on its course of possible manifestation, and this is quite distinct from a barbaric or inhuman world that privileges the visibly external and seeks to disregard life and its unique forms of showing in preference for neutrality.[49] Both models (lifeworld, world of life) offer entirely different proposals of the activities of manifestation. For Henry the world as the great "horizon of horizons" is to be subjected to the primordiality of the self-affectation of life.

This approach likely would have received a less than enthusiastic reaction from Heidegger for its seeming to be an all too subjectivist account of the world. How might one arrive at some level of objectivity by associating life with interiority, and the world with exteriority? Is this problematic not reducible to the dichotomy between "inside" and "outside," which both Husserl and Heidegger sought to dispel?[50] How can life-as-lived be distanced from a world relation? As Waldenfels expresses this concern in a slightly different manner, "doesn't the negative characterization of self-affection as nonintentional, nonrepresentational, and nonsighted or nonecstatic bear a constant reference to the world-relation that it suspends?"[51] Waldenfels' worry is that by starkly abandoning the world's value, one is in fact apophatically affirming it. One can accept that the world relation (*Weltbezug*) indeed is held together by life, yet might not the self-affectivity of life provide for a lived intelligibility of living; of something to *live for* that one finds in the world? Also, might this bring us back once again to the seemingly stark contrast between the invisible and visible that Henry's work has rejected since the 1960s?[52]

Henry does not answer these questions directly, but for them he does provide some consolation. He turns to the example of the two senses of how "the body is the appearing of the world." First, while bodies are revealed in the "exterior" world, they still harbor interior elements experienced via sensual qualities. Second, the body is the opening through which this world itself is accessed through a transcendental outside of self as such.[53] The body is the culmination of phenomenon and manifestation as we properly are living out our worlds. Again, the world has its basis in one's life as lived, and perception is replaced with a deeper being-affected.

These reflections on life and world are depictive of Henry's applications of phenomenology: "other sciences study specific phenomena [yet] ... phenomenology explores what allows a phenomenon to be a phenomenon." The in-depth study of things does not make or force things into appearance, and thus it becomes a matter of *how* they enter into conscious experience as they affect me and matter to me as a living being who receives impressions. The givenness of things concerns how *they dynamically* come into manifestation and how they draw our attention to their active appearing aside from their ontic status. We give attention to what continues to give, not to what is given finally and conclusively, for something "is only if the appearing appears in itself and as such that something, whatever it may be, can in turn appear, can show itself to us." Phenomenology is interested in things-as-appearing in their unique how, which leads to a unique "life experience." Every phenomenon has the potential to change my life.

With a decidedly Heideggerian tone, Henry suggests that appearing itself can even obscure the thing's appearance; that what seems to be given in a straightforward and obvious manner is distinct from this kind of appearing. The experience of "objects in their how" (*Gegenstände im Wie*, as Husserl puts it) occurs via the world as it, itself, appears. While one does not "perceive" the world per se, one indeed finds oneself "affected" by it. Objects-in-their-how are "lived with" and, as made manifest in the world, entail that one operates with implicit, and therefore in-need-of-unfolding, conceptions of phenomenality. For Henry, "the conception of phenomenality that is derived from the perception of objects in the world ... is ... in the final reckoning, the appearing of the world itself."[54] The world appears in its affective experience, by its giving objects in their how, and through our conscious making intelligible (via "the movement through which it throws itself outside" by setting its phenomenal data "at a distance") of its phenomenality. The world needs to be studied phenomenologically by showing (*faire-voir*), *through the act of revealing*, the means through which life initiates relation with the outside.

Again, distance implies exteriority, and allows for the visibility of things to appear, and for Henry it is life that ultimately provides meaningful relations with the world and its objects beyond its more ontic presentations and visible manifestations. The interiority of life can be arrived at and experienced in such an inconspicuous way in the world because life is: (a) not under the jurisdiction of the world's oversight; (b) has its own self-revelation whose essence is self-affectivity; (c) maintains an instantaneous and unmediated excitation; and (d) cannot be reduced to any of the forms of phenomenal presentation that the world typically is known to champion.[55] Appearing goes hand-in-glove with being-moved and it is not a docile, emotionless endeavor. Appearing affects.

Summing up, Henry's understanding of the world is the transcendentally second order of experience that is temporally and spatially after one finds oneself affected by the world, which indeed relies on the autoaffection of life in its self-revelation. To be affected in and by the world is to experience oneself living. Affections are the primal first experience one has with oneself, and they immediately provide intelligible content for us about ourselves in the momentary presencing of our world. However, we so often overlook both world and life, despite their being the most overt and obvious of experiences. In this sense, life does not hide in a supernatural and utterly invisible dimension, but hides in plain sight in an immanent, and therefore characteristically taken-for-granted time and place that is the world of life. If life is inconspicuous, so is the world that appears according to life's affectivity.

Being in (but not of) the Religious World of Life

The Relations between World and Life

It is possible to interpret the world of life in its religious element, one according to which an experience of an inconspicuous God might be given description. First, it is helpful to arrive at some of the means of relation between world and life, building on Heidegger and Henry's insights. One product of the preference for clarity and distinction is the unfortunate exclusion of that which demands an entirely different kind of attention. The contemporary and especially non-phenomenological means of interpreting world is marked today by a totalizing attendance to what appears directly, clearly, and obviously, and by its marginalizing or, at best, subjectivizing and individualizing the experiences of things that are not commonly understood in their spectacularity. However, the case of life reveals how these relied-up ways of seeing end-up overlooking precisely the very most obvious of experiences. This is especially the case in the context of religious experience. One way not to overlook life, and therefore to experience it in its radicality, begins first with bracketing this direct kind of seeing so that the world's phenomenality might appear. Since life is marked by inconspicuousness, and because life is the means to attaining the phenomenality of the world (which life is responsible for animating), then the world can be understood and experienced anew as imbued with life.

This points to how there is a religious world of life that is inconspicuous. First, the world cannot be presupposed as an invisibly operative essence, whose content and means of showing are utterly unknown and inaccessible, otherwise, it becomes a new Absolute, thereby occupying the ontotheological position Heidegger sought to abolish. Yet since the world is powerless, even if one does not challenge its neutrality or indifference (which are presupposed often by phenomenology's attempting to make its practitioners presuppositionless) it cannot operate quietly as a metaphysical source, and thereby must be capable of phenomenological description. The world cannot maintain the status of being an absolute nature, for it has no poetic or creative potential to sustain itself. The world is not alive (unless, of course, one ascribes to a pantheistic or panentheistic view). Second, the world is inconspicuous in its status as ever-present and operative, yet generally ignored and subsequently absent. The attempt to think the world (what it is, how it appears, and its means of presentation) first comes with a banality and commonality that inhibits its being thought. The world's supposed neutrality and indifference often births indifference to its status, despite its guise of banality.

Third, as animated by life, the world is that which we are *in*, and this *inness* is to be interpreted through sensations, impressions, affections, and moods that thereby speak the truth (as disclosure and enclosure) about the world and its social underpinnings. Affections are the couriers of relation between ourselves and the world (not only its phenomenal data) thereby granting access to the world in a way that does not discount ontic and everyday things in the world, but rather elevates them to the status of revealing the mysteries of Being. As Heidegger taught, not one thing, no matter how seemingly banal, lacks the potential to communicate on behalf of the uncanny. It in fact only is because *Dasein* is enmeshed in the space and time of the world that *Dasein* is capable of somehow offering an intelligible description (as the constitutor of meaning) of the world's phenomenal appearance, its worlding or worldhood beyond abstraction. Despite Henry's occasionally misleading language of exteriority and interiority (especially in the context of thinking the world), which appears to at first rely on the visible and invisible dichotomy, a closer look at his work reveals that he frequently reiterates the need to house transcendental life in the immanent here. This demonstrates that Henry also does not entirely wish to abandon immanent reality, but rather to reinstate how the world's modes of presentation are all but comprehensive, especially in their lacking the ability to provide a horizon for detecting what is the *most* obvious—life.

Although Henry and Heidegger offer differing accounts of the life vis-à-vis world relation, they both insist that the world's supposed neutrality does not prohibit it from appearing to us in its phenomenality, which is unlocked by the keys of affective "living" (Henry) or "dwelling" (Heidegger), which are thereby infused in, and subsequently bring into affective experience, the easily overlooked world.[56] What is utterly unique about Henry's "phenomenology of life" (and distinct from Fink and Patocka's respective cosmological approaches) is that it brackets the "how structure" of taking-something-as-ordinary, and turns to affection as a means of presenting an intelligibility that is not putatively obvious. Affections or moods are the pressure points of living and dwelling that act as levers for disrupting the everyday world of life and bracketing how one takes something to be obvious. Understood in its inconspicuousness, life does not reenchant or act simply as the invisible hand of inspiring the world's phenomenal data, but perhaps more radically, is one essential player in the discombobulation of experience as a confrontation. Again, this does not involve a giving-up and getting-over of the world by conjuring an invisible, unseen, and inaccessible space or essence, but rather a turn to the paradoxical nature of the world itself and how affection cues relations with it.

This radicalizes world views, which when thought phenomenologically could be exposed as the entrapments and calculatory apparatuses that prohibit thought to which affects and moods give rise. As Heidegger recognized in his *Phenomenological Interpretations of Aristotle*, it is not enough to investigate critically our beloved *Weltanschauungen*. Although the systemic and synoptic order of characterizing the various values in/of life-as-lived in the world must be investigated, the world's presentation itself (or worlding) is in need of being challenged.[57] This refashions world view not according to *how* one *interprets* the world's manifestations, but how one affectively can perceive the coming into appearance of the world itself.

An investigation into the ongoing tensions between world and life can be summarized to have four steps, all of which open onto a religious world of life. First, a description of the world in a way that attends to its dynamism is necessary, as a world view void of life is dead and not depictive of a lived reality. Second, it is helpful to observe how representations of life make-up the world-view and are integrated within it. Third, the obvious and clear must be deprivileged, for they remain a hindrance to seeing the most obvious (what is alive). And fourth, the various points of necessary and irresolvable tensions between life and world should be acknowledged, for they might furnish productive and affective moods or pressure points.

Without such tensions, there is stagnancy, and where there is stagnancy there is no life. Yet tension is both nondialectical and nonsynthetic, as it is depictive of the inconspicuous condition of the world vis-à-vis life relation, which allows things to appear paradoxically by blurring or making their data unclear. This blurring can lead to the possibility of a religious *poesis* (creating, building) precisely because the pragmatic clarity and totalizing effects the world tends to distribute might be disturbed. In other words, blurring or distortion is the clarion to affective, poetic, and active engagement of the life of living religiously.

The Religious World of Life

When the world (or the everyday "life world") is understood in the context of Heidegger's interpretation of Heraclitus' *phusis*-infused *cosmos* and Henry's concept of life (as "world of life"), the inner-tension of the world of life can inspire a shock that allows for the experience of what oscillates between them—The Inconspicuous God. This shock is the distortion of the ability to see clearly, distinctly, and obviously, and therefore to bracket-out the spectacles of everyday life responsible for various totalities that command our social imaginaries. Put more succinctly, when the differentiations of life and world collide, they can provide the conditions by which a religious experience can be acted on. If Inconspicuousness is a primary trait or characteristic of God then religious life needs to be trained on it.

It is precisely the tension between life and world that concerned Jesus in his prayer for his followers before going to the cross (John 17). More particularly, it was a matter of his followers' conflictive relation of being *not-of* (ἐκ, having an ek-sistence from somewhere otherwise than) the world, while simultaneously being sent (ἀπέστειλα) *into* (εἰς) the world (κόσμου) in a radical way ("They are not of the world, even as I am not of the world. Sanctify them in the truth; Your word is truth. As You sent Me into the world, I also have sent them into the world." John 17:16–18, NASB). As not-of, their life is from elsewhere than the order of the *cosmos*, yet as sent-into (the proper definition of "apostle") their life is found *in* the world.

While holding a conflictive tension, these two folds of Jesus's prayer are not contradictory. More broadly, Johannine literature refers to *cosmos* in different ways: (a) more negatively to those who do not recognize God's truth (John 1:10, e.g.); (b) more positively to space as a product of God's accomplishment (John 1:9); or (c) more neutrally to people, whose dwelling is the world (John 3:16–17) or where they simply "are" (John 8:23). In each case, the world is never something to which one is called to remain indifferent or abandon. The tension enacted by this "not-of" and "sent-in" is a matter of taking the world itself into view. It only is by being in the world that it is possible to take each new apperception toward a new creative typification (in Husserlian terms) of nonabstracted life. This experiential *sent-inness* is essential to experiencing the inconspicuous God who also occupies the world; and the experience of *not-ofness* is the clarion to redound to the affects of life, which the *cosmos* in and of itself is incapable of providing.

Often overlooked in this passage is the verse sandwiched between Jesus's prayers concerning this being-in/not-of-ness. Yet it points to a carbureting factor that helps bind this in/of relation together: "Sanctify them through thy truth, thy word is truth." (John 17:17). Their being sent in/not-of the world uniquely hangs on the revivification of *aletheia*, which is not, as one might render it today, a matter of adequation or being propositionally correct per se. To Greek ears, this word *aletheia* would have signaled to something not unlike the discombobulation of one's illusions so that a different reality can be experienced. In this case, the prayer consists of the hope that the disciples' world-relation would be brought under investigation and subsequently altered through a fundamental experience with truth, which constitutes, in this case, sanctification. Sanctifying is to be understood as a "clearing away" that gives a refreshed inspiration—life.

It is the aforementioned confrontation between having life not of this world, while being inherently sutured to it as apostles (as "sent ones") that allows for their experience of the religious world of life. The prayer begins (in John 17:2) with the wish to give life (a "never ending" life), the truth of which is not found in a solipsistic consciousness, but in a counterexperience of being looked back at by a life unending and not commanded by the specific orders (and ways of seeing) that a traditional conception of *cosmos* champions and teaches. Yet simultaneously, this religious world of life is experienced also via one's sent-inness, which prevents any totalizing asymmetry with the world in toto. The response is religious insofar as one is to learn from this experience how to endure differently via the distortion of the world's clarity, and the presentation of a religious life grounded, founded, and integrated in an inconspicuous reality.

In the case of Jesus's prayer for his disciples, the in/not-of relation of the world is what allows active participation with the inconspicuous God. The in/not-of relation is their truth. Life is not born of the world, yet the world's banalities are those into which one is sent. Dwelling in the world of religious life in this way cuts against the grain of the visibility and invisibility paradigm, deprivileging what shines in spectacularity, and simultaneously what is incomprehensible. It now becomes a matter of how such a God, in the form of a word of Christ, is to "dwell richly" (Colossians 3:16). This is what the next chapter seeks to develop via the work of Lacoste and a liturgical reduction to "in-dwelling."

Notes

1. Craig Calhoun, "Rethinking Secularism," *The Hedgehog Review* 12 no. 3 (2010): 36. It was the paradox of time that Augustine sought to teach, and according to Calhoun, Augustine emphasized "the importance of this connection to the eternal for their ability to cope with the travails of the temporal world."

2. Eugen Fink, *Spiel als Weltsymbol* (Stuttgart Germany: Kohlhammer Verlag, 1960), 192. See also S. Fink, *Sein, Wahrheit, Welt: Vor-Fragen zum Problem des Phänomen-Begriffs* (Den Haag: M. Nijhoff, 1958).

3. As Calhoun interprets, for Taylor "Cause and effect relationships are understood in this-worldly terms as matters of nature, technology, human intention, or even mere accident." This marks Taylor's immanent frame. Ibid., 36.

4. Further, for Barbieri, "One way of orienting ourselves in the world involves focusing on the very quality of *worldliness*, and this is what we do when we reflect on the secular and the varied roots and cognates associated with it: *saeculum*, secularity, secularism, secularization." William A. Barbieri Jr., "The Post-Secular Problematic," in *At the Limits of the Secular: Reflections on Faith and Public Life*, ed. Barbieri Jr. (Grand Rapids, MI: Eerdmans Publishing, 2014), 129.

5. For Descartes, extension is what constitutes the substance of "the world:" "extension in length, breadth, and depth constitutes the nature of corporeal substance." ("Nempe extension in longum, latum et profundum, substantiae corporeae naturam constituit."), René Descartes, "Principles of Philosophy," in *The Passions of the Soul and Other Late Philosophical Writings*, ed. Michael Moriarty (Oxford: Oxford University Press, 2015), 155. See here Heidegger's engagement with his "Analysis of Worldhood and Descartes Interpretation of the World," in *Being and Time*, trans. Richardson (New York: Harper, 1962), 122–28. Elsewhere, Heidegger claimed that "Descartes' *Meditations* already gained the insight that everything real—ultimately this whole world—has being for us only in terms of our experience and cognition, and that even the performances of reason, aimed at objective truth with the character of 'evidence,' unfold purely within subjectivity." Martin Heidegger, 'Phenomenology,' Draft B (of the Encyclopaedia Britannica Article) with Heidegger's Letter to Husserl" in *Becoming Heidegger: On the Trail of His Early Occasional Writings*, 1910-1927. eds. Theodore Kisiel and Thomas Sheehan. Chicago: Northwestern University Press, 2007. Available at: http://religiousstudies.stanford.edu/wp-content/uploads/PHENOMENOLOGY-ENCYCLOPAEDIA-BRITANNICA.pdf

6. Quoted by Henry from the French version of Husserl's *Leçons*. Michel Henry, "Phenomenology of Life," in *Veritas: Transcendence and Phenomenology*, ed. Conor Cunningham and Peter M. Candler (London: SCM Press, 2007), 124.

7. And he continues "men recognize thoroughly the absurdity of the dualistic interpretation of the world, according to which nature and spirit are to be looked upon as realities (*Realitäten*) in the same sense. In all seriousness my opinion is this: there never has nor ever will be an objective science of spirit, an objective theory of the soul, objective in the sense that it permits the attribution of an existence under the forms of spatio-temporality to souls or to communities of persons." Edmund Husserl, *The Crisis of European Sciences and Transcendental Phenomenology. An Introduction to Phenomenology*, trans. David Carr (Evanston, IL: Northwestern University Press, 1970). See here also Dermot Moran, *Husserl's Crisis of the European Sciences and Transcendental Phenomenology: An Introduction* (Cambridge: Cambridge University Press, 2012).

8. Husserl, *The Crisis of European Sciences and Transcendental Phenomenology*, Part III B: "The Way into Phenomenological Transcendental Philosophy from Psychology" § 58: "For the transcendental philosopher, however, the totality of real objectivity—not only the scientific objectivity of all actual and possible sciences but also the prescientific objectivity of the lifeworld, with its 'situational truths' and the relativity of its existing objects—has become a problem, the enigma of all enigmas. The enigma is precisely the taken-for-grantedness in

virtue of which the 'world' constantly and pre-scientifically exists for us, 'world' being a title for an infinity of what is taken for granted, what is indispensable for all objective sciences." Then in § 59: "the lifeworld—the 'world for us all'—is identical with the world that can be commonly talked about. Every new apperception leads essentially, through apperceptive transference, to a new typification of the surrounding world and in social intercourse to a naming which immediately flows into the common language." For Husserl, the Greeks knew better that the worlds we take to be "natural" are in fact representations of the world: "The historical environing world of the Greeks is not the objective world in our sense; rather it is their 'representation of the world', that is, their own subjective evaluation, with all the realities therein that were valid for them."

9. Martin Heidegger, *Sein und Zeit*, ed. Friedrich-Wilhelm von Herrmann (Frankfurt am Main: Klostermann, 1977), 65, Martin Heidegger, *Being and Time*, trans. John Macquarrie and Edward Robinson (New York: Harper & Row, 1962), 93, 96.

10. See Heidegger, *Sein und Zeit*, § 7 for the subversion of appearing as merely that which "comes into light" into that which also is "covered over." What appears to us retains perhaps the most layers of being hidden or unseen.

11. Heidegger, *Being and Time*, 136. My interpretation of Heidegger's offering a means to think beyond the "secular hypothesis" may be controversial in the context of contemporary interpretations of his work in French phenomenology, most especially by Lacoste, to whom this challenge is issued in a later chapter of the present study. As Shrijvers thinks, for Lacoste, Heidegger's understanding of "world" is "secular:" "Lacoste asks whether Dasein, and the hermeneutic of its facticity is not merely a hermeneutics of secularization. Can and must we assume that this 'being-in-the-world' and its corresponding anxiety is the most original and fundamental characteristic of human existence?" Joeri Schrijvers, "Jean-Yves Lacoste: A Phenomenology of Liturgy," *Heythrop Journal* 46 no. 3 (2005): 314–33.

12. Henry, "Phenomenology of Life," 252.

13. Michel Henry, *I Am the Truth: Toward a Philosophy of Christianity* (Stanford, CA: Stanford University Press, 2003), 41. For Henry Life "is incapable of giving itself to a perception, of becoming visible in the truth of the world." then on 46 Heidegger mistook the "phenomenological presupposition according to which 'to show oneself' means 'to show oneself in a world,' in the ek-static truth of its 'outside.'" Indeed when "truth is reduced to that of the world, to a horizon of visibility . . . life, stripped of truth, of the power of revealing, finds itself reduced to something that shows itself in the truth of the world, in the illumination of its 'outside'—finds itself reduced entirely."

14. Henry critiques that "there exists no mode of knowing other than Galilean science, that is to say, modern physics." Henry, *I Am the Truth*, 260. It was in *Essence of Manifestation* that Henry began the process of reducing phenomenology to its affective basis or dimension. Michel Henry, "Author's Preface," in *Essence of Manifestation*, trans. Girard Etzkorn (The Hague: Martinus Nijhoff, 1973), xii. This remained essential to his work, as in one of his last collections, *Words of Christ*, man is described as fundamentally affective, as "the human essence is the heart" and "affectivity is the essence of life." Michel Henry, *Words of Christ* (Grand Rapids, MI: Eerdmans Publisher, 2012), 12.

15. Henry continues along such lines, insisting that "there is a path of thought which explains the privilege accorded by classical philosophy to obviousness, to matters that seem self-evident. It is easy to recognize behind this privileging of the self-evident the reign of the visible which dominates the development of our culture." Henry, "Phenomenology of Life," 253.

16. Maurice Merleau-Ponty, *Phénoménolgie de la perception* (Paris: Gallimard, 1945). For Merleau-Ponty, "mais tout sein und zeit est sorti d'une indication de Husserl et n'est en some qu'une explication du 'natürlichen Weltbegriff' ou do 'Lebenswelt' que Husserl, à la fin de sa vie donnait pour theme premier à la phenomenology."

17. Heidegger, "Phenomenology Draft B," 22. And as Heidegger later puts it this means the "transcendental constitution of the *Existenz* of the factical self. This factical self, the concrete human being, is as such—as an entity—never a 'worldly real fact' because the human being is never merely present-at-hand but rather ek-sists. And what is 'wondersome' is the fact that the existence-structure of Dasein makes possible the transcendental constitution of everything positive." Heidegger, Ibid., 22.

18. Martin Heidegger, GA 61, *Phänomenologische Interpretationen zu Aristoteles: Einführung in die phänomenologische Forschung* (Frankfurt am Main: Vittorio Klostermann, 1921), 90. Martin Heidegger, *Phenomenological Interpretations of Aristotle: Initiation into Phenomenological Research*, trans. Richard Rojcewicz (Bloomington: Indiana University Press, 2001). A careful, more thorough study of Heidegger's understanding of world would entail a close investigation of the 1935–1936 *The Origin of the Work of Art* in which the world is described as the opening in the field in which the real is manifested, but also provides a kind of "illumination" for what appears to appear.

19. Heidegger, *Sein und Zeit*, 65; Heidegger, *Being and Time*, 93, cf. 92.

20. Martin Heidegger, GA 32, *Hegel's Phenomenology of Spirit*, trans. Parvis Emad and Kenneth Maly (Bloomington: Indiana University Press, 1988), 98.

21. Martin Heidegger, *Poetry, Language, Thought*, trans. Albert Hofstadter (New York: Harper & Row, 1971), 53.

22. Heidegger, "Phenomenology draft B," 18.

23. And he continues "If we vary the factical world into any world that can be thought, we also undeniably vary the world's relativity to conscious subjectivity. Thus, the notion of a world existing in itself is unintelligible, due to that world's essential relativity to consciousness." Ibid., 16. For Sheehan, "Heidegger insisted that world-as-such," understood as the meaning-giving context, is an essential correlative of transcendental constitution and cannot be bracketed out. He "rejected Husserl's claim that the transcendentally reduced ego could not be the human ego *stricte dicta*." Heidegger, "Translator's introduction to 'Phenomenology,' Draft B (of the Encyclopaedia Britannica Article) with Heidegger's Letter to Husserl" in *Becoming Heidegger: On the Trail of His Early Occasional Writings, 1910-1927*, eds. Theodore Kisiel and Thomas Sheehan (Chicago: Northwestern University Press, 2007), 304–06.

24. Heidegger, *Being and Time*, 31.

25. Ibid., 80.

26. Ibid., 93.

27. Ibid., 103, 107.

28. Ibid., 92, 99.

29. Martin Heidegger, "Seminar in Le Thor 1966" in *Four Seminars*, trans. Andrew Mitchell and François Raffoul (Bloomington: Indiana University Press, 2003), 8.

30. For Heidegger, "Everyday opinion seeks truth in variety, the endless variety of novelties which are displayed before it. It does not see the quiet gleam (the gold) of the mystery that everlastingly shines in the simplicity of the lighting. Heraclitus says (Fragment 9): 'Asses choose hay rather than gold.'" Martin Heidegger, "Aletheia: Heraclitus Fragment

B 16," in *Early Greek Thinking*, trans. D. F. Krell and F. A. Capuzzi (San Francisco: Harper Collins, 1984), 122. From Martin Heidegger, GA 7, *Vörträge und Aufsätz* (Pfullingen: Verlag Günther Neske, 1967).

31. For Heidegger, "we know too much and believe too readily ever to feel at home in a questioning which is powerfully experienced. For that we need the ability to wonder at what is simple, and to take up that wonder as our abode." Or put more simply, "Wonder first begins with the question, 'what does all this mean and how could it happen?'" Heidegger, "Aletheia: Heraclitus Fragment B 16," 104.

32. Heraclitus asks "how could anyone remain concealed?" Heraclitus' "question is not first and foremost a consideration of concealment and unconcealment with regard to the sort of men whom we ... like to interpret as carriers ... of unconcelament. Heraclitus, expressed in modern terms, thinks the reverse. It ponders the relation of man to 'the never-setting' and thinks human being from this relation." Ibid., 109.

33. As noted by Schenk-Mair, Fink's cosmological thinking and "concept of the world is derived from Heraclitus' physis." Katharina Schenk-Mair, *Die Kosmologie Eugen Finks* (Würzburg: Königshausen & Neumann, 1997), 11.

34. Heidegger, "Aletheia: Heraclitus Fragment B 16," 111. And if we "change the negative expression into a completely affirmative one, we then hear for the first time what the fragment means by the 'never-setting'—i.e. the ever-rising." See also 112: This turn of speech is not found in Heraclitus. But the negative phrase does entail "the not setting ever." This can also refer to the "upsurgence" or "emergence"—the rising.

35. "The not setting ever, means both revealing *and* concealing—not as two different occurrences merely jammed together, but as one and the same." Ibid., 12.

36. Ibid., 113 "self-revealing loves self concealing" and "*phusis*—essence [*das Wesen*], [is] the 'what' of things." For Heidegger, concerning Heraclitus' fragments 1 and 112, Heraclitus "does not think *phusis* as the essence of things, but rather thinks the essential unfolding (*Wesen* as a verb), of phusis."

37. For Heidegger, "Die φύσις ist die Unscheinbare. Das Aufgehen als das, was uberhaupt das gelichtete Offene für ein Erscheinen gewährt, tritt selbst in allem Erscheinen und in jedem Erscheinenden zuruck und ist nicht ein erscheinendes unter anderen." Martin Heidegger, GA 55, *Heraklit. 1. Der Anfang des abendländischen Denkens (Heraklit)* (1943). *2. Logik. Heraklits Lehre vom Logos* (1944) (Frankfurt am Main: Vittorio Klosterman), 142. "Die φύσις kommt nicht innerhalb des aufgehenden und aufgegangenen auch vor, so wie ein Erscheinendes, sondern sie ist in allem Erscheinenden das Unscheinbare, aber keineswegs 'das Unsichtbare', wie die schon genannten philologischen übersetzungen fälschlicherweise übersetzen. Die φύσις ist nicht das unsichbare, sie ist imgegenteil gerade das anfänglich gesichtete, das, obzwar zunächst und zumeist, ja oft überhaupt nie eigens Erblickte." Ibid., 143.

38. Heidegger, "Aletheia: Heraclitus Fragment B 16," 117. For Heidegger, "We say 'world', and think it improperly so long as we represent it exclusively, or even primarily, after the fashion of cosmology or philosophy of nature. World is enduring fire, enduring rising in the full sense of *phusis*. Though we are speaking of an eternal world-conflagration here, we must not first imagine a world which is independent and is then set ablaze and consumed by some ever-burning torch. Rather, the worlding of world ... are all the Same."

39. Ibid., 119, 121–22. As he puts it on 121, "We are too quick to believe that the mystery of what is to be thought always lies distant and deeply hidden under a hardly penetrable layer of

strangeness. On the contrary, it has its essential abode in what is near by, which approaches what is coming into presence and preserves what has drawn near." Ibid., 121.

40. Henry, *I Am the Truth*, 45. Henry gives credit here to Heidegger for initiating this thought on life in *Sein und Zeit*. As Henry quotes Heidegger, "Life, in its own right, is a kind of being, but essentially it is only accessible in Dasein."

41. Staudigl interprets Henry to be claiming, in effect that "affectivity is the most primordial mode of revelation of both our self and the world." Further, "Animated by a radical form of the phenomenological reduction, Henry's material phenomenology brackets the exterior world in a bid to reach the concrete interior transcendental experience at the base of all exteriority." Michael Staudigl, "From the 'Metaphysics of the Individual' to the Critique of Society: On the Practical Significance" of Michel Henry, "Phenomenology of Life," *Continental Philosophy Review* 45 (2002): 339–61. See also Michel Henry, *Words of Christ*, trans. Christina Gschwandtner (Grand Rapids, MI: Eerdmans Publishers, 2012), 73. For Henry, "Life ... is not a thing, a being, or a genre of a particular being, a set of phenomena specifically called 'biological' and that contemporary biology reduces to material processes, insensible." and "life as we experience it, which is our life, is in itself a revelation—this unique form of revelation which who reveals and what is revealed are one and the same. For this reason, I have called it a self-revelation.... Living actually consists in this 'experiencing oneself,' 'being revealed to oneself'."

42. Henry, *Essence of Manifestation*. Henry clearly took cue on this point from Husserl's Vienna lecture in developing his phenomenology of "life." For Husserl: "Now, life on the level of nature is characterized as a naïvely direct living immersed in the world, in the world that in a certain sense is constantly there consciously as a universal horizon but is not, merely by that fact, thematic." Thematic is that toward which man's "attention is turned. Being genuinely alive is always having one's attention turned to this or that, turned to something as to an end or a means, as relevant or irrelevant, interesting or indifferent, private or public, to something that is in daily demand or to something that is startlingly new." Edmund Husserl, *Philosophy and the Crisis of European Man* (Vienna lecture), trans. Q. Lauer (New York: Harper and Row, 1965), 166. Jean-Luc Marion interprets Henry to not "privilege" the invisible, as "the invisible and the visible belong to the same world, hence *to the world* itself." Marion then quotes Henry, who states that "the invisible is not the antithetical concept of the visible." It indeed makes more sense to describe the relation (and at points univocity) between the visible and invisible. Jean-Luc Marion, "The Invisible and the Phenomenon," in *Michel Henry: The Affects of Thought*, ed. Jeffrey Hanson and Michael R Kelly (New York: Continuum, 2012), 21, cf. 23.

43. In *Essence of Manifestation*, Henry bemoans the types of truth our world today champions, a truth that signifies "d'une monde absolu" (an absolute world) as a calculatory apparatus. See Michel Henry, *L'Essence de a manifestation* (Paris: Presses Universitaires de France, 1963), 361.

44. "Unaquæque res, quantum in se est, in suo esse perseverare conatur." "Each thing, as far as it can by its own power, strives to persevere in its being." Baruch Spinoza, "Ethics," in *The Collected Works of Spinoza, vol. I*, ed. and trans. Edwin Curley (Princeton: Princeton University Press, 1985), 61. Descartes (in his *Principles of Philosophy* II. 3) develops his own version of this proposition, which states that each and every thing, in so far as it can, always continues in the same state.

45. Henry, "Phenomenology of Life," 251.

46. Ibid., 244.

47. Ibid., 246.

48. The "reality that constitutes the world's content is life." Henry, *I Am the Truth*, 107. See here László Tengelyi, "Selfhood, passivity and affectivity in Henry und Levinas," *International Journal of Philosophical Studies* 17 no. 3 (2009): 401–14. For Tengelyi "Henry is convinced that the events of the world are only occasional causes of our feelings. It is our affectivity itself which makes it possible for the world to exert an influence upon our interior life. In other words, it is, in each case, our particular 'attunement' that exposes us to an affection by the world."

49. See here Michel Henry, *La barbarie* (Paris: Presses Universitaires de France, 2008), 210.

50. In "Phenomenology of Life" Henry claims to develop this out of Heidegger's work. As Henry interprets, for Heidegger, "The world is the ek-static horizon of visibilization inside of which everything can become visible, and the second part of Being and Time declares explicitly that this 'horizon' concerns exteriority, the 'outside of self' as such." The world is identified here with temporality, and temporality is nothing other than "the originary 'outside of self' in and for itself." As Heidegger puts it, "*Zeitlichkeit ist das ursprüngliche 'Außer-sich' an und für sich selbst.*" Heidegger, *Sein und Zeit*, 329.

51. Bernhard Waldenfels, "Antwort auf das Fremde. Grundzüge einer responsiven Phänomenologier," in *Der Anspruch des Anderen. Perspektiven phänomenologischer Ethik*, ed. Bernhard Waldenfels and Iris Därmann (Munich: Fink, 1998), 35–49.

52. For Gschwandtner, "On the one hand, Henry's stark distinction between the 'truth of the world' and the 'Truth of Life,' his insistence on the invisible over the visible, and his rejection of the 'things of the world' in general and modernity in particular, may strike many readers as gnostic … in favor of the 'supernatural' or 'spiritual.' He certainly has been accused of such dualism, yet any such criticism would rely on a rather superficial reading and fundamental misunderstanding of the divisions he outlines. Henry advocates a material phenomenology, a phenomenology of utter immanence. What is most real is what is most immediate, namely our experiencing ourselves within our own feelings and affections, in our flesh directly. This is not a philosophy of transcendence or other-worldliness. Henry is trying to articulate what is invisible not because it is so far away, but precisely because it is so close and immanent that we cannot gain the distance from it that vision or observation would require." Christina Gschwandtner, "The Truth of Christianity? Michel Henry's Words of Christ," *The Journal of Scriptural Reasoning* 13 no. 1 (2014). Available at: http://jsr.shanti.virginia.edu/back-issues/vol-13-no-1-june-2014-phenomenology-and-scripture/the-truth-of-christianity-michel-henrys-words-of-christ/.

53. Henry, "Phenomenology of Life," 256, cf. Ibid., 257. Henry's "Phenomenology of Life" originally was delivered in 2000 at the Munich Academy of Fine arts, and as the translator notes "A month before he died in July 2002, Henry confirmed, in discussion with Joseph and Joëlle Llapasset, his belief that this article conveys the essence of his whole philosophical project."

54. Ibid., 241–43. Then in *The Essence of Manifestation* Henry states that "The invisible … constitutes the 'how' of the revelation of the essence of revelation and determines this 'how' phenomenologically." Henry, *Essence of Manifestation*, 440. Further, "The invisible is nothing which might be beyond the visible, it is nothing 'transcendent,' it is the original essence of life such that, since it takes place in a sphere of radical immanence, it never arises in transcendence and, moreover, cannot show itself in it." Ibid., 453.

55. For Henry, "as intentional, consciousness is nothing other than the movement through which it throws itself outside: its 'substance' exhausts itself in the coming outside

which produces phenomenality. The act of revealing in such a coming outside, in a setting at distance, is what constitutes showing (*faire-voir*)." Henry, "Phenomenology of Life," 243, cf. Henry, *I Am the Truth*, 34. There, he continues in this trajectory: "Life designates a pure manifestation, always irreducible to that of the world, an original revelation that is not a revelation of any other thing and odes not depend on anything other, but is rather a revelation of self, that absolute self-revelation that is Life itself." And then, See also Henry, *Words of Christ*, 39: "According to the definition that I have proposed, life is what is experienced in itself, immediately and without distance. It reveals itself, that is to say reveals itself to itself, or, as one can also say in philosophical terms, it is self-revelation [*auto-révélation*]." There is an "insuperable certainty specific to each of the impressions we feel" and a certain immediacy to our being affected.

56. And here Heidegger sounds strikingly similar to Henry: "when I make a general and (as is required) a rigorously consistent reduction to my mind, the world that has been rendered questionable in the transcendental inquiry is certainly no longer presupposed—and the same for all minds as regards their purity. Here in this context of statements about the purely mental, the world that has straightforward validity for these minds themselves is not the focus of attention, but rather only the pure being and life of the very minds in which the world appears and naturally, via the corresponding subjective modes of appearance and belief, acquires meaning and validity." Heidegger, "Phenomenology draft B," 17. Translated from Edmund Husserl, "Ergänzende Texte, A. Abhandlungen," in *Gesammelte Werke, vol. IX, Phänomenologische Psychologie*, ed. Walter Biemel (The Hague: Martinus Nijhoff, 1962; 2nd edition, 1968), 256–77, 595–99, 600–03.

57. Heidegger, GA 61, *Phenomenological Interpretations of Aristotle*, 34.

4 Inconspicuous Liturgy: Lacoste, Heidegger, and the Space of Godhood

It is not without some bit of irony that Heidegger's last seminar in 1973 took place where he lived and dwelled, in his home. The "Zähringen seminar" as it has come to be called, not only introduced Heidegger's "phenomenology of the inconspicuous" but also provided an extension of his concept of dwelling (*wohnen*), which marks the paradoxical essence of Dasein as perennially anxious concerning its placeness, because wherever Dasein is, it is always not present in any traditional sense of that term. Dasein is both present where it finds itself, and absent in its seeking its beyond-itself, and thus presence and absence find their intertwining already in Dasein, whose being is marked by a staying and dwelling that extends from its stativity as there.

One thing that holds this there/here together is the notion of surplus. Heidegger sought to extend the Husserlian *Überschuss* or surplus to form a fundamental way in which we undergo the experiences (*Erfahrungen*) of things as they are not determined in and by themselves, but by what is beyond them in categorial intuitions. My experience of the inkwell is not determined whatsoever by its objectivity or substance, its visible content or *hyle* (such as the wetness of the physical ink, or the wood of which the well is composed). To extend commentary introduced in chapter 3, the surplus of this experience of the inkwell as such is provided by me, and in/through the flow of givenness the experience is held together. Otherwise, the sensual intuition cannot synthesize the vast and at times overwhelming stream of conscious data that spring from it. Given also are damns built in the steady flow of data.

In Platonic terms, one sees the inkwell as such, but one does not see the substance or physical stuff of which the inkwell is composed in the same way. Heidegger's tonic insight and correction of Husserl in these regards was that the givenness of the surplus (categorial intuition) was primordial to the experience of the sense data: this surplus is not "added to" (the *Über* of *Überschuss*) the sense data, but rather precedes that data "even if it is *seen* differently from what is sensibly visible."[1] It is according to this at first seemingly rudimentary insight that a different kind of seeing is initiated. This seeing can go beyond the sort of conscious experience that seeks to grasp, grip, and take up what is given by actively memorializing and intentionally recollecting the intelligibility of its data at will, as purposed. Instead, for Heidegger there is a kind of experience that relies more on intuition than intention, and fundamentally gives itself over to the primordial surplus that categorial intuition breathes into the otherwise flaccid and lifeless sensual data, the *hyle*. Heidegger does not call this type of seeing a nonexperience, but indeed reframes experience beyond conscious control. Experience is instead a confrontation.

This even can be traced all the way back to Heidegger's (very) early insight in *Phenomenology of the Religious Life*: "'Experiencing' does not mean 'taking-cognizance-of' but a confrontation-with, the self-assertion of the forms of what is experienced … [and] it has both a passive and an active sense."[2] To question experience in its phenomenological sense is to question the content *and the forms* of the experienced—the intertwining of the how and the what that appear and make appear the taken-for-granted. This is essential to arriving at the "one thought only" of which Heidegger claimed himself to be the promoter: to think the provenance and basis of truth, which was the way in which relation with the disclosure/enclosure with/in the world is shifted into an encounter. A fundamental experience with the disclosure/enclosure of things can bring one face to face with a "poetic" (*poesis*, creative) dwelling: "to stand in the presence of the gods and be struck by the essential nearness of things."[3] To bring the distant here, and to set the here at a distance is a primordially poetic endeavor. Being *in* is, paradoxically, also a being-out-in-the-open that poetically creates and consequentially instills the wonder of it all. Could there be a reduction that allows for the experience of such a paradoxical confrontation, more specifically of living religiously, or are such experiences damned to the solipsistic and private theatres of consciousness?

These concerns of experience and dwelling from 1973 have striking premonitions of aspects of Lacoste's "liturgical turn" to "place." This work was initiated in the 1990s and engaged in a displacement of the meaning of the word "liturgy," which he recently claimed "has no philosophical past whatsoever."[4] Lacoste concludes his "Le monde et l'absence d'oeuvre" with the assertion that "our aptitudes to experience in fact exceed our aptitude to experience the world."[5] The world itself must be brought into a fundamental questioning or reduction that involves a means to see, perhaps even know something or someone on its outside. For Lacoste, there is one thing we tend to always presuppose whenever we discuss our being in the world: placedness. It is according to this question of place, which concerns *where I am*, that allows for an articulation of the relation between man and the Absolute, which ultimately feeds-back into the matter of *who I am* most fundamentally. Experience at its core is the basis of the study of phenomenology, and Lacoste seeks to alter this basis in a way that deformalizes its seemingly straightforward nature, thus influencing the rules of phenomenology.

One way he does this is by suturing any possible positive description of experience to its inherently indwelling opposite, nonexperience. Religious Experience is nonexperience. The Absolute's place is nonplace. This paradox can be exemplified in the life of the recluse, whose desires to most radically "be there" (wherever he is) are accomplished through the act of retreating. The Recluse, in being nowhere to radically be there demonstrates that "symbolically, his place is a nonplace."[6] It is possible to be somewhere by being nowhere, and this paradox finds its highest potential to transgress experience in what Lacoste names the "liturgical reduction." While his use of the word "liturgy" is not antithetical to how that term traditionally has been understood according to particular confessional rites, Lacoste reduces these rites to their core: Liturgy is the means by which it is possible to organize an inquiry into the humanity or core essence of man by recognizing the fundamental relation one has with nonman. In this way Lacoste inverts the claim made by Feuerbach (that "anthropology is the secret of theology") to now reveal that the Absolute is the forgotten key of anthropology.

This liturgy institutes a phenomenological twist on the Augustinian soul-before-God as now a restless, active, and dynamic being-before, *esse coram Deo*. It is what Lacoste calls "the resolute deliberate gesture made by those who ordain their being-in-the-world a being-before-God, and who do violence to the former in the name of the latter" for, as he puts it in *Expérience et absolu*, liturgy exceeds being in the world, "la liturgie exceed l'être-dans-le-monde."[7] These violations and transgressions consist in Liturgy's institutions of "nonplaces" or spaces where determinations enter into a new order of signification: "No immanent logic of place resides in liturgy;" Liturgy exceeds "the relation to the earth," it "can open up a space where neither world nor earth is interposed between man and God," it "exacerbates our not-being-at-home in the world and is a critique of our relation to the earth," and does "justice to the complexity of the question of place in a way that a phenomenology in which the world and earth constitute the ultimate or the nontranscendable par excellence cannot."[8]

This all leads to an inherently radical conclusion: a liturgical reduction can go beyond phenomenology's many prejudices, which subsequently limit and restrict experience itself to the nontranscendable experience within the world. Liturgy redefines place, tears down the walls between interior and exterior, and perhaps most importantly, enacts a transgression, through an introduction of a radically eschatological vision, whereby "the world ceases to be a horizon, and appears as it is not, as a being that one can contemplate as a totality." Bracketing the world allows for the subsequent arrival at another understanding of placedness, and the liturgical act can thereby redefine place itself, no longer as a being-there but as a more dynamic being-toward. By being-before-not-man in a finally free act of being-toward, the world as a horizon vanishes, and thereby furnishes an interrogation of the humanity of man (as the subtitle of his book suggests). This is one goal the liturgical reduction seeks to accomplish in its radical suspension of *place-specificus* and therefore, perhaps also *place-generalis.*[9]

Lacoste's development of the questioning of experience via the nonexperience and nonplace of religion is a profound one for theological thinking, and in my view, thoroughly reflective of Heidegger's own positions regarding the aforementioned here/there distinction. Lacoste's liturgy is a theological illumination of *Being and Time* and an application of the antinomy of *wohnen* (dwelling) initiated by Heidegger.[10] Lacoste provides another means of confronting how religious phenomena shift between visibility and invisibility, and his attack on the privacy of feeling (which is an essential driver of various fideisms) attests to this fact. For Lacoste, religious experience must be turned from the primacy of any Schleirmacherian (and subsequent Modern, German Protestant Theological) elevation of an intuitive life that reaches its penultimate passion in its most immediate feelings.[11] As Lacoste knows, any reduction of nonplace must avoid being reduced to an ultimately metaphysical (and ontotheological) logic, which would lead back to an ipseity that entraps religion once again in the immediacy of emotion. Liturgy also must allow for a confrontation with the totality of ontotheology.

This is one example of how Heidegger's work is an essential backdrop against which Lacoste questions experience, and develops the liturgical reduction.[12] Yet his contrasting between his work and that of Heidegger at points is suspect. Although Lacoste claims his logic of liturgy to concern "subverting the Heideggerian logic of being-in-the-world,"[13] there is not one reference (not even a footnote) in *Experience and the Absolute* to Heidegger's thorough analysis of "world" in "The Worldhood of the World" found in *Being and Time* (to which our present study has already attended in detail in chapter 3). Secondly, Lacoste appears to conflate Heidegger's interests with an antitheistic impulse, as Dasein and the later turn to the fourfold "concern themselves solely with an atheistic world and a familiar earth."[14] Yet Heidegger specifically addresses what he called "the cheap accusation of atheism" as early as 1928. And thirdly, Lacoste pitches his liturgical reduction against Heideggerian Being there, and claims that his approach to reconceive place no "longer is ... to be thought of as a being there, but as being toward."[15] Yet the many interpretations of Heideggerian Dasein as being-there are drastically imprecise, for in Heidegger's own words: "'Dasein' is a key word of my thinking and thus the occasion for major misunderstandings. For me, 'Dasein' does not mean the same as 'Here I am!' but rather—if I might express it in a perhaps impossible French—être le-là. And the le-là is precisely *aletheia*: disclosedness—openness."[16] Thus, to what degree is Lacoste's understanding of liturgy reliant on an incomplete understanding of Dasein as a static being there, the Dasein that Heidegger had already opened up to the other of "there," the open clearing?

These three problematic interpretations (Dasein as being there, the atheistic Heidegger, and the staticity of being-in-the-world) of "Lacoste's Heidegger" are employed in this chapter as thematic springboards for a deeper application of Heidegger's work to Lacoste's "liturgy," ultimately leading to the proposal of an "inconspicuous liturgical reduction." Lacoste's reduction, after all, seeks to disorient the totality of place through a unique exercise, and in 1973 Heidegger referred to how there is a "domain" or "clearing of the appearing of the inconspicuous" in which one performs "an exercise in a phenomenology of the inconspicuous."[17] The place and clearing goes hand-in-glove with such an exercise, and this exercise is employed here to extend Lacoste's contribution toward one means of accessing a place or more general space that is inconspicuous due to its overfamiliarity. Since dwelling is a living-being-in, it is matter of questioning also how the inconspicuous God dwells.

Experience is Irreducible to Consciousness

It hopefully is clear by now what is at stake in Lacoste's project. The question then becomes whether he can succeed in negotiating the passage between ontotheology on the one hand, and a limitation of the transcendental horizon on the other, and yet do so in a way that provides a kind of knowledge that is not under the ultimate jurisdiction and oversight of subjective consciousness. One matter it may come down to is whether or not there is a means of questioning experience in its seemingly agreed-upon forms of social acceptance while remaining a transcendental-going-out-of-oneself. He claims liturgy can do this: "Liturgy does not annul the a priori laws governing existence. But it does prove that transcendental forms of experience do not constitute the entirety of our capacity for existence, and that the humanity of man does not let itself be determined exclusively by what comes to experience always, everywhere, and to everyone."[18]

Humanity is not governed by the experience of the world, but by something else. By subverting one's simple acceptance of being-in-the-world, and replacing it with a being-before-the-nonexperienceable, one is afforded a kind of epiphanic verticality that can pierce through the screen of the world.[19] At the very least it is possible to attempt to bracket the world, and in doing so yield to the nonexperiential. The horizon of nothingness (which, in the end, is no horizon of experience) alters present experience and furnishes affections or intelligibility. Whatever rules are in place concerning what it means to exist (ek-sist, to be simultaneously in and out of) notwithstanding, being-before-God (the active bringing of oneself before the nonexperiential) helps prove and provide for an evidential experience that is not reducible to what can come about via transcendental consciousness.

Transcendental consciousness, the going out of oneself to find something other than oneself, is not necessary for one to be-before the nonexperience of the

Absolute. Further, this being-before-the-Absolute makes me more human than ever before. It provides a means of being human in a fundamental way that demonstrates that intuition and awareness need not succumb to a supposedly neutral theatre of the secular and public world. In part, this is because the dynamics of being before God are built on an experience that is a nonexperience, which God *is*.[20] The liturgical reduction displaces one's ego, and leaves one emptied and impoverished (via *kenosis*) because the Absolute is precisely such a nonexperience.[21] How, in the more particular aspects, can this be the case, especially if Lacoste's depiction of religious experience is to go beyond a subjective, ego-oriented feeling?

The reduction to liturgy itself must remain, to some degree, indescribable, for it is the point of access to the nonexperience, thus providing for a nonplace from which place can be observed, and a new topology established. Lacoste wants a topology that overturns how we typically understand the here-there relation: "As regards our relation to this 'here' or this 'there,' liturgy is capable of subverting it in a remarkable way."[22] Similar to how Marion seeks to *invert* the intuition-intention relation established in Husserl's transcendental phenomenology, Lacoste hopes to *subvert* how we typically understand the here-there relation. His approach to doing this involves demonstrating how liturgy (in its "remarkable way") provides for a kind of involvement (in a nonconsciousness-orienting way) with God, with whom one's relation is characterized as "before." Yet Lacoste asks of this relation rhetorically: "Do consciousness and what it bears witness to suffice to take account of the relation between man and the Absolute? Or, more radically, is it necessary to speak in terms of consciousness to take account of this relation?"[23] That which consciousness bears witness to in this case are the structures of thought that one laminates onto all experience: Here cannot be there. The beyond, in the now, cannot be experienced. All experience is determined by the horizons of this world.

One of Lacoste's most interesting wagers is that these rules of consciousness can indeed be bracketed long enough for one to have a nonexperience, and this leads to the conclusion that consciousness cannot bear the meaning of liturgy (it can only know the reasons for it). This being-before leaves one with a certain kind of knowledge about the Absolute, yet it is a knowledge that turns back the conventional rules or forms of structure (which accord to a topology of how we typically understand place) that classify our world. The nonexperience in this sense not only provides an opening onto the nonplace of the Absolute, with which one is in relation liturgically, but also a clearing that astoundingly is reliable as a meaningfully present intelligibility. What is meaningfully present about such an experience of nonexperience is that there is a noticeable "'liturgical disorientation of consciousness' or to return to a distinction already put forward, of the 'soul' putting consciousness in question."[24] The soul and consciousness (one ontic, the other ontological, perhaps) check and balance one another. One reflects on one's own conscious grasping and challenges its preunderstandings and preferred modes of seeing, and Liturgy provides a unique form of warrant that allows for this reflection.[25] A testimony can be offered of such a liturgical disorientation of consciousness, for in being before God as the absolute nonexperience (again, for Lacoste it matters little if we call it God or the Absolute), not only is the individual soul being put into question, but also along with it, the entirety of the world and its horizons. This marks the excess and profusion of inexperience over experience.

Lacoste seeks to establish a means of nonexperience (or as it might be called, a "pre-experience"), but it seems as if what he really is after is an experience that is not under the oversight of consciousness. This is a move that Heidegger in some sense initiated, for the experience of the inconspicuous, or what does not directly shine, is to some degree experienced without its being grasped or graspable by consciousness. In regard to that which is experienced inconspicuously, there can be no conscious grasping. To some degree, Lacoste recognizes that Heideggerian *erschlossenheit* "is prior to every act of consciousness that Dasein is 'open' to the world: the world takes possession of man and the function of his opening on the world is to underpin his acts of consciousness."[26] The first part of this interpretation is unquestionably true of Heidegger. There is something prior to consciousness. Yet the later part appears not to take into account that world itself is opened-up via its own disclosure.

It was in the Zähringen seminar that Heidegger made explicit how he sought to establish the possibility of a kind of seeing prior to consciousness, even suggesting of Being (as he did in his earlier *On Time and Being*) that it is to be aligned more closely with the dynamic *es gibt*. Overall, the last four seminars of Heidegger culminate in an intense engagement with being-historical thinking (*Seynsgeschichtliches Denken*), and an abandonment of fundamental ontology *in nuce*. In attempting to think "more Greek than the Greeks" it is not a Being of static presence that is developed, but an ontology of sending or givenness. It was a static reliance on Being that the Greeks, and subsequently Husserl, attempted to encircle and ultimately describe according to consciousness's grasp. Husserl's intentionality-rich approach "remains trapped in immanence" and limited to a metaphysics of presence.[27] One reason for this is that irrespective of any attempt on Husserl's part to no longer underwrite the inside/outside distinction, consciousness still begins with an inside. And for Heidegger, phenomenology must begin with an intuition that disables the inside of intention, namely, by finding oneself thrown out there in the world. This is the fundamental experience of Dasein, but it is in this being-thrown that one can come to regard anew what is in the world. This is not a world that shuts down all possibilities beyond its scope, but a world that continuously opens-out onto one's making-anew the world itself; making and shaping a "worldhood."[28]

It is not, as Lacoste may hyperbolize, a world that limits a priori the horizon of experience to what can appear only according to the horizons of the world, but rather a world that already entails its own opening-up. Being itself is this clearing-opening. So therefore, being-in-the-world entails being precisely in relation with its "unworld." And this is all consistent with Lacoste's own hopes: to establish what Lacoste calls a nonexperience, which is reducible to simply meaning before-conscious-grasping. It opens onto how things can appear to us, unsuspecting to thought. This is one reason why Heidegger calls being-in-the-world an "irreducible fact, always already given, and thus radically 'prior' to any conception of consciousness."[29] The world's priorness is not static, but essentially ever-giving. Since being-in-the-world is fundamentally being-open, this suggests that Heidegger also had developed an opening onto nonexperience a priori of conscious grasping.

This leads to a challenge to Lacoste's interpretation of Heidegger: if Heidegger's being-in-the-world fundamentally is not a holding back of man to the horizon of the stativity of the world as traditionally understood, and therefore not a limitation of the absolute to the immanent, then had Heidegger not initiated already a turn to nonworld to a further degree than Lacoste seems to give him credit?[30] There is indeed in Heidegger's thought already a way of experiencing that is *not* reducible to consciousness or the oversight of an atheistic vision. Heidegger makes this explicit. "Appearing," which under Heidegger's watch becomes "announcing," can show itself by not showing itself; the presence of something unseen can appear like latent "sickness symptoms" (*Krankenerscheinungen*). While Heidegger refers to other means of appearance, for example, what can signal to showing in and of itself, or what can straightforwardly and ontically appear, there is also a kind of appearing that can be understood as pronouncement of an intelligible thing *without* that thing showing itself. There is also the possibility of phenomenal appearances that only announce on behalf of the active, yet invisible, presence of other phenomena never clearly disclosed. At the very least, it seems that for Heidegger as well as Lacoste, something (which Heidegger still calls "experience") exceeds a being conscious.

Subverting the Logics of Place and the Inconspicuous

This raises the possibility of bringing more clarification to how Lacoste's nonexperience functions: "What does it mean to speak of a liturgical reduction, and above all, how does one do it?"[31] This question recently posed by Lacoste, ten years after the English publication of *Experience and the Absolute*, comes with an immediate two-fold answer: "It means, in the first place, that the 'thesis of the world' can be put in suspension; for without that the Absolute itself (or God, it matters little) is the object or the victim of such a suspension." This is an indirect way to the Absolute, for the absolute thwarts such suspension. Without any suspension of the world, God would be rendered only according to the horizon of the world, which is only capable of showing certain features of the Absolute that would necessarily need to conform to the world and its forms of presentation. Lacoste presumes here that the Absolute must be wholly other than the logics and imaginaries of the world, which have a distinct formation of place. Then Lacoste suggests of the liturgical reduction, that "it means, secondly, that God can intervene phenomenologically in the strange mode of the irreducible, and that God's phenomenality necessarily refers to an exterior of consciousness."[32]

God as irreducible reminds us of claims made by Lacoste in other works concerning God's standing outside any suspension or bracketing that phenomenology can offer. Yet, if God is irreducible in the world, then to experience the nonexperience of the Absolute one must bracket the entire world. Thus, the Absolute can enter the world as that which subverts the world, as that which renders the world's horizon, from the outside of the world, estranged. Yet importantly, this experience of the Absolute via *coram deo* is not to be founded on the efforts of an egocentric, feeling-oriented, fideistic basis: The Absolute's phenomenality, which is the intertwining of the way a thing appears alongside its *what*, is exterior to consciousness. These answers to the question "what is liturgy?" led Lacoste to conclude that a liturgy is not prohibited on phenomenological grounds: "Thus one can say that a reduction is feasible, and that it is faithful to the things themselves, in which we take leave of the 'natural attitude' in order to permit God to appear as God—and in which we thus take the liberty to let appear in *actu* nothing but God and us, whereas all that is not God and not us is reduced to what it is in the field of consciousness."[33]

This is all only to demonstrate that the Absolute can appear as absolute and total without totalizing (Levinas), and do so according to the Absolute's complete glory, which is disorienting, blurring, and striking. The absolute deformalizes totality absolutely by employing a phenomenality that unravels its rules of comprehension.

If Phenomenology it is to remain committed to its efforts of calling into question who we are, then it therefore must be opened up to the nevertheless ambiguous beyond-the-world. Liturgy is poised to accomplish this task. In a way not unlike Nietzsche's Zarathustra, who proclaims that man must be overcome for man to remain man, Lacoste suggests that to overcome such a man, the sense of place and topography also, in tow, must be overcome and transgressed.[34] It especially is in this context of transgressing the world that Lacoste often refers to Heidegger. In an earlier work Lacoste claims his logic of liturgy concerns "subverting the Heideggerian logic of being-in-the-world."[35] In so far as Heideggerian being-in-the-world does not already subvert itself, Lacoste's claim on liturgy here remains untested. Lacoste appears to negatively evaluate the world in general as if it is diametrically opposed to the logic of the Absolute which/who appears in a way that distorts appearance itself in/to consciousness. It should be noted here that one must beware the metaphysical remnants to which it is all too easy to cling unquestionably, even when (and perhaps *especially* in) a rejection of metaphysics. But the easily reverted-to dichotomy between the Absolute and world also must not be ignored. Heidegger's own words could provide a tonic caution to any attempt to establish such a dichotomy: "the reversal of a metaphysical statement remains a metaphysical statement."[36]

It is not questioned here that Lacoste offers, through liturgy, something Heidegger never could in any explicit way. The liturgical reduction is inherently intertwined with nonworld, and fundamentally aims at the Absolute by naming it "irreducible." A fundamental contribution Lacoste provides to phenomenology is the inevitable reckoning one must undertake, not with one's coming "death" via angst, but with what Schrijvers interprets as "the terror of the nonexperience," which we already know, for Lacoste redefines the term "experience" according to this anxiety.[37] Yet still, it is odd that a central aspect of Lacoste's liturgical reduction involves a seemingly total suspension of the world. Instead of relying on Heidegger's approach in these regards, Heidegger is employed as a backdrop against which Lacoste's position is cast. As mentioned, there is not one reference in *Experience and the Absolute* to Heidegger's most important engagements with "The Worldhood of the World." Whether a mistake, or a purposeful omission, there is no explanation on Lacoste's part for neglecting to engage Heidegger in these contexts.

As I addressed in chapter 3, which considered Heidegger's world in closer detail, Heidegger by no means sought a world closed-off to the possibilities of God, but rather challenged any attempt to "enclose" God within it as *causa sui*. Even when it comes to such a thing as "the world," which to the Modern mind becomes a neutral theatre on which things appear naturally and obviously, one cannot avoid that for Heidegger "possibility" is higher (more important and fundamental) than "actuality." And when taken in the context of Heidegger's fundamental critique of Husserl's *Lebenswelt*, which according to (the especially early) Heidegger, ultimately reduced human experience to the *umwelt* or environing space, it becomes clear that for Heidegger the world should not be drained of real, life-as-lived-experience (*Erleben*). Indeed, Heidegger did not seek to be "absolutely without world, world-alien, a sphere where the breath is knocked out of you and you cannot live."[38]

Life as lived, and a world that corresponds to it's being lived-in, is in direct opposition to a world that is supposedly neutral for an ego to engage transcendentally and come to clarity for clarity's sake. Heidegger wanted to face up to what many considered irrational, not to justify its senselessness, but to show how the world is inherently bound to nonworld. Thus, *Being and Time* offers a study of the world *as a phenomenon*, which is *ordered* according to its character traits of worldliness. Heidegger arrived at the paradox that since we are the constitutors of the world we therefore can bracket it by describing it, as one would from the belly of a whale, from within, which opens onto the sense of an outside that is unique and inconspicuous. The inconspicuously hidden of the world has openings onto its outside from within it, thus merging (in a way inspired by Husserl, but perhaps never achieved by him) the intertwining of inside/outside in a radical way. Can this intertwining be thought of in terms of the sacred?

Does Reference to the Immanent Limit the Transcendent? On the Sacred

It is out of concern for any limitation to the horizons of experience that Lacoste develops his liturgical reduction, as he seeks to provide for the possibilities of an experience of the sacred without reducing its effects to the play of numinous feeling and sentiment. In *Experience and the Absolute*, liturgy both subverts and confirms earth and world.[39] It is such a confirmation that, like any good act of worship or being-before-God, becomes the affirmation of all that such an Absolute has made—the world itself and its enrapturing horizon. What makes subversion so unique is that it does not negate entirely the subverted, but reappropriates it in some fashion.

Yet in this context the liturgical reduction is pitted against Heidegger's sacred, and Lacoste does this for a number of reasons. First, Lacoste thinks that *Being and Time* limits the horizon of experience to what can be described according to the neutrally public, open, and acceptable space for all: "The central (but not exclusive) intention of *Being and Time* is to unveil the fundamental structures of experience such as they are everywhere, always and for everyone."[40] For experience to be universal in this sense is to limit the potential and possibilities of appearances that extend beyond the solipsistic horizon. Second, he thinks Heidegger's later turn to the sacred and the divinities of the fourfold is reducible to a vague spirituality that only prolongs the false equations of religious experience with religious feeling or a variation of a nonknowledge-based sense of the infinite once championed by Protestant theologians; those who sought to provide legitimization of religion in the face of challenges posed by Modern thought. It is to such sentimentality that Heidegger succumbs; what Lacoste recently called "a vague encounter with the sacred" in supposed "divine entities without a face."[41]

I find Lacoste is correct in suggesting that those four terms of location (earth, sky, mortals, and deities), the *Geviert* or Fourfold, "mark out the space in which Being is meted out, and over which sovereignly reigns, even over the gods themselves, the sacred—*das Heilige*." Lacoste reduces this vague spiritual notion to the fact that instead of God being the sovereign, the sphere of immanence exercises over the fourfold a greater power than whatever the divine could produce.[42] The form or mold of the sacred oversees the content any divinity could fill it with.

Thus, Lacoste concludes, under the *Geviert* one can only become "acquainted with an immanent sacred (*deviennent familers d'un sacré immanent*)," and therefore not with a transcendent God.[43] While this may be a fair critique of Heidegger's engagements with the sacred via the Fourfold, is it a sustainable one that can refer to Heidegger's work overall, namely that the sacred is bound to an immanence that holds power over any potential being-before-God? Is it not precisely this immanent or transcendent distinction that Heidegger, in the first place, sought to overcome, especially given his engagements with *das Unscheinbare*? What, after all is the sacred for Heidegger?

The sacred (*das Heilige*) is the *space* according to which there is wonder and awe (*Scheu*) at Being, a space described as the "open clearing" (*Lichtung*) in which the utter otherness, expansive excess, and presencing of Being is experienced as the real basis of the world.[44] In an earlier turn to legitimize life as fundamental to consciousness, Heidegger first tried to do so through Christian life. Yet after concluding that phenomenology could not be established through religious experience, he moved on to his project of expressing a fundamental ontology without metaphysics. He doesn't address themes central to religious experience again until his engagements with Hölderlin (around 8 year later), and it is then that the sacred takes on a disposition of that which prefigures and can go without the existence of Gods, or more appropriately, their flight, or salvation.[45] It is fundamentally not the world that furnishes the ground for one's accessing and living in sacred space, but rather precisely the opposite: this sacred clearing allows for the worlding of the world. This marks the primal, yet hypersensual sense of being that man has forgotten.

Further, Heidegger's sacred also comes along with a cultural critique. In Hölderlin's "Flight of the Gods" such a flight is partly due to the modern machination of the human condition toward a progress that has sought to replace one's sacred relations—this spacing that provides wonder at Being.[46] A reinstallation of this kind of sacred is a prescription for what ails the technological condition of man, entrapped in an implicit and seamless totality. After all, "can it be denied that Heidegger's 'turn' was conditioned by his quest for the Sacred, through his reinterpretation of Hölderlin?"[47] This question posed by Janicaud is of interest, especially in arriving at whether or not it is possible to conceive of the sacred as anything more than a metonym for *Lichtung*. The sacred represents the aforementioned "wonder of wonders" that the world is without a ground, and that we can make sense of things, have meaningful relations with them, and engage with what is given in a way that all things, even the simple, can be reenchanted. Since Being enacts a fundamental withdrawal, it can only be captured in its retreat via distance. This is one reason why the "space of Godhood" (*Wesensraum der Gottheit*) is this clearing of the sacred, as a clearing away and resetting of space that reenchants experience.[48] This all occurs in our place, our home, where we live and dwell, in which "the world's night is . . . the sacred night (*heilige Nacht*)."[49] This is the ordinary space out of which the mysteries of the uncanny can be experienced. Yet this ordinary space is not the profane or secular place supposedly conceived according to an atheistic horizon of being-in-the-world as Lacoste seems to worry.

For Heidegger we are neither bound to nor delineated by the world's horizon and limited domains of places. As Krummel recently posed "This sense of the sacred would prefigure any positing of boundaries within its expanse that would subsequently differentiate it from the profane."[50] Since this sacred is prior to boundaries, it indeed is more like space than it is like place. Places are specifically identifiable, localized, purposed, fixed (e.g., a car is not a place), demarcated zones, and distinct from other places. Conversely, spaces are more abstract, vacant, invisible, built around content, and that in which things are extended. The sacred is not the opposite of the profane, but the chaotic clearing that unpredictably, unforeseeably, and *poetically* creates the world. And perhaps more like spacing, it dramatically redefines place. For Lacoste to develop a nonplace, it would need to be safeguarded from being reduced simply to the more abstract space, which the sacred appears to represent for Heidegger.

To reiterate, Heidegger's engagements with the sacred arose in the context of the critique of technology, from which, as he comes to phrase it later, "only another [*noch ein*] God can save us now."[51] This is not the God of theology, nor is it the God of atheism.[52] Yet it is some other God who can overcome (through a pure differentiation) the threat of Nihilism that modern technological advancements uniquely pose in their underwriting of a supposed autonomous subjectivism that results in the banality of things and the ultimate economical quantification of even human beings.[53] This all reduces Being itself to an at-any-point-accessible standing reserve (*Bestand*).[54] Our privileging of unconcealment finds its nihilistic manifestations in technology, and the sacred is experienced in the active refusal of categorial experience championed by such nihilistic forms of calculation. This nihilism is treated as one version of our ontotheological condition, namely, of attempting to make everything clear and apparent to ourselves. Perhaps the most Godly thing to do, as Heidegger puts it in a different context in *Identity and Difference*, is to put these Gods (before whom one cannot sing or dance) "to death."[55]

Still, Lacoste is especially concerned that Heidegger already precludes, or at least seriously limits, the relation one might have with a transcendent God. In one important sense, Lacoste's concerns are valid, but if and only if one's relation with transcendence entails a disembodiment, and a metaphysical beyond which no man still living on this earth can go. Although Heidegger seeks an immanently based sacred (which is one reason why he establishes Being as ontically inaccessible, as ontologically always already there as the nearest to us, yet paradoxically "farthest away"), it is precisely for the sake of getting beyond the God of *causa sui*, before whom any such adoration is impossible. On the one hand, it is possible to limit and subsume this God to the logics of this world and thus to foreclose any possibility of wonder at such a God. Yet on the other hand, the opposite reaction of emptying God of all content, potential qualities, or divine features can be as equally ontotheological, and it is against this possibility that Lacoste's work must be safeguarded.

Anselm's dictum that God is "that than which nothing greater can be conceived" does not act, in every case, as irreducible. Otherwise, the irreducible replaces the Absolute as the de facto name of God, and the empty throne is kinged, not by an unknown God, but by unknowability itself; that is, a vacuity that provides no room for thought and no trace of content for wonder. No one worships the unknown as such. Yet one can worship the unknown God, whose qualification or divine attribute as unknown may provide enough destabilization for endless enchantment. Without this recognition, Lacoste's hopes for a "post metaphysical theology" may be reducible to a neoplatonic *phusis* that Heidegger originally sought to overcome in his attempt to demarcate what it could mean to employ phenomenology as "post metaphysical."[56]

Yet it may be the case that Lacoste reads Heidegger differently in these regards, for after all, Lacoste does not reference the possibilities that Heidegger's "phenomenology of the inconspicuous" might entail. Indeed, Lacoste recognizes, for example, in his work on negative theology, that there are two spheres of knowledge: comprehension (*Connaissance*) and awareness (*Savoir*), which must be taken and understood in conjunction with one another. He arrives at the claim that God is incomprehensible precisely on the grounds that God is known to some degree.[57] God exceeds (as *Res semper major*) being a thing, as what can be grasped momentarily, and as Lacoste put it recently "we think the definitive from within the provisional," which entails that our provisional understanding or knowledge can never entirely see or grasp that which is definitive in its entirity.[58] Despite Lacoste's interpretations of Heidegger's sacred as a limitation of the nonexperiential, Lacoste's approach appears to exude aspects of Heideggerian phenomenology of the inconspicuous, the exercises of which initiated the possibilities of a kind of seeing irreducible to what the fangs of the will might seek to grasp and conceptualize. What is seen is experienced in a radical *there* that estranges that *there*. Despite being conscious of its absence, whatever is inconspicuous paradoxically can be presented in a place. Phenomena that give themselves inconspicuously are presented and to some degree known (*Connaissance*), yet uniquely hide from being comprehended (*Savoir*) while still sufficing to create intrigue at the unknown's enigmatic presentations.

And it is precisely due to their presentation in a place that it is possible to discuss a distinctly Heideggerian "nonplace" via the sacred. If it is truly the case, as Malpas recently has argued, that Heidegger's being and dwelling (especially after the 1940s) is a matter of place, and if the inconspicuous initiates a turn *within and out of* a place dwelled in via the presencing of absence, then it is not prohibited to suggest that the nonplace to which Lacoste refers was to some degree prefigured in Heidegger.[59] Another reason for believing this suggestion is that in "The Appearing and the Irreducible," Lacoste's working against Husserl's understanding of the human as reducible to a subjectively conscious being is again strikingly similar to a tonic correction Heidegger supplied to this aspect of Husserl's work in the Zähringen seminar through demonstrating that being-conscious can by no means govern all experience.[60] This is a problem fundamental to considering the irreducibility of God because it is a matter of what one accepts as warrant to be of (or from) God in revelation. Lacoste claims God to be irreducible and outside the bounds of phenomenology, yet again, could this irreducibility also become a name, and therefore prescribe a limit onto God?[61]

Lacoste seems to recognize the difficulty of such a question, and claims that, on strictly phenomenological grounds, the world must be bracketed, for even if one claimed a religious experience, it would need to be (not unlike Hume's miracles argument) described according to what those experiences furnish for description "within really 'needing' to attribute to it an extramental origin, and a fortiori a divine origin."[62] Were there to be a revelation of the Absolute, it likely would be so excessive that it would present more concealment than clarity. Any a priori methodological limitation placed on the Absolute will be nonphenomenological, and for this reason Lacoste fashions the liturgical reduction to operate in a way that distills the relation between oneself and the Absolute, a nonexperience that is known to be unknown, and before which one finds oneself placed.

The Place of Nonconsciousness

As already made clear, Lacoste seeks something bereft of the calculatory apparatus of consciousness, but also distinct from those numinous feelings that in recent years have trapped the intelligibilities of religious experience. On this matter, *Experience and the Absolute* associates the deep connective tissue between consciousness and being-in-the-world: "Does not our inherence in the world fundamentally have to do with consciousness? To this question, which is not formulated in *Sein und Zeit*, the book [Lacoste's] responds unambiguously."[63] Modern man's privileging of consciousness (*la conscience*, *Bewusstsein*) has demanded a fundamentally different understanding of the world, and Lacoste is aware that Heidegger wished to locate the opening that creates the possibility of consciousness, the fundamental disclosure of *Erschlossenheit*. Yet are *Sein und Zeit* and Heidegger's subsequent proposals regarding the *before* of consciousness truly that affirming of the intersutured nature of world and consciousness?

The opposite appears to be the case! Much like Lacoste's critiques of a Husserlian world that is enclosed and unavailable to the absolute's in-breaking,

Heidegger's challenges of Husserl's immanent-oriented consciousness are on the grounds that it seeks to calculate the appearance of things: "If we inquire into the character of the presence that reigns in the 'making-present-to-oneself,' which every consciousness is, we must admit that this making-present-to-oneself takes place in immanence. Whatever I am conscious of, it is present to me—which means: it is *in* subjectivity, *in* my consciousness."[64]

Here Heidegger dissociates Dasein from Husserlian consciousness, and the world that is purported to entrap it. He does so by returning, as Lacoste often does, to the question of the world as a place. Heidegger's dwelling can be associated with "the clearing of the appearing of the inconspicuous."[65] This clearing, like Dasein's "dwelling" is lived-in in a strange way, for it is there that presencing itself presences, and this is how Being works (not beings, or Being in general). Being, the constant theme of the Zähringen seminar, gives itself in its inconspicuous presencing, which brings to presence (in a new way) what is present. This all occurs in this region (*Bereich*, which can also be translated as "space") or spacing of the inconspicuous.[66]

What makes Being inconspicuous is that it opens onto something not entirely unlike Lacoste's "nonplace," but one that is experienceable, for within it are indications. These indications do not signal simply to other things somewhere else, but rather what presently and actively is indicating "what shows and lets be seen, in that it depicts what is to be seen."[67] This is the kind of *indwelling* indication that is always already here-yet-not-here, which amounts to (as addressed in chapter 2) a tautology or even involution, which can be found in Parmenides' Fragment 8, verse 29: "The same dwelling in the same, it lies in itself." Can this "dwelling in" be thought of in a radical way that inconspicuously reveals or conceals the sacred, not only as a dwelling-in, but also as an in-dwelling?

The answer could perhaps be "yes" if it is truly the case that Dasein is not simply a being-there, but also a being-*out*. Dasein should be seen as a radical redefinition of consciousness itself. The *sein* of *Bewusst-sein* is deformalized and inverted to its "ek" or *out*: "being in Da-*sein* says being-outside-of" as the mode of Dasein is "ek-statically being the there."[68] In *Experience and the Absolute* Lacoste refers to l'être-là, being-there: "Liturgy suggests a redefinition of place: no longer is it to be thought of as a being there, but as [a means of] being toward" (la liturgie est de toute façon une manière d'être-là.).[69] As mentioned earlier, the misunderstanding of Heideggerian Dasein as "being there" was a major source of frustration for Heidegger, who even addressed the matter in French, naming it not l'être-là but "être le-là." The "le" makes all the difference, and Heidegger would like for us to hear the direct implication of a relationship with the closure/disclosure of *a-letheia*.[70] A consciousness-oriented phenomenology needs to be openedup to the other of "there," and the "da" of Dasein is not demonstrative (*nicht demonstrativ*) of "there" as a place (*dort*) but instead refers to the ecstatic "being-out." The "da" refers to the absence of a there and to the temporal and spatial *lichtung* of Being, which is an infinite expanse of possibility (as opposed to reality or actuality).[71]

As this being-open, Dasein always maintains a quasi-transcendental relation with the world in which it dwells uniquely, finds meaningful presence, and grapples with its anxieties and cares. As addressed in chapter 3, Heidegger comes to imbue this world (*Kosmos*) with a paradoxical twist by opening our understanding of it out onto the "nonshining" or *unscheinbar.* There is an inconspicuous phenomenality and zone always already there for any experiencing beyond a conscious and totalizing grasp.[72] As reiterated in the Zähringen seminar, "In *Being and Time* ... the 'thing' has its place no longer in consciousness, but *in the world* (which again is itself not immanent to consciousness)."[73] Is this world described by Heidegger, and subsequently the experiences of things that have their place in this uniquely radical *there* as irreducible to the grasp of consciousness, a fundamentally atheistic one?

Extending Lacoste's Liturgical Reduction

Even at the time of writing *Sein und Zeit,* Heidegger was keenly aware of the many claims that he was an atheist, to which he responded in 1928: "It is preferable to put up with the cheap accusation of atheism, which, if it is intended ontically, is in fact completely correct. But might not the presumably ontic faith in God be at bottom godlessness? And might the genuine metaphysician be more religious than the usual faithful, than the members of a 'church' or even than the 'theologians' of every confession?"[74]

These questions ultimately kept Heidegger from proffering a response through the provision of a viable theology (which had he done so, he claimed, it would have been a science that never even included the word "Being"). Yet it was not to a decidedly atheistic horizon that Heidegger was committed. Heidegger rejected the enclosure of the world and the West's preferences for technologically enhanced actualities over possibilities, and knew all too well that any naming of God ultimately could amount to foreclosing God from being Absolute. Still, Lacoste certainly is on good grounds to ask what it is before which Heidegger finds himself truly willing to worship, and if it is not some vacuous, empty spacing, or contentless version of Otto's "numinous" holy. Lacoste's accusation of Heidegger is that his sacred, not unlike Otto's, cannot account for God: "God must not be assimilated too quickly to the sacred or to the numinous." This numinous feeling championed by Schleiermacher, and perhaps prolonged in any attempt to "feel the presence of the 'divine' of which Heidegger speaks" should not be confused with what the liturgical reduction seeks to accomplish: the relational opening, being-before the Absolute in precisely the Absolute's nonworldly place.[75] The Absolute, before whom or what one trembles for its stripping one bare of a world or dwelling, calls into question any evident "atheism of life."[76]

This is one reason why Lacoste proposes a liturgical reduction to be a kind of firstresponse to any vague or vacuous conceptions of religious experiences as numinous or spiritual feelings. He attempts to articulate in phenomenological terms what inherently can transgress phenomenalities (the intertwining hows and whats of phenomenology and its analyses). This may provide a deeper sense of what Heidegger was insinuating when he referred to dwelling and nondwelling, which can be described fundamentally as *Unzuhause*—not-being-at-home.[77]

Two questions can be posed to Lacoste's liturgical reduction that demonstrate the need for further specificity. First, in an experience with the Absolute, how can the world in its entirety be suspended without discarding also what it means to dwell? If dwelling is rethought as having momentary flashes of utter and complete nonplacedness or putatively nondwelling, then has not the paradox of dwelling been lost entirely if the world is bracketed completely? Second, if in the experience (or nonexperience) with the Absolute via *coram deo* one is not dwelling in the world, then how can it ever be possible for this nonworldly experience to ultimately feedback into truly transgressive, world-altering differentiation? Is it possible truly to access the beyond-world then return to it in a way that the world in fact is rendered strange? Does not leaving the world, even if only for a temporary suspension or epoché, entail an eventual returning to it and its everyday proceedings and forms of presentation? Dwelling permanently in a nonplace is not an option, and ultimately, if there are no worldly evidences (in language, culture, etc.) that can be described in a community (even if composed of true believers), then what is it that keeps these religious nonexperiences from being merely subjective? What keeps them therefore from being reduced back to the mystical, numinous feeling of the transcendent-heavy, hidden, and Platonic *eidos* Lacoste fervently combats?

A response to these questions concerning the liturgical reduction could be fashioned in terms of inconspicuousness. First, as inconspicuous, liturgy would need to not abandon the predicates on which nonworld paradoxically is based. The dichotomous pitting of the world/not-world would need to be overcome through the provision of a place that holds within it, its own nonplace.[78] Yet this nonplace, and any reference to it, would need to come back to, and have been originally birthed out of, what is everyday and mundane. The validation of this place or dwelling would not be based in or of this world. Yet simultaneously the nonplace *from within* the dwelling could entail both Heidegger's *ecstasis*, and Lacoste's *enstasis* via a fundamental intertwining that both the world and the Absolute might give to thought.[79] It is *enstatis* that provides for a fundamental shifting of liturgy via inconspicuousness.

Before addressing this *enstatis*, it is helpful also to consider how transgression is inherent to the enterprise of any liturgical suspension of the world. Lacoste establishes the possibilities of a particular kind of seeing that embraces the paradox of place and nonplace. Yet it remains essential that dwelling be characterized by detectingfromwithin what is the most unhomely (*un-heimlich*) or uncanny. Lacoste's reformation of Husserl's "originary ground of belief" to reflect on how "what appears to us lets the nonphenomenal appear as well," demonstrates that it is out of appearance that nonappearance gains its force of momentum. Lacoste unorthodoxically claims that even for Husserl "perception grasps—*Auffassung*—simultaneously the visible and the invisible."[80] It is this simultaneity (based on how there are things outside the field of consciousness) that could be described as inconspicuous.[81] This is a nonappearing that is still present yet not presently meaningful, and therefore only consciously absent.[82] Lacoste's work is not bereft of reflection on the inconspicuous, and his work bears the marks of overcoming the matrixes of opposition that plague our thinking concerning religious experience. He mentions the inconspicuous or inapparent in explicit terms only briefly, pointing to how it cannot be controlled by any reduction, suspension, or logic: "not every logic of the inapparent . . . allows access to the inapparent," for it must be "given to us otherwise" as it "only appears—as hidden and masked—when we know it is there." Yet if one ever is to access it, it will be by way of the liturgical act, which affords the confrontation that allows for an *au-delà* or way beyond "the sacred and profane, and thus beyond their dialectic."[83] As opposed to any attempt to escape being-in-the-world, liturgy should be expressed according to what I proposed in the previous chapter to be a nondichotomous description of the relation between the world/nonworld. In a broader, inter-personal, and social nexus according to which we organize life, the Absolute is not accessed by fleeing the world, but by attending to it as a marginalized and latent *here* within this world. The opening onto nonplace is to be found *in* the place that, inconspicuously, has become most familiar to us.

Inconspicuous Liturgy

As the point has been made repeatedly, Heidegger knew that it is precisely that which is familiar and closest to us that ontologically is the furthest away.[84] And what, in this particular context of space or place, has become the most familiar? A response to this question leads back to the concern of *enstatis* or being in. Lacoste's project teaches of being before the Absolute, yet this being before must also be thought in the context of dwelling, which is an antinomy. To dwell is to be in, to subsist, and uniquely take up space (Spinoza) *in*. As described in the book of Acts, it is the Absolute, or God *in* "whom we live (ζῶμεν), are set into motion (κινούμεθα), and have our being (ἐσμέν)" (Acts 17:28). Living, moving, and dwelling all orbit around this preposition "in" (ἐν), which pertains to an accordance between the realm, state, or condition of *how* one *is* with the place in which one is, resides, or takes refuge (e.g., the English word "inn").

Yet perhaps more radically, this "in" can be inverted from one's being-in or even being-before-the-Absolute, to the Absolute's *being in* us. In Heideggerian terms, it is Dasein who has become the most latent, and therefore in its overfamiliarity, its "out" is a radical "in." An inconspicuous liturgy would suspend all that is not about becoming the "ἐν;" an "inn" for the Absolute to dwell (οἰκεῖ). The reduction to being this "in" would be a deformalization that is a response to the question posed by St. Paul: "Do you not know that you are the temple of God and that the Spirit of God dwells in [οἰκεῖ ἐν] you?" (I Corinthians 3:16).

If the liturgical reduction is an active suspension that aims to deformalize the world long enough to be-before-the-Absolute without entirely rejecting the world, and if phenomenology calls for attendance to what is the closest (within the world), yet furthest from conscious awareness, then the whence that phenomenology can pursue in regards to the Absolute must be understood as uncannily close, even taking on a mundane or banal form.[85] The Absolute does not float in indeterminate space, but is so close that it dwells familiarly within us. A supernatural laminate need not be presupposed in order to be attuned to what is dwelling in oneself, and an inconspicuous liturgical reduction suspends everything (even one's subjectivity) that is not always already *there in*.

This of course raises a number of theological problems, such as matters of panentheism, the interrelations of the trinity, and a pneumatological determinism in regard to divine participation.[86] Yet on phenomenological grounds, this inversion of the "ἐν" could prove instrumental in further safeguarding religious experience from being reducible to pure sentiment (one major fear of Lacoste's) and ontotheology. In seeking a nonspectacular Absolute, an inconspicuous liturgical reduction would suspend what gives itself immediately by turning to what is the most immanent—the Absolute's indwelling. The goal here is not to uncover, reveal, or bring further clarity to the Absolute. That not only is impossible, but also a form of revealing/uncovering that ignores the Absolute's ability to be inconspicuous. Since Lacoste's liturgy seeks to furnish the highest demonstration of possibility *for man*, it is of use to see that this takes place also *in man*.[87] In the same chapter as Paul's reference to Christ as *Eikon* (as the "image of the invisible God") is the claim that the truest riches of mysterious glory are qualified by the realization of "Christ in you" (Col. 1:27). As noted in previous chapters, the glory of these mysteries is a para-glory, not in the least because it occurs in man. Thus, being-before-the-Absolute entails a radical turn to confront (as being before) the closeness of what/who indwells.

There are two final aspects of an inconspicuous liturgical reduction worth mentioning. First, it allows for an indirect or peripheral confrontation with the indwelling Absolute. As the Absolute becomes total, it ultimately discharges the absoluteness of totality, and along with it, its spectacular phenomenality. What prevents the Absolute from reduction to pure ontological totality is how, as Levinas knew, the Absolute (despite being an abusive word) has "meaning only . . . in the rupture of phenomenology, to which the face of the other gives rise."[88] Such a rupture allows for the challenging of a deceptive totality, and does so in accordance with the acts of man that poetically (actively and creatively) access a space of Godhood that is built-out-from-within. Since desire is qualified by a privation, of wanting what is not-here-within, this reduction can bring reform to a subjectivity obsessed with identifying itself with its transcendental outside. The specific type of glorification of the Absolute, in this case, involves its inconspicuous status, as a not-outside, thus making it capable of deformalizing the inside. To repurpose Heidegger here, such a domain would be a sacred dimension of *Gottheit*.

Second, and in following Lacoste, the Absolute is not *suspended* or bracketed, but rather what is suspended is all-that-is-not-Absolute. Under this formulation, this reduction at first appears to be a phenomenologically inspired apophatic or negative theology. Yet this is no pure privation since this reduction happens *in* and through me, despite my not being-at-one with the Absolute. And despite seeming panentheistic, I and the Absolute are not indeterminately intertwined, but instead make up two separate phenomenalities. As a dwelling, my phenomenality is in my role as the proxy of relation (not unlike Heidegger's *Krankenerscheinen*, or "sickness symptoms"), as a medium by which the clearing of Godhood is pronounced. One here becomes a living testament or symptom of the Inconspicuous God, whose "whence" or glory shines in the most ordinary and overlooked of phenomena precisely despite my insufficiencies in housing the Absolute. The dual movement of this liturgy is that my subjectivity is set aside, while attention is given to the *in me* that putatively *is not* me. This dual movement, of the Absolute-in-me-yet-entirely-different-from-me can find expression in Nietzche's dictum that "when you stare for a long time into an abyss, the abyss stares back into you."[89]

The mores of our present age, weaned on media-frenzied illusions and representations, have inverted the traditional relation between distance andfamiliarity and forgotten its abyssal Absolute. Today the distant has become the most familiar, thus making the familiar, as Günther Anders knew, even more and more distant. What is necessary in order for the totality of such spectacular phenomenality to be overcome is an Absolute capable of transcending this paradigm by tarrying not only within the familiar, but also by turning ever so subtly one's attention to the Absolute within whatever has become marginalized (the Absolute's gazing back, if you will). Yet this marginalization is eternal, never fully made to open or be revealed, thus still giving reason for wonder, anticipation, and praise. As Colossians 3:16 continues, being the dwelling of God should induce a unique kind of adoration (a "singing to God with gratitude"). This is what the next chapter seeks to describe via the work of Jean-Luc Nancy.

Notes

1. Martin Heidegger, "Seminar in Zähringen 1973," in *Four Seminars*, trans. Andrew J. Mitchell and François Raffoul (Bloomington: Indiana University Press, 2003), 66. Concerning the Husserlian "idea of 'surplus'" (*Überschuß*), Heidegger explains: "the 'is' through which I observe the presence of the inkwell as object or substance, is a 'surplus' in relation to the sensuous affections. But in a certain respect the 'is' is given *in the same manner* as the sensuous affections: the 'is' is not added to the sense data; it is 'seen'—even if it is *seen* differently from what is sensibly visible. In order to be 'seen' in this way, it *must* be *given*."

2. Martin Heidegger, *The Phenomenology of the Religious Life* (Bloomington: Indiana University Press, 2010), 7.

3. See Martin Heidegger, GA 4, *Hölderlin and the Essence of Poetry* (Frankfurt am Main: Vittorio Klostermann, 1936).

4. Lacoste engages liturgy in "a displacement of meaning" as "The world has no philosophical past whatsoever." Jean-Yves Lacoste, "Response to Gschwandtner, Hart, Schrijvers, and Hackett," *Modern Theology* 31 no. 4 (2015): 676. Regarding the "meanings" of philosophy and theology, see Lacoste's most recent attempts to rebridge the gaps between them in Jean-Yves Lacoste, *From Theology to Theological Thinking*, trans. William Chris Hackett (Charlottesville, VA: University of Virginia Press, 2004).

5. See also Jean-Yves Lacoste, *Le monde et l'absence d'œuvre et autres etudes* (Paris: Presses Universitaires de France, 2000), 101. There, Lacoste reiterates, shortly before the publication of *Experience and the Absolute* into English, that liturgy determines Dasein as not defined or limited by its being-in-the-world. Necessary is "une surdétermination des conditions natives de l'expérience. On peut donner un nom à cette surdétermination: nous dirons par convention que le Dasein et le mortel sont capables de liturgie." ("an overdetermination of native conditions of experience. One can give a name to such an over-determination: we will suggest by convention that *Dasein* and the *mortal* are capable of *liturgy*.") Jean-Yves Lacoste, *Le monde et l'absence d'oeuvre et autres etudes* (Paris: Presses Universitaires de France, 2000), 16. See here also Jean-Yves Lacoste, *Expérience et Absolu: Questions Disputées Sur l'humanité de l'homme* (Paris: Presses Universitaires de France, 1994), 1.

6. Kevin Hart recently drew the connection between Lacoste's counterexperience and his distaste for the association of religion with numinous "feeling:" "Husserl's phenomenology is not put to the side because of its rigorous attention to experience; that is of immense value, Lacoste thinks, since phenomena come only by way of experience. His hostility with regards to 'experience' in Experience and the Absolute is confined to Schleiermacher's inflection of *Erlebnis* in religion, which Lacoste takes to undergird the whole of the philosophy of religion." Kevin Hart, "Poverty's Speech: On Liturgical Reduction," *Modern Theology* 31 no. 4 (2015): 641–47.

7. Lacoste, *Expérience et Absolu*, 27. "Liturgy exceeds being-in-the-world." Jean-Yves Lacoste, *Experience and the Absolute: Disputed Questions on the Humanity of Man* (New York: Fordham University Press, 2004), 39.

8. Ibid., 22, 28, 39, 74.

9. Ibid., 22, 175. Further, "Liturgy is in fact the very concept that precludes the ruinous opposition of the interior and the exterior, of the 'body' and the 'soul': by thinking in terms of liturgy, we are constantly compelled to think in terms of place." For these reasons, and for others, "liturgy suggests a redefinition of place: no longer is it to be thought of as a being there, but as being toward." Ibid., 22.

10. For another engagement on how Lacoste transitions liturgy from Heidegger's being-in-the-world, see Jean-Luc Marion, "Lacoste ou la correction de l'analytique existentiale," *Transversalités* 2 no. 110 (2009): 169–175. For Marion: "Le travail de Jean-Yves Lacoste prend son origine—son origine philosophique du moins, car cette origine trouve elle-même son sens dans une lumière théologique—dans la lecture de Sein und Zeit, plus précisément de l'analytique existentiale du Dasein" ("The work of Jean-Yves Lacoste originates—at least, its philosophical origin, which itself finds its meaning in a theological illumination—in the reading *Being and Time*, more precisely the existential analytic of Dasein"), 169. (Author's translation). Here in this essay, Marion claims of Lacoste's liturgy that it can be characterized as a passage from the evidence of being in the world to the possibilities of a theological reduction.

11. Indeed, for Lacoste "the God with which liturgy confronts us does not necessarily belong to the field of experience." Lacoste, *Experience and the Absolute*, 22. For Gschwandtner, Lacoste "hesitates to call this 'experience' because he tries to stay away from a reduction of religious experience to feeling or affectivity. Instead he engages our 'being-before-God' in language deeply influenced by but also quite critical of Heidegger's phenomenological approach." Christina M. Gschwandtner, "The Vigil as Exemplary Liturgical Experience: On Jean-Yves Lacoste's Phenomenology of Liturgy," *Modern Theology* 31 no. 4 (2015): 648–57. For Schleiermacher, the truest essence of religion is in "the immediate consciousness of the universal being of all finite things in and through the infinite, of all temporal things in and through the eternal." Further, "to seek and to find this infinite and eternal factor in all that lives and moves, all growth and change, in all action and passion, and to have and to know life itself only in immediate feeling—that is religion." Friedrich Schleiermacher, *On Religion: Addresses in Response to its Cultured Critics*, trans. Terrence N. Tice (Richmond: John Knox, 1969), 79.

12. For another engagement with Lacoste's work through a Heideggerian lens, see William Chris Hackett, "What Is Called Theological Thinking," *Modern Theology* 31 no. 4 (2015): 658–65. There, Hackett turns to Heidegger's 1938 essay "The Age of the World Picture" to compare Lacoste's *penser* with Heidegger's *Denken*.

13. Jean-Yves Lacoste, "Continental Philosophy," in *The Routledge Companion to Philosophy of Religion*, ed. C. Meister (London: Routledge Press, 2007), 657.

14. "If phenomenology . . . furnishes us the coordinates with which to coherently question who we are, and with which to rigorously debate what we are, will it not also provide us with the means to understand how *Dasein*, how *mortals*, who concern themselves solely with an atheistic world and a familiar earth, with the sky and the deities, can also be concerned with a God with whom they maintain a relation steeped in ambiguity?" Lacoste, *Experience and the Absolute*, 2, 22.

15. Lacoste continues, "liturgy suggests a redefinition of place: no longer is it to be thought of as a being there, but as being toward." Ibid., 22.

16. Martin Heidegger, "Lettre à Monsieur Beaufret (23 novembre 1945)," in *Lettre sur l'humanisme*, ed. and trans. Roger Munier (Paris: Aubier, Éditions Montaigne, 1964), 182. And in Martin Heidegger, *Zollikoner Seminare. Protokolle—Gespräche—Briefe*, ed. Merdard Boss (Frankfurt am Main: Vittorio Klostermann, 1987), 156. Martin Heidegger, *Zollikon Seminars: Protocols—Conversations—Letters*, ed. Medard Boss and trans. Franz Mayr and Richard Askay (Evanston: Northwestern University Press, 2001), 120.

17. Thought must be brought "into the clearing of the appearing of the unapparent." Martin Heidegger, "Letters to Roger Munier (dated Feb 22, 1974)," in *Martin Heidegger,*

ed. Michel Haar (Paris: Editions de l'Herne, 1983), 115. Prior to that, on April 16, 1973, he writes "for me it is a matter of actually performing an exercise in a phenomenology of the inapparent; by the reading of books, no one ever arrives at phenomenological 'seeing.'" Martin Heidegger, "The Appendix" in *Four Seminars*, trans. Andrew J. Mitchell and François Raffoul (Bloomington: Indiana University Press, 2003), 89.

18. Lacoste, *Experience and the Absolute*, 109.

19. For a phenomenological engagement with "epiphany" and vertical givenness, see Anthony J. Steinbock, *Phenomenology and Mysticism* (Bloomington: Indiana University Press, 2007).

20. For Gschwandtner, "it is less an experience than an openness to experience." Further, "Liturgy functions as a challenge to ordinary experience. It shows something deeper and more fundamental than Dasein's experience of being-in-the-world." Christina M. Gschwandtner, "The Vigil as Exemplary Liturgical Experience: On Jean-Yves Lacoste's Phenomenology of Liturgy," *Modern Theology* 31 no. 4 (2015): 648–57.

21. Faith is not phenomenologically identifiable. See Jean-Yves Lacoste, *La Phenomenalite de Dieu: Neuf Etudes* (Paris: Cerf, 2008). As Schrijvers suggests, one cannot put one's faith "in suspension." Joeri Schrijvers, "God and/in Phenomenology: Jean-Yves Lacoste's Phenomenality of God," *Bijdragen, International Journal in Philosophy and Theology* 71 no. 1 (2010): 88.

22. Lacoste continues, "We are not, for all that, claiming that liturgy discloses all its secrets in the elucidation of its relation to topology." Lacoste, *Experience and the Absolute*, 39.

23. Ibid.

24. Ibid., 152.

25. "We can describe every experience, even inexperience, as the 'experience of consciousness,' and therefore in terms of intentionality. But … this enables us to do no more than verify the presence of whoever is praying or is attempting to pray, and to verify the disappointment occasioned when knowledge coincides with inexperience." Ibid., 149.

26. "We must always begin by referring to the excess of inexperience over experience, to the point of the pure and simple negation of experience." This is where Lacoste's "restlessness" or desire for the Eschaton is an attempt to get beyond the limits of world. Ibid., 40, 192.

27. Heidegger, "Seminar in Zähringen 1973," 70.

28. Ibid., 64.

29. Ibid.

30. Lacoste even recognizes Heidegger's "Origin of the Work of Art" as the initiation of some "other than world," and Lacoste agrees with Heidegger that works of art exceed the presence of the world.

31. Lacoste, "Response to Gschwandtner, Hart, Schrijvers, and Hackett," 679.

32. Ibid.

33. Ibid.

34. Liturgy can bracket the world and open onto a nonplace via prayer. Lacoste, *Experience and the Absolute*, 27.

35. Lacoste, "Continental Philosophy," 657.

36. Martin Heidegger, "Letter on Humanism," in *Basic Writings*, ed. David Farrell Krell (New York: Harper & Row, 1977), 232.

37. For Schrijvers "Where in *Sein und Zeit* the confrontation with finitude takes place in angst, the liturgical person has to reckon with the terror of the nonexperience." Joeri

Schrivers, "Jean-Yves Lacoste: A Phenomenology of Liturgy," *Heythrop Journal* XLVI (2005): 314–333. For Lacoste, "If a phenomenology of what I am here calling 'liturgy' is possible, will we not . . . [be able to] redefine what we commonly understand by the term 'experience?'" Lacoste, *Experience and the Absolute*, 2.

38. Martin Heidegger, GA 56/57, *Zur Bestimmung der Philosophie* (Frankfurt am Main: Vittorio Klostermann, 1919), 75, 78, 112. Heidegger did not want to leave "lived experience behind. To be sure, something of the experiential still comes along with me—but no one knows what to do with it, so they invent the convenient label of the 'irrational' for it." Ibid., 117.

39. Lacoste, *Experience and the Absolute*, 87.

40. Ibid., 104.

41. Lacoste, "Response to Gschwandtner, Hart, Schrijvers and Hackett," 677.

42. Lacoste, *Experience and the Absolute*, 16. "The sovereignty that the sacred (or that of Being) exercises [over the fourfold] . . . substantially enlarges the sphere of immanence."

43. Ibid., 18.

44. Martin Heidegger, GA 3, *Kant und das Problem der Metaphysik* (Frankfurt am Main: Vittorio Klostermann, 1929), 258–59. This is at points similar to Bataille's conception of the sacred, as the ungraspable appearance of what is usually covered over in ordinary life. This is conceived as a distinction between substance (material) and the sacred. See Georges Bataille, *Visions of Excess: Selected Writings 1927–1939* (Minneapolis: University of Minnesota Press, 1985).

45. The sacred, as a space in the clearing of being, allows us to return to the important question, "How, and in what way can the world be without a ground?" As Krummel put it, "for Heidegger, what the thinker thinks of as "being" here, even as it withdraws from his conceptualizations, the poet calls "the sacred."" J. W. M. Krummel, "The Originary *Wherein*: Heidegger and Nishida on 'the Sacred' and 'the Religious'," *Research in Phenomenology* 40 no. 3 (2010): 378–407.

46. See Heidegger on Hölderlin's, "Flight of the Gods" (GA 39, *die Flucht der Götter*), *Hölderlins Hymnen "Germanien" und "Der Rhein"* (Frankfurt am Main: Vittorio Klostermann, 1934), 80. See here also the recent English translation of Martin Heidegger, *Hölderlin's Hymns "Germania" and "The Rhine,"* trans. W. McNeill (Bloomington: Indiana University Press, 2014).

47. Dominique Janicaud, *Phenomenology and the Theological Turn* (New York: Fordham University Press, 2000), 31.

48. Martin Heidegger, GA 9, *Wegmarken* (Frankfurt am Main: Vittorio Klostermann, 1998), 339. Martin Heidegger *Pathmarks*, trans. William McNeill (Cambridge: Cambridge University Press, 1998), 258.

49. Martin Heidegger, GA 5, *Holzwege* (Frankfurt am Main: Vittorio Klostermann, 2002), 272. Martin Heidegger, *Off the Beaten Track*, ed. and trans. Julian Young and Kenneth Haynes (Cambridge: Cambridge University Press, 2002), 202.

50. Krummel, "The Originary *Wherein*," 378–407. See here Martin Heidegger, GA 3, *Kant und das Problem der Metaphysik* (Frankfurt am Main: Vittorio Klostermann, 1929), 258–59. Under Krummel's assessment, in both "What Are Poets for?" and "Letter on Humanism," Heidegger employs "the threefold scheme of gods, godhood, and sacred: gods are to be understood only in light of the dimension of the godhood (*Gottheit*), but godhood can be present only in the domain of the sacred—the 'essential space of the godhood' (*Wesensraum der Gottheit*) that, in turn, is the 'dimension for gods and god' (Dimension für die Götter

und den Gott).... And this means the truth of be-ing as the clearing, making room for beings from the far side of being.", 392.

51. "Nur noch ein Gott kan uns retten." This was originally an interview conducted on September 23, 1966, and later printed in *Der Spiegel* May 31, 1976. Martin Heidegger, "'Only a God Can Save Us Now': An Interview with Martin Heidegger," trans. David Schendler *Graduate Faculty Philosophy Journal* 6 no. 1 (1977): 5–27.

52. Further regarding this divinity, for Heidegger "The era is defined by the god's failure to arrive, by the 'default of god.' But the default of God ... does not deny that the Christian relationship with God lives on in individuals and in the churches; still less does it assess this relationship negatively. The default of god means that no god any longer gathers means and things unto himself, visibly and unequivocally, and by such gathering disposes of the world's history and man's soujourn in it." Martin Heidegger, *Poetry, Language, Thought*, trans. Albert Hofstadter (New York: Harper & Row, 1971), 91. Martin Heidegger, GA 5, *Holzwege (1935–1946)*. 2nd ed. (Frankfurt am Main: Vittorio Klostermann, 2003), 269.

53. Regarding these gods, Hubert Dreyfus thinks that Heidegger "sees the pursuit of autonomy as the cause of our dangerous contemporary condition. He counters the Enlightenment vision with a nontheological version of the Christian message that man cannot be saved by autonomy, maturity, equality, and dignity alone." Heidegger's concern, then, was that there is a "technological impulse that wishes to quantify the dignity of shared, meaningful, concerns." And that "this conviction underlies his dangerous claim that only a god ... can save us from nihilism." Dreyfus continues, "Our current condition is defined by the absence of a god." Hubert Dreyfus, "Nihilism, Art, Technology, and Politics," in *Cambridge Companion to Heidegger*, ed. Charles Guignon (Cambridge: Cambridge University Press, 1993), 312–13.

54. Martin Heidegger, GA 65, *Beiträge zur Philosophie (Vom Ereignis)* (Frankfurt am Main: Vittorio Klostermann, 1999), 125. Martin Heidegger, *Contributions to Philosophy: (From Enowning)*, trans. Parvis Emad and Kenneth Maly (Bloomington: Indiana University Press, 1989), 87.

55. Heidegger notes that "the godless thinking which must abandon the god of philosophy, god as *causa sui*, is ... perhaps closest to the divine god [göttlichen Gott]." Martin Heidegger, *Identity and Difference*, trans. Joan Stambaugh (Chicago, IL: University of Chicago Press, 2002), 72.

56. Jean-Yves Lacoste, "Presence and Parousia," in *The Blackwell Companion to Postmodern Theology*, ed. Graham Ward (Oxford: Blackwell, 2005), 396.

57. As Gschwandtner interprets, "God can be known, but not ultimately comprehended." Christina M. Gschwandtner, *Postmodern Apologetics: Arguments for God in Contemporary Philosophy* (New York: Fordham University Press, 2012), 180.

58. Further "we cannot but anticipate the definitive." Lacoste, "Response to Gschwandtner, Hart, Schrijvers and Hackett," 683.

59. For Malpas, Heidegger's Being and "place" are bound together. Jeff Malpas, *Heidegger's Topology: Being, Place, World* (Boston: MIT Press, 2008).

60. Jean-Yves Lacoste, "The Appearing and the Irreducible," in *Words of Life: New Theological Turns in French Phenomenology*, trans. C. Gschwandtner and ed. Bruce Ellis Benson and Norman Wirzba (New York: Fordham University Press, 2010), 51. For Lacoste, "On one hand, Husserlian phenomenology has a goal to pave a way toward our more primitive experiences—*Experience and Judgment* says that better than any other text of

the corpus. Yet on the other hand, primitive experiences put the human being into play as a being of consciousness, and a systematic inquiry into consciousness or into subjectivity (at issue here is only a part of our humanity) is the only mode of exploration Husserl knows."

61. Ibid., 62. Lacoste continues, "'Existence' of God, 'existence' of my pipe, can the two be said univocally? One perceives intuitively that the answer must be 'no'; and thus that certain existences appear to us as 'reducible' and others as 'irreducible'; this intuitive certainty merits that one regard it as established."

62. Ibid., 64.

63. Lacoste, *Experience and the Absolute*, 10.

64. Heidegger, "Seminar in Zähringen 1973," 70.

65. Ibid., 79.

66. As mentioned in the introduction, Figal demonstates the fundamentally inconspicuous nature of "space" (*Raum*). Günter Figal, *Unscheinbarkeit. Der Raum der Phänomenologie* (Tübingen: Mohr Siebeck, 2015).

67. Heidegger, "Seminar in Zähringen 1973," 79.

68. Ibid., 71.

69. Lacoste continues, "liturgy suggests a redefinition of place: no longer is it to be thought of as a being there, but as being toward." Lacoste, *Experience and the Absolute*, 22. "Liturgy is somehow a means of being-there." Lacoste, *Expérience et Absolu*, 209.

70. Heidegger, "Lettre à Monsieur Beaufret (23 novembre 1945)," 182. And in Heidegger, *Zollikoner Seminare. Protokolle—Gespräche—Briefe*, 156. Heidegger, *Zollikon Seminars*, 120.

71. Thomas Sheehan recently described this important distinction: "In *Being and Time* this clearing is called the Da of Da-sein. This word Da should never be translated as 'here' or 'there' but always as 'openness' or 'the open' in the sense of that which is thrown-open." This "Ex-sistence is thrown" into its openness "but not of its own accord." And Sheehan continues: "So too Da-sein should not be translated as 'being-there,' 'being-here,' or 'being t/here.' Heidegger insists that the Da of Da-sein is not a locative adverb at all ('here,' 'there,' or 'where'): 'Da ibi und ubi.'" Thomas Sheehan, "What after All Was Heidegger About?" *Continental Philosophy Review* 47 no. 3 (2014): 249–74.

72. Martin Heidegger, "Seminar in Le Thor 1966," in *Four Seminars*, trans. Andrew J. Mitchell and François Raffoul (Bloomington: Indiana University Press, 2003), 8. See also a closer engagement of Heidegger's appropriations of Heraclitus in chapter 2 "Inconspicuous Worlds."

73. Heidegger, "Seminar in Zähringen 1973," 70.

74. Martin Heidegger, *The Metaphysical Foundations of Logic*, trans. Michael Heim (Bloomington: Indiana University Press, 1984), 165, footnote 9.

75. Lacoste, "The Appearing and the Irreducible," 63. Therefore "our theology is never founded on the limited basis of our experience of God. We can feel his presence, or what we take as such, but we can just as much feel the presence of the 'divine' of which Heidegger speaks, or worse, we can confuse one with the other."

76. Lacoste, *Experience and the Absolute*, 105. For Lacoste, "The atheism of being-in-the-world and the paganism of earthly existence correspond here to the evident atheism of life."

77. Lacoste already noted (ibid., 11) that being in the world is fundamentally "determined as *Unzuhause*, as a not-being-at-home, a nondomiciliation." See also Lacoste, ibid., 12: "Whoever recognizes himself to be a foreigner in one place, according to the ordinary usage

of the concept, possesses a homeland in another. The metric of 'here' is autochthonous to some other 'there.'"

78. Lacoste indeed initiates an overturning of this dialectic. See ibid., 86.

79. "Enstasis is perhaps more originary than all ecstasis." Lacoste, "Response to Gschwandtner, Hart, Schrijvers and Hackett," 677.

80. This is all in the context of a critique of Janicaud's presumption or "major philosophical blunder" that "phenomenology deals only with the visible ... and that the play of sensory 'matter' ... gives access to the visible and the visible only." Jean-Yves Lacoste, "Perception, Transcendence and the Experience of God" in *Veritas: Transcendence and Phenomenology*, ed. Conner Cunningham and Peter M. Candler Jr. (London: SCM Press, 2007), 5. Aspects of this essay were also published in Jean-Yves Lacoste, "More Haste, Less Speed in Theology," trans. Oliver O'Donovan in *International Journal of Systematic Theology* 9 (2007): 263–82.

81. Lacoste, "Perception, Transcendence and the Experience of God," 2. Lacoste suggests that such an invisible/visible oscillation is already in Husserl, and briefly engages the problematic between sensical and categorial intuitions: "In the Husserlian treatment of perception there is no need to 'describe' a cube in order to know it. We see the cube although sensation[s] 'present' only part of it to us[.] The cube is here 'in the flesh,' *leibhaft da*. And yet what is presented here and now is not the whole thing." Under this analysis, a cube is considered a cube only because one synthetically perceives the different sides of it through performing the Husserlian "finishing act" of consciousness. For Lacoste, it is this finishing act that allows us to see that we rely on *what is putatively not given* or does not appear in our establishment of a cube *as* cube. As Lacoste observes, "most of the furniture of the universe [is not present to] the field of my consciousness." Further, "perceptive experience deals also with the nonperceived." Ibid., 4. Elsewhere, Lacoste suggested that Phenomena and their appearances "do not give us the thing itself—but they give it to us obscurely." Jean-Yves Lacoste Lacoste, "The Work and Complement of Appearing" in *Religious Experience and the End of Metaphysics*, ed. Jeffrey Bloechl (Bloomington: Indiana University Press, 2003), 71.

82. Elsewhere, Lacoste even refers to an "unconsciousness" that is a kind of "seeing" without consciousness. This could furnish another avenue to explore the inconspicuous. Lacoste, *Experience and the Absolute*, 149.

83. Jean-Yves Lacoste, *Etre en danger* (Paris: Cerf, 2010), 117–18.

84. Martin Heidegger, *Being and Time*, trans. John Macquarrie and Edward Robinson (New York: Harper & Row, 1962), 15.

85. This also is not prohibited on the grounds of Lacoste's own liturgical reduction, which is primarily a suspension of relations *with* God, not just being-before God. Liturgy designates "the logic that presides over the encounter between man and God writ large." Lacoste, *Experience and the Absolute*, 2. Hart puts this nicely: "[The] Liturgical reduction, in turn, leads us to a place at the heart of being human where there is no desire for appropriation. It is less a place than a relationship with God in which we are exposed to our ontological poverty." Hart, "Poverty's Speech: On Liturgical Reduction," 641–47. This also may be consistent with Hans von Balthasar (who exerts deep influence upon Lacoste) for whom one is to turn to God, not in order to realize one's own possibilities, but the possibilities that God's holiness enacts. In the case of turning to the indwelling of the Absolute, one can be reminded of the grace of God without it being a "glorification" of man.

86. See here Jürgen Moltmann, *God in Creation*. For Moltmann, "God the Holy Spirit ... is *in* all created beings ... [If] we understand the Creator, his creation, and the goal of that creation in a Trinitarian sense, then the Creator, through his Spirit, *dwells in* his creation as a whole, and in every individual created being, by virtue of his Spirit holding them together and keeping them in life. The inner secret of creation is this *indwelling* of God." Yet Moltmann openly professes to a panentheistic position, while still rejecting pantheism, for "Without difference between Creator and creature, creation cannot be conceived of at all; but this difference is embraced and comprehended by the greater truth which is what the creation narrative really comes down to, because it is the truth from which it springs: the truth that God is all in all. This does not imply a pantheistic dissolution of creation in God; it means the final form which creation is to find in God." Ibid., 89. Jürgen Moltmann, *God in Creation: A New Theology of Creation and the Spirit of God*, trans. Margaret Kohl (San Francisco: Harper & Row, 1985), xii. For more on this Trinitarian, Pneumatological problem see Moltmann's *The Spirit of Life*, where he references an "immanent transcendence" kind of indwelling. Jürgen Moltmann, *The Spirit of Life: A Universal Affirmation* (Minneapolis: Fortress Press, 2001), 34.

87. Lacoste, *Experience and the Absolute*, 105. Liturgy is what *makes* us human.

88. Emmanuel Levinas, *Entre Nous: Thinking-of-the-other*, trans. Michael Smith and Barbara Harshav (New York: Columbia University Press, 1998), 167.

89. Friedrich Nietzche, *Beyond Good and Evil: Prelude to a Philosophy of the Future*, ed. Rolf-Peter Horstmann and Judith Norman (Cambridge: Cambridge University Press, 2003), 69.

5 Inconspicuous Adoration: Nancy, Heidegger, and a Praise of the Ordinary

Adoration is a participation in the active deformalization of the everyday and ordinary. Broadly conceived, when adoring, one sets apart and aside some particular thing as uniquely distinct from everything else. As the Latin *adorare* expresses, the *ad* (to) is the change of indicator that signals to an act that relates directly with a formal speech or "saying" (*oratio*) by differentiating it and making it one's own. This making-ones-own, which is part and parcel of deformalizing the speech, shifts the adored from having a formal status and integrates it into the life of the adorer. Adoration creates divisions, dividing lines, and distinctions between things and oneself, and in this sense, adoration is as passive as it is active—one adores what is deemed striking, and one in turn is affected or struck by the adored.

Yet this striking entails that adoration leaves one speechless beyond any formal address. One is "set straight" (*dirigere*) to the phenomenon by setting it "apart" (the *di* of *dirigere* originates in *dis* or "apart"). To address is to be directed "to" (*ad*) what has announced itself in its own form and manner, but in a way that corresponds to the adored, which prevents its own phenomenalization from crystalizing into a static concept. Here, the adored leaves no clear and calculable traces behind to allow the adorer to address it in any complete way. If formalized, the adored runs the risk of becoming an idol, a status that cannot sustain the act of adoration for very long. To avoid idolization, it becomes necessary to relate with the adored through an active setting-apart that gives glory—as the doxology teaches—not only to the adored as a set of characteristics or traits, but as a formation that operates with a phenomenality utterly unique to it, and unlike any other.

These reflections on adoration appear consistent with the position of Jean-Luc Nancy, for whom the disenclosure of things in their wonder is what invokes a call to adoration. Not only is adoration an act of differentiating, but it also is an act whereby, more precisely, one adores and thereby differentiates the great differentiator. In recent years, Nancy has described how there is a theological innervation that innately is integrated into what it means to be human today in western societies. His turn to a deconstruction of Christianity began with the attempt to get away from what he saw to be the banal polarities between atheism and theism, and it is in Christianity that he found a kernel of hope for such a project, as Christianity paradoxically marked both the end of religion and its beginning. One essential core of this beginning is its form of adoration, which operates according to faith in differentiation itself. Religion more broadly, in his estimation, is scored by antiadoration for it no longer harbors the means and modes to one's engaging in a fundamental relation with the wondrous. As such religion becomes bored with itself, and through its tiring doctrines attempts to carve out in society its own forms of legitimation and rationality.

What is necessary then is not a religious reason, but means by which the disenclosure and transcending of reason itself might be accomplished. In his analysis, this is what Christianity sought to achieve. Christianity (and despite Nancy's own atheistic impulses), in its humble beginnings, initiated a new form of understanding *how* things relate and share a border, boundary, or touch line (see *Noli me Tangere*). Christianity teaches that we no longer are to accept as immediately valid or operative the many dichotomies that have tended to plague religious dogmatism, as Christianity points to an entirely new understanding of truth. Truth presents itself and that which is revealed in it via the twin operations of opening and closing, which Nancy comes to name "disenclosure," which is his redux-version of Heidegger's paralogism of "disclosure" (*Ent-ber-gen*, an "unholding" or opening-up-to-the-unsafe). Yet, Nancy's insertion of the "en" here indicates an important difference, and entails the active opening up to the perhaps passive dispolarization that is capable of being experienced in or by truth as it grips us. While we typically understand truth as that which we "grip" (as the German *Begriff* or concept is rooted in "Griff," a grip or "handle") through our creation of concepts, truth also does a certain gripping. What ultimately is necessary then is to experience the truthing of truth via a kind of faith, not in a purely inconceivable or ambiguous other, but in *othering* itself. This othering is not simply the creator of the world (as the monotheisms teach), but more radically, the world's great differentiator. God *is* differentiation, which provides an entirely new and radical meaning to the "a" in atheism by God deformalizing God's own self. How one relates with the obfuscation this differentiation creates marks a faith that ultimately should lead one to adoration.

It likely was Nancy's radical atheism that kept him off Janicaud's blacklist of phenomenologists to have hijacked phenomenology for theological purposes. Yet, Nancy has demonstrated a profound (and confessed) reliance on Heidegger, who Janicaud primarily blamed as a generative father of the theological turn. Thus, to what degree might Nancy employ a "phenomenology of the inconspicuous" and how might it be differently intonated than those generally associated with the theological turn? One answer has come from the editors of the recently published *Retreating Religion*, who claim that against modernity's negation or suppression of religion, those of the theological turn (e.g., Henry, Marion, Chrétien) attempted to "reintroduce absence into presence, bringing the nonapparent toward a new state of appearing" and that "by contrast, the path Nancy seeks to enter is entirely different."[1] That is, inapparency or inconspicuousness has emboldened these thinkers with a new confidence to resuscitate metaphysical remnants of theologies past and their inherently supernatural and invisible phenomena.[2]

As the editors of *Retreating Religion* recognize, Nancy also employs this concept in his work, but in a slightly different way: "Nancy shares an interest in what these advocates of a theological turn in phenomenology see as phenomenology's blind spots" and the turn to these blind spots are based on "Heidegger's critical revision of the principles of phenomenology."[3] The difference in Nancy's work is that it explores "the way religion and secularism, theism and atheism are still entangled in our time." Not unlike Nietzsche's attempt to dissolve the distinctions between existence and nonexistence (namely, of God) Nancy demonstrates how the nonpresence (and by proxy absence) of God places on us the demands to find means of articulating how we are supposed to relate with this nonpresence. Nancy is not seeking a lever by which to give a new voice to religion and to reconcile philosophy and religion once again, but to find means of relation with the "blind spots of presence" that cannot be "filled in" with adding God "to its field of inquiry."[4] Attending to these blind spots, as the editors of *Retreating Religion* note, is what it means to engage a phenomenology of the inconspicuous or inapparent: "By these blind spots they mean, first, the 'unapparent,' the 'nonappearing,' or, as Nancy would say, absence as opposed to, or as a 'remainder' of, the apparent, of the appearing in presence and second, the other person, others as well as the Other of transcendence—God—all of whom are tacitly marginalized or even negated by phenomenology's preoccupation with the ego and its presence to itself."[5]

Thus, in spite of Nancy's potential disagreements with the theological turn on how to apply the unapparent, nonapparent, or inconspicuous, he still advocates for a subversion of phenomenology that follows Heidegger's embrace of the paradoxes of appearance and nonappearance. The question indeed becomes *how* Nancy attends to these margins, blind spots, and inconspicuous spaces, especially in regard to the precarious border between philosophy and theology, over which one never can be too careful in attempting to cross. For on the one hand, if what is inconspicuous is never to be experienced, then it is reducible to an ontotheologically constituted metaphysics; yet on the other hand, if what is inconspicuous is reducible to utter visibility, then it likely removes itself from being worthy of adoration. The path Nancy seeks is a subversion of these extremes by offering more detailed accounts of how the borders between them can be described.

Such an assessment of Nancy's work can be enriched by investigating it alongside Heidegger's "*Phänomenologie des Unscheinbaren*," which despite Janicaud's oft and repeated references, *not once* is uttered by Heidegger in the context of supporting theology, invisibility (*unsichtbar*), or the supernaturally transcendent. For Janicaud, "without Heidegger's *Kehre*," which entails the eventual turn to the inapparent, "there would be no theological turn. Assuredly."[6] Yet, this approach of Heidegger's calls to repentance both any reliance on such invisibility *and* any straightforward visibility that might entail a methodological and calculated atheism. Inconspicuousness implicitly offers another warning to anyone (irrespective of religious background) tempted by idolatry in any form, namely, by challenging explicitly the often incorrectly drawn borders between visibility and invisibility.

Without explicitly barring theological reflection, the approach to inconspicuousness is reflective of the deep ambiguities of Dasein's means of relation with the "clearing" (*Lichtung*) and the oscillatory movement between concealment (*lethe*) and disclosure (*aletheia*). Beyond the surface distinctions between visible/invisible, this approach opens onto an investigation into how phenomena have many forms of hiddenness, not only in their not-yet-appearing or utterly incomprehensible mystery, but in their paradoxical presentation of giving themselves as inconspicuous. There indeed are phenomenal experiences that abandon what traditionally is understood in terms of phenomenality. To reiterate from previous chapters, what is *unscheinbar* can refer to the marginalized, the wallflower, or the overlooked, as its root *der Schein* (license, ticket, warrant) entails the permission of a thing to be. Since in the Zähringen seminar Heidegger turned to a somewhat ambiguous description of what he found to be of phenomenological import in Parmenides's tautological thinking, it is helpful to turn once again back to how Heidegger employs the work of Parmenides's "Being," with which one cannot enter any genuine relation according to "concepts," for in conceiving (*begreifen*), there is the gesture of taking possession as opposed to more intuitively taking something into view.[7] One need not develop concepts in order to see or to be led, as Parmenides once ambiguously called it "to the 'that it is.'"[8]

It is in his seminar on Parmenides, in the winter term of 1942/1943, that Heidegger begins to explore the interrelations between the inconspicuous, Being, and mystery. There, mystery is described neither as entirely unexplainable, nor as remaining-to-be-explained, but as harboring a secret kind of concealment "characterized by its inconspicuousness."[9] This is because, as noted in the Zähringen seminar, presence itself is manifested, or to employ the tautology, "presence presences," which entails that presentation can operate without an ontology that seeks a total grasp of what appears. When thought of in this light, Heidegger's *Phänomenologie des Unscheinbaren* can be understood as an approach to how particularly mysterious phenomena harbor the uncanny means of simultaneously revealing and hiding, and doing so within everyday experience. What is mysterious is not referential to what is yet to appear or be unveiled, but to what hides *in its* appearance and very phenomenalization. It is an event of apparition, which never is to be exhausted, no matter how much phenomenological or transcendental bracketing takes place. In fact, any direct explication of the intelligibility of this mystery entails that one has in fact already precluded such phenomenality, which undermines precisely such directedness or intentionality by being appropriative. One cannot be appropriated by what is fully explainable. As developed in the last chapter, being-before the Inconspicuous God entails a paradoxical confrontation or relation, and adoration could be seen as the response to such liturgy.[10] St. Augustine's question, "what do I love [or adore] when I love my God?" still remains pertinent today, and it is as much a question of the definition of adoration as it is about God, who not only operates according to a *what* but also a *how*. "What is adoration?" and "what is God?" are sutured to one another and point to the question of God's *how*.

The remainder of this chapter places Nancy's notions of "adoration" and differentiation alongside Heidegger's developments of disclosure and truth to propose a means by which the inconspicuous God might be adored. For Nancy, adoration is not "appropriation" but, via truth as disenclosure, an expression of being-appropriated-by, namely by what he calls (in *Adoration: The Deconstruction of Christianity II*) a divinity of pure differentiation. This differentiation disrupts attempts to see and focus with "clarity" (which certainly is a characteristic that is never *adored*) as God is a matter of passing into withdrawal as an opening-up void. Such abyssal differentiation turns things out, and this process is worthy of adoration. Yet it goes unaddressed by Nancy that there is also a version of pure differentiation responsible for negative socialities as the driver of spectacles and simulacra through a kind of nightmarish diversity. This differentiation and diversity can birth passivity by destining subjects through "enframement" (Heidegger). Nancy's version of differentiation is in need of being distinguished from this kind of negative diversity. Further, description of the notion of adoration as inconspicuous can be helpful here, for as inconspicuous it can be an act that relates to differentiation in a counterspectacular way, as the adored resided within the rejected and marginalized. The phenomenality or *how* of God points to God as a formation. Forms necessarily withdraw and are interwoven into everyday life in a way that leaves them on the touch line or boundary of phenomenalization.

Nancy's Appearance and Nonappearance as "Drawing-out"

To extend Nancy's engagements with adoration, it is helpful to turn first to his conception of appearance, which is considered closely in *The Pleasure of Drawing*. There, it is not the clearly visible that is of interest, but rather what gets marginalized in appearance or is the remainder or residue of what comes to appear (*scheinbar*). The line, margin, or boundary for the *what* of appearances and their ensuing dichotomies can be accessed. *The Pleasure of Drawing* demonstrates how this possibility can be understood by turning to how drawing and the arts entail their own disenclosure of reason that opens uph the world from within the world, and onto what has not been given easily to visibility.

To draw is not to reproduce, but to access and cocreate lines. It is through the cultivation of spaces, contours, and shapes that the present/absent dichotomy can be challenged in a radical way, namely, through its activity of initiating the making appear. There are two ways of understanding this coming into appearance—as appearing and appearance. First, one can witness the work of "appearing" itself and how it uniquely operates in the particular instance of what is drawn. Second as "appearance," something (an image, line, etc.) is brought into visibility that was otherwise dormant, latent, or merely ideal. We might suggest that for Nancy it is the synthesis between the drawing-out or coaxing of an image that represents the visibile "appearance," and that it is the drawing-in to the "appearing" itself that defines what it means for something to appear.

The word "draw" originates in the Latin *apparere*, which is the movement of coming into sight, the action of making-appear or luring something into open space. The suffix *parere* entails the coming forth, the making-visible (*la paraître*), and the coming into appearance (*l'apparaître*) of that which was either not-before in existence, or perhaps present-yet-hidden. Although drawing is of a line, and therefore to a certain degree "of the order of divisibility" (*dividere*), its movement draws attention to "the infinity of becoming visible" as "the movement through which appearance is possible [and] cannot itself be finished."[11] Appearing inherently is deceptive in its often entailing an appearance that shrouds its excessive and infinite potential.

The meaning of appearance for Nancy can be understood better through a reflection on art, which he explicitly describes as inconspicuous: "In its own way, art remains inapparent, and it is not the coming into appearance (*paraître*) or phenomenality that presents it—in short, one must be sensitive not just to the form but to the withdrawn movement of a formation."[12] That is, appearance-as-making-visible does not account for the making of art, as art also amounts to an attendance to what uniquely hides. In this sense, drawing, which is typically understood in its function of making appear, entails the seemingly opposite movement of with-*drawing* in a formation—what it veils in its formatting of the visible. Drawing sets into motion a dividing line (*dividere*) that opens-up a negative space or absence that comes into presence inconspicuously. Drawing creates and frames space, and the essence of art is just as marked by its capabilities to bring about withdrawal as it is by its bringing something forth or forward. This is, in part, because "art itself" (*l'art elle-même*) appears from the abyss (*le gouffre*) unexpectedly and seemingly from nowhere. This invisible sense of art is not conceived in Platonic terms, but instead embarks on a more radical dissolution of the dichotomies between presence and absence. Perhaps this is why art is named by Nancy to be inapparent, for art, like Nancy's god, is capable of creating by arriving and passing by simultaneously.

This all is quite close to Heidegger's treatments of presence and withdrawal, which especially become pertinent to any reflection on his well-known engagements with *vorhanden* and *zuhanden*, and the ways in which things draw the most attention when they are not functioning, and therefore to some degree are absent. This insight is not depictive simply of one of many operations of Being. Instead, it plays a formative role in how Being is to be understood. This kind of *Zuhandenheit* (what is readily within reach) is named the most rudimentary, ontological-categorical meaning or "voice" (*Bestimmung*) of Being itself.[13] And thus absence is integrated into what it means for something (even an ontic thing) to appear.

The basic thrust of this position is operative in Nancy's challenge issued to the absence/presence problematic on which we often rely in thinking God. God is not to be understood as an alterity or an other. Instead, God is alteration—othering and change itself. God *is* difference, and this active differing and sub-altering complicates any notion of revelation. Revelation (again, *a la* Nancy via Heidegger) is also a revealing of a productive absence; productive in its provision of a kind of quandary or fixed attention on that which (or perhaps who) defaces the absent/present paradigm. For Nancy, this moment and place at which real presence is in departure or withdrawal, is when faith becomes actualized according to the birthplace or creative event.

Adoration and Truth as Disenclosure

These reflections on appearance foreground how Nancy engages Christianity, the truth of which may lead to one's relation with differentiation, and ultimately acts of adoration. There are three ways in which the features of Heidegger's "phenomenology of the inconspicuous" seem comparable to features of Nancy's "adoration." First, Nancy often relies on a concept of truth (and reflective of Derrida's deconstruction) that is the play between closure/disclosure. Second, Nancy's adoration is the activity of being-betrothed to something outside-here, an extraordinary in the ordinary and everyday. And third, Nancy's view seems to support the Heideggerian notion that the uncanny and mysterious is manifested in and through the finite, but in a particular way distinct from other finite experiences.

As briefly mentioned, in his lectures on Parmenides in the winter term of 1942/1943 Heidegger noted how he preferred "disclosure" (*entbergen*) over unconcealment, and it is on this conception that Nancy's disenclosure fundamentally gets developed. The French *déclosion* relates closely to *déclore*, which refers to the tearing down of walls, the cutting down of hedges or bushes that encastle one's garden or yard. Disenclosure therefore marks the opening-up of reason for which both Christianity and the arts hold a unique potential.[14] Christendom (which is distinct from Christianity) imbues and permeates the whole of Western thought, and provides a means through which the various laminates of reason and human experience might be exfoliated. "The whole of our thought" says Nancy "is through and through Christian," and thus, to deconstruct Christianity, is to deconstruct our thinking, which, in a gesture of adoration, leads one toward the excessive sense of the world. To adore is to turn, within the world, to what it opens-up-onto. It is in this opening-up of Christianity's "black box" that the altering potential of reason can become disenclosed. That is, after Christianity's deconstruction, one finds an inconspicuous remainder in the aftermath or margins of this deconstruction: "The dis-enclosure of reason is the effect, or rather the remainder, of deconstructed Christianity, of religion's having withdrawn from itself, pushed off from its observances and beliefs."[15] A true Christianity that follows in the way of Jesus is one continuously deconstructed. Beyond its dogmatic forms of religion, Christianity always retains a challenge to the quietly operating intricacies of reason, which dogmatic religion threatens to keep contained.

These observations indeed are close to Heidegger's focus, in the Parmenides Seminars, on the meaning, sense, and differences between *aletheia* (unconcealedness) and *lethe* (concealedness) in Greek thought and culture. Truth as "disclosure" (*entbergen*) for Heidegger "comes closer to the essence of the Greek *aletheia*" than "unconcealedness" (*Unverborgenheit*) because it is a matter of an existential and active releasement.[16] The ways something hides or is concealed directly corresponds to the disclosure of that which is, or previously was, enclosed, and still retains characteristics of this prior status. Disclosure is the more active opening up that is a simultaneous closure. For example, a picture frame reveals precisely in its closure by limiting the field of experience. There are various forms in which the hidden might conceal (e.g., sheltering, withdrawing, mystifying), yet the overall forms of relation between *lethe* and *aletheia* are beyond the general modes of experience on which we often rely.[17] Another reason for the preference of disclosure over unconcealedness is that the aforementioned forms of relation should not be confused with the common interpretation of a thing's being-concealed as the merely not-yet-known in the horizon of scientific unconcealment. There indeed are different types or modalities according to which concealment (*lethe*) might conceal, and Heidegger believes that his notion of disclosure can depict this movement more accurately.

Further, truth is the manifestation of truth *as* disclosure. Heidegger's disclosure is inherent to the essence of Dasein, as the opening up, not simply of truth, but also that truth is the very nature as this act of disclosure, which in and of itself, is brought to appearance. That is, even disclosure is laminated with varying levels of that which can be unconcealed. This indeed amounts, as Heidegger notes, to a tautology. One aspect of disclosure that is of particular interest in juxtaposing Heidegger and Nancy is that the truth of the uncanny, which is always already concealed in the ordinary, normal, and everyday is the very nature of the "divine for the Greeks."[18] This concept of the divine as the uncanny in the common entails that it is the maker of this differentiation, and operates as the leverage between the mysteries of the uncanny, and the ordinary nature of the common. Truth "truths" by this inconspicuous differentiation. The most ordinary and common harbors perhaps the greatest potential for the uncanny, for it is the most lived with and dwelled-in. The discovery, for example, that my mother is an axe-murderer would furnish a high degree of the feeling of uncanniness, estrangement, or not-being-at-home by calling into question the very distinction of the ordinary or extraordinary, on which my entire belief structure and worldview generally hinges.

The most uncanny experiences are those that provide a glimpse of the true potential of what we take for granted.[19] Indeed, for Heidegger, the uncanny is only insofar as it is birthed out of the ordinary, and therefore marked most essentially by its inconspicuousness, which "grazes beings like the shadow of a cloud silently passing."[20] The "uncanny is the simple … the inconspicuous" and gives itself only insofar as it has quietly operated as-overlooked, in which the uncanny divine can appear and reappear. A strikingly similar kind of divinity is referred to by Nancy as early as 1987 in *Des lieux divins*, "The god may very well be made manifest selfsame with the heavens, or with the sea, or with the skin of man or the animal's gaze; it may be that he is manifest selfsame with everything that is open and offered and in which he has dispatched himself."[21]

The sacred divine to which Heidegger turned in his more numinous, poetic phase in the description of the fourfold appears to be taken-up by Nancy in his description of an uncanny making manifest of the divine in the ordinary things of nature. It is not so much the naturalness of these things that makes them proper vehicles for the uncanny, but more specifically, their propensity, as natural and ordinary, for being overlooked. Thus, the divine finds place in what most easily is made-to-ordinary, and this divine revelation is simultaneously a closing-over through disguising. This all comes to play in the kind of inconspicuousness to which Nancy more implicitly attends in his deconstruction of Christianity and adoration.

Although uninterested in developing any explicit "return of religion," Nancy demonstrates how the modern West has sought to negate and suppress its own most truly operative imaginaries and commitments, which are Christian "through and through." Overall, the deconstruction of our implicit Christianity can be a lever of disenclosure, opening, unfolding, or unifying the inside (the enclosed) with the outside (the disclosed).[22] In this sense of deconstruction, one relates with phenomena that cannot appear in any traditional sense, and must remain inconspicuous; those that slip somewhere between the yet-to-be deconstructed according to the multifaceted modalities of Christianity—the aforementioned cause of deconstruction—and those that will ever-remain-hidden.

Inconspicuousness characterizes the touch line or relation that is drawn between these two types of experiences with hiddenness.

This touch line has phenomenal content. "Touch" is described by Nancy as a momentary, blink-of-the-eye occurrence that by its nature cannot last, yet leaves the traces of a dashed dividing line (*dividere*) that unifies into a relation. This kind of touch characterizes disenclosure, which entails the productive interlocking of the present and the absent, ultimately leading to an "open world without myths and without idols."[23] It is in this world that adoration can occur, namely, of differentiation beyond idolization and any assurances whatsoever. As one experiences the truth that is disenclosure, one engages fundamentally with differentiation through adoration. Without assurance, and beyond good and evil, both disenclosure and adoration quietly operate in reason's margins as an unveiling that disfigures reason itself.[24] This is an interminable process prodded on by how one chases after the inexplicable in order, not necessarily to arrive at new knowledge, but to see reason's other challenging it. This opening-up and challenging of reason provides the occasion for the adoration of differentiation, which, not unlike Lyotard's *différends*, produces angst-ridden, aporetic, and irresolvable enigmas. To adore, then is to address for as long as possible these touch lines of relation inherent to the productivity of or in differentiation.[25]

Adoration as an Opening to the Outside-Here

This supplies some explanation for why adoration can be described as the active sustaining of being-enraptured or uniquely beholden to something extraordinary that integrates uniquely and colors distinctly everyday, ordinary life. Adoration is "a word addressed to what this word knows to be inaccessible (*sans accès*)" and absent.[26] This relation with the adored therefore is marked by a paradox—the absent is *addressed*, which requires some navigation or guiding sense. Thus, to address the inaccessible and absent is to be directed to a nonpresent opening. This entails the adorer's being "set straight" (*dirigere*) to the object of address by setting it apart. Given the lack of supernatural otherworldliness in Nancy's work, adoration is necessarily a means of addressing here the unpredictable manifestations of the uncanny, which precisely is in the flow of immanence. This points to an "outside here" with which one might relate by setting apart the act itself from other acts. Nancy draws the distinction between *adoratio* and *oratio* ("Adoratio: la parole adressée. Oratio: parole solennelle") to show the difference the "ad" makes between adoration and oration. An oration is a formal speech, while adoration is what *addresses* what is worthy with a speech unique only to the adored.[27]

This indeed again is close to Heidegger, who in his lectures on Parmenides consistently states and reiterates that the uncanny is only in the ordinary. One can only arrive at phenomenological seeing by addressing the unordinary goings-on that are always already at work. Nancy's adoration can be seen as the appropriate and appropriating response to such Heideggerian mystery. Heidegger claims that as foreign "the mystery thus becomes a 'residue' still remaining to be explained. But since technical explaining and explicability provide the criterion for what can claim to be real, the inexplicable residue left over becomes the superfluous."[28] Superfluousness is what gets overlooked or rejected for its dull quality, which creates ambivalence. It is the left overs of what is claimed to be legitimate via a technical or scientific procedure to get a grip (*Begriff*) on its reality. It is in this sense that the truly mysterious is rejected as insignificant and illegitimate because it provides no raw material for a technical kind of construction or seeing. One simply does not know what to do with it. As Schuwer and Rojcewicz render it in the English version of the *Parmenides Seminars*, *unscheinbar* is insignificant in that it sources the concealment unique to mystery to operate in the form of camouflage. And "therefore this inconspicuousness (*Unscheinbarkeit*) must explicitly protrude everywhere and must always be concerned with safeguarding its outward appearance."[29] The inconspicuous nature of mystery is that it can protrude anywhere as this superfluous, ambivalence-creating waste without being recognized and detected.

Since there is no warrant to interpret Nancy's adoration as committed to an entirely inconceivable and invisible entity, his acts of adoration must take place instead in nominal, marginal spaces of ordinary life. And since one never actually can reach the uncanny (Heidegger) or the mysterious content of one's adoration (Nancy) in its entirety due to its inconspicuous nature, the directedness of adoration is not an intentional effort but an extensional one. We adore by *extension* and stretching out (*tendue*) as opposed to attempting to calculate that to which we are directed. Instead of a phenomenological intentionality based on the modern myths of subjectivity, extension transcendentally reaches not toward the outside, but rather the dividing line established between the outside and the inside. To extend toward the infinite opening and the disenclosure of reason? This is adoration. It is the unschematizable address to, and hope for relating with, that which exceeds everything, even the very notion of incomprehensibility.

The Touch Line between Opposites

The question of the immanent opens onto the third way Nancy's work can be treated through Heidegger's "inconspicuous," namely in the nature of this uncanny world beyond, in the finite, which gives itself on the touch line between closure and disclosure. Adoration is not a means of addressing what would be conceived as the absurd in everyday life (such as flying spaghetti monsters), but instead takes place at the most basic point of transgression of phenomenal appearance—the infinite *in* the finite, for the beyond is within (*en-deçà*). Yet to reach this "in," which is not some "backworld" (*arrière-monde*'), one must turn away from the description of things in their ontological status, which smothers the various breaches in and within the finite, and one must turn toward the touch lines and boundaries of sense, and the potential *outside* of phenomenal experience *within* the world. This is because the world does not have parts or multiple dimensions but rather is simply "the exposition of what exists to the touch (*touche*) of sense, which opens within it the infinity of an 'outside.'"[30] Even the physical touch reminds us, as Merleau-Ponty once taught, that it is not concepts that rule our experience, but our affective involvement with things-as-sensed. The world is the space of touching, and is that which touches its own infinite and differentiating outside.

What these—somewhat sophistic—reflections ultimately call for is a radical reinterpretation of revelation and finitude which "would not exist if in the very act of naming it we did not allow it to transpire that we exist and that the world exists as an opening onto infinity, via infinity."[31] Were the finite not infinitely open to what is beyond it, then it would forfeit its plasticity, and its status as a temporally situated immanent; the raw material of which would remain in stasis—lifeless and flaccid. A most radical definition of the finite is that it characterizes what is *bound to change*, and the finite must have a lever for this differentiation, otherwise it becomes an infinite straight line, and therefore abandons its status as finite. Yet, these openings within the immanent occur only briefly, like flashes of lightning that are capable of altering the state of all that is given. Yet again, this does not point to an invisible back-world, but to a thoroughly excessive immanent, the constant newness, differentiation, and creation of which proves some operative power that is irreducible to what can be detected through our modern forms of conceptualization. Since, as Merleau-Ponty once noted, Heidegger's interests were always in what can be announced or given in and of this world, a description of the inconspicuous is of no exception, and cannot be inflected theologically toward an essential, supernatural laminate, which Nancy seeks to avoid entirely.

It no longer is enough to demand, as Wittgenstein did, that "the sense of the world must lie outside the world."[32] Instead, to access sense we are to attend to the touch line between the outside and inside. Adoration occurs when we can make some intelligible sense of our situated relation with this touch line. Here Nancy appears to offer a tonic fusion of Wittgenstein and Heidegger by going further than suggesting that all phenomena must have a finite manifestation, and that sense belongs on the outside of the total and finite. For Nancy, there is a not-so-easily detectable sense that pervades all things: while extending toward an outside, one still wakes up every morning and finds oneself "in the midst of the world." What one senses are "manifestation[s] of what is not manifest" in any straightforward sense, as an *outside here*.[33] Wittgenstein's "sense" along with Heidegger's "inconspicuousness" can be synthesized; and thus, Nancy offers a new understanding of revelation, namely, as disfiguration: "What 'revelation' introduces is ultimately a disfiguration. Revelation is not a doctrine. What is revealed is not concerned with content-based principles, articles of faith, and revelation does not unveil anything that is hidden: it reveals insofar as it addresses, and this address constitutes what is revealed."[34]

Thus, for Nancy the form of revelation is the estrangement of all that is or can be given, and this estrangement is a disfiguration bound to the personal address in the neutral zone between inside and outside. True experiences of revelation begin with the *unheimliche* form or means through which the content of *what* is revealed can lend to a release of control. Not to be confused with the discovery of new information or content, revelation operates as a form and formatting through a uniquely bivalent closure and disclosure of what is already here. One then relates with revelation via an extension toward that which has been differentiated or disfigured, and it is precisely the making strange or making uncanny that characterizes revelation. An experience of revelation takes place in the turning to address of adoration, in the posture of speaking to and about the disfiguring *le touché*, the touch line.

This bivalency of closure or disclosure is one reason Nancy's adoration is applicable to *phenomenality*, which includes the synthesis of the sets of acts of phenomenology with the various potential intelligibilities and meanings a thing can hold. Although adoring is an act according to which the suspension and setting apart of a phenomenological epoché is not prohibited from supporting, its action presumes a certain intelligibility of a *phenomenon*—a thing to be adored that is announced uniquely as shrouded. Perhaps most important about Nancy's version of adoration is that it calls for a rigorous engagement with finitude. Therefore, even as a radical atheist, he can suggest that Socrates and Christ alike present how there is "another life in the midst of this one" and that "the truth of this world [operates] as the outside that presents itself right here, an outside that is 'divine.'"[35]

This position is about more than a claim to have discovered "transcendence in immanence," and ultimately challenges and disfigures the immanent here itself and any strong overemphasis on its infinitude. Others associated with the theological turn generally are critiqued for attempting to conceive forms of transcendence as features of phenomenality, and this led to the question Janicaud posed 25 years ago: must one choose between the "unconditional affirmation of transcendence and the patient interrogation of the visible"?[36] Janicaud's answer was an emphatic yes, for the policing of the "rupture with immanent phenomenality" is necessary in order to be as true as possible to Husserl's originally held "principle of principles," which sought to delineate its method to accept only for phenomenological investigation and suspension the immanent givenness of phenomena that appear in this world, and along an unsuspecting horizon of experience. For Janicaud, a methodological atheism is not only recommended for phenomenological thinking. It is entirely necessary. Yet what of an atheism that is not methodological, and one that challenges the presupposed closures of what is in-and-of-the-world in a somewhat nonneutral way? This seems to be closer to Nancy's version of atheism.

Inconspicuous Adoration

Nancy conceives the intentional horizon of visibility as full of openings (*ouverture*) onto what does not appear easily, for there are always irreconcilable yet productive blind spots of finite life. The emphasis on the disfiguring work of differentiation is not to make compatible the impulses of theology and phenomenology, but to estrange the appeared from appearing, ultimately threatening the disciplinary optimisms of both disciplines, which often seek to achieve ever-greater forms of clarity and distinction of their subject matters. Although it may be enjoyed, clarity is never adored. Differentiation, however, is worthy of adoration because it is the form that productively obscures finite reality and any supposed quarantining of the appearing from the margins of appearance. For him, the elsewhere is within.[37] This work of differentiation is the closest Nancy gets to divinity, for as "neither a known being *nor* an unknown one," God is "the 'void that is opening up.'"[38] This void operates at the level of absence and withdrawal in consciousness, as the question of God is "no longer one of being or appearing" but rather of "passing."[39] An experience of this passing concerns something's being withdrawn-from-presence, and thus, any presentation of this God will present simultaneously this God's withdrawal. God is an abyssal differentiation that turns things out, helping us set them apart.

Yet what characterizes Nancy's position as in this case unique is precisely what puts it under threat of an inherent ambiguity in need of attention. The seeming distrust of forms of knowledge that could confront, challenge, and extend faith is underpinned by adoration's directed *extension* toward divine *differencing*, the generality of which could amount to a dangerous potential. As Baudrillard knew, the playful celebration of diversity in and of itself can become nightmarish in a spectacle-dominated world. And even worse, when difference is grafted onto the infinite, this results in a production of images that amounts to a simulacra-saturated hyperreal that even presents itself as more real than finite reality. The hyperreal infinitely simulates in an order of totality as a "deterrence machine" that constantly reinvents, produces, and circulates diversions. Simulation generates modes of a real without origin and the "sovereign difference" between one thing and another gets replaced by pure "difference."[40] This pure difference results in the simulacrum of divinity itself and its subsequent multiplication and dispersion in the form of a complex machinery of idols.

Plato referred to "simulacra" that repeat themselves through differentiation, with no original version copied; Lefebvre referred to a rerouting of difference within the obsession with "neo;" and Jameson pointed to an appetite for the consumption of images or "pseudo-events."[41] How can Nancy's emphasis on pure differentiation resist the concern that simulation has become the master of diversity? Has Nancy succumbed to such a celebration that has eclipsed the important distinction between what Malabou recently described as "flexibility" and "plasticity," the former of which being but a political tool weilded for fashioning conformity within a totality?

One way to circumvent these concerns of the generality of diversity is to consider it in more specific terms. What *kind* of difference can hold back the simulation of infinite production, diversion, and the "substitute Images of the divine" Adorno warned us about? What sort of diversity is worthy of adoration? One answer: Only a differentiation that is an ever-prescient threat to idolization. Since idolization gains its momentum from spectacularity, then this divine differentiation must counteract such spectacularity by being woven into the tapestry of marginal, everyday life. Only then can it escape domestication and control of nightmarish reproduction. This calls for reflection on an inconspicuous adoration, which can be thought in terms of "the adored" and the adorative act.

First, adoration is distinguished by attention and address. It attends to what stands out, and it addresses or speaks formally *to* the adored. An active setting-apart takes place in participation with the adored, who obfuscates and differentiates the ordinary. Since adoration is aimed at and is addressed to what differs in its presentation, and since the dominant mode of presentation today often is beholden to a nightmarish and spectacular diversity, the adored presents its out-of-placedness in a marginal and not-so-spectacular way. It differentiates insofar as it does not strut its glory and uniqueness, but instead expresses a humble omnipotence that is always different, counter-to-expectation, and unlike any nightmarish difference, does not encourage passivity. This ability to ever-be-different is what marks the power of the holy, and what sustains its worth of adoration.

This of course runs contrary to how holiness typically is understood. As noted by Nancy, the life of Christ is unique insofar as it depicts someone who remained constantly aware of an outside-here. It generally is presumed that the holy presents its spectacularity in glorious light and distinction as a purely out there. Yet, as the concrete lived experience of Christ represents, there is an entirely different or divine form of integration and incarnation that in most cases runs counter to spectacularity. Christ "the visible image (εἰκὼν) of the invisible (ἀοράτου) God" (Colossians 1:15; 2 Corinthians 4:4) entered the world in a marginal barn among animals and dirt. Despite multiple manhunts, Christ eluded religious authorities by blending in with his surroundings. Christ befriended the overlooked and rejected. Christ worked as a marginal carpenter. If these traits are not just happenstancual but indeed are depictive of divinity, then the holy iconicity of God and the means by which this God is adored should also be rethought. This holiness of the adored is not marked purely by a content or *what* that is different, but a differentiation of the different as the pinnacle formation or line between the present and absent. The holiness of the adored is the-setting-apart, precisely of the most banal "here" and lived with.

As for an inconspicuous adoration, it does not conceive or grasp the adored, but extends toward it through an address. As the doxology expresses, adoration typically is understood as the giving of glory to, and the right reflection of the source of illumination. Yet, an inconspicuous adoration turns to the acts of the adored, which differentiate and reinvent the realities it inhabits. Since adoration in general gains its force of meaning from separation, it is an act of attending to what does not usually grab attention. Inconspicuous adoration, like the adored, follows in the subversion of the relation between the ordinary and the extraordinary.

Inconspicuous adoration adores by turning to what generally is rejected as ordinary because it is precisely not what is thought to be extraordinary that is truly worthy of adoration. One adores, not what is inconceivable, but what actively resists pure conception while still providing content for the adorative act to be sustained. The adored is able to keep the tension between the familiar and the distant in place, and in the adorative act one turns to what drives this point of distinction and separation. In this sense, inconspicuous adoration cocreates the drawing of lines of separation, and to borrow from Nancy, addresses the movement of a formation through extension. It is not merely a God of content or attributes to which one remains beholden but also and perhaps more so, a *God of formation*. What do we adore when we adore the inconspicuous God?—the form itself, which limits, not through what Heidegger called in his essay on technology a "destining" or "determining" enframement, but rather through a disenclosing frame or form that creates a touch line that encourages the adorer to reach whatever it opens up. Only such a great differentiator that operates the levers of closure and disenclosure is worthy of adoration.

As an act, this adoration marks a return to what is rejected, and seeks out, by merit of its rejection, its unique forms of presentation that elude totalizing comprehension. This adoration involves tarrying with the marginal long enough to experience the neutral zone or touch line that divides what one deems ordinary (familiar) from what is taken as extraordinary (distant). In this act, one adores that which or who stands out by not-standing-out-as-usual. The disfiguring work that the inconspicuous God enacts is in the adorer's identification with the-of-little-value and rejected, leaving the adorer caught happily somewhere between insignificance and infinite differentiation. And thus, to Augustine's (reformatted) question "what do I adore when I adore my God?" it is possible to proffer a small proviso: it is not difference-as-content that is adored, but rather the form responsible for creating it; the differentiation that overcomes the spectacles underwriting the many hegemonic dichotomies to which we resort when attempting to conceive the holy. Adore this Inconspicuous God by locating something worthy of praise in what is rejected as ordinary. It now becomes a matter of whether or not it is possible for these experiences of adoration to furnish their own evidence, which inherently is intersocial and proclamatory.

Notes

1. Ignaas Devisch, Laurens ten Kate, Aukje van Rooden, and Alena Alexandrova, *Retreating Religion: Deconstructing Christianity with Jean-Luc Nancy* (New York: Fordham University Press, 2012), 34.

2. In reference to his own work, Nancy asserts that "this is the end of negative theology as well as the end of a phenomenology in general, albeit that of the inapparent." Jean-Luc Nancy, *The Creation of the World, or Globalization*, trans. François Raffoul and David Pettigrew (Albany, NY: State University of New York Press, 2007). Jean-Luc Nancy, *La creation du monde ou la mondialisation* (Paris: Galilée, 2002), 72, 98.

3. Devisch, ten Kate, van Rooden, and Alexandrova, *Retreating Religion*, 34.

4. Ibid., 34–35. As Laurens ten Kate proposes, "Contrary to the 'theological turn in phenomenology,' which tries to give God a place in the phenomenal world, reactivating his phenomenal status as the 'nonapparent,' Nancy does not adopt a restorative approach with regard to the problem of God's presence/absence." Laurens ten Kate, "God Passing by: Presence and Absence in Monotheism and Atheism," in *Retreating Religion: Deconstructing Christianity with Jean-Luc Nancy*, ed. Ignaas Devisch, Laurens ten Kate, Aukje van Rooden, and Alena Alexandrova (New York: Fordham University Press, 2012), 140.

5. Ibid., 34.

6. Dominique Janicaud, *Phenomenology and the "Theological Turn": The French Debate* (New York: Fordham University Press, 2000), 31.

7. Martin Heidegger, "Seminar in Zähringen 1973" in *Four Seminars*, trans. Andrew Mitchell and François Raffoul (Bloomington: Indiana University Press, 2003), 80–81. For Heidegger realizes that what he is referencing is "clearly a tautology. We are here in the domain of the inapparent: presencing itself presences. The name for what is addressed in this state of affairs is: *TO EON*, which is neither beings, nor simply being, but … presencing: presencing itself."

8. Ibid., 79. In "The Origin of the Work of Art" Heidegger once again refers to Parmenides's "that it is": "The 'that it is' of createness, emerges into view most purely from the work. To be sure, 'that' it is made is a property also of equipment that is available and in use. But this 'that' does not become prominent in the equipment; it disappears in usefulness. The more handy a piece of equipment is, the more inconspicuous it remains that, for example, such a hammer is and the more exclusively does the equipment keep itself in its equipmentality." Martin Heidegger, *Poetry, Language, Thought*, trans. Albert Hofstadter (New York: Harper & Row, 1971), 63.

9. Martin Heidegger, GA 54, *Parmenides*, trans. André Schuwer and Richard Rojcewicz (Bloomington: Indiana University Press, 1992), 63.

10. For Steinbock, "Phenomenology has shown . . . that what is primary is the relation itself." Anthony Steinbock, *Phenomenology and Mysticism* (Bloomington: Indiana University Press, 2011), 225.

11. Jean-Luc Nancy, *The Pleasure in Drawing*, trans. Philip Armstrong (New York: Fordham University Press, 2013), 93.

12. Yet, "being sensitive to it is not necessarily to be a 'connoisseur' (a word that usually belongs to the artistic scene but in effect to love, therefore to share this movement of form that desires itself, that desires its sense." Ibid., 57.

13. For Heidegger, "Zuhandenheit ist die ontologisch-kategoriale Bestimmung von Seindem, wie es 'an sich' ist." Martin Heidegger, *Sein und Zeit* (Tübingen: M. Niemeyer, 1967), 71. For an earlier treatment of this concept in *Sein und Zeit*, see 15–16.

14. Nancy's "The Deconstruction of Christianity" ("La déconstruction du christianisme") was first published in 1998 in the French review *Les Etudes philosophiques*. For Nancy "*toute* notre pensée est de part en part chrétienne. De part en part et toute, c'est-à-dire nous tous, nous tous jusqu'au bout." Jean-Luc Nancy, "La Déconstruction du Christianisme," *Etudes Philosophiques* 4 (1998): 503–19.

15. Jean-Luc Nancy, *Adoration: The Deconstruction of Christianity II* (New York: Fordham University Press, 2012), 43. This text was originally published as *L'Adoration*: *Déconstruction du Christianisme* 2 (Paris: Editions Galilée, 2010).

16. Heidegger, *Parmenides*, 12, cf. 64. When it comes to matters of unconcealment, "we are here only broaching a realm whose fullness of essence we hardly surmise and certainly do not fathom, for we are outside the mode of experience proper to it."

17. Ibid., 14. There are different types of closure and unconcealedness. Unconcealedness "can mean concealedness is taken away, cancelled, evicted, or banned, where taking away, cancelling evicting, and banning are essentially distinct." Heidegger further clarifies these on 61–63. As for those differing modes of concealment (which are not according to the will of man, but Being) they include: concealing (displacing, setting aside), going away or being absent, sheltering and saving the concealed for what it is, preserving, destroying, distorting, withdrawing, mystifying (leaving within a known treasure "a residue still remaining to be explained"), and finally a reference to what he calls an "ambush" sort of mystery.

18. Ibid., X. cf. 104: "That which within the ordinary comes to presence by his own look is man. Therefore, the sight of the god must gather itself within the ordinary."

19. In fact: "as soon as we consider the simple unavoidable essential domains, which are for a historiographer naturally of no consequence, since they are inconspicuous and noiseless, then, but only then, do we see that our usual basic ideas, i.e., Roman, Christian, modern ones, miserably fail to grasp the primordial essence of ancient Greece." Ibid., 43.

20. For Heidegger, "The uncanny is also not what has never yet been present; it is what comes into presence always already and in advance prior to all 'uncanniness.' The uncanny, as the being that shines into everything ordinary, i.e., into beings, and that in its shining often grazes beings like the shadow of a cloud silently passing, has nothing in common with the monstrous or the alarming. The uncanny is the simple, the insignificant, ungraspable by the fangs of the will, withdrawing itself from all artifices of calculation, because it surpasses all planning." Indeed "the astounding for the Greeks is the simple, the insignificant. Being itself. The astounding, visible in the astonishing, is the uncanny." Ibid., 101.

21. Jean-Luc Nancy, "Of Divine Place," in *The Inoperative Community*, trans. Peter Connor, Lisa Garbus, M. Holland, and S. Sawhney (Minneapolis, MN: University of Minnesota Press, 1991), 123.

22. While in the first volume of the deconstruction of Christianity Nancy suggests that there are "dangers that religion invariably poses to thought, to law, to freedom and to human dignity," in the second text he claims that Christianity, in its self-deconstruction over the centuries, is a matter of interest to us as a causal basis of democracy, freedom, social and political goods. Jean-Luc Nancy, *Disenclosure: The Deconstruction of Christianity I* (New York: Fordham University Press, 2008), 2. See also Nancy, *Adoration*, 38.

23. For Nancy, such "an open world is a world without myths and without idols, a world without religion if we understand by this word the observance of behaviors and representations that respond to a claim for sense as a claim for assurance, destination, accomplishment." Nancy, *Adoration*, 38.

24. To reiterate, as the editors of the recent *Retreating Religion* understand, according to Nancy "the nonapparent . . . can never end in a reconciliation, however subtle its form, with phenomena." Devisch, ten Kate, van Rooden, and Alexandrova, *Retreating Religion*, 34.

25. Nancy, *Disenclosure*, 1. Then in *Adoration*, Nancy poses religion as that which persistently threatens the "disenclosure" of reason (and perhaps phenomenology, also), which can open onto a new form of "adoration."

26. Nancy, *Adoration*, 2.

27. "Adoratio: la parole adressée. Oratio: parole solennelle, parole avant tout tenue, tension de la voix, de la bouche et de tout le corps parlant. Parole dont le contenu est inséparable voire indiscernable de l'adresse. Langage soutenu qui se distingue de sermo, langage ordinaire." Nancy, *L'Adoration*, 28–29.

28. Heidegger, *Parmenides*, 63.

29. Heidegger continues "In this way the mysterious is only what is left over, what is not yet accounted for and incorporated within the circuit of explicative procedures." Indeed "The secret in the mystery is a kind of concealment, characterized by its insignificance, in virtue of which the mystery is an open one." There is indeed "another kind of concealment within the mysterious is displayed by the clandestine, under the cover of which, e.g., a conspiracy simmers. There the concealment is the character of an extended yet at the same time tightly knit ambush, lying in wait for the moment of the sudden outburst. The inconspicuous is here too. But now it takes the form of camouflage and deception. Therefore, this inconspicuousness must explicitly protrude everywhere and must always be concerned with safeguarding its outward appearance." Ibid., 63.

30. Nancy, *Adoration*, 3, 12, 27.

31. Ibid., 3.

32. For Wittgenstein "The sense of the world must lie outside the world. In the world, everything is as it is and happens as it does happen. *In* it there is no value—and if there were, it would be of no value. If there is a value which is of value, it must lie outside all happening and being-so. For all happening and being-so is accidental. What makes it nonaccidental cannot lie *in* the world, for otherwise this would again be accidental. It must lie outside the world." Ludwig Wittgenstein, *Tractatus Logico-Philosophicus* (London: Kegan Paul, 1922), § 6.41.

33. Nancy, *Adoration*, 52. The respective meanings of Christ and Socrates both refer to "another life in the midst of this one" and their respective deaths open "the truth of this world as the outside that presents itself right here, an outside that is 'divine' if you like." Ibid., 29.

34. Ibid., 41.

35. Ibid., 29.

36. Janicaud, *Phenomenology and the "Theological Turn,"* 26.

37. Nancy is against any culture of the beyond: "The 'elsewhere' is not, however, a beyond; it is not a transcendence, in the sense understood by theologies, nor is it a simple immanence, in the sense understood by those theologies that have been inverted into atheism. This elsewhere is in us ... [and] ... it is being itself as it proves to be, once detached from its ontological bindings." Nancy, *Adoration*, 102.

38. Jean-Luc Nancy, *God, Justice, Love, Beauty: Four Little Dialogues* (New York: Fordham University Press, 2011), 29. See also Jean-Luc Nancy, *Noli Me Tangere: On the Raising of the Body* (New York: Fordham University Press, 2008).

39. Nancy, *Disenclosure*, 111, 165.

40. Jean Baudrillard, *Simulacra and Simulation* (Ann Arbor, MI: University of Michigan Press, 1994), 2, 13.

41. Fredric Jameson, *Postmodernism, or, the Cultural Logic of Late Capitalism* (London: Verso, 2008), 17.

6 Inconspicuous Evidence: Janicaud, Religious Experience, and a Methodological Atheism

Following Husserl's conception of phenomenology as *Erste Philosophie* (first philosophy), could there be a "first theology," and would phenomenology be the approach that makes up its basic method, thereby altering how its evidence is understood? Although an answer in the affirmative would entail a host of problems, phenomenology is developed as a descriptive enterprise of the givenness or presentation of phenomena that ontologically and chronologically are constituted prior to any evidential character of epistemological justification. An essential goal of phenomenology is a presuppositionlessness that does not limit an accurate description of what appears. Although in many cases the content of an appearance is not limited to what is within reach of those to whom that which appears presents itself, it seems undeniable that explicit and inadvertent limitations often are placed on phenomena. Some phenomena are deemed never to appear; others are quarantined to the realm of meaninglessness by merit of not providing sufficient connectivity of signs that suture the individual to the experience; and still others simply are overlooked due to their not attracting attention because they do not follow the order of a glamorous clarity.

This raises the related concern of warrant, and the means by which one can arrive at it and base one's life on it, especially in the case of certain exceptional limit phenomena. As the German *Schein* refers, warrant can be understood as that which appears to self-justify itself. The adjective inconspicuous or *unscheinbar* (traceable to the fifteenth century) is entirely dependent on this root *Schein*, which variously is referred to today as a warrant, license, or ticket. *Der Fahrschein* is a travel pass that permits one by law to ride the train; *Den Anschein* is a "guise" that diverts attention to counterfeit warrants; and a *Parkschein* is the ticket obtained to enter a garage. Broadly understood, *Schein* points to a thing's status as clearly candor, trustworthy, and capable of being attained and understood with little trouble as evidential. What is evidential entails an intersocial and communal defense predicated on how others interpret a specific situation. This is perhaps one reason why in a 1992 interview Levinas famously referred to how the science of relation with the other, an "original ethical event would also be first theology."[1]

While at first glance it seems possible to conceive it as such, *unscheinbar* is not the simple inversion or negation of warrant. When the root *Schein* is paired with *bar*, *scheinbar* refers not to that which is obvious, but to what *seems* or *appears* to be the case. It is not actuality to which it points, but rather potentiality. *Schein* refers to warrant, what is *scheinbar* seems in potentiality, and in this case, what is *unscheinbar* must be understood in its ability to obscure even the *potentia* of *potential* from within what is actual. It functions with the positive ability to elude any direct conjecture concerning its status.

This notion can be applied in the context of the content of a phenomenology of religious experience, which must be accounted for in ways that correspond to the form of their presentation, and that thereby challenge the traditional conceptions of evidence. Yet as a phenomenology, this is not quite so simple, as it initiates a double-bind: What is given phenomenological description must be presuppositionless and not import what cannot be valid to the senses, yet what is religious should abandon the clarity creating, justificatory apparatus that might burden any acts of faith. On the one hand, there is the danger of phenomenology sliding into epistemology and the de facto abandonment of the primacy of phenomenological description as first philosophy; and on the other, there is an approach that appears to shun community instituting power, and in theory allows any and all phenomena warrant to appear to a subject without any explanation or defense. Does phenomenology's having the status as a method already limit what it is capable of achieving for thought and experience, and would a presupposition about God (or any other presupposition), hinder us from having what Merleau-Ponty once called a horizon "unsuspected" by thought? Further, does use of the word "evidence" in the context of religious experience already bog it down with demands of its being defended; demands that the experiencer likely cannot even meet in the first place?

In some ways, this double-insistence of a phenomenology of religious experience began to be worked out uniquely by Dominque Janicaud, who, as mentioned in the introduction to the present study, pejoratively named *Le tournant théologique de la phénomenénologie Français* in 1991. His critiques did not concern these thinker's theological conclusions per se, but rather their basic approach to how they attained warrant to employ phenomenology to draw them. Reliant on Husserl, Janicaud casts phenomenology as able to address only what might appear within our subjective world of experience (*Erfahrungswelt*) as putatively obvious (*selbstverständlich*) and immediately given. As stated by Husserl, the generative father of phenomenology, the golden rule is to resist claiming as true anything that we "cannot make essentially transparent to ourselves by reference to consciousness and on purely immanental lines."[2] The immanent, "really real" is the place, means, and laminate according to which we engage the reductions of things, irrespective of the content that might appear. This world, and not any other, is the meaning-giving theatre that sets the stage for how claims are made, and how those claims in turn stake their claim on us.

What appears must do so unsuspectingly. Phenomenology seeks the description of phenomena independent from assessment according to the axiomatic content and justifiability of such phenomena. The approach was controversially and enigmatically accorded by Husserl in § 58 of *Ideen* to be "methodologically atheistic" for the necessity of its having a horizon of "pure consciousness" that infinitely remains open to whatever might appear.[3] Under Janicaud's restricted interpretation, this presuppositionlessness must be total and uncompromising. Therefore, any attempt to employ the method of phenomenology in regard to theology runs the risk of subverting the approach to the presuppositions of an invisible and metaphysical laminate. In fact, any reference to the invisible, at least according to Merleau-Ponty, must be to an invisible "of this world," and this rule is in place to safeguard us from both ontotheology and delusional hallucination.[4]

Throughout Janicaud's work his interest was in developing a phenomenological minimalism that sought to protect the method from any delusional transcendence that "in its various guises and at its various levels" persistently sought to infiltrate immanent life. The transcendence of God and any invisible hinterworld "must remain excluded from the new field of study we have to create, insofar as this field must be a field of pure consciousness."[5] The phenomenologist must not abandon Husserl's enterprise of constitution, not succumb to seeking out the most "originary," and not inadvertently return to an idealist, *metaphysica specialis*. This does not mean that theology cannot arrive at its own conclusions in a relevant and unique way. In fact, since its inception phenomenology has demonstrated a sustained interest in religion, for example in the work of Scheler, van der Leeuw, Stein, S. Frank, Hering, or Duméry. Yet, it does mean that phenomenology, a unique method crafted for attending only to "appearing and its manifestations" cannot be enacted when "the game is fixed" by presupposing theology's supernaturalisms.[6] Janicaud especially was suspicious of the work of the recent phenomenological theologians because he thought they ignored the distinctions between phenomenology and religion all together, reinstalling theology as the queen of the sciences, and even subjecting the method to theological bases. It is clear that for Janicaud, theology cannot be first philosophy.

Indeed, the spirit of Husserl's method in fact was intended to develop some means of sorting out what delimits wonder, and in order to experience the ontological realities of the world. Yet when brought into the context of religious phenomena, this spirit gets pushed to its limit, for Husserl also initially names phenomenology "first philosophy," which entails that it is a method that is fundamentally generative to all methods. It is a paradoxical method in the sense that it plays by certain rules, but in a way that epistemology does not control and oversee its interests, activities, and conclusions. This leads to a problem that would at best dampen and at worst hamper any phenomenology of religious experience: what are the religious concepts that one might prelaminate on experiences, and what are those that must be precluded from the outset? Is it a matter of minimalistic purity that protects the unity of the phenomenological method, and if so, is not purity already a concept?

The aims of the remainder of this chapter are threefold. The first aim is to address some of the inherent problems of a phenomenology of religious experience through Janicaud's references to Heidegger's approach to the inconspicuous. The second aim is to introduce these problems into the broader philosophical discussion regarding the topic of religious experience in phenomenology of religion. And after locating a red thread that helps address Janicaud's concerns, a third aim is to put forward a proposal as to what evidence could look like when it comes to a phenomenology of religious experiences. Since previous chapters have developed the notion that experiences of revelation are more often than not integrated in everyday life, it is here taken for granted that religious experiences, broadly understood, operate likewise. This does not bar the types of experiences that are miraculous or spectacularly supernatural, yet it does accept that the general infrequency (not to mention uncontrollability) of these events calls for a description of other kinds of religious experiences in their everyday element and function. This type of religious experience covers the range of finesse and subtlety the Absolute plays in everyday life, operating in a way that is more difficult to name and detect due to the synthetic unity between integration and marginality. This paradox—that the power of divinity is integrated in the marginal—is a fundamental mystery underlining religious experience.

Phenomenological Theology and Janicaud

Despite the many and varied responses to, and criticisms of Janicaud's particular claims over the years, he was wise to recognize that the work associated with the theological turn hinges on Heidegger's approach to the inconspicuous. This topic:

> places us at the crux of the matter where everything is decided: at the point of rupture between a positive phenomenological project and the displacement of its "possibility" toward the originary [*originaire*]. What troubles some can gratify others. If the "phenomenology of the unapparent" finally makes all rule-based presentation of the phenomena vacillate in favor of a hearkening to a world whorled with silence, here—against all expectations—is a line extended toward the originary, the nonvisible, the reserved. Ready to renounce a thematic phenomenology, the candidates to the theological heritage will content themselves with a phenomenology of points and dots.... If the "phenomenology of the unapparent" is to be interpreted not as a regression, but as full of promise, then the most audacious soundings stand permitted.[7]

"Unapparent," which here is used to translate *unscheinbar* or inconspicuous, is named the ultimate "sick root" of this particular phenomenological movement, providing these thinkers a counterfeit warrant to seek limit phenomena on the unstable border between philosophy and theology. For Janicaud, it is not so controversial that Heidegger called into question Husserl's approach to the intentionality of consciousness for its solipsistic constitution of phenomena. It is not problematic that Heidegger's turn to the arrival, sending, or announcing of phenomenal intelligibility is brought back to the self-presentation of the phenomena themselves (and not to the solipsistic endeavor of a method).[8]

Yet, Janicaud's overwhelming concern was in regard to these inconspicuous phenomena because they were invisible, ultimately disturbing our experience of time consciousness. Years after his well-known work on *The Theological Turn* became famous, Janicaud returned to the question of *das Unscheinbare* in 1997 in *Chronos* in the subsection "La tentative d'une 'phénoménologie de l'inapparent'" (the attempt of a "phenomenology of the inconspicuous"). There Janicaud claimed that this approach Heidegger began to develop in the Zähringen seminar sought to alter Husserl's understanding of time, suggesting in particular that "the formula 'phenomenology of the inconspicuous,' which is both paradoxical and enigmatic, seems to complicate the problem of the place of clarity."[9] (*la formule "phénoménologie de l'inapparent', a la fois paradoxale et sibylline, paraît compliquer le problem au lieu de l'éclaire.*). Clarity is what phenomenology seeks, and that "the inconspicuous, in the most essential sense, as that 'phenomenality par excellence,' while neither immediate nor ontic, also cannot be reduced to an eidetic intention."[10] This of course is consistent with Heidegger's turn from Husserl's intentionality-rich approach, yet as Janicaud warns, without intentionality, phenomenology remains passive and at the mercy of what "intuitively" appears, and that "the inconspicuous is that which does not appear at first glance and escapes even the most common experiences" (*l'inapparent comme ce qui échappe à l'expérience la plus courante, ce qui n'apparaît pas de soi-même au premier regard.*). Without intentionality, we all become passive, which makes us timeless. The inconspicuous acts as a "disturbance" within a phenomenology that must seek (at least to some degree) some form of immediacy. This is one reason why the inconspicuous "reserves the most problematic of 'phenomenalities' in the temporal dimension."[11]

Just one year after the publication of *Chronos*, Janicaud returned to the topic of the inconspicuous in *La phénoménologie eclatée* (*Phenomenology Wide Open*, 2005), which questioned the possible "openness" of phenomenology and its limits. Heidegger's phenomenology of the inconspicuous is referred to as a significant and new meditative form of thinking that hopes to develop a deep proximity between the what and the how. It seeks "to train sight and hearing to get as close as possible to phenomenality" as "*une phénoménologie de la proximité*."[12] An approach to proximity, in this case, concerns the presencing of presence and the closeness/farness approach/withdrawal interaction that always is taking place in the grand experience of Being. This is what Heidegger calls "tautological thinking," which concerns a return to "the first self-evident insight of phenomenal appearing: time temporalizes, saying speaks, the world worlds."[13] As shown in previous chapters, Heidegger's tautology seeks, through the middle voice, a deprivileging of both intention and intuition in order to furnish a means of using such dichotomies to take thought further. Tautological thinking is a patient working-out of dichotomies in order to arrive at how concepts that typically are polarized in fact share fundamental attributes.

This points to the dynamic nature of the world, and how we are to engage it. As noted by Janicaud, this approach unravels our relation with the world as a private theatre for entertainments and spectacles: "The 'phenomenologist of the inconspicuous' is no longer an ideal spectator of the truth of the world and of its essences: he learns to inhabit the world 'at arm's length' from the withdrawal of things."[14] It is only by tautological thinking that we arrive at a true understanding of what is proximal, and how distance creates nearness, and how the familiar must become distant in order for any interest to be taken in it. A phenomenology of the inconspicuous insists on bringing the absent and the present into carburation so that we do not succumb to those spectacular forms of presentation that tend to keep the many matrixes in operation.

However, under Janicaud's analysis Heidegger's approach eventually fails on one essential account: it seeks to allow for the possibility of bringing into appearance what does not appear, and how "appearance does not appear" in general. Janicaud's concerns are valid in regard to religious experience, yet are incorrectly formulated in regard to Heidegger's approach. One reason for this is due to how the French "inapparent" can be translated as "invisible," and how this does not at all account for what Heidegger refers to as *unscheinbar.* This is exemplified in Janicaud's seemingly all too quick reduction of a phenomenology of the inconspicuous to being at its core antithetical to phenomenology's approach to the things themselves: "It will no longer be a matter of suspecting a return to the 'theological' for the phenomenologies of the invisible (*Inapparent*) … but rather to ponder if phenomenology must not be radically atheistic in order to succeed in its project to attain, describe, and speak of the 'thing itself.'"[15] This incorrect translation of Heidegger's notion seems to be the root of Janicaud's misunderstanding, and it is confusion over which (in general) Heidegger expresses downright frustration: "The inconspicuous [is] by no means to be confused with 'the invisible' as the already mentioned philological translations incorrectly render it."[16] Heidegger's approach to the inconspicuous is, at its core not *l'inapparent* but rather *a peu en evidence* or *peu frappant* (lacking in evidence, and the ability to be spectacular). Janicaud did not recognize how a phenomenology of the inconspicuous gains its intelligibility through a characterization of how phenomena are composed of a positive synthetic unity between lacking evidence and not being spectacular.

Janicaud recognizes however, that this approach is an important one. He ultimately is led to ask: "Is this 'phenomenology of the inconspicuous' to be called an oxymoron, a supreme paradox, or a disconcerting impossibility?"[17] It is here that Janicaud points his finger squarely in the face of the problem of evidence in regard to any paradoxical religious experience. Pausing for a moment these phenomenological investigations, it is helpful to turn to the question of religious experience more broadly.

Religious Experience and Warrant

The nascent development of a philosophical approach to religious experience in many ways was initiated by William James, and subsequently critiqued over the last century in regard to the warrant or illegitimacy of such experiences on epistemological grounds. James did not seek to legitimize religious experiences, but rather to provide some meaningful intelligibility to their description, ultimately tying them to their "mystical elements." He considered religious experiences to maintain four interlocking aspects: ineffability in their negativity, offering noetic knowledge in their subsequent fashioning of thought, transiency in their temporal constitution, and passivity in their intuitive reception. James arrived at the conclusion that the warrant for such experiences is provided individually, and need not be presented to and verified by other subjects.

In fact religious experiences provide a fundament for life, which then feeds into philosophy. It is not the other way around. This is because of the subjective basis of "warrant." In a way that Lacoste surely would disapprove, James followed Schleiermacher in the qualification of the "religious" as based on the subjective and affective life of moods, which James often considered to offer deeper and mediatory sources of religious explanation. James makes this explicit, as exemplified in the following three observations: First, "Feeling is private and dumb, and unable to give an account of itself." Second, "I do believe that feeling is the deeper source of religion, and that philosophical and theological formulas are secondary products, like translations of a text into another tongue." And third, "Mystical truth exists for the individual."[18] This reliance on the matrix of affections/moods/emotions entails, for someone like Lacoste, that "the (sad) characteristic of 'religious experience' is that it is always my experience" lacking an intersocial integration.[19]

Despite the problematic nature of James's subjective basis of religious experience, he draws close attention to a deep problematic between how religious experience and—what for now could be called—"philosophical experience" provide differing conceptions of *experience* itself. What is the basis of these differing understandings of experience? James makes a subtle, and often overlooked observation. Religious experience is paradoxical and shrouds its warrant enigmatically:

> its results are mysteries and enigmas, declines to justify them rationally, and on occasion is willing that they should even pass for paradoxical and absurd. Philosophy takes just the opposite attitude. Her aspiration is to reclaim from mystery and paradox whatever territory she touches. To find an escape from obscure and wayward personal persuasion to truth objectively valid from all thinking men has ever been the intellect's most cherished ideal. To redeem religion from unwholesome privacy, and to give public status and universal right of way to its deliverances, has been reason's task.[20]

James's provision of a paradoxical, personalist, testimony-based warrant for religious experiences indeed did not include an explicitly viable means through which other persons are to accept them as legitimately authoritative and putatively nondelusional. Yet his feeling-centric, "cosmic or mystic consciousness" was described as sutured to "persevering exercises" or spiritual "disciplines" (like those of Saint Ignatius) that can "detach [one] from outer sensations."[21] As James knew, such exercises range from reclusion from the world, to immersion in it, yet all of them produce within the exercisers some peculiar characteristics. Like St. Teresa, who held that religious experiences could be "proven" as trustworthy through the checks and balances of scripture and a life-well-lived, James sought warrant for religion whereby one could at least self-justify these occurrences in life. Yet it seems this was the closest James could get in describing these experiences in their subjective, mystical, and indeed invisible element.

As mentioned in chapter one, for many philosophers today, paradoxes usually are understood as only eloquently stated, yet indefensible contradictions. In unambiguous terms, and as James's view supports, philosophy wields the tools of logic in overcoming contradictions. Since a paradox is the unity of seemingly contradictory opposites, it also becomes a target of philosophical dissolution. More continentally oriented philosophers, of course, often find solace in this aspect of what Kierkegaard determined to be central to thought itself, yet these thinkers also have the tendency to justify the jettisoning of religion from the social sphere by merit of the psychological or cultural contradictions religion is claimed to entail against an accepted humanist ideal. And more analytic philosophers often find it difficult epistemically to justify paradoxes as means of expressing truth or a correct depiction of reality. Thus, religious experiences, which are underwritten by their paradoxical nature, often are deemed to have no doxastic merit or authority; or worse, are merely the result of a delusion or psychological aberration.

This is a common critique leveled at religious experiences by many today especially in response to the arguments propounded (for example) by Swinburne,

Plantinga, or Proudfoot that religious experience provides a kind of internal evidence for a justified or "warranted" true belief in God's existence.[22] For example, Michael Martin draws attention to the vastly broad, nonuniform, noncoherent, and often contradictory accounts that the discrepancies among religious experiences often hold. One naturally cannot accept as valid *all* of these accounts for they present putatively different gods and distinct claims.[23] A sweeping justification of the plurality of religious experience "in general" is impossible, and as Martin wisely notes, there are not only differences among the world religions, but also contradictions between them. Yet, without playing by the rules of Martin's epistemology, or trying to argue that his analysis of the conflicting accounts of the supposed verifiability of many seemingly conflicting supernatural accounts is problematic, it is possible to challenge his definition of religious experience as "an experience in which one senses the immediate presence of some supernatural entity" and on which the "paradox" is relied in describing it.[24]

Martin's (seemingly a priori) rejections of religious experiences emanate from, and revolve around how presence is preunderstood in the context of this special entity, and the paradox is merely the means of describing what one already preaccepts regarding religious experience. Although Martin is right to include the paradox within his definition of religious experience, it seems more so the case that the paradox figures much more prominently, even down to the core of what constitutes truth (which previous chapters have addressed extensively). Phenomenality itself is enacted via a slippage between *what* is given and *how* it is given, pointing to a dual-operation. Thus, any straightforward understanding of "presence" already entails at least some degree of paradoxical constitution.

Phenomenologies of Religious Experience

This raises the concern as to whether or not there could be something like a paradoxical warrant or evidence inherent to religious experiences. Since such a paradox would operate at the level of consciousness, which not only grasps things in directness, but also indirectly, it may provide for its own kind of warrant achieved through the explication of the consistency, trustworthiness, and effortful nature of *how* a paradox operates. This also could result in the provision of at least some socially explanatory power, even if the claims made regarding such experiences are not accepted by everyone (as nearly no claim ever is). Three figures in particular stand out for their employments of phenomenology toward the theme of evidence in religious experience: William Alston, Merold Westphal, and Anthony Steinbock.

It was to a more Husserlian phenomenology that Alston remained committed in his approach to the question of religious experience, which he distinguished between the sensory and nonsensory (mystical experiences).[25] For Alston, since our meaning giving conceptions of phenomenality follow along sensory lines, and in conjunction with the semiotic structure of differentiation in what and how we experience such phenomena, religious experiences also can be funded by a "direct" model. For this reason, experience is univocal, whether it be of God or a coffee mug. In part, this is because one in fact arrives at the same phenomenological problems when one attempts to denote, describe, and ultimately defend generally "ordinary" perceptual experiences, just as much as they do of religious experiences. My claim to having been reading the newspaper at the café this morning could be rejected by anyone as delusional for any number of reasons. Yet it would take a very extreme circumstance or provision of evidence in order to convince me out of my belief that I indeed was at the café this morning. In part, this is because all experiences begin with one's "taking something as" such and such, and then after the fact assigning epistemologically oriented "causal contributors" to such an experience.[26]

Ultimately, Alston attempts to circumvent the ascribing of religious experiences to feelings and moods, and instead to one's immediate, yet still subjective "direct" experience of a personal God. This is how Alston employs phenomenology for religious experience: "If the experience is given a perceptual construal from the start, we will at least have to take seriously the view that a claim to be perceiving God is prima facie acceptable on its own merits, pending any sufficient reasons to the contrary."[27] Perception, or taking-something-as, is the basis of all reality, and indeed is an entirely presumed and acceptable means by which life can be organized. This taking-as is applicable to providing some social legitimacy to religious experiences so long as one is not bombarded with irresolvable contradictions in attempting to act in accord with such claims. This move, in other words, of placing the experience of God under "direct" sensory experience, allows warrant to think such an experience as veridical "rather than delusory" so long as defeaters to that particular experience are not presented. If defeaters are presented, their evidence must be overwhelming in order to counteract the initial experience.[28]

Westphal seems to leverage a more existentialist phenomenological account between understanding the meaning-giving conceptions of religious experience as justifiable, and the possibility that such social justification is not, in the first instance, entirely necessary. The matter of religious experience is conceived according to two problematic notions, both of which leave it in the hands of solipsistic feeling: to either distill or "isolate the affective moment of religious life" or "to identity religious experience with mystical experience."[29] Westphal's approach is to turn to self-transcendence as a means of seeing how religious experience is mediated by volition, feelings, and concepts, as all three are always at work and necessary for human experience in general. Taking cue from the existentialists, the angst and ever-looming threat of noetic self-deception entails the life-long endeavor of pursuing the experience of God, an endeavor that begins with surrendering one's static concept of self. Since transcendence is possible if and only if one can first self-transcend, explication of religious experience must begin here.

But none of this furnishes any epistemological assurance that things truly are as they seem. This is because religious experience is fundamentally a matter of faith. And faith, by definition, necessitates a lack of calculable guarantees. Since faith necessarily is precarious, the demands that epistemology places on religious experience to furnish evidence could ultimately eradicate the acts of faith. Westphal then turns to whether or not there is an evidence that at least provides a version of confidence: "Can we be confident that this prayer is offered to a truly transcendent God . . .? Unfortunately not." Yet regarding the words of prayer it is possible to "stipulate that their sincerity is attested by the appropriate deeds" even though "sincerity is no guarantee against deception."[30] Again following Kierkegaard, Westphal develops a personalist account that is attuned to the ever-looming possibility that I am being deceived. In the end, religious experience "cannot provide any evidence for truth as objectivity until it has passed the test of subjectivity." This is because "evidence" is an epistemologically-controlled notion. Is it possible to discuss evidence otherwise?

Similar to Westphal's personalist account, yet still (at least implicitly) in favor of a Jamesian/Schleirmacherian numinous "feeling" as the basis of religious experience is the work of Anthony Steinbock. For Steinbock religious evidence has been fatally misdiagnosed according to the strict contours of presentation. Instead religious experience maintains its own sphere of evidence, and must "*be taken on its own terms* and not subordinated to how objects are given to us in perception, or evaluated according to philosophical narrow-mindedness, or accepted or rejected according to presuppositions of religious belief." This sphere of evidence he calls epiphany or "vertical experience" that is opened up by vertical givenness, which goes beyond, and even is capable of surmounting the presentative evidences of "reason and knowledge."[31] It is possible to be afforded an account of a "special" order of human experience that allows for the discernment and description of a basic structure of religious experiences that have their own evidential basis.

From religious experience to realigious transcendence, the modality of religion is a Waldenfelsian "hyper-phenomenon" that is about relation with the inter-Personal (with a capital P), which denotes relation with the holy and absolute—a being like no other.[32] For Steinbock, living religiously entails an engagement in, and articulation of the modes of vertical experience that pertain to the religious sphere as they are given. The modality of religion is a particular sort of hyperphenomenon irreducible to "cultural, ethical, biological, or aesthetic" aspects of life, and therefore must be described according to its own form of evidence.[33] Steinbock qualifies this evidence (again, called epiphany) not according to some vague, neutral, or multidirectional giving, but according to a radically personal and inter-Personal regioning where one experiences oneself as a subject of another's directionality or attention. He ultimately criticizes Heidegger's all too often meandering *denkweg* as oftentimes directionless and "misleading."

Inconspicuous Evidence and Religious Experience

This all sets the stage for a synthesization of these three thinkers' works into a reflection on a different kind of evidence that allows for a description of religious experience, and a means by which the aforementioned epistemological double-bind can be reduced to its deeper core. Steinbock convincingly argues for a sphere of evidence unique to the givenness of religious experience, yet with a highly feeling-centric and perhaps fideistic account, does not seem to provide for the necessity of the essential aspect of religious life that guards against delusion through truth. Phenomenology is too enmeshed in the holistic lattices of everyday life in order for its descriptive approach to distance itself from its liturgies and activities, which are not antithetical to reason's evidences. Westphal's personalist account properly distinguishes itself from a fideistic and emotive basis paradoxically by tying faith to its potential deception, yet this position may risk distancing itself from a Heideggerian notion of "truth," abandoning truth to the form of *Adequatio*, leaving "evidence" in the hands of epistemology. And although Alston develops his direct model as a type of evidence, he does not provide an account of *how* one undergoes such experiences consciously, and how the paradoxes of religious experience can be sustained in the context of evidence, which is intersocial by definition.

These are of course loose caricatures that run the risk of being all too reductive. Yet they serve to illustrate how attempts to develop a phenomenology of religion necessarily lead to a number of problems, to which a description of a paradoxical evidence of religious experience could furnish a response. Independent from any need to epistemically justify religious experience, there is still an internal demand that religious experiences place on us as inherently social. To disavow the coconstitutive dynamics of religion indeed may be an implicit betrayal of the religious, which for someone like Levinas, is most fundamentally founded through relations with the other, as ethics is the fundament of both phenomenological experience and "first theology." Further, the use of the broad and swathing term "religion" may be far too reductive because it may sacrifice the pure reflective differences of religions in favor of describing their unity. Is it necessary that any descriptive use of the phenomenological reduction in terms of "religion" ultimately ends in a version of pluralism that inadvertently eradicates the unique intelligibilities of these different means of relation with the Absolute?

Without having a clear answer that solves immediately these two problems, it is in this context that it becomes possible to put forward a composite definition of religious experience: If religion were to be defined as the initiation of, or the being-open-to the fundamental and effortful relation between oneself and what one takes to be a personal, meaning-giving, and life changing potential; and if experience were taken as the means of latching-onto-as-meaningful particular circumstances in the steady stream of consciousness, then a "religious experience" could be described as the momentary capturing of the intelligibility of data that is part and parcel of such efforts of being-open to this meaning-giving, life changing, and personal potential. Experience, the very confronting and capturing itself, takes on a distinctly unique intonation when the attempt is made to furnish a doxastic explanation of that which by necessity eludes conscious description.

This rough sketch of a definition sets a condition for the illustration of the role of inconspicuousness in providing one step in overcoming the double-bind that entraps religious experience. If there are unique evidences or warrants (*scheinen*) that might be understood to underwrite the philosophical validity of paradoxical phenomena, then religious experience could be funded in a way that demonstrates its unique forms of legitimacy without its intelligibility being reduced to the twin concerns of the oversight of modern epistemology and the gravity of a fideistic and solipsistic subjectivity. To reiterate, the "un" in *unscheinbar* does not entail the utter privation of *Schein* or warrant, but only that whatever *is unscheinbar* does not present its warrant clearly and obviously in the way that other phenomena might. Usually evidence is a phenomenon in and of itself that is achieved by isolating information relevant to another phenomenon, then applying it back to the whole context to learn something new about it. One locates what stands out as isolatable. Yet in the case of religious experiences, it could be suggested that the means to attaining the evidences of their phenomenality operates by locating what cannot be isolated from the whole.

Religious experience has its own form of inconspicuous evidence, and this is the case for at least three reasons. First, religious experience shrouds its evidence in a unique way because the vast intelligibility of the content is so overwhelmingly significant that it cannot be extracted from the form of presentation. Such evidence, as shrouded, calls for something far more demanding: a life lived religiously whereby the integration of the holy within everyday life is sought out. It is only throughout the course of one's life of living religiously that the evidences of these experiences become intelligible. As established in the last chapter, this is why the act of adoration must be a directedness toward a unique phenomenality that "gives" through deformalization.

Second, and as in every case of evidence, the evidence of religious experience is sutured to the character of that which one is attempting to "prove" or describe. The informative content of this evidence provides an intelligibility that teaches us something about that to which it refers. In this unique case, the "that" of proof of a religious experience would be some putative givenness of the holy. Therefore, to offer a proof of this Absolute would be to begin with a certain knowledge of God-as-provable. This thereby would disqualify the Absolute self-presentative ability to not appear. Provability, in this latter case, would entail that the Absolute can be conjured, and must appear when and if one summons its evidences to clarity. Instead, the evidences of religious experience lack this temporal immediacy. Indeed, if this evidence were readily available and conjurable, it immediately would undermine the power and omnipotence of that which is conjured. Instead, religious experience attests to an experience of that which protects and shrouds itself from such conjurability.

Third, if religious experience indeed is depictive of the supreme principle of divinity, then the presentation of this supreme principle, by merit of its omnipotence, most often would not *force itself* into presentation or direct accessibility. What is supreme has no need of asserting itself in a show of power. And in fact, it is a by far more powerful expression of power to not assert itself, and to be integrated in the whole in a nondetectable way. The subtlety of divinity, or in this case, the supremacy of the supreme, rests on its positive ability to not be displayed evidentially.

As convincing as these three points may be, each lean religious experience in a decidedly more apophatic direction, therefore it is necessary to provide two positive indications as to how this "evidence" is at all worthy of the name. First, it is an evidence above all evidences. True, it is not isolatable, which is one characteristic that we generally conceive to be appropriate to evidence. And true, it is not a body of information that undeniably can be asserted empirically. Yet, this evidence does furnish some kind of affirmation, and it does so by merit of its unique integration in all that remains relevant to life. It is an evidence above all evidences because it is integrally holistic, and thereby (at least for the religious experiencer) applicable to any and all other evidences that seem pertinent to their life. A belief or proposition can be deepened because this affirmation—which is not bereft of content—has gone through the trials and tests of faith, which is integral to religious experience.

Second, the means by which religious experience is provided warrant is through investigating and detecting that which uniquely harbors the ability to shroud itself and integrate itself holistically. The evidence is not purely apophatic, for in this case privation is an ability—it is a resource-of-lacking. If the Inconspicuous God presented its evidential character entirely, it would forfeit its phenomenality as divine. Its unique ability is to holistically integrate and affect the whole, not just particular aspects of it. This is evidential of phenomena that at first seem apophatic as a purely "nonpresent." Yet, this integration is positive, as it laminates layers of intelligibility—or as Marion might suggest, saturation—that prevents it from being clearly or neutrally confronted. A religious experience whose evidential character is limited to only particular moments of life is quarantined, and as such it would lack integration and effective potential.

And third, the evidence of religious life is paradoxical. It is not isolatable, yet it is experiential; its proofs do not stand out, yet this ability to integrate is a sign of dynamic *potentia* (which omni-potence must entail). This comes full circle to the paradox according to which religious experience operates: religious experience attests to relation with supreme power, yet this power is in its ability to not display its power.[34] In a phenomenological key, these experiences gain their effectiveness from an evidence that is not impoverished of the ability to prove itself, but the opposite. As the holy ciphers itself into the world, at a million points throughout the whole, it still has succeeded in keeping its warrant nonisolatable. That is a most true power and ability, one founded in the inconspicuous capacity to elude the dichotomy between the warranted and the nonevidential, which in the end, amount to a generative reliance on the same thing: The division between a thing and its evidence, which implies the evidence is distant, isolatable, and not integral to all aspects of—especially everyday and marginal—life. It now becomes necessary to investigate how "having" faith in an Inconspicuous God might be possible.

Notes

1. Emmanuel Levinas, *Is it Righteous to Be? Interviews with Emmanuel Levinas*, ed. Jill Robbins (Stanford: Stanford University Press, 2001).

2. Edmund Husserl, *Ideen zu einer reinen Phänomenologie un phänomenologischen Philosophie, vol. 1, Husserliana, vol.* III/1, ed. K. Schumann (Den Haag: M. Nijhoff, 1976), 176.

3. Janicaud, *La phénoménologie éclatée* (Paris: Editions de l'Eclat, 1998), 124. See here also Dominique Janicaud's engagement with "Athéisme Méthodologique," *La phenomenology éclatée*, 43.

4. Maurice Merleau-Ponty, *The Visible and the Invisible*, trans. A. Lingis (Evanston, IL: Northwestern University Press, 1968), 151.

5. Dominique Janicaud, *Phenomenology and the "Theological Turn": The French Debate* (New York: Fordham University Press, 2000), 68. See here Edmund Husserl, *Ideas Pertaining to a Pure Phenomenology and to a Phenomenological Philosophy: General Introduction to a Pure Phenomenology*, trans. F. Kersten (The Hague: Martinus Nijhoff Publishers, 1982), 134.

6. Janicaud, *Phenomenology and the "Theological Turn,"* 43. To these questions, Yates responds by asking back, "If phenomenology and theology "make two," does this make atheists of phenomenologists? To press the point, what if pretensions to rigorous neutrality

were themselves already ideological, or even religious in the negative sense?" Christopher Yates, "Checking Janicaud's Arithmetic: How Phenomenology and Theology 'Make Two,'" in *Analecta Hermeneutica* 1, no. 1 (2009): 83.

7. Janicaud, *Phenomenology and the "Theological Turn,"* 30–31, cf. 28–29.

8. On this particular point, see László Tengelyi, "New Phenomenology in France," *The Southern Journal of Philosophy* 50, no. 2 (2012): 295–303.

9. Janicaud, *Chronos: Pour l'intelligence du partage temporel* (Paris: Bernard Grasset, 1997), 143.

10. Janicaud in general concludes that Heidegger's Zähringen seminar serves to throw more decisive light on the radical change that Heidegger wished to have upon the theory of time. Dominique Janicaud, *Chronos: Pour l'intelligence du Partage Temporel* (Paris: Bernard Grasset, 1997), 157–58.

11. "Or quelle est la phenomenalite par excellence qui, ni immediate ni ontique, ne se laisse pas non plus réduire à une vise eidétique? C'est precisement celle qui reserve la plus problématique des 'phenomenalities': la dimension temporelle." Ibid., 159. See also Janicaud, *Phenomenology and the "Theological Turn,"* 28–31. And Dominique Janicaud, *Phenomenology "Wide Open": After the French Debate*, trans. Charles N. Cabral (New York: Fordham University Press, 2005), 100, footnote 14.

12. Janicaud, *Phenomenology "Wide Open,"* 75. See also Janicaud, *Chronos*, 109.

13. Here Janicaud argues that such an approach can be conceived as a "minimal phenomenology," yet "to call this unusual phenomenology 'minimal' is not to belittle it. Rather it is to give the fullest sense to this very difficult attempt to train sight and hearing to get as close as possible" to understanding experience and that "The 'practical studies' of the later Heidegger (like the exercises in *Daseinanalyse* from the Zollikoner seminar) are undertaken in this vein." Janicaud, *Phenomenology "Wide Open,"* 73. This was originally published in French as *La phénoménologie eclatée* (Editions de l'Eclat, 1998).

14. Janicaud, *Phenomenology "Wide Open,"* 75.

15. Ibid., 9. *La phénoménologie eclatée*, 19: "il ne s'agira plus de suspecter un retour au 'théologique' chez des phénoménologues de l'inapparent, de l'Autre, de l'auto-affection ou de la donation pure, mais de se demander si la phénoménologie ne doid pas être."

16. Essential for Heidegger is the meaning of "das Unscheinbare, aber keineswegs 'das Unsichtbare,' wie die schon genannten philologischen übersetzungen fälschlicherweise übersetzen." Martin Heidegger, GA 55, *Heraklit. 1. Der Anfang des abendländischen Denkens (Heraklit)* (Frankfurt am Main: Vittorio Klosterman, 1943). And 2. *Logik. Heraklits Lehre vom Logos* (Frankfurt am Main: Vittorio Klosterman, 1944), 142.

17. "Cette 'phénoménologie de l'inapparent' nomme-t-elle un oxymore, un supreme paradoxe, une déconcertante impossibilité?" Janicaud, *La phénoménologie eclatée*, 106. On this point see also Janicaud's earlier work, which came before his critique of the theological turn, namely. Dominique Janicaud, *La puissance du rationnel* (Paris: Editions Gallimard, 1985); See Dominique Janicaud, *Powers of the Rational: Science, Technology, and the Future of Thought*, trans. Peg Birmingham and Elizabeth Birmingham (Bloomington: Indiana University Press, 1994).

18. William James, "Religious Experience," in *Philosophy of Religion: Selected Readings*, 4th ed., ed. Michael Peterson, William Hasker, Bruce Reichenbach, and David Basinger. Oxford: Oxford University Press, 2009), 40, 44–43. This is a selection from William James, *The Varieties of Religious Experience* (New York: New American Library, 1958).

19. Jean-Yves Lacoste, "The Appearing and the Irreducible," in *Words of Life: New Theological Turns in French Phenomenology*, trans. Christina M. Gschwandtner and ed. Bruce Ellis Benson and Norman Wirzba (New York: Fordham University Press, 2010), 63.

20. James, "Religious Experience," 44.

21. Ibid., 40. James continues: "as a matter of psychological fact, mystical states of a well-pronounced and emphatic sort *are* usually authoritative over those who have them. They have been 'there,' and know. It is vain for rationalism to grumble about this." Ibid., 41.

22. See also Wayne Proudfoot, *Religious Experience* (Berkeley, CA: University of California Press, 1985). There, Proudfoot identifies noetic, reason-giving qualities upon which religious experiencers rely in identifying theological experiences according to nonnaturalistic conceptions of explanation. See also Keith Yandell, *The Epistemology of Religious Experience* (Cambridge: Cambridge University Press, 1993).

23. For Martin, "Religious experiences are like those induced by drugs, alcohol, mental illness, and sleep deprivation: They tell no uniform or coherent story, and there is no plausible theory to account for discrepancies among them." Michael Martin, "Critique of Religious Experience," in *Philosophy of Religion: Selected Readings*, 4th ed., ed. Michael Peterson, William Hasker, Bruce Reichenbach, and David Basinger (Oxford: Oxford University Press, 2009), 68.

24. Ibid., 65. Martin also notes that mystics often rely upon (or more pejoratively, retreat to) paradoxes in describing such experiences, as their intelligibilities exceed normal vocabulary.

25. Alston refers to nonsensory experience as "mystical experience." William P. Alston, "Religious Experience as Perception of God," in *Philosophy of Religion: Selected Readings*, 4th ed., ed. Michael Peterson, William Hasker, Bruce Reichenbach, and David Basinger (Oxford: Oxford University Press, 2009), 52. See also William P. Alston, *Perceiving God* (Ithaca, NY: Cornell University Press, 1991).

26. William P. Alston, "Religious Experience as Perception of God," in *Philosophy of Religion: Selected Readings*, 4th ed., eds., Michael Peterson, William Hasker, Bruce Reichenbach, and David Basinger (Oxford: Oxford University Press, 2009), 50. Yet still, Alston's account of religious experience is oriented around a subject's individual experience, which in his phenomenological orientation, is not to be countered by others: "We would need strong reasons to override the subject's confident report of the character of her experience." Alston describes this phenomenologically and in greater detail beyond causal thinking: "not every causal contributor to an experience is perceived via that experience. When I see a house, light waves and goings on in my nervous system from parts of the causal chain leading to the visual experience, but I don't see them." We make causal explanations after experiences of what we take to appear, and "we learn this by first determining in many cases what is *seen*, felt, or heard in those cases, and then looking for some causal contribution that is distinctive of the object perceived." Ibid., 52.

27. Alston's view of direct experience of God "contrasts with the widespread view that 'experience of God' is to be construed as purely subjective feelings and sensations to which supernaturalistc causal hypothesis are added." Ibid., 53.

28. Ibid., 57. Alston concludes: "If my arguments have been sound, we are justified in thinking of the experience of God as a mode of perception in the same generic sense of the term as sense perception. And if God exists, there is no reason to suppose that this perception is not sometimes veridical rather than delusory."

29. Merold Westphal, "A Phenomenological Account of Religious Experience," in *Philosophy of Religion: Selected Readings*, 4th ed., ed. Michael Peterson, William Hasker, Bruce Reichenbach, and David Basinger (Oxford: Oxford University Press, 2009), 80. As Westphal notes, transcendence "can mean that which is beyond, the transcendent. Or it can mean going beyond, transcending. For the Augustinian tradition the two are united, and transcending is toward the transcendent." Westphal, like Lacoste, may be counter-Schleiermacherian in his attempt to "isolate the affective moment of the religious life from the cognitive and volitional, and to identify religious experience with the former." Ibid, 81.

30. Ibid., 84.

31. Anthony Steinbock, *Phenomenology and Mysticism* (Bloomington: Indiana University Press, 2011), 33, 115–157. See also 33, 138, 116.

32. See here Bernhard Waldenfels's treatment of religious transcendence in *Hyperphänomene. Modi hyperbolischer Erfahrung* (Frankfurt am Main: Suhrkamp, 2012), 353–412.

33. Steinbock, *Phenomenology and Mysticism*, 22.

34. On this specific point, see here John Caputo, *The Weakness of God: A Theology of the Event* (Bloomington: Indiana University Press, 2006).

7 Inconspicuous Faith: Chrétien, Heidegger, and Forgetting

While I was obeying his order to feed and get the horses ready for the field . . . Covey [the master] sneaked into the stable . . . and seizing me suddenly by the leg, he brought me to the stable floor. I now forgot my roots, and remembered my pledge to stand up in my own defense. Whence came the daring spirit necessary to grapple with a man who, eight-and-forty hours before, could, with his slightest word have made me tremble like a leaf in a storm . . . My resistance was entirely unexpected, and Covey was taken all aback by it, for he trembled in every limb.

—*Frederick Douglass*[1]

Imagine . . . a human being who does not possess the power to forget, who is damned to see becoming everywhere; such a human being . . . would see everything flow apart in turbulent particles, and would lose himself in the stream of becoming.

—*Friedrich Nietzsche*[2]

Believing, furnishing evidence, and even adoring all are predicated on acts of forgetting. This is because forgetting is inherent to the nature of truth itself. The root of truth, *a-letheia* (ἀλήθεια), is founded in *lethe* (λήθη), which despite its many possible meanings most essentially means "forgetting." Once the privative alpha (ἀ) or "un" is added to *lethe*, truth becomes straightforwardly "un-forgetting." *Lethe* also can be translated as oblivion, can characterize what is forgotten (e.g. someone's being "oblivious"), and involves what is latent or escapes notice (Greek *lanthanein*) as inconspicuous. What is latent is present and capable of emerging or developing, yet absent from conscious awareness, and the Latin *latentem* refers to what is dormant, secret, or simply unknown due "to being hidden" (*latere*). As abstract as it may sound, truth could be defined as a remembrance that has gone through the trial of loss instantiated by fundamental experiences with the covered-over-ness of forgetting, latency, or oblivion.

Yet *lethe* has not always been capable of being understood in a positive element. In Greek mythology, which greatly has influenced Christian theology and Hamartiology, the river Lethe (or "Unmindfulness") flowed endlessly through

Hades in its stream of oblivion. The river represented the goddess (or demon) Lethe, who personified forgetfulness. The river, whose sounds produced feelings of drowsy drunkenness, was drank from by the inhabitants of Hades in order to forget a past earthly life. Dating to third-century BC Greek literature, forgetting even was taken to be a sin of committing to nontruth. Apollonius referred to Aithalides, whose soul was not overwhelmed by Lethe and was gifted with unfailing memory.[3] And in the *Republic*, Plato suggested that *lethe* may refer to the total nature of our flawed earthly existence. When souls faced the penalty of judgment, "a new cycle of life and mortality" awaited them as they "marched on in a scorching heat in the plain of forgetfulness until they arrived at the river Lethe to drink and then forgot all things."[4] It should come as no surprise then that *lethe* came to be used to refer to sin, as the cultural preferences for the remembrance and privileging of memorization had become evident.

Yet it is possible to describe forgetting in a more phenomenological sense. It is not difficult to conceive that forgetting can be either active or passive. Passive forgetting would be the product of the selective attempt to remember things one deems to be essential to a period of time. For example, to spend an hour in the city yet to remember only my croissant at the café is to forget all of the innumerable perceptions I deemed unworthy of remembrance, such as the color of the flowers on the table, the smell of the waiteress' perfume, or the coffee stain on the newspaper. Such forgetting is a matter of fact and is essential, for indeed, as Nietzsche notes, "without forgetting, it is utterly impossible to live at all."[5]

Active forgetting would involve the attempt to forget the intelligibility of a particular experience. In cases of trauma, for example, it may be preferable that an event's details be blotted from memory. Or in the case of sin, as Kierkegaard held, "it is blotted out, it is forgiven and forgotten."[6] Both types of forgetfulness fund the possibility of treating the nature of truth itself as at points empowered by its "unremembered," which remains operative although generally unacknowledged. What, then, of a forgetting that employs aspects of both types: a passive overlooking, and an active attempt to send something amiss from the grasp of the mind? This would amount to an active attempt to passively overlook.

It is in this direction that Jean-Louis Chrétien, another thinker associated with the theological turn, develops a phenomenology of religion in its experiential element.[7] Since phenomenology itself is a set of acts, they can correspond to, and need not be in competition with other acts, such as liturgy, ritual, or prayer. These acts all correspond to a wrestling with truth, and under Chrétien's development, forgetting is a kind of active bringing-to-truth whereby what confidently is taken to be the case is surrendered in order to be rendered-open to what is absent, yet affective. In this sense, the active attempt to overlook some intelligibility can be an inherent source religious experience: namely, for its overcoming of what seems to yearn for our attention, for its openness toward the presently absent, and for its putting away of the "old" in order for the new to become. The content, therefore, of what comes to be experienced has been there all along, and turning to the means by which the hidden operates within the nonhidden is the seeking of truth at its most fundamental level. It is this operation that underwrites a kind of inconspicuous faith.

This chapter addresses one aspect of faith in its "how," and demonstrates means by which it can be understood through a particular lens of inconspicuousness. It does so by developing—out of a synthesis of the work of Heidegger and Chrétien—three ways forgetting can be seen as essential to the faith experience. Faith indeed is an "act." Yet it is not an act like others, and as an inherently interpersonal act, it is achieved through means other than simply a direct "willing" of faithfulness or trying to be faithful. Yet it also is not possible to achieve faith through total surrender or nonwilling. Instead, faith is achieved through the middle voice of faith—faith faiths via an active counterwill (as a form of surrendering) in the act of forgetting, and is inherently interpersonal. Faith is sustained by the merit of this interpersonal nature, which contributes to making the "object" of faith inconspicuous.

These claims are underwritten by Heidegger's reflections on forgetting and testimony, and relate closely to Chrétien's notion of the unhoped for or content of this forgetting, which concerns what is here, now, always, and already. As the French *l'inespéré* refers, this unhoped for is a hope for what is impossible to ever dream of hoping, and to achieve this, forgetfulness must be total. Forgetting runs in conjunction with an inconspicuous faith by merit of instantiating an active attempt to overlook something in favor of not simply the "new" but, more radically, a disclosure of the new from within the old that has been there all along. Inconspicuousness is what characterizes the content and proof of faith, bringing a wished-for reality to life.

Heidegger and Forgetting

On the matter of forgetting, it is helpful to start with Heidegger, who often referred to the inherent relation between forgetfulness and truth. There are four different ways Heidegger's references to forgetfulness could be characterized. The first seems to have been initiated by Husserl to some degree in the context of the natural attitude, of taking-for-granted (and thereby forgetting) the world and self. Heidegger takes this more critical notion of forgetting or overlooking and embalms it in the hope that things-as-revealed (provided they are given through Being) are not fundamentally missed, overlooked, or forgotten. In the 1946 "Letter on Humanism" he described the "fundamental experience" of lack of attention to Being as *Seinsvergessenheit*, or the "forgetfulness of Being," which is a more negative covering-over of the clearing of Being. The fundament of this formulation gets referred to alternatively throughout his work as a *Lichtungsvergessenheit* (clearing forgetfulness) or *Ereignisvergessenheit* (appropriation-forgetfulness) that closes over any potential wonder (θαυμάζειν) at the openness of the meanings and intelligibilities of things.

A second sense of forgetting points to how our reliance on technical life has left us oblivious to what is known as the ontological distinction between Being and *beings*.[8] Such a distinction is what allows us to relate existentially with Being or wonder-creating "clearing" in a way that concrete, ontic life of the natural attitude is suspended in preference for what might appear unexpectedly. It is by living in the in-between of these two aspects of Being that their difference can be experienced more fully and productively.

Third, varied usages of *Verlassenheit* ("forsakenness"), employed in the context of God and Being, mark the inevitable product of these more negative kinds of forgetfulness, such as *Gottvergessenheit*.[9] The forgetting of God or Being comes with the consequence of abandonment/forsakenness (*Gottverlassenheit* and *Seinsverlassenheit*, respectively), which refers to how "Being leaves beings to themselves and denies itself to them." When Being abandons beings, their relation with *Entbergung* (the "unconcealing of being as such") is putatively absent.[10] This forsakenness amounts to the absence of absence—the absence of withholding, withdrawing, or refusing. Yet we are unaware of this forsakenness, due to a certain veiling of the feeling of abandonment. As described in *Beiträge zur Philosophie*, the three veils (which we ourselves are complicit in constructing) that cover up our general feeling of *Seinsverlassenheit* are our obsessions with calculation, speed, and "the massive" (*massenhaft*, a universal or pragmatic, wholesale applicability).[11]

These veils also can be seen as corresponding to Heidegger's later developments of the sacred. The sacred clearing allows for the worlding of the world, yet man has "forgotten" this primal yet hypersensual sense of Being. In Hölderlin's "Flight of the Gods," such a "flight" partly is due to the modern machination of the human condition toward a supposedly enlightened "progress" that has sought to replace one's sacred relations—this aforementioned spacing or clearing that feeds our wonder at Being.[12] Yet, as it remains clear from Heidegger's overall work, the blame here does not fundamentally rest on humankind's shoulders, for the active *Wesen* of Being or the divine holds an agency that flees on its own accord. Nevertheless (and as addressed in detail in chap. 4), any salvation from the technological condition of man comes in part with a quest for the sacred. This was one essential element of Heidegger's great "turn," as Janicaud asks rhetorically, "can it be denied that Heidegger's 'turn' was conditioned by his quest for the Sacred, through his reinterpretation of Hölderlin?"[13]

Fourthly, there is also a sense of oblivion *inherent within* Being, and this is not due to man's forgetting of the ontological difference as *Seinsvergessenheit*, or any abandonment of the gods. Being withholds a fundamental notion of itself within itself, never to be revealed: "Being does not come to the light of its own essence." And in bringing beings into appearance, "Being itself stays away. The truth of being escapes us. It remains forgotten."[14] As mentioned briefly in chapter 2, the a priori of Being never fully comes into the light of appearance, for its truth, although recognizable as truth, keeps itself at a distance, ever retaining its element of oblivion or forgetfulness. Nevertheless, this is not a privation, as Being is what brings-to-present and therefore is the closest of things despite being forgotten. The task is not to bring Being into further manifestation per se, but rather to be appropriated by its *lethe*, to be instilled with the wonder of what *Vergessenheit* ("oblivion") has concealed or withdrawn from presence.

This kind of forgetfulness, however, must be understood as radically more than a general forgetfulness. Anytime we forget, we actually are able to trace out the contours of that which was forgotten—we remember that we forgot. For example, I can remember that I have forgotten what year Heidegger gave this seminar, or what I had for breakfast on Tuesday. Yet I do not forget *that* I had breakfast, and attempting to recover the forgotten indicates that it is something with which I still am in relation. In this case, forgetting is also remembering, as I realize that something *has* been forgotten. It is in similar terms that, as Steinbock puts it "remembering attempts to overcome forgetfulness by recapturing what was forgotten and making it present again."[15] In short, when remembering *that* I forgot, the forgetting is not total.

Yet there are indeed cases in which forgetting itself has become forgotten. This amounts to a complete forgetting. In section 9 of "Overcoming Metaphysics" (*Überwindung der Metaphysik*, 1936–1946), Heidegger ties the very process of this overcoming to the "oblivion" or forgetting of Being. Overcoming incorporates this oblivion; it does not seek to unveil everything, for that would decidedly be a means of development championed by our technical and mechanical age. Such an age is exemplified by the total mobilization of nations ramping up for conflict, and how "the 'World Wars' and their 'totality' already are consequences of the abandonment of Being."[16] It is this kind of double-forgetting that Chrétien insists to be an essential aspect of Heidegger's work:

> Heidegger frequently insisted on the doubling of forgetting: to truly forget, forgetting is not yet enough, for forgetting in memory that one has forgotten is only a mode of remembering—a mode that, precisely, permits us to rediscover what was forgotten. Complete forgetting, he shows, is forgetting the forgetting, disappearance of the very disappearance, where the covering over is itself covered over. This doubling, or second power of forgetting must in truth be posed as first: it is not a higher form of forgetting that succeeds another form exponentially, for the forgetting that does not forget itself constitutes on the contrary a first memory, a first opening to overcoming the forgetting.[17]

It may in fact have been Kierkegaard who was the first to describe this forgetting, and therefore influence Heidegger and subsequently Chrétien in these regards: "one is not ignorant of what is forgotten, since one is ignorant only of what one does not and never has known; what one has forgotten, one has known. Forgetting in this highest sense is therefore not the opposite of recollecting but of hoping ... to forget is in thinking to take away being from that which nevertheless exists, to blot it out."[18]

This forgetting actively foils hopes and expectations. The relation between hope and this sort of forgetting about forgetting itself is what Chrétien comes to investigate in closer detail.

Chrétien and Forgetting

For Chrétien, turning to the familiar to find something unfamiliar within it provides for a productive confrontation with our overwhelming preferences for a posteriori knowledge. To forget is to offer "to God of memory" and for one to be "stripped of memories and lose them." This is the act by which God enters into memory and renarrates its contents. Divine surplus is what makes forgetting great: "forgetting alone, if it is great, places us in accord with this excess." There is an interpersonal element at work within this act of forgetting, for the remembered "will be recovered ... but in a different form; it will have become malleable, receptive to divine action, instead of being the organ of attachment to what escapes it or has already escaped."[19] The excessive divine action is what in this case waits for us to fulfill our part or role in the forgetting process, and to surrender temporarily the self-sustained ability of remembrance.

The task is directed toward absence "because memory is the place of presence," which lacks dynamic faith. The role we play in forgetting is an act of *kenosis* or self-emptying through which "forgetting produces an ignorance of self that is positive." As already developed in relation to Lacoste, this would be a being-liturgical or *coram deo* that forgets everything (and everyone) else. This is why, despite the potential that an "uncovering" or even a "correctness" (*Adequatio*) may provide for experiencing the Inconspicuous God, Chrétien's *The Unforgettable and the Unhoped For* "is dedicated to forgetting and its diverse forms."[20]

Yet this kenosis is unique in that it is not merely negative. Forgetting is not the emptying out of memory, and there is a productive nature of forgetting in that it "founds and gives." In loosening the conscious grip (*Griff*) on "the remembered," one is free to forget the past as it does not constitute in total one's humanity. To forget in this sense also is to be in the truth more radically by bracketing the more ontic form of truth that more often than not privileges "uncovering" and revealing in the present. This allows for closer attendance to what is becoming present and absent.[21] Chrétien refers to this as a bracketing of crystalized and past memorialized deposits of knowledge, and, as reiterated more recently, "my present condition prohibits me from imagining figuratively."[22] Indeed, somewhat enigmatically, this is an active bracketing that takes place in the form of a *kenotic* prayer: one comes to be appropriated *by* the truth that becomes, paradoxically, "unforgettable" (*Alastos*) by breaking the chains of totality and its illusion of knowing.

Chrétien of course is not ignorant to the fact that there are forms of bad-faith immemorialization that amount to a forgetting of forgetting as a total loss or imprisonment in ignorance. Such forgetting marks our "earthly" condition. It is this notion that compounds into one of Chrétien's greatest insights, which is that this bad-faith form of forgetting (to which Heidegger refers in regard to *Seinsvergessenheit* etc.) is underwritten by a remembrance or memorialization that is ill conceived. There is an intelligibility that is taken out of context, disguised in the form of a spectacular truth that prohibits further thinking. As opposed to the attempt to eradicate memory (which the ancient Greek myths of *Lethe* promulgated), it is necessary to see that the root of this problem "is stimulated not by forgetting itself, and not by the powers of the sensible, but by what of the truth subsists in us."[23]

Strangely, it is the remembered that underwrites ignorance, or the ignorance of ignorance. This ignorance also prohibits the-unhoped for. When leaning on past acts, thinking becomes sedimented into *habitus* or sedated into dispositions. Hope is not characterized by attempting "to calculate one's conduct in probabilities, thus remaining in the realm of economics. Only the unhoped for ... is ... the anchor and resource against what is unforeseen in life."[24] There must be a particular kind of forgetting-of-forgetting in order to break the spell of ignorance.

Unhope and Potentiality

This unhoped for concerns the interrelated matters of possibility and potentiality. For Heidegger, this potentiality is exemplified by the act that no matter how banal or mundane, all things retain the possibilities of being conduits of Being. Where Marion would insist on "poor" or "common law" phenomena that are not "saturated" by merit of their being products of technological life, for Heidegger all things bear *potential* to be conduits of an Uncanniness that "itself in its essence is the inconspicuous [*unscheinbar*], the simple, the insignificant, which nevertheless shines in all beings."[25] All things bear the marks of an instantaneous controvertibility from one intelligibility into another. When all that is around me has become banal, Being has been forgotten, and I have lost touch with this controvertibility. This is one reason why Heidegger described the meanings of Being according to an inversion of Aristotle's preference for actuality (being-in-*energeia*, or ενεργεια) over potentiality (being-in-*dunamis* δυναμις). As Heidegger insisted, "Higher than actuality stands potentiality."[26] The over-preferencing of actuality leaves Being reliant on the terms of objective "presence," thereby subordinating Being's potentiality or possibility, which fundamentally operates in paradoxical ways. Although potentiality/possibility here is preferred as a kind of social corrective, being-actual *and* being-possible are to be understood to hold a synthetic and nondialectical unity.

After Heidegger's development, one way this role of potentiality can be articulated further is in terms of inconspicuousness, which furnishes consciousness with the ability to see and experience concurrently two opposite forms of intelligibility, in ways that can surprise and provide newness to/for thought in its potentiality without being distant from reality. Potentiality is not to be confused with the putatively *new and spectacular* (with which our technological societies constantly bombard us), but with a *new in the banal*. Potentiality is the means of operation of Chrétien's unhoped for, which functions in association with faith and is instantiated by an active forgetting. It is unhoped for because an "intention" of faith is not capable of controlling what will or could come. It is not in the realm of actuality that this hope is based. Put more positively, what we do not hope for is more powerful, for it insists on the intersocial element of a unique kind of surprise that does not impress us in a spectacular way. If hope were a matter of spectacular fulfillment, then faith could be taken as the key to supplanting it. Yet faith operates inconspicuously and not so straightforwardly, seeking to attain a unique kind of knowledge that motivates it.

Faith in Its How: The Interpersonal Nature of Faith

If to forget is to make a kind of sacrificial offering out of one's memory, and if forgetting is inherently a part of the faith act, which is interpersonal by nature, then this interpersonal offering must be understood beyond the traditional interdicts, namely, of trust and belief. Faith surely is not merely the ascent of information or articles of "belief." In his proclamation of the "death of God," Nietzsche surely was not derailing a culture that had forgotten "information" or creeds regarding God, but rather was commenting on their loss of faith acts. Faith surely has some element of "the state of being ultimately concerned," as Tillich famously claimed, and at least some unique form of being grasped by what "transcends us unconditionally."[27]

Yet faith also goes beyond a mere "trust" and into a specific form of its own evidence, aside from what is seemingly trustworthy. Surely, faith operates with confidence and fidelity; it is a "trust in that which gives value to the self" and a "loyalty to what the self values," as Niebuhr insisted.[28] Yet faith is more than trust because it instills an absolute loyalty that no single human (who one could "trust") could ever be capable of conjuring. One problem with a modern understanding of faith is that it often has been conceived mostly in its subjective and therefore solipsistic element. As Chrétien put it quite recently, "One must not for a single moment lose sight of the fact that biblical hope, just like faith, is a personal link with the personal God."[29]

If there is an interpersonal nature of faith, then does it not entail interpersonal activity that, like all interpersonal activities, requires some element of difference from within itself? Faith is quintessentially interpersonal, as Balthasar knew, "because faith interiorly strives away from the believer on into the light of God and to the evidence to be found in God alone; but the *quaerens* must be complemented by an *inveniens* which is compatible with the earthly state of the believer."[30] The faith act is instantiated by other, interpersonal acts, and therefore its evidence, proof, or warrant always will remain lacking to some degree. Faith thus cannot be attained through an iron volition that wills it into existence. How, then, does it grow to the point of attaining a unique kind of "religious" knowledge?

One answer: faith operates as a synthetic and interpersonal act between oneself and God. This can be taken in conjunction with the conception of faith developed by the writer (likely St. Paul) of Hebrews 11:1: "Faith is the substance of things hoped-for, the evidence of things unseen." The "unseen" reality has a proof that corresponds to it uniquely. This proof or evidence is faith. Although it has elements of its own self-justification, faith is not a proof like any other proof. This *Schein* or "justification" has a circular nature: faith is a produced act of hope, and it is the "filling" or content that inspires hope and brings it to life. It fills one's wished-for reality with content, which inherently is interpersonal. Faith (as an interpersonal act) simultaneously is the content and proof of a wished-for and inconspicuous reality.

Testimony and Witness

In the case of the Inconspicuous God, there is not always a genuine experience that provides, as Gadamer claims in reference to the truth of understanding, an "encounter with something that asserts itself as truth."[31] Some phenomenal experiences are exempt from this kind of self-assertion. This can be exemplified in the case of testimony and witness, the means of expression of interpersonal faith. That to which one testifies usually does *not* assert itself in any spectacular sense. The testimony gains its power from the fact that the testified is *not* self-evident; otherwise, there never would be any need of testifying. Furthermore, the one in whom faith is placed does not disband, delegitimize, or bring to completion the faith act, but rather sustains it precisely by not asserting itself as thoroughly comprehensible. In faith, as Ricoeur knew, "the Absolute and its presence is constituted. It is only about this that testimony testifies."[32] Ricoeur points to a "middle voice" that is both active and passive. How does one testify about the Absolute, and what is the content of the testified that can attain a positive description?

This question is reflective of Heidegger's earliest treatments of Christian life in 1920. He interpreted St. Paul as providing a new conception of the life of faith that is inherently intertwined with the coconstituting and intersocial elements of proclamation and witness (which Ricoeur distinguished from testimony). This intertwining is not about the communication of what one comprehends, but rather how and what one does *not know.* Only that for which one awaits in faith and hope is worthy of "proclamation."[33] What at first appears merely to be an apophatic claim of negative theology harbors something uniquely capable of phenomenological description: sutured to such "testimony," faith-as-lived is always already intersocial. Its qualities of being shared and proclaimed are constitutive of the faith act as interpersonal.

"Witness" is the communication of the unknown, how one arrives at its structures of/for the continuation of thought; and giving-witness is a making-social of the recognition that something greatly alters the social fabric of life in one's radically having-re-become. This witness or testimony is based on the "how structure" of having. And "having" in this religious and paradoxical context entails the elucidation of the contents, relations, and enactments of *how* one bears witness to this unique having, its moments of appearing that alter not only the individual life but also the social tapestry in which one finds oneself. In the context of faith, having is a kind of *not* having, even a kind of forgetting. This realization that one "does not have" creates suspense for the to-come. The phenomenological suspension of forgetting, to which St. Paul referred, infuses the world with suspense. Again, this can be understood as more than an apophatic description of the Absolute.

Inconspicuous Faith: or, How to Forget

Suspense (especially in the phenomenological sense of "bracketing" or the *epoché*) may be a good way of describing the faith act, which circularly *calls* for a conversion, not only of the self but also of one's past, by forgetting not merely what one knows but also how one attains the faith-act itself. Forgetting is one act within our capacity to bring about faith. As Chrétien understood, the giving-up of one's memory is an offering to the Absolute, which then can forge new pathways of faith and thus sustain it. Inspired by Chrétien and Heidegger, there are three ways that forgetting can be thought to support the interpersonal activities of faith: denoticing, counternoticing, and covering-over.

First, forgetting is a means of denoticing, which entails a double movement: not only is it opening up to the new, but it also is a disclosure of the new from within the old that has been there all along. It disturbs the relation between what is obvious or "in the way" (*ob viam*), and what is thought never to be brought to full disclosure. To a limited degree, this denoticing could be compared to St. Paul's call to "take every thought captive" in order for faith to be developed. Thoughts that are not taken captive rule the mind and life of faith, and instead themselves take captive through a totalizing control of phenomenalization. By not taking thought captive through forgetfulness, past faith acts can only be memorialized and crystalized, therefore lacking in vitality. Denoticing temporarily brackets past faith acts.

This can be expressed in more Husserlian terms. Denoticing provides a means by which it is possible to see the present condition by withholding judgment on what has been taken to be the intelligibility of a particular event or thing. Denoticing can assist in taking every presupposition captive, which allows one to experience the fullness of *thinking* in a way that brackets the thoughts captured. Faith must operate with a complete presuppositionlessness that does not prohibit, in judgment, what could be the case. This is a holy "setting apart" or clearing away of memorialized judgments that allows for new means of faith that are entirely unsuspected by thought. As Chrétien understands, unhoping provides for us precisely what we do *not* hope for; if we could hope for it, then the provider of one's hopes would attain a level of being controlled by the hoper.

A second way that forgetting can be developed in regard to faith is through a counternoticing. This leads back to the question posed in the introduction to this chapter: What of an active attempt to passively overlook? Counternoticing is different from denoticing, for it actively takes the remembered and relocates and renarrates it in another context. This gives the remembered an entirely different intonation, for the sake of attaining a unique kind of knowledge. In the case of St. Paul, this knowledge and the act of forgetting are carbureted by an interpersonal faith. In Philippians 3:9–13, the essential nature of forgetting in order to reach the ultimate goal of following Christ is described. As stated in verse 10, this goal is to supersede all other goals.

The goal is a unique kind of knowledge—to "know Christ." This is an interpersonal knowledge attained by an interpersonal faith that produces and creates a basis for righteousness; and in order to enact this righteousness, one's own past righteousness, via ethical mandates and self-regulation, must be released or forgotten (Philippians 3:9). Faith is not constructed or self-made, yet there is *one act* of will that can achieve the overall goal, which is a product of the interpersonal nature of faith that develops righteousness: one can actively forget (3:13). A phenomenology of faith, as Chrétien notes, entails that forgetting "in each instance throws us and opens us to preoccupation with what lies before us," and this is precisely the imagery St. Paul developed in this context of faith.[34] To accomplish this, something like denoticing needs to take place.

Third, forgetting is a means of covering-over. This is not "hiding" but rather the placement of a sheer laminate over the remembered. This is the active "a" of *aletheia*, which is not just the subtraction or negation of something, but also an addition of something to it. Veiling veils only aspects of the remembered, not its entirety. This is why covering-over is not antiremembrance but counterremembrance. This forgetting furnishes an individual with the ability to establish new faiths in the unseen by suspending what "stands out" spectacularly in their history. Some past achievement or event must be dehad, which could be understood as similar yet still distinct from Heidegger's "letting go" of *Gelassenheit.*[35] In being both active and passive, this understanding of forgetting is found in a middle voice. The giving of memory as an offering is a "letting"; in this case, giving is letting or giving-way. The middle voice in this instance would be "faith faiths."

Broadly conceived, these acts of forgetting (which can be intonated phenomenologically) are within the capacity to attain such knowledge, which runs in conjunction with an inconspicuous faith (inconspicuous by merit of its lack of clarity, yet still possessing its own evidence). By continuing a reflection on the words of Paul, "I do not consider myself yet to have taken hold of it [this knowledge of Christ]. But one thing I do: Forgetting what is behind and straining toward what is ahead." (Philippians 3:13). Without the past at least to some degree being forgotten it becomes, as Nietzsche once put it, "the gravedigger of the present."[36] And, as St. Paul taught, learning to release and give over to oblivion certain thoughts (*epilanthanomenos*, or ἐπιλανθανόμενος) is how faith actively is lived-with.

Inconspicuous Faith

This allows for three final reflections on faith as inconspicuous. First, when faith is sutured to forgetting, it becomes inconspicuous because the means of attaining faith cannot be through a direct grasping. As noted, one cannot "will" faith into action, yet it also remains impossible to will a nonwilling in efforts to become more faithful. Instead, the middle voice of faith ("faith faiths") gets underwritten by an active forgetting that helps bring faith about. Faith operates with the goal of attaining a kind of knowledge that furnishes a warrant unlike any other, and faith faiths and deforges by putting the faith act itself out of focus. Like the task of driving a car, in which the focus is on driving but not on the car itself, the act of faith is brought about by an active willing of forgetting so that the various aspects of a given moment of faith can become pertinent.

Second, the notion of "faith in" may be formulated poorly. Being interpersonal, faith is always a "faith-with" and therefore cannot be attained solipsistically, as faith is the relation with the Absolute. Yet, as inconspicuous, the subject/object of faith does present itself and does provide enough evidential content for an experience of an act of faith. It is here that the notion of forgetting needs to be understood as radically inherent within acts of faith as a forgetting of old beliefs and their produced outcomes in order to be, as Lacoste reminds us, *coram deo* in a way that all else gets bracketed. Forgetting, however, should not be understood as purely negative or apophatic, as it actively laminates the ordinary (*Vulgäre*), mundane, lived-in, and habitual (*Gewöhnliche*) with a presuppositionlessness that allows for faith-participation without faith-determination.

And, third, faith is achieved via an active-passive, a covering-over that alters the experience of that which remains uncovered. Faith is irreducible to trust, an act of will applicable to any person. It specifically concerns the relation with the interpersonal Absolute, who cannot be an "object of faith." Yet faith also is irreducible to belief systems and worldviews as it renews and recontextualizes the individual's sense of presence. Faith-as-belief-system and faith-as-trust with an Inconspicuous God can be brought into unity through an act of forgetting. In the end, what most totally is "unforgettable" is characterized as such precisely because it is what uniquely eludes and absconds conscious memory's grasp. Yet it does so while simultaneously leaving something behind, something unhoped for or, said inversely, something *never-to-be-despaired-over.*

Notes

1. Frederick Douglass, *My Bondage and My Freedom* (New York: Miller, Orton, & Mulligan, 1855), 186–187.
2. Friedrich Nietzsche, "Unfashionable Observations," in *The Complete Works of Friedrich Nietzsche, vol. 2*, ed. Ernst Behler (Stanford, CA: Stanford University Press, 1995), 89.
3. As described by Apollonius, Aithalides, son of Hermes, gifted with unfailing memory, "has long since been lost in the inexorable waters of the Akheron, yet even so, Lethe (Forgetfulness) has not overwhelmed his soul [unlike the other dead, he remembers his past lives and retains his memory in the underworld]." Rhodius Apollonius, *The Voyage of Argo: The Argonautica*, trans. E. V. Rieu (Harmondsworth: Penguin Books, 1971), 642, §1.
4. Plato, "The Republic, Book X," in *The Dialogues of Plato*, trans. B. Jowett (Oxford: Clarendon Press, 1990), 617, 621.
5. Nietzsche, "Unfashionable Observations," 89.
6. Søren Kierkegaard, *Works of Love: Some Christian Reflections in the Form of Discourses*, trans. Howard and Edna Long (New York: Harper & Row, 1964), 295–96.
7. For recent studies on Chrétien's balancing between religion and phenomenology, see Andrew L. Prevot, "Responsorial Thought: Jean-Louis Chrétien's Distinctive Approach to Theology and Phenomenology," *The Heythrop Journal* 56, no. 6 (2015): 975–87. See also Joshua Davis, "The Call of Grace: Henri de Lubac, Jean-Louis Chrétien, and the Theological Conditions of Christian Radical Phenomenology," in *Words of Life: New Theological Turns in French Phenomenology*, ed. Bruce Ellis Benson and Norman Wirzba (New York: Fordham University Press, 2010), 181. Davis, for example, develops a connection between Henri de Lubac and Chrétien, and demonstrates how Heidegger's distinction between manifestation (*Offenbarkeit*) and revelation (*Offenbarung*) is employed by Chrétien to defend the saliency of employing phenomenology in a "religious" way.
8. Martin Heidegger, *Holzwege* (Frankfurt am Main: Vittorio Klostermann, 1980), 360.
9. Martin Heidegger, "Phänomenologie und Theologie," in *Wegmarken*, 2nd ed. (Frankfurt am Main: Vittorio Klostermann, 1978), 53.
10. Martin Heidegger, *Nietzsche, vol. 3, The Will to Power as Knowledge and as Metaphysics*, trans. J. Stambaugh, D. F. Krell and F. A. Capuzzi (San Francisco: Harper & Row, 1987), 18, 155.

11. Martin Heidegger, GA 65, *Beitrüage zur Philosophie* (Frankfurt am Main: Vittorio Klostermann, 1989), 120. See Michael Inwood, *A Heidegger Dictionary* (Oxford: Blackwell, 1999), 74.

12. Martin Heidegger on Hölderlin's "Flight of the Gods" (*die Flucht der Götter*), in GA 39, *Hölderlins Hymnen "Germanien" und "Der Rhein"* (Frankfurt am Main: Vittorio Klostermann, 1934), 80.

13. Dominique Janicaud, *Phenomenology and the "Theological Turn": The French Debate* (New York: Fordham University Press, 2000), 31.

14. Martin Heidegger, "Nietzsche's Word: 'God Is Dead'," in *Off the Beaten Track*, ed. and trans. Julian Young and Kenneth Haynes (New York: Cambridge University Press, 2002), 197.

15. Anthony Steinbock, "The Problem of Forgetfulness in Michel Henry," *Continental Philosophy Review* 32 (1999): 279.

16. "Die 'Weltkriege' und ihre 'Totalität' sind bereits Folgen der Seinsverlassenheit." Martin Heidegger, "Überwindung der Metaphysik" ("Overcoming Metaphysics"), in GA 7, *Vorträge und Aufsätze* (Frankfurt am Main: Vittorio Klostermann, 2000), 91. Prior to that, on 90, he refers to the development and order of mechanization: "All dieses ist schon eingespannt in den Mechanismus der Rüstung des Ordnungsvorganges. Dieser selbst ist bestimmt durch die Leere der Seinsverlassenheit, innerhalb deren der Verbrauch des Seienden für das Machen der Technik, zu der auch die Kultur gehört."

17. Jean-Louis Chrétien, *The Unforgettable and the Unhoped For* (New York: Fordham University Press, 2002), 2.

18. Kierkegaard, *Works of Love*, 295–96. For a synthetic outline of different "types" of forgetfulness as developed from Freud, Kierkegaard, and Nietzsche, see also Miroslav Volf, *The End of Memory: Remembering Rightly in a Violent World* (Grand Rapids, MI: Eerdmans, 2006).

19. For Chrétien, "Every divine action disturbs: it foils our expectation and our calculations, our hopes and our fears, in a striking manner." Chrétien, *The Unforgettable and the Unhoped For*, 77. See also 99.

20. Ibid., xx, 34.

21. Ibid., xx, 23. For Chrétien, "Attentive study to the Platonic thought of recollection . . . shows that this first forgetting constitutes its irreducible nucleus. But this forgetting is a forgetting that founds and gives, a forgetting that opens a properly human temporality, which is that of search for the truth and for oneself," xx. One reason for this is because "the original opening to the truth can not be thought according to the presence of the present," 23.

22. Jean-Louis Chrétien, *Under the Gaze of the Bible*, trans. John Marson Dunaway (New York: Fordham University Press, 2015), 84.

23. Chrétien, *The Unforgettable and the Unhoped For*, 34–35: "The pre-possession—obscure, latent, unarticulated—of truth is that which throws us into the illusion of knowing. That which remains in a sense outside the reach of forgetting, the unforgettable character of what in essence belongs to us, forms what can make us forget supremely and fall into the worst sort of illusion. The pre-possession of science is taken for science: here would be ignorance at its limit." Continuing, "This double ignorance marks the deepest fall, the imprisonment par excellence, since it prohibits even the search for truth and paralyzes our desire. It is from this that philosophy must first and foremost deliver us," 35.

24. Chrétien, *Under the Gaze of the Bible*, 71.

25. Martin Heidegger, *Parmenides*, trans. André Schuwer and Richard Rojcewicz (Bloomington: Indiana University Press, 1992), 105.

26. "Höher als die Wirklichkeit steht die Möglichkeit"; Martin Heidegger, *Being and Time*, trans. John Macquarrie and Edward Robinson (New York: Harper & Row, 1962), 34; see also Martin Heidegger, *Sein und Zeit*, ed. Friedrich-Wilhelm von Herrmann (Frankfurt am Main: Vittorio Klostermann, 1977), 51–52.

27. Paul Tillich, *Dynamics of Faith* (New York: Harper One, 2009), 231, 256.

28. Richard Niebuhr, *Radical Monotheism and Western Culture: With Supplementary Essays* (Louisville, KY: John Knox Press, 1993).

29. Chrétien, *Under the Gaze of the Bible*, 78.

30. Hans Urs von Balthasar, *Glory of the Lord I: Seeing the Form*, trans. Erasmo Leiva-Merikakis (Edinburgh: T & T Clark, 1982), 136.

31. Hans G. Gadamer, *Truth and Method*, trans. Joel Weinsheimer and Donald G. Marshall (London: Bloomsbury, 2013), 504.

32. Paul Ricoeur, *Essays on Biblical Interpretation*, trans. Lewis Seymour Mudge (Philadelphia: Fortress Press, 1980), 144.

33. Martin Heidegger, *The Phenomenology of Religious Life* (Bloomington: Indiana University Press, 2010). This includes his "Introduction to the Phenomenology of Religion," from the winter semester seminars of 1920–1921.

34. Chrétien, *The Unforgettable and the Unhoped For*, 35.

35. For more on *Gelassenheit*, see Martin Heidegger, GA 83, *Seminare: Platon—Aristoteles—Augustinus* (Frankfurt am Main: Vittorio Klostermann, 2012). See also Ian Alexander Moore, "*Gelassenheit*, the Middle Voice, and the Unity of Heidegger's Thought," in *Perspektiven mit Heidegger*, ed. Gerhard Thonhauser (Freiburg: Karl Aber, 2017).

36. Nietzsche, "Unfashionable Observations," 89.

8 Inconspicuous God: Levinas, Heidegger, and the Idolization of Incomprehensibility

Truly you are a God who hides himself, O God of Israel, the Savior.
—Isaiah 45:15.

THE INDO-EUROPEAN ROOT of "the very notion of 'god' (*deiwos*)," as Benveniste points out, in its most "'proper meaning,' is 'luminous' and 'celestial.'"[1] Perhaps this is one reason why it generally is taken for granted still today that, as Debord put it, "what appears is good, and what is good appears," and why modes of manifestation generally are associated with light rather than dark, with clarity and obviousness rather than with obscurity and marginality. Yet, many phenomena actually become intelligible precisely in and through their giving themselves in an obscurity and marginality. Dark matter is presented to space in its being shrouded in nonvisibility, despite its being fully immanent and constantly altering the environments in which it persistently intrudes. The blurry smile of the Mona Lisa enigmatically only can be seen through a peripheral glance that eludes the conceptual grasp of directedness. The darkness of dark matter is integral to its activities, and the blurriness of the smile is essential to any experience of the Mona Lisa.

Some experiences with phenomena are given inconspicuously through one of the many potential modes of shifting between what Heidegger would call "concealment" (*Verborgenheit*) and "disclosure" (*Entbergung*). This shifting can be thought in terms of darkness or obscurity (a *Dunkelheit* that does not lend to complete and utter invisibility). The intelligibility of such things is given or brought into presence (*Anwesenheit*) through their sense data taking on various shades of obscurity, ranges of mystery, or degrees of hiding. There is a productive and effectual means of relation that one might have with an obscurity that does not reflect or shine in the way most phenomena might. Indeed, givenness, manifestation, and their similar cognates give, along with the content revealed, layers, and degrees of concealment. They hide in their giving, veil in their manifesting, and attest to how both the content *and* the form of phenomenality are experienced in varying shades of illumination and obscurity.

This paradoxical relation between darkness and light, which influences our understanding of presence, reaches its highest potential and challenge in the question of the givenness of God to thought.[2] Anselm defines God as the "cannot be thought," that is, not thought in a way that allows comprehension through access to God as *causa sui*. Yet even to think that God *cannot* be thought *is* to already operate with a given thinking of God—God therefore becomes "the unthinkable." Levinas referred to this problem, which is evidenced in the brilliant title *Of God Who Comes to Mind*. There is a certain pregivenness of what Levinas called (in *Enigma and Phenomenon*) the "enigma" that marks how the "Other" is manifested without presenting itself; how this "God" therefore is given to "experience" in its inaccessibility. God *is given* as inaccessible. The enigmatic character of Levinas's "Other" is marked by a riddle and paradox: the Other that one cannot think becomes experienced as the unthought. This is the God *who comes* (or is given) to mind (*De Dieu qui vient à l'idée*), who is not to be called a "phenomenon" for "God is . . . other than the other (*autre qu'autrui*), other otherwise."[3] God's givenness remains purely different.[4]

Intelligible description of this God or Other requires an understanding of transcendence that shrouds God from a totalizing and conscious grasp, thus making room for reception and revelation. Many have interpreted that Levinas holds to an entirely unexperiencable and incomprehensible God whose invisibility and inaccessibility bar any possible idea of the infinite. He indeed seeks an infinite Alterity irreducible to solipsistic interiority ("the infinite cannot be thematized").[5] Yet, the most interesting thing about Levinas's "God" is not that it ends in a nonproductive incomprehensibility per se, but that God's infinity becomes incarnate in the nearest people among us, those entirely foreign neighbors, marginalized victims, and strangely inconspicuous others. The God who comes to mind does not do so through a supernatural experience per se, yet this coming (which both is present and Messianic) does provide a certain rupture in the immanent ordering of things.

Although the infinite is not infinitely obscure or abstract, it enigmatically and inconspicuously is presented in traces on the faces of people. Yet one must take the time to look, and to do so in a different way. This looking does not produce an enlightenment that brings the gazed-up into further clarity, but rather entails the unfolding of a deeper sense of wonder that protects things' phenomenal intelligibility in obscurity.[6] Through acting ethically, one sees and is impacted by the Other, whose ambiguity sends shockwaves throughout the system according to which one attributes intelligibility to things. This initiates an entirely inconspicuous, yet productive, relation that is more about the dark and obscure "in overflowing this play of lights" than a consciousness "tending to the full light" as Levinas puts it.[7]

Any attempt to grasp the infinite directly is unethical and impersonal in its totalizing (and "sameness" making) tendencies. Even as absolutely absent God still brings some intelligibility forth, and manifests a response from me in the faces of these mundane others.[8] Thus, instead of Levinas reducing God to a supernatural "inconceivable," God is renamed according to an infinity of immanent faces, even though those faces are obscured from any totalizing conceptualization. The paradoxical role of Levinas's divine is that its absence always leads back to the immanent responsibilities placed on me by a very particular, and nonabstract other, to whom I can respond "here I am!" He then reaffirms this notion: "That which we call God can only take meaning starting from the relations with others. It is only beginning from these relations that God can 'manifest' himself."[9] Levinas understood that despite not naming the *Tetragrammaton*, its seemingly empty form eventually is filled with content. Although it is an apparently opposite endeavor to "unname" God, this false optimism is part and parcel of the attempt to conceive things by bringing them into light as phenomena. At best, the enigma of the manifestation, presentation, and givenness of God *to thought* therefore can be thought in its unique presentation.

This naturally points to an important double bind. One cannot think even the word "God" without returning to this enigmatic quality, yet *not thinking* still demands that one operates with an aboutness of at least the idea of God, which likely does not come into appearance directly or clearly.[10] It becomes necessary, then to conceive what kinds of givenness out of which things operate, and how, as Steinbock puts it, they "also 'give' the sphere of the Holy."[11] To inquire into this aboutness or givenness is to radicalize the question "is there a God?" (*Gibt es einen Gott?*) on phenomenological terms of the *es Gibt* of God, namely, by asking instead "how is God given, and to what modes of givenness might God correspond?" This of course is inspired by Marion's *God without Being*, which sought to test phenomenology as a first step in theology that brackets God's Being as a foundational, epistemologically arrived at *causa sui*. To respond to this question, it is necessary to turn to how the givenness and *hows* of God often oversee the meaning-giving content of *what* is given.

The ways in which even the very idea of the "idea" have been conceived through the centuries attests to a privileging of one particular type of *how*: clarity, luminescence, and distinctiveness. For Descartes, the "idea" of infinity is understood as a kind of "appearance" that is productive. As developed in the Greek *idea* (from *idein*), which originates in the Greek *opan* ("to see") to have an idea is to see or grasp something that appears due to its being brought into distinction. This of course can be related to *phainesthai* (from which phenomenology gains its namesake), in terms of what is illuminated or brought into public view.[12] Yet is God such an idea, appearing in such a way, or might God be thought more accurately according to modes of obscurity and darkness? Following Levinas's attempt to think God not as a shining phenomenon, could the enigmatic character of God be thought according to an unshiny (*nicht glänzend*) inconspicuousness?[13]

Gaining inspiration from Levinas, Marion, and Heidegger, this chapter seeks to think more carefully the givenness of God, which here is conceived in terms of inconspicuousness. Irrespective of whether or not one thinks "there is" a God, there is or "it gives" (*es gibt*) the thought of God, which appears in particular ways. One way of characterizing such modes of appearance can be developed through a consideration of the particular types of hiddenness God might employ. There is a multidimensionality of the concealedness/disclosure relation at work within givenness (*Gegebenheit*) or presencing (*Anwesen*), and this might help in safeguarding our thinking from reverting to the dead-end of thinking God as inconceivable, which may amount to idolization.[14] Inconceivability inadvertently becomes an absolute, and putatively is not a proper name for "God."

The givenness of God here is thought according to two formulations (inconspicuous phenomena and inconspicuous givenness). The attempt here is not to invert the light/dark paradigm in any purely apophatic way, but rather to display how intelligibility comes about in an oscillation between light and dark, between forms of *nondichotomous* presence and withdrawal. Since throughout the present study Heidegger's "phenomenology of the inconspicuous" has been engaged in detail according to the Zähringen seminar, this chapter will consider some of the premonitions of such inconspicuousness nascent in *Being and Time*, then apply them back to the question of givenness.[15] After considering how the notion of inconspicuousness could be extended and applied to show the efficacy of conceiving of a particular modality or type of givenness, this approach then will be applied to a consideration of the givenness of God as inconspicuous.[16] Inconspicuousness provides a potential avenue on which the enigmatic phenomenality of God can be understood as a present-absent without reverting to the cause/effect structure that has entrapped the thought of God as *causa sui*.

Premonitions of Inconspicuousness in *Being and Time*

In general, getting beyond such a paradigm and structure to describe with more detail such hiding and veiling marks an essential goal of Heidegger's work. Although one aspect of the performance of the *epoché* concerns the uncovering of the hidden or not-yet-appearing, there are other types of hiddenness, among which *Unscheinbarkeit*—which "appears in all things"—might be classified.[17] Inconspicuousness points to how things tease and withhold to keep attention: the more one attempts to force a direct expression of the intelligibility of a particular inconspicuous phenomenon through inspecting it, the more it does not admit to such expression, and therefore presents itself as withdrawn from experience.[18] It is in this sense that things can retain, in their being overlooked, particular layers of *Dunkelheit*, which can refer to both obscurity and darkness. It is in inconspicuousness (*Unscheinbarkeit*) that the ordinary weds the obscure, and the mysterious finds expression. Despite any phenomenon's full and direct presence, it is simultaneously enacting a dynamic withdrawal without our conscious, watchful awareness, and in this sense, phenomena fluctuate in the dark of consciousness.

This provides a general backdrop for interpreting *Sein und Zeit*, which bears but one rather insignificant use of the word *unscheinbar*.[19] Yet with more than 130 uses of "appearing" (*erscheinen*) and its many variations, there is a way in which inconspicuousness highlights, as Jean-François Courtine also argued, the facets and strata of the uncovering of the appearing of phenomena due to the inevitable association with *Being*, *aletheia*, and the covering/discovering (e.g., *verbergen*) relation inherent within them. Appearing (*erscheinen*) refers to that which shows itself from itself and of itself, and thus this self-showing carries its own ways of seeming (*erscheinen*) to appear. To *not appear* is related directly to that which only *seems* to appear, and it is essential to note that inconspicuousness is not to be confused with this dyad of not appearing and appearing: "Indeed it is even possible for an entity to show itself as something which in itself it is *not*. When it shows itself in this way it 'looks like something or other.' This kind of showing-itself is what we call 'seeming [*Scheinen*] ... [And] signifies that which looks like something, that which is "semblant," "semblance" [*das "Scheinbare" der "Schein"*]. [Further] "phenomenon" as that which shows itself... [and] 'phenomenon' as semblance ... are structurally interconnected.'"[20]

Things may be given as they actually appear to be. Yet, in their being given, they can be mobilized as signposts to point to, or indicate something else. This kind of appearing is a thing in its "seeming." Every reference or attention to Being entails the covering up of another strata of Being, and for something to appear to be (i.e., to reflect Being itself) is not for that thing to straightforwardly give itself, but for it to seem (in the sense of surmising the status of something) or be a resemblance of something else, in a radical moment of discursive recollection.

In one sense, this is the act of association, which is the attempt to make what is camouflaged somehow intelligible. The experience of a phenomenon's appearance, or seeming to be something, immediately leads one to make an association between it and something else that one has already previously experienced. At root, seeming is association. In another, different sense, the inherent connection between a phenomenon's being both showing and seeming produces another understanding of phenomenon as a thing that shows itself in its seeming, in its associability, and in its status as tentative and temporally structured. A thing's being given could, at any point, seem to be given otherwise, although without contradicting the way it was, in the first instance, given. *Appearing* inherently implies an immediate referral or relationship between at least two seemingly contradictory intelligibilities within a given phenomena that provoke differing affections in us.

Although *unscheinbar* is not referenced here, Heidegger does refer in this context to specific cases of phenomena that do not directly give themselves or shine, but indeed may seem: "This is what one is talking about when one speaks of the 'symptoms of a disease.'"[21] This can be exemplified in a sort of phenomenon that employs other phenomena as a proxy on their behalf. The *appearance* of a *Krankheitserscheinung* (sickness symptom) indicates (*indizieren*) itself precisely as that "which does not show itself," yet is still announced or introduced, namely as a disturbance in a healthy body.[22] To follow the example, the sickness is *unscheinbar* insofar as it only indirectly shows itself, and deploys symptoms to speak for its seemingly invisible, yet affectively experienced activities. In such cases the phenomenal experience is with the indication itself, a proxy for that which remains uniquely hidden or disguised. Yet profoundly, the recognition is made that the symptoms are not the originary phenomenon, but only manifestations of it or ambassadors on its behalf.

This sheds more light on appearance, which can be understood, not so much as a *what* to be seen, but as an announcement of something's potentially meaningful presence; an announcement that comes in the form of symptoms, sketches, or syntax.[23] That which *can* show itself acts as an ambassador that announces a phenomenon's unseeability. This is accomplished through phenomena that tend to specialize in translating on behalf of other phenomena. In these cases, a thing's appearance must bear the marks of a "double signification: first, appearing, in the sense of announcing itself as not-showing-itself; and next, that which does the announcing [*das Meldende selbst*]—that which in its showing-itself indicates something which does not show itself."[24] And then thirdly (and perhaps most importantly) "appearing" can be the term used to designate the more "genuine sense" of "'phenomenon' as showing-itself."[25] This insight is relevant not only for particular phenomena like sicknesses. It points to a means of phenomenality essential to the *Lebenswelt.* And if we remain ignorant of the distinction made between these three kinds of appearance, we will remain bewildered. As the next section of *SuZ* indicates, phenomenon should be understood in this third, more genuine sense of appearing, and as Heidegger crucially argued—from before *Sein und Zeit* up to his graveside in Meßkirch in 1976—*Sein*, especially as *Lichtung* and beyond its metaphysical sense of *Seiendheit*, belongs *to*, and displays its unique glories within what shows itself and appears.

The two aspects or movements of a phenomenon's self-articulation (their showing and being shown) are not easily distinguishable from one another, so much so that these two movements often are one and the same. Within them is a subtle indication that they bear within themselves a strata or layer that is incapable of being signified or presented, yet this indication is indeed a phenomenon in itself that says something about that which does not appear. The phenomenon never fully shows itself, but this not-showing is still part and parcel of the phenomenon as shown. Not-shining is a phenomenon in and of itself. In this limited sense, the inconspicuous nonappearing appears.[26] As mentioned throughout the present study, in the Parmenides Seminars Heidegger eventually unfolds a number of ways in which aspects of things or matters do not come to light. Things in their hiddenness can be, for example, undiscovered, disguising, accidentally covered over, or actively buried over (*verdecken*, the most commonly relied on means of defining hiddenness). In this seminar inconspicuousness is distinguished from these forms of hiding and is even named the primary character trait of mysteriousness itself.[27] Indeed, for something to be named "mysterious" it must have some form of presencing itself as somehow enigmatic and absent. The mysterious can indicate itself as inherently confusing as shining falsely. And to see properly this conflagration, the attempts to conceive of (*in Be-griffe fassen*) a phenomenon must be surrendered.

This teaches that phenomenology is no longer a tool that simply permits us to see something as it truly is, but rather one that initiates a deformalization precisely of the seen by darkening or obfuscating its data.[28] Such obfuscation can properly draw one into the phenomenon's self-disclosure, as phenomenology is refashioned as a tool for considering the absence of phenomena, with which one still might relate.[29] As inconspicuous, phenomenology can lend to reflection (*nachdenken*) on the "positive characterization[s]" of the overlooked, which precisely is "the closest thing."[30] To enter into this kind of experience, the will to bring the not-yet-in-the-light into fuller clarity is to be suspended. This approach to unshining might bear on the question of the givenness of God, the unique obscurity of whom surely exceeds and eludes any totalizing gaze.

Inconspicuousness and Givenness

Given the subtlety of Heidegger's references to inconspicuousness, it remains applicable to understanding specific phenomenal experiences with hiddenness. As such, it could be an approach that allows for various kinds of seeing (though again, not conceiving) the given symptoms of what does not appear straightforwardly, and toward accessing that which those symptoms represent. More specifically, inconspicuousness might lead to a greater encounter with the media between seemingly contradictory phenomena as they withdraw (*proodos*, or "move away") and arrive (*epistrophè*, or "returning") in appearance. As a means to understanding some experiences, inconspicuousness helps to describe a point of access to a very precise moment at which there is a simultaneous presencing and absencing of a thing's intelligible data.

If inconspicuousness can be understood as operative at such a fundamental level, then it can be integrated within the very meaning of things-as-given, marking a kind or variation of givenness (the coming-into-being-given) itself. Givenness is a helpful concept for any extension beyond an economy of exchange, calculation, and modes of causality that tend to over-condition experience. Givenness points to the sheer excessiveness of the faculties themselves; not only is the thing excessive or saturated, but also the very way in which something is given. As noted, Marion successfully has provided for (in my view) "saturated phenomena" that also saturate the field of vision and experience. The active seeing of things projects onto them, prior to their being given, dynamic strata of expectation and anticipation. A value of givenness in these regards can be exemplified in the understood preference for categorial intuition over sensual intuition, which at any point can be bracketed in preference for a return to the immediate impressions of sense data.

Yet it should not be taken for granted that givenness is an inherently religious form of appearing. Phenomenology always has endorsed an active wrestling with different modes of appearing and revealing, and this likely is why theology has been a constant dialogue partner for those found among its ranks. Both Scheler and Heidegger, as early students of Husserl, held to the systematic distinction between revelation (*Offenbarung*) and manifestation (*Offenbarkeit*) for this very reason.[31] Levinas, in *Totality and Infinity*, upheld this line between revelation and givenness as disclosure, which subsequently inspired the work of Marion, who still claims to be true to the distinction between theological revelation and phenomenological manifestation or givenness more broadly.[32] One thing all of the aforementioned thinkers agree on is that manifestation is in itself often an obscure phenomenon that obscures other phenomena.

Although these distinctions between the modes of appearing for philosophy and theology often are helpful to delineate, givenness can be seen as a most neutral mode out of which phenomenality appears. All things that *are* have come into being, and this dynamic mode of Being is even referred to by Heidegger as a kind of "givenness." Yet all of this does not entail that there is but one univocal givenness. The way in which things are given vary greatly, and therefore there are different forms or variations that correspond to the type, level of saturation, or excessive force out of which a phenomenon is given.[33] Givenness also takes on characteristics according to the type of phenomena it wishes to reveal, sustain, and maintain. From the outset, then, it is not prohibited to refer to inconspicuousness as a kind or type of givenness; that is, at least in the context of God. Does it not make sense, then, to conceive of the manifold ways in which God could be given to thought prior to attempting to determine whether or not God exists? This could be a productive means to theological thinking, especially since God (generally) is not given in any direct or shining way (those who mystically see or audibly hear God directly notwithstanding).

One way of addressing the *how* of the thought of God could involve a description of an inconspicuous givenness. To ask, "how can God be given?" is distinct from asking, "can God be given?" The former question, which is of more interest here, can be stated otherwise: "what is the how character and characteristics of presentation of such a givenness of God, should that givenness occur?" The latter question (can God be given?) still is construed metaphysically, namely because it ascribes the name "God" first and foremost according to the *causa prima*, because it seeks of a "yes" or a "no" in answer to that question, and due to its bringing that thought to an ultimate conclusion that is not instantiated by a dynamic God first and foremost. An inconspicuous givenness, that is, an approach to the givenness of that which is inconspicuous, is marked in general by its phenomena's unique renouncement of their *being given*. The gift given follows its way of being given, separating from the static being of presence, renouncing being, and thus not falling prey to a metaphysics of presence.[34] To think beyond the metaphysical confines of God as unknowable or ultimately hidden, it can be helpful to draw a distinction between inconspicuous phenomena and inconspicuous givenness in the consideration of arguing for God as inconspicuous.

Inconspicuous Phenomena

Inconspicuous phenomena act as such insofar as they do not accord to the rules of appearance, yet simultaneously are unable to be jettisoned immediately from experience as invisible. As inconspicuous, they slide back and forth between the visible and the invisible, and they distort the sense of relation with reality due to being both concealed (*lethe*) and uncovered (*a-letheia*). This inconspicuousness can be exemplified quite well with a vision metaphor. As Kandel notes, "our peripheral cone vision, which cannot perceive details well, employs a holistic analysis that enables us to see" in ways often better than "foveal vision." It remains possible to "perceive things in peripheral vision . . . that we miss in central vision."[35] Some phenomena can be grasped only peripherally as they require a more holistic or broadening vision for their particular presencing to be experienced. Some phenomena tend to disguise themselves in the peripheries of conscious experience. Like quicksand, the more one struggles to grasp them through foveal means, the deeper one sinks into misunderstanding them.

There are three ways these inconspicuous phenomena can be thought. First, such phenomena can be given to experience through various forms such as hiding (e.g., hiding a treasure), surrogating (announcing itself via another phenomena), or screening (e.g., a translucent curtain through which light is refracted). They can be experienced as they immanently come into presence, with their data corresponding to the type of hiddenness they, at that particular point, enact or incite. My back pain could be experienced as inconspicuous in either the form of a passive, latent concealment (I do not notice it by merit of being distracted by a simultaneous knee pain) or in the form of an active camouflaging (I took pain medication that now covers it up).

A second way of understanding such phenomena can be exemplified in the case of Heidegger's *Krankheitserscheinungen*, which are present-at-hand only through and by proxy—as immanent phenomena that serve to indicate the presence of that to which they point. Yet, there is still a sense in which such phenomena transgress what typically is called "immanent" experience. Like dark matter, these phenomena would intrude into otherwise closed spaces of visibility and thereby employ the space surrounding them to communicate on their behalf, usually without their being perceptible to the faculties. They are given by offering accord between the visible and inconspicuous, giving simultaneously something graspable/detectable through conception, and something that eludes conception and produces ambivalence. The immanently detectable data of a thing given, most often and unfortunately are trumped by the data that one, in the first place, originally conceived.

Thirdly, inconspicuous phenomena can be understood according to everyday experience, whereby conceivable intelligibility is preferred over that which is not conceivable. This strangely is inconsistent with what we know about how we experience the intelligibility of phenomena. To employ once again the horse example: his hair, teeth, and muscle all fully are present and operative to my senses, yet they hide from me in favor of my true idea of the horse and what I take it that a horse *does*. Seeing a horse may raise the negative association I attribute to horses due to my falling off one as a young child, or it may lead me to the particularly romantic mood that the sight of a beautiful horse insights. In both cases, sense data slips into darkness, yet without too much effort, can be brought to bare in the experience and subsequently deformalized. The data of a thing that are most present of the horse are that which become the most inconspicuously given to me. For a horse to be a horse, and not be a blob of hair, bone, and muscle, these sense perceptions of the horse must render themselves inconspicuous in favor of the horsehood itself, and vice versa.

The more a thing enters conceptualization as a phenomenal appearance (or in the case of God, the more God reaches the level of spectacularity) or nonappearance, the less it becomes possible to interact dynamically with it. And the less it can be interacted with dynamically, the more it attains stativity. The more it attains stativity, the more likely it is that the phenomenon will be overlooked, ultimately prohibiting one from ever having any intuition as to what *is* inconspicuous.[36] In the case of phenomena that arrive inconspicuously, one can experience the profusion of what simultaneously both is here and not here through a kind of phenomenological seeing that is not unlike the aforementioned aspects of peripheral vision in that their arrival or announcement require a unique kind of seeing that corresponds to *how* they are given.

The Inconspicuous God

Inconspicuous phenomena can present themselves in the shifting of thought from categorial to sensual intuition, can give themselves liminally through a proxy, and can be engaged through sifting-out the type of hiddenness according to which their data are or can be given. In the case of God's inconspicuousness (God's status as a phenomenon notwithstanding), it generally would involve twin experiences that form that specific phenomenal experience: God's simultaneous entry and withdrawal from the very appearance in which God arrives. There are three ways God can be understood as inconspicuous. A first would be in one's overlooking the features of how God very well could be introduced in a new way to thought. In which case, God-like-data one previously had been given—and at one point was taken to represent God—is preferred over an actively differentiating God. Such God-like-data are second order phenomena or attributes of God, not God per se. To recall once again the horse analogy, wherein "horsehood" is a categorial intuition preferred over what actually appears at that moment, it is out of habit that one prefers the doctrines or preunderstood means of how God is assumed to always already be given, instead of any potentially new ways and means of God's being given.

Second, God could be given to thought as inconspicuous through the active and intentional sifting-through of the various forms of inconspicuousness, hiddenness, or latency God might enact. By being attuned to the active thoughts of God that are often hidden or overlooked, one might first determine the nature of the present experience with inconspicuousness out of which God might be giving Godself. There may be cases in which the thought of God is a constant source of troubling, pain, and therefore actively is covered-over or anesthetized. In which case, this overlooking would need to be engaged actively so as to not overcome it, yet to experience it more deeply as a constant scandal (*skandalon*, σκανδαλον) to what one takes for granted concerning the thought of God, which in this case is "covered-over" through a kind of anesthesia. Or, there could be thoughts of God that are incongruously simple, ordinary, or insignificant, which of course are modes to which inconspicuousness deeply relates. An engagement with God as inconspicuous in this sense would entail a closer attention to the simple and marginal in a way that wonder is incited precisely at such phenomenal overlooking. The dull and marginal most often retain the most hidden and mysterious potential (*dunemei*, "dynamite") for life change. The realization that something had been there all along, and subsequently overlooked, holds a powerful effect.

A third understanding of God as inconspicuous could be that not-so-inconspicuous phenomena are animated to indicate or speak in lieu of God. Levinas's reflections on "the face" illustrate this point perfectly. The uncanny and mysterious means of God would be rendered experienceable in and through what is taken to be ordinary, and in such cases, God would only appear in the immanent as nonappearing. God would be given-as-resistant to the overly preferred means and modes of "bringing to light," and in this case one is provided the opportunity to deformalize previous conceptions of God that do not incite adoration.

In these briefly sketched cases, it seems that accessing an inconspicuous God in an obscure yet present experience, in and through a substantiality that cultures and preconditions that experience, may help broaden a more holistic perspective through which aspects of the mysterious or uncanny God can be seen uniquely.[37] Instead of seeking God as such, the seeking of God would become much more indirect. This would result in an antinomic kind of epiphany (from *phainesthai*, what shines or appears) that draws attention to our present relationship with the ordinary. It is in the somatically seen or affected that the Holy arrives on the limited horizon of human experience. God can be given "in the hyle" so to speak, of sense perceptions, sounds, objects, or callings. Such things do not speak on behalf of a God in an invisible blind spot, yet direct grasping cannot earn or merit an experience with such a God. Yet it may be possible, on the blurry edges of an indiscriminate line between that which does and that which does not provide sufficient illumination for conclusive conceptions, that intuition can become aware of what intention fails to grasp. Something of God has been given, which would signal to God's own givenness, a kind of inconspicuous givenness.

Inconspicuous Givenness

Inconspicuous givenness has a very subtle, yet consequential difference from their aforementioned corresponding phenomena. It may not be necessarily the case that phenomena only are *characterized* by inconspicuousness, but perhaps also that inconspicuousness can mark a *way* in which things are given; in which case, such a givenness gives so that inconspicuousness itself is part and parcel of the experience. It can incite feelings of being on the verge of the border between the seen and unseen; of something being overlooked; of being in the presence of an uncanny strangeness; of something having passed through the peripheries of consciousness in a way that eludes both confirmation and denial. Inconspicuous givenness gives in its provision of the disorientation of one's sense of presence. Yet, the givenness of inconspicuousness is effective despite any potential illusions, diversions, or distractions, and operates by giving one little control over its unique movements. And again, this all incites a fundamental ambivalence.

As effective, this kind of givenness alters the entire environment in which things are to appear, as well as the way in which one relates with what at first would be nonvisible. Such givenness does not come with an automatic, self-understood (*selbstverständlich*) justification of how it gives; for its mode of apprehension likewise is inconspicuous. Yet such givenness is not invisible (*unsichtbar*), for the experience is capable of giving so that aspects of the phenomenon become visible. This might turn attention and affect to a kind of movement that momentarily disorients even the preunderstandings of how something is covered-over or unveiled. This givenness gives by withholding the given from being recognizable as visible or invisible.

Inconspicuous givenness gives via an indicator that provides just enough data to intuition so that the givenness itself remains nearly inexplicable. Although the tendency is to see only what is illuminated, this type of givenness gives even without offering a sense of "seeming" (*scheinen*). The nonshining of something directly corresponds to the margin one allows for its unique withdrawal or making-nonappearance. The experience of the givenness of inconspicuousness in this sense would come in a marginality that may carry with it the effects of boredom at its ordinariness, thus further contributing to the given phenomena's overlooked nature. When this suspension is performed, givenness actively gives reasons for forfeiting the preunderstandings of phenomenality, yet does so by offering an indication—a sliver of detectability or intelligibility that furnishes just enough data to confirm the experience.

The Inconspicuous Givenness of God

This all hopefully remains applicable to thinking God "in God's how." The actual content of the appearance (i.e., the phenomenal data) in this case is of less consequence than the form of its transmission or givenness, at least for that moment at which one is more attuned to such givenness, and not to the phenomena given. The content would enact but a liminal appearing in preference for seeing the form and how it shapes the content. While this inconspicuous givenness exclusively gives (along with its phenomenal content) obscurely, alongside that sense of obscurity comes a corresponding idea of God-as-overlooked. That is, some thing or some data that corresponds to God is given, or appears in the peripheries of thought, which thereby provides occasion for the thought of God. This givenness gives the intelligible sense of something having been overlooked, some mode of access appropriate to God's being given that is irreducible to comprehension.

In this case, God would be given by coming out of obscurity and returning into it simultaneously. This movement would prevent God's becoming a phenomenon in the sense of shining or coming into the light of full manifestation. The tautology that Heidegger once developed out of Parmenides's work could help phenomenology overcome the "genuine philosophical embarrassment" of self-imposed dichotomies. The endeavors of *aletheia* are to unconceal *as* they conceal in giving. One finds the *there is* or *it gives* of God as God comes into, and simultaneously departs from conscious thought.[38]

The effective reign, or Kingdom of God is commensurate with God's inconspicuousness, which enacts the very movement of veiling God's own mysteriousness. It is not the clarity of God that makes God effective, nor is it God's incomprehensibility, but rather God's ability to hide between the two in obscurity. This givenness of God presents data that transgresses through obscuring. The obscure appearing or veiling of God comes in tow with means to access somehow this inconspicuous God.

In the final analysis, this might be achieved through phenomenology, which today is employed to emphasize different kinds of seeing. Such a method can seek the inherent depth structure of things through close inspection of the minutia of what is visible or not-yet-apparent. It might employ a horizonal seeing that gains its force from adjusting to the far-sighted and distant, spherical curvature of experience; as it rotates and brings further clarity, the more one attends to it. It even can be used to engage a "vertical" (Steinbock) seeing that entails an attunement to religiously intonated hyper-phenomena, epiphanies whose evidences stand out and beyond what has become normalized. It is in this context that a phenomenology that is inconspicuous seeks to stretch attention toward what dangles on the edge between what is enlightened and what is in utter darkness. This is not necessarily an inversion of Husserlian intentionality, per se (in the way that Marion's "saturated phenomena" are accessible to intuition, yet irregardable by intention), but instead, hopefully a way of experiencing the givenness of that which cannot be directly aimed at, yet at the same time is something at which one might be directed.[39] This kind of directedness would not be quite so direct. This aim would not be centered on its target in a straightforward way, and in the case of the givenness of God, one would aim indirectly by merit of deformalizing God's having-been-given (via forgetting) in a way that God's actively being-given can take place through what is inconspicuous or marginal. This indirectedness might help release one's grip (which conceptualizes) so that the means by which God inconspicuously autorejects spectacular phenomenality can be experienced.

Beyond Inconceivability

From the obvious references to God in terms of light (in the primary texts of many faith traditions), to the seemingly opposite insistence on God's incomprehensibility, a *Deus absconditus* easily can be reduced to a de facto *ultimatus obscurare*. At the very least, a phenomenology of the inconspicuous givenness of God can push back against the temptation to quarantine God to the invisible, incomprehensible, or entirely inaccessible, and can do so in a way that is irreducible to an apophatic or negative detheologization. As Heidegger frequently bemoaned, the forms of the unknown often are mistaken for being metonymically univocal for mysteriousness. And as a result, the unknown ends up exacting a totalizing power over thought by negating and prohibiting thought itself. Or, as Levinas knew, it becomes necessary to return to immanent life to access the mysteries that do not easily come into view; mysteries that, by merit of their mysteriousness, deformalize our understanding of presence.

It may be that the attempts to leave God inconceivable fail due to being more idolatrous on the account of still conceiving, albeit silently and without words, features of God, thus still not escaping the gravitational pull St. Paul referred to as idolatry (Romans 12:3). In which case, a new metaphysics can arrive not so much in the Nietzschean twilight of the idols, as light fades from refracting on them, but in those idols' inevitable and stillborn dawn: In the place of woodcarvings stands an empty vacuity filled by any unchecked, momentary fancy or whim. If idolatry, as Bloechl recently put it "is an event of comprehension, of holding something up in a light that can be crossed effortlessly by an imperial gaze" then it should be addressed how a proper counteridolatry is not an extreme antiidolatry, which would amount to the same. Necessary is an appropriated adoration that takes place within the most ordinary and marginal moments of life.[40] The category mistake often made is that openness is openness as such; that naming something unknown can cease or terminate the swarm of thought. Yet as Levinas once demanded, irrespective of predispositions, one "cannot escape God."[41] Whether in the form of an Anselmian "that than which nothing greater can be conceived," a Cartesian "idea of God [that] is given" or a "Marionian" synthesis between the two, that "as irreducible, the idea of God is given as that which one cannot have," the thought of God will be given, and even may be inescapable.[42]

The two approaches to inconspicuousness that have been developed here—inconspicuous phenomena and inconspicuous givenness—hopefully furnish description of the givenness of God that might go beyond the seemingly inevitable consequences of idolization when thinking of God. To think actively the givenness of God as inconspicuous could be a means of dismantling (or as Heidegger put it "overcoming") the various matrixes of opposition that underwrite our ontotheological condition. The new paradigm introduced by St. Paul for interpreting "the invisible," as *eikōn tou theou tou aoratou* ("Christ is the visible image [εἰκὼν] of the invisible [ἀοράτου] God." Colossians 1:15) proposes an iconicity, not for its own sake, but one that seeks to counter the social imaginaries idolatry tends to autopresent. "Christ, who *is the image* of God" (2 Corinthians 4:4) is the *Eikon* according to which God gives Godself by escaping any direct and conscious grasp, yet still leaving inconspicuous traces behind for intelligible meaning-making. Not unlike the "dazzling darkness" to which pseudo-Dionysius referred, the inconspicuous God is not simply different from idols, but fundamentally counteracts them and their preferred form of ideal phenomenality. This God does so by being obscure, which in this case bespeaks an inherent quality of integration, and enigmatically incites a sense of ambivalence. Inconspicuousness helps articulate how God's incarnate integration and *omni-potence* can instantiate a unique sphere of effective reign today, in a totalizing and spectacle driven world.

Notes

1. Emile Benveniste, *Indo-European Language and Society*, trans. Elizabeth Palmer (London: Faber and Faber, 1973), 445–46.

2. See also John P. Manoussakis, "The Phenomenon of God: From Husserl to Marion," *American Catholic Quarterly* 78, no. 1 (2004), 53–69. For Manoussakis, "The field where philosophical thinking runs the greatest risk of losing itself (but also, the field where it receives the greatest promise to regain itself) is that which concerns the question of God. The thought of God is, par excellence, that which does not belong to thought ... yet ... as a question and as a problem posed to philosophy, is raised always within philosophical thinking, which it endlessly confronts."

3. See Emmanuel Levinas: *God, Death, and Time*, trans. Bettina Bergo (Stanford: Stanford University Press, 2000), 224. Emmanuel Levinas, *De Dieu qui vient à l'idée* (Paris: Vrin, 1982). Concerning how this "Enigma" is distinct from how we are to understand "phenomenon," see Emmanuel Levinas, "Enigma and Phenomenon," in *Emmanuel Levinas: Basic Philosophical Writings*, ed. Adriaan T. Peperzak, Simon Critchley, and Robert Bernasconi (Bloomington: Indiana University Press, 1996), 65–77. Emmanuel Levinas, "Enigme et phenomene," *Esprit* 33 (1966): 1128–142.

4. Levinas, *Emmanuel Levinas*, 141.

5. Emmanuel Levinas, *Totality and Infinity: An Essay on Exteriority*, trans. Alphonso Lingis (Pittsburgh, PA: Duquesne University Press, 1969), 211. In reference to Descartes's "infinite," Levinas continues, "If to think consists in referring to an object, we must suppose that the thought of infinity is not a thought." Ibid., 211. This can be read back into claims made in the preface of *Totality and Infinity*: "The idea of infinity (which is not a representation of infinity) sustains activity itself" and "is the common source of activity and theory." Ibid., 27.

6. This is why, for Levinas "Ethics is first philosophy." See here Jeffrey Bloechl, *The Face of the other and the Trace of God: Essays on the Philosophy of Emmanuel Levinas* (New York: Fordham University Press, 2000).

7. Levinas, *Totality and Infinity*, 27–28. Here, Levinas appears to reduce Heidegger's work to a privileging of "disclosing." Levinas says of his own project that "in accomplishing *events* whose ultimate signification (contrary to the Heideggerian conception) does not lie in *disclosing*. Philosophy does indeed discover ... but ... without discovery (or truth) being their destiny." Ibid., 28. Given Heidegger's engagements with the attempt to reinscribe closure within the very nature of *aletheia*, especially in the 1930s in relation to Heraclitus and Parmenides, this may be an unfair criticism.

8. Emmanuel Levinas, *Humanism of the other*, trans. N. Poller (Urbana: University of Illinois Press, 2006), 38–40.

9. Emmanuel Levinas, *God, Death, and Time*, trans. Bettina Bergo (Stanford, CA: Stanford University Press, 2000), 185.

10. Similarly, from Caputo's perspective: "I think that phenomenology provides the most successful, important, and meaningful way to think about God, with the proviso that this would always be a phenomenology that confesses the limits of what we can say about God. A phenomenological approach to God is necessary and inescapable, not only for religion ... but also for phenomenology itself." John Caputo, *Religion With/out Religion: The Prayers and Tears of John D. Caputo*, ed. James H. Olthuis (New York: Routledge Press, 2002), 176.

11. See also Anthony J. Steinbock, "Saturated Intentionality," in *The Body: Classic and Contemporary Readings*, ed. Donn Welton (Malden, MA: Blackwell Publishers, 1999), 178–99.

12. Plato's "idea," of course, is a representation of something else in consciousness. As duly noted by John C. Marcado, "A phenomenology of God, then, would seem to require a phenomenology of the unthinkable, of what cannot be given even to thought, such less to experience." John C Marcado, "Nothing Gives," in *Japanese and Continental Philosophy: Conversations with the Kyoto School*, ed. Bret W. Davis, Brian Schroeder, and Jason M. Wirth (Bloomington: Indiana University Press, 2011), 147.

13. For a deeper engagement with this question, see Jean-Yves Lacoste, "Perception, Transcendence and the Experience of God," in *Phenomenology and Transcendence*, ed. Conner Cunningham and Peter M. Candler Jr. (London: SCM Press, 2007), 1. For Lacoste in these regards, "God is admittedly no thing. And when he dares be present in the world as a thing, he does so in the sense perception perceives only as a sacramentum: the rest is unperceivable." Lacoste engages "one or two things about the way God appears while transcending his present apparition."

14. Phenomenology is to be a nonmetaphysical science, which is why Michel Henry claims that, "while the other sciences study specific phenomena—physical, chemical, biological, juridical, social, economic, etc.—phenomenology explores what allows a phenomenon to be a phenomenon." Michel Henry, "Phenomenology of Life," in *Phenomenology and Transcendence*, ed. Conner Cunningham and Peter M. Candler Jr. (London: SCM Press, 2007), 241.

15. As mentioned in the introduction to this study, Taminiaux claimed that the "Zähringen seminar" taught simply that, "there is an excessiveness at the very heart of seeing" as intentionality is "transfixed with excessiveness" to see things coming into appearance. Jacques Taminiaux, "Heidegger and Husserl's Logical Investigations in Remembrance of Heidegger's last Seminar," *Research in Phenomenology* 7, no. 1 (1977): 79.

16. I find this view to be consistent with Steinbock's: "the attempts to merely describe empirically the variety of religions and religious experiences ... fail to ask how the Holy or the other person is given." Steinbock later notes, 230, the need to conceive different "kinds" of givenness. Anthony J. Steinbock, *Phenomenology and Mysticism: The Verticality of Religious Experience* (Bloomington: Indiana University Press, 2007), 158.

17. See also Gérard Guest, "Aux confins de l'inapparent: l'extrême phénomenénologie de Heidegger," *Existentia* 12 (2002): 123.

18. To reiterate Merleau-Ponty's claim once again, Heidegger "seeks out a direct expression of being while showing on the other hand that it does not admit of direct expression." ("*cherche une expression directe de l'être don't il montre par ailleurs qu'il n'est pas susceptible d'expression direct.*") Maurice Merleau-Ponty, *Notes de Cours, 1959–1961* (Paris: Gallimard, 1996), 148.

19. "*Die Beschaffung, Sichtung und Sicherung des Materials bringt nicht erst den Rückgang zur 'Vergangenheit' in Gang, sondern setzt das geschichtliche Sein zum dagewesenen Dasein,*

das heißt die Geschichtlichkeit der Existenz des Historikers schon voraus. Diese fundiert existenzial die Historie als Wissenschaft bis in die unscheinbarsten, 'handwerklichen' Veranstaltungen." Martin Heidegger, *Sein und Zeit*, ed. Friedrich-Wilhelm von Herrmann (Frankfurt am Main: Vittorio Klostermann, 1977), 394.

20. Heidegger, *Sein und Zeit*, 28–29, Martin Heidegger, *Being and Time*, trans. John Macquarrie and Edward Robinson (New York: Harper & Row, 1962), 51.

21. Heidegger, *Sein und Zeit*, 29; Heidegger, *Being and Time*, 52.

22. Ibid. "Here one has in mind certain occurrences in the body which show themselves and which, in showing themselves as thus showing themselves, 'indicate' something which does not show itself. The emergency of such occurrences, their showing-themselves, goes together with the Being-present-at-hand of disturbances which does not show themselves. Thus appearance, as the appearance 'of something', does not mean showing-itself; it means rather the announcing-itself by something which does not show itself, but which announces itself through something which does show itself. Appearing is a not-showing-itself."

23. Ibid. "All indications, presentations, symptoms, and symbols have this basic formal structure of appearing, even though they are different among themselves."

24. Ibid, 30; Ibid, 53.

25. Ibid.

26. Ibid. The phenomenon "is something that proximally and for the most part does not show itself at all: it is something that lies hidden, in contrast to that which proximally and for the most part does show itself; but at the same time it is something that belongs to what thus shows itself."

27. "The secret in the mystery [*Das Geheime des Geheimnisvollen*] is a kind of concealment [*Verbergung*], characterized by its insignificance [*Unscheinbarkeit*, i.e., inconspicuousness] in virtue of which the mystery is an open one." Martin Heidegger, *Parmenides*, trans. André Schuwer and Richard Rojcewicz (Bloomington: Indiana University Press, 1992), 63. Martin Heidegger, GA 54, *Das Geheime des Geheimnisvollen ist eine Art der, die sich durch ihre auszeichnet, kraft deren das Geheimnis ein offense ist* (Frankfurt am Main: Vittorio Klostermann, 1982), 93.

28. It is on this point in particular that Heraclitus "the obscure" becomes a formidable source of inspiration for Heidegger in the early 1940s.

29. Heidegger, *Sein und Zeit*, 36; Heidegger, *Being and Time*, 60.

30. Heidegger, *Being and Time*, 69, ref 9.

31. Max Scheler, "Formalismus in der Ethik und die Materiale Wertethik, vol. 2," in *Gesammelte Werke*, ed. Maria Scheler (Bern: Francke, 1966).

32. For Steinbock, "Levinas' work [*TI*] which, despite the fact that it seems to qualify the Other as what is not able to be given, makes a clear distinction between givenness as disclosure and absolute givenness or givenness as revelation." Steinbock, *Phenomenology and Mysticism*, 12.

33. For an important engagement with, and extension of Marion's description of givenness and saturated phenomena, see Gschwandtner's recent *Degrees of Givenness*, in which the argument is made that givenness is not univocal, and for these reasons, various "givennesses" are in need of being explicated. Christina Gschwandtner, *Degrees of Givenness: On Saturation in Jean-Luc Marion* (Bloomington: Indiana University Press, 2014).

34. This is one reason why Marion holds that "the gift gives itself precisely to the strict degree to which it renounces to be, excepted from presence, undone from itself by undoing

the subsistence in it." Jean-Luc Marion, *Being Given: Toward a Phenomenology of Givenness* (Stanford, CA: Stanford University Press, 2002), 127.

35. Eric Kandel, *The Age of Insight: The Quest to Understand the Unconscious in Art, Mind, and Brain: From Vienna 1900 to the Present* (New York: Random House, 2012), 246.

36. Par excellence, the gift works "as a pure loss, which in order to give itself, it [the gift] must in effect disappear, it thus appears at the price of pure disappearance in it of all subsistence." Neither subsisting nor being-stable, and in excessively giving in such a way that it is not the point of focus or attention, the gift gives *as* a loss. This is what Marion calls a "gift beyond gift," which is a strange gift because it gives nothing, and "since this strange gift gives nothing (nothing real, not a thing), it frees itself in order to give the condition of the given." This gift, the first gift, gives the very condition of the gift. Again, these are not conditions that are subject to causality but those provided by givenness, which in effect, "gives" its own ratio. This is another reason why attempting to first conceive the existence of God before the possibility of God's givenness may be doomed to fail. Jean-Luc Marion, "Sketch of a Phenomenological Concept of Gift," in *Postmodern Philosophy and Christian Thought*, ed. Merold Westphal (Bloomington: Indiana University Press, 1999), 127–28.

37. The inconspicuous appears in the most ordinary of matters, "but," says Heidegger, "it is the substantiality that, in its non-appearance, enables what appears to appear. In this sense, one can even say that it is more apparent than what itself appears." Martin Heidegger, "Seminar in Zähringen 1973," in *Four Seminars*, trans. Andrew Mitchell and François Raffoul (Bloomington: Indiana University Press, 2003), 67. In the Christian tradition, for Caputo, "the very appearance of Jesus is conditioned upon his nonappearance . . . inasmuch as we need the 'condition' in order to apprehend him as the Incarnation." Caputo, *Religion with/out Religion*, 176.

38. See here Jean-Luc Nancy, *Disenclosure: The Deconstruction of Christianity* (New York: Fordham University Press, 2008). Recall that for Nancy, God *is* differentiation by being "he who passes by."

39. It is in this sense (but perhaps only in this sense) that inconspicuousness is similar to the invisible, as "invisible, from *viser*, designates what cannot be aimed at, meant, or intended." Marion, *Being Given*, 363, note 41. Marion's Saturated Phenomena are an inversion of Husserlian intentionality as they are not capable of being aimed at, yet saturated with intuition that overwhelms intention. The phenomena "will therefore be invisible according to quantity, unbearable according to quality, absolute according to relation, and incapable of being looked at [irregardable] according to modality." Ibid., 113. This is taken up and altered by Manoussakis, for whom "inverted intentionality" entails the looking-in of God: "God appears while He remains invisible; He appears, nevertheless, in me and only in me, a fact that indicates that, insofar as I am the Other for God, an Other that He can look at and be in relationship with, God is in need of me as the horizon that possibilizes His (otherwise impossible) appearance. The human self, and therefore every human self, is understood as the sacred place of God's epiphany." John Panteleimon Manoussakis, *God after Metaphysics: A Theological Aesthetic* (Bloomington: Indiana University Press, 2007), 68.

40. Bloechl's position on "darkness" is a bit more extreme than my own in terms of its intelligibility: "If we associate that light with intelligibility, then 'darkness' must signify a condition in which we are no longer in the presence of intelligible things. As one moves from experience by light to experience in darkness, the world and everything in it cease to appear intelligible." Further, "what distinguishes darkness from anything given in the light is the

fact that it gives itself without possibility of being ordered, and we know this: the deeper we enter true darkness, the more inclined we are to surrender any attempt to search for order. This surrender of all comprehension leaves us exposed in a way that can never be the case during the daytime, when experience always navigates ordered relation and any gaps that might interrupt them." Jeffrey Bloechl, "The Twilight of the Idols and the Night of the Senses," in *The Experience of God*, ed. Kevin Hart and Barbara Wall (New York: Fordham University Press, 2005), 160–61.

41. Emmanuel Lévinas, *Autrement qu'être ou Au-delà de l'essence* (La Haye: Le Livre de Poche, 1974), 165. Emmanuel Lévinas, *Otherwise Than Being* (Pittsburgh, PA: Duquesne University Press, 1998).

42. As Marion puts it: "How does the idea appear to us? Here again, as a given, or according to the most minimalistic acceptance, as a pure given: '*Si detur Dei idea*' (*ut manifestum est illam dari*)." That is, if the idea of God is given (as it is manifest that it is given) it appears as a "pure" given. The idol shows what it shows, and does not hold anything to be revealed: "the title 'God' does not grant access to this 'God,' but in that very instant, offers a perfect view of the one who produced or recited the word. In other words, it all comes back to the question of the idol. The idol, and this once again bears repeating, is not an illusion or deception, but simply shows perfectly that which it shows, without a shadow, and without concealment or withdrawal. But it only reveals that which it is aimed at—namely, the one who does the aiming, not that at which he aims." Jean-Luc Marion, "*The Irreducible*" trans. Jason W. Alvis. The Journal for Cultural and Religious Theory, 2018.

The Spectacle of God: Inverting the Sacred/Profane Paradigm

But for the present age, which prefers ... representation to reality ... truth is considered profane, and only illusion is sacred. Sacredness is in fact held to be enhanced in proportion as truth decreases and illusion increases, so that the highest degree of illusion comes to be the highest degree of sacredness.

—*Feuerbach*[1]

We are beings nourished exclusively on substitutes.

—*Anders*[2]

What is the dominant and preferred paradigm of presentation today, and how might an inconspicuous God (who operates according to unique phenomenalities) figure as an intervention into this dominance? A phenomenology of the inconspicuous cuts against the grain of a spectacular phenomenality that employs glamorous events as its allies in creating passivity. When applied to conspicuous or *conspicere*, which have roots in *spek*, scope, or *specere*, the privative "in" counters any autofocus on phenomena that force themselves into immediate attention. What presents spectacularly ultimately leaves little room for attention to anything else, forcing its subjects into a passive acceptance of its self-pronouncement, and reinforcing its totality through the social bond via a *spectaculum* or public display. In terms of presentation, a spectacular phenomenality is a dispossession that manufactures alienation by giving the sense that one truly is active, all the while underwriting human passivity even by way of contemplation, critical thinking, or abstract *theoria*.

It seems both Husserl and Heidegger always had in mind Aristotle's distinction between four types of wisdom and revealing (*episteme*, *theoria*, *phronesis*, and *techne* in book six of *Nicomachean Ethics*), and how *theoria* was, especially in fourth-century BC Greece, the highest form, as a spectator theory of knowledge. Husserl already had deployed phenomenology as "first philosophy" in order to supply a new hypergenesis of *episteme* and *techne* by establishing a descriptive approach to what appears in conscious experience. He even had installed a fail-safe within phenomenology not to revert into abstraction by insisting that one's essential insights be gained from the everyday *Lebenswelt*. Yet, as Heidegger came to realize, such phenomenological findings often so easily remain trapped in *theoria* without being refracted back into everyday life. Thus, one of Heidegger's aims was to fashion a form of thinking that would be irreducible to a distanced, spectator *theoria* and its concern with principle (via some clear production of signs in a compressed environment of propositions). In this sense, it could be argued that Heidegger's thinking is a form of *phronesis* that is concerned with the ontological conditions of being-in-the-world, yet in a way that actively resists the reduction to a pragmatic practicality or ethical use value. Necessary for Heidegger was a new mindfulness of concrete, everyday concerns in a way that the findings automatically were integrated back into the pertinence of daily existence, and in a way that passivity can be counteracted.

Such a hope is observable in his 1949 presentations in Bremen on modern technological advancement (better known as *The Question Concerning the Essence of Technology*), which on the one hand bemoans what many at the time supposed to be the fate of the modern age, while on the other attempts to avoid a reactionary, antitechnological, Luddite response. Although technology (as *techne*) is one among many essential modes of revealing, modern machination is disturbing in that it has led to the predominance of one type of *poiesis*-less revealing, which calls for the unreasonable demand that technology extract and store energy from everything that it touches. This biopolitical setting-in-order has sought to make standing reserves of nature, bringing it into a monstrous and resourceful accessibility.[3] Responsible for this gathering, which has made man merely its employed orderer, is the *Ge-stell* or enframing championed by Modern technology, which embodies the dangerous destining of revealing, and blocks the shining forth of other forms of unveiling.[4]

Three points especially are of interest to us here in these brief concluding remarks. First, *Ge-stell*, the dominant paradigm of contemporary life, deceptively shrouds its phenomenality or givenness, thereby marshaling thinking into a symbolic computation of representations. Second, there is a saving power that can redeem the endangered from enframing because such a power is "of a higher essence than . . . though at the same time kindred to" the endangered, bringing it "for the first time into its genuine appearing." And third, it is not from without that this saving power lies distant, but rather from its being embedded within: "The essence of technology must harbor in itself the growth of the saving power" incarnated within this dangerous destining of *Ge-stell* via a unique, more primordial, nondeceptive concealment.[5]

All three of these points seem taken for granted by Guy Debord in his 1967 analysis of *La société du spectacle*, in which he implicitly updated Heidegger's analysis via Feuerbach's understanding of his present age's being ruled by illusions. Feuerbach observed that "only illusion is sacred" and that the more skilled a spectacle is at capturing attention (all the while shrouding its operations), the higher the degree of sacredness is attributed to it. Feuerbach also observed that the incarnation of God is not "a peculiar, stupendous mystery, after the manner of speculation dazzled by mystical splendor; on the contrary, it destroys the illusive supposition of a peculiar supernatural mystery."[6] This milieu of hyperrealities and digital spectacles demands that Feuerbach's observation here is extended. No longer is it only that illusion is sacred, but more extremely now, the sacred has become univocal to the illustrious or spectacular to the point that all else that does not immediately grab attention is profane. Since appeal to the sacred is fueled by its unique mysteriousness, this dominant form of spectacular presentation, which inspires an unending passivity, captures attention in the form and pretense of adoration, thus intertwining focused attention with an often-unconscious praise. The most sacral of experiences and glorious divinities must display the greatest degree of spectacle, and therefore what nevertheless appears, yet lacks in illustriousness, becomes profane. God therefore has become a spectacle.

The Spectacle as a Form of Phenomenality

As Debord concluded, Spectacles produce through mulching and recycling content that, alongside their appearance, present a sense of diversity. They are accepted by merit of their melding of commodity value and appearance. This has resulted in a separate pseudoworld of autonomized images that turn creative and active life against itself, underwriting a totality of human passivity like never before. As everyday commodities exemplify, a spectacle has a certain shelf life, and once it gets too familiar, a new spectacle replaces it—*ad infinitum*—that is capable of maintaining the carburation of distance and familiarity unique to this form of presentation. Each spectacle changes and disavows the previous one: "That which asserted its definitive excellence with perfect impudence nevertheless changes."[7] Spectacles orchestrate waves of enthusiasm that seek to prohibit our recognition of these spectacles' replacement of one another, despite their insisting that they alone are worthy of adoration.[8] This of course is how totalitarian power works: by diverting attention from one thing long enough to cover the lie that it is its own illusion, and by subsequently nourishing pseudofreedoms toward inconsequential commodities, all in order to traffic in numbness and passivity.

As Heidegger knew, enframing leads to a sense of being concrete, and as Debord made explicit, the stratification of labor and activity can be underwritten by contemplation and abstraction, which feeds back into the passivity that spectacular phenomenality hopes to create.[9] Henry also drew attention to something like this spectacular phenomenality, calling it *media*, which entails the ignorant negation of any immediate and affective life, supplanting it with a derealizing structure of the world. As Henry bemoaned, with "the horror of the spectacle that was offered for their delight" in entertainment also comes an impersonal, empty, and lifeless gaze. Henry cast the final blame on the Galilean a priori of scientific advancement in modern industrialization, which insists on all things' mediation, and thereby short circuiting any potential for attention to what Henry thought to be the ever-important, auto-affective, immediate life. This kind of advancement, claims Henry, "can no longer offer anything but the terrifying spectacle unfolding right before our eyes."[10] Henry helps us see that spectacles have a genesis in a kind of phenomenality.

An observation initiated by, yet underdeveloped by Debord is that the spectacle is not simply a phenomenon, "visual deception," or mere faction of society, but rather "represents the dominant *model* of life" in a monopolizing *Bildung* and educational formation that leaves its subjects waiting to be shocked by yet another new appearance. Spectacularity becomes "an identification of all human social life with appearances" in a way that "is fundamentally spectaclist" and nourishing this obsession with appearing. This points beyond the Hegelian recognition of the tendency to privilege the faculty of sight, and toward how a spectacular phenomenality teaches the autoprivileging of *what* actively grabs attention, ultimately diverting toward its own ends. To involute Debord's claim that "what appears is good; what is good appears," it is possible to see that, today, whatever does not appear clearly or lacks pure signification marks the privation of good; that whatever does not come into illumination is not good and therefore deceptive. The preference for illumination entails that any god that does not appear is little more than that than which nothing greater can be *deceived*.[11]

This points to how spectacular phenomenality has become a quietly operating social imaginary or deep worldview by suturing itself to a pseudomaterial theology.[12] This phenomenality enacts its domination by setting apart, on the subject's behalf, that which is valuable as a commodity from that which is useful, and this has resulted in the creation of a false privation that viciously circles back to the privileging of illusions and the illuminated. False privation (the feeling of great need) has led to a subjugation reinforced by what Lukács noted to be "the fact that people's activity becomes less and less active and more and more contemplative."[13] The more successful the commodification, the greater this privation, and the greater this privation, the deeper the metaphysical domination of the phenomenality of the spectacle. Like addictive drugs, spectacles present with their content of spectacularity an augmented survival that seeks to colonize all social life.

Such phenomenality goes hand in hand with a yearning for direct apprehension and for things to be brought into one's own possession. This marks the unique cultural shift, as noted by Günther Anders, from "being" to "having." Although Debord attempted to extend Anders's work toward a second shift, from "having into appearing," it remained underemphasized how directedness and focus lead back into seeking possession.[14] Spectacular phenomenality teaches that apprehension of all that appears is achieved through calculation, self-containment, and domination. While spectacles are shiny diversions, spectacular presentation, as a means, form, or *how* of appearing is (following Heidegger's notion of *Ge-stell*) far more cunning, shrouding its presentative quality and integrating its operations within normalcy and neutrality.[15] This directedness has become a dominant paradigm that self-justifies and disguises its mediations through a claimed reliance on clarity and distinction.

On hearing the phrase "clear and distinct," one of course is reminded of Descartes, for whom those perceptions are self-evident and indubitable. His clear and distinct ideas are not sense perceptions per se, but a means of grasping propositions or providing warrant for an argument. The proposition "triangles have three sides" (to which Kant furnished further specificity via synthetic and analytic propositions) is clear and distinct because it is relatively simple and self-evident to perception insofar as the conclusion already is contained within the proposition. For Descartes, this is *how* consciousness *grasps* information, constantly sorting out the clear from the unclear; the valuable from the insignificant. What is perceived as clear and distinct calls for metaphysical certainty, and this certainty, for Descartes, is the telic end of thinking. Whatever is clear and distinct necessarily is *Adequatio*—correct, true, and to be affirmed unquestionably as valid for meaning making. The seeking of clarity, and the hoping for truth, often collapse into being one and the same.

In a more phenomenological context, truth is to be sought first and foremost through focusing consciousness on the specificity of things themselves and their modes of presentation. In regard to this focusing, as Merleau-Ponty notes, "on the side of the object it means to separate the region focused on from the rest of the field … [and] on the side of the subject it means substituting for overall vision … an observation, that is, an isolated vision that the subject directs at will."[16] A focusing of the mind separates something by isolating it and privileging it beyond other things within the field of experience. Yet, one unforeseen consequence of this focusing and isolation is that the focuser may end up abstracted into what Anders called the "ivory tower of perception."[17] One so easily falls prey to the tendencies of abstract *prehension*, of perceiving and accessing consciousness while ignoring conscience, and thereby lacking in reflection on the lived involvement with that which is perceived.

Instead of a closer relation/confrontation with things, the *aim* (which already knows its target and intended outcome) too often gets reduced to a theoretical expansion of perceiving things in their distinction. In some cases, clarity "for clarity's sake" reduces truth to clarity, leaving clarity as the whitewashed yet camouflaged means of spectacular phenomenality. Seeking clarity in a way void of conscience lends to a distanced abstraction that in turn numbs the *poesis* of creative life. Every totality has rules that oversee its authority through the nourishment of passivity, and a spectacular phenomenality can be underwritten by an abstract *theoria* that (following the root *specere*) remains *skeptesthai* by setting things apart and isolating them outside their given context. Here the spectacle inflicts the wound of passivity and calmly balms it with a momentary fix of spectacular clarity.

The Spectacle of God

If all of this furnishes us at least some indication as to one of the dominant forms of presentation today, then it must be considered to what degree it operates with its own unique theology. God's forms of presentation tend to be overly associated solely with either a spectacular "allure," or what seems to be its opposite, yet actually is the same: an inconceivability that amounts to God no longer being thought. God is supposed to be alluring and dazzling (so the story goes), and if there is nothing presented that meets such criteria, then the idea of God is named "inconceivable" and protected from being reduced to a finitude that would amount to blasphemy. Yet (and surely apophatic theologians would find reason to disagree on this point) such a protective measure so easily leaves God no longer worth thinking about, inadvertently sacralizing, once again, what is spectacular. This amounts to all experience becoming grist for a spectacular phenomenality and its own hegemonic divinity. This "spectacle of God" could be interpreted in at least three ways.

First, the spectacle *is* God, or becomes godlike. Since it is not merely content that we worship, but also forms of presentation or phenomenality, and since the dominant paradigm of presentation today is that of the spectacle, then this phenomenality becomes paradigmatic also of God. Whatever is left after any supposed detheologization is a husk of divinity that has an even deeper metaphysics that ultimately retains some character traits of a supreme principle. When blindly reliant on a spectacular phenomenality, whatever constitutes the ability to cocreate a diversity of spectacles as a spectacle-maker becomes divine, and conceived in terms of a plurality of difference and dynamism. Not unlike the enframing about which Heidegger remained concerned, the spectacle-maker operates by actively partitioning, isolating, and organizing phenomena. The spectacle-maker is worthy of adoration because it creates difference, leaving any other supreme being or God as but one among many temporalized entertainments, which are rendered incapable of leaving any lasting influence. God as the spectacle-maker replaces and supersedes any other God that could be imagined.

Second, God operates *according to* spectacles. Following the possessive "of," there are spectacles *of* God to which one resorts because they provide illusions of comfort from lives of fragmentation and partitioning, which spectacular phenomenality in the first instance created. What is prized in modern life as "specialization" leaves the specialist detached from the whole and committed to its parts, and these parts are illusions that falsify or falsely represent God. These illusions widen the distance between the spectator and the spectacle of God, reinstalling idolization by merit of the multitude of idols that claim to represent God. These idols are resorted to because they are the product of direct apprehension, the prized means of spectacular phenomenality. Such forms of having and apprehension, however, are impoverished and merely are reflective of a Debordian "technologically equipped primitivism."[18]

And third, God is *a* spectacle. God has been quarantined within a ghetto of the spectacle, and as such, reduced to being a part of the false privation process initiated by commodity value. Not only is God adjoined to the mere provision of the commodity, but God has become but one commodity and spectacular relation among many, as one celebrity capable of capturing attention long enough until another spectacle overcomes it. The partitioning of society has left God to be one "good" among goods, a particular good with little permanence and potence. Although great glory may be attributed to God, it is possible that, if misunderstood as synonymous with spectacularity, such glory reinforces the quarantining of divine mystery into being but one temporary distraction from the woes of modern machination, of which Heidegger warned.

Although elevated to the plane of glory, or at best a celebrity of a higher order, God becomes limited to presenting or phenomenalizing Godself via spectacular phenomenality. This all entails a theology in which God becomes incapable of being integrated, incarnated, and having any effective, omnipotent influence on all aspects of everyday life. This leaves God's phenomenality limited and therefore beholden to an autonomized system of production. Instead, God must be counterspectacular, or as this book has sought to demonstrate, inconspicuous.

Only an Inconspicuous God Can Overcome the Spectacle

As Heidegger knew, the modern overprivileging of "uncovering" can be remedied only by another kind of revealing/manifestation from within the totality of enframing. Necessary is what Debord called a *Détournement* that has the unique ability to disrupt the steady flow of spectacular life. Only what is inconspicuous is capable of counteracting the determinism of what Benjamin insisted to be a "false, errant totality—the absolute totality" that autoassigns its pertinence to us and makes us complicit to its presentation.[19] The ending (*barkeit*) in *Unscheinbarkeit* must be emphasized, as it refers to how what is inconspicuous retains the ability to alter the "whole."[20] It does so by integrating with and alongside what has become the most marginal and common. Even when such phenomena are "revealed" they still "prove to be infinitely inconspicuous" as not appropriable by totality, and furnishing an attitude of ambivalence.[21]

An inconspicuous God is able to resist becoming a part of any totality, but perhaps more importantly, also "not-becoming-a-totality-in-its-own-right."[22] Inconspicuousness characterizes the phenomenality of a God that operates modestly and humbly within the lattices of societal frameworks in a way that is irreducible to "incomprehensibility," which has the potential to become the *via negativa* of a spectacular phenomenality. From Eliade's "hierophany," to Otto's *das ganz andere* (wholly other), many descriptions of the sacred often isolate it from its lived conditions. Instead, as inconspicuous, divine phenomenality might be aligned more so with the profane, thus allowing the most marginal, common, or poor to operate with the highest degree of sacredness by merit of their unique ability to hide or house the incarnated.

The phrase "God is inconspicuous" can be understood in a number of ways, but it is hoped that proper attention has been paid here to the core notion that God's form of presentation—God "in God's how"—must be taken seriously. Inconspicuousness is but one way of understanding this *how* of God, and it is relied on insofar as it characterizes what presents through a counter activity, delegitimizing the meaning-giving conceptions of glory through a paradoxical holiness or counterglory. It is in this sense that, as Levinas often put it, God appears "otherwise," namely by eluding conscious grasp and renouncing the pregiven understandings of God's phenomenality. Yet, such elusion tells us infinitely more than we tend to imagine: it indicates who and what God associates Godself with, it tells us about the space of "Godhood," and points us to the means by which religious experience hangs tenuously in the balance of everyday life. Religious experience is not just for specialist saints who claim to have experienced life-altering supernatural events, but rather also is worked out by people who have to find ways to live religiously (often sloppily, and not so seamlessly) in the busy, hustle and grind of everyday life. This points to how God operates in a certain marginal and inconspicuous way, despite the overwhelming noise of a western social imaginary that demands God only to operate to the contrary. It is hoped that the concept of inconspicuousness can help furnish particular means by which the implicit rules of these imaginaries can be rendered questionable.

As each of the chapters have demonstrated, through reliance on the work of those associated with the Theological turn, such an inconspicuous God calls for an "inconspicuous revelation" (chap. 1) because its phenomenality is counter to expectation, which usually anticipates such manifestation to be spectacular. There is an "inconspicuous religious lifeworld" (chap. 3) because life, which is inconspicuous, destabilizes any totalizing neutrality of the world in a way that calls us to become the carburetors of the tensions between life and world. There is an active inconspicuous liturgy (chap. 4) that might open from within what has become the most familiar to us, a dwelling of the Absolute or a space of "Godhood." Then, the adoration of this God is inconspicuous (chap. 5) because it finds the adored to have the uniquely divine ability to be on the touch line between the ordinary and the obscure as ever-differentiating from itself. This may furnish an evidence for religious experience that is inconspicuous (chap. 6) by merit of its resistance to isolation, its witnessing to a destabilizing omnipotential, and its ability to furnish a proof that is reflective of its paradoxicality. Faith can be understood as inconspicuous (chap. 7) because it is experienced and achieved indirectly via the *covering over* of some past memorialization, and thus "faith faiths" through an active–passive movement. And finally, God's givenness is inconspicuous (chap. 8) because God, by being marginal, overcomes the brutish matrix of opposition between a univocal spectacularity or incomprehensibility; both of which can lend to a numbing effect on theological reflection and therefore devotion.

The developed notion of the inconspicuous God points to how God-as-otherwise is not a not-given purely as a renunciation of immanent life, but is integrated incarnately within whatever for us has become taken for granted. It becomes necessary to see differently not only *what* but also *how* one's perception itself is taken for granted, especially in the case of God. This book has attended to just some of the reasons why we cannot stop at the description of God's attributes or content, otherwise we may inadvertently rely on inherently ungodly forms of phenomenality, circling back to idolization. Such an invisible and subtle ideology of the spectacular phenomenality of God could amount to man's becoming complicit to the surrendering of thought, namely, of God. Such an unthought "God" would be ungodly as the-thought-out, the not-to-be-thought, the "being" whose nature cannot be thought. Stated otherwise, a God that remains out-of-thought is no God at all.

Notes

1. Ludwig Feuerbach, *Preface to the Second Edition of The Essence of Christianity*, trans. George Eliot (New York: Harper Row), xxxix. This claim from Feuerbach is how Debord opens *The Society of the Spectacle*. Why might the notion of illusion, as a sacred manifestation of transcendence interest Debord? Because the pejoratively conceived "spectacle" of western society seeks to reconstruct and copy with a material realism the various sacred logics that mediate its sense of ecstasy.

2. Günther Anders, *Die Antiquiertheit des Menschen, Ausgabe in einem Band, vol. 1* (Munich: Beck Verlag, 1980), pt. II, § 10.

3. Martin Heidegger, *The Question Concerning the Essence of Technology* (New York: Harper & Row), 1977.16.

4. Ibid., 22, 28. Then in "The Turning" Heidegger specifies that enframing "is that setting-upon gathered into itself which entraps the truth of its own coming to presence with oblivion. This entrapping disguises itself, in that it develops into the setting in order of

everything that presences as standing-reserve, establishes itself in the standing-reserve, and rules as the standing reserve. Enframing comes to presence as the danger." Ibid., 37.

5. Ibid., 28, 34. See here also Jean-Pierre Dupuy, *On the Origins of Cognitive Science: The Mechanization of Mind*, trans. M. B. DeBoise (Cambridge: MIT Press, 2009), 13.

6. Ludwig Feuerbach, *The Essence of Christianity*, trans. G. Eliot (San Francisco: Harper Torchbooks, 1957), 52.

7. Guy Debord, *Society of the Spectacle*, trans. Ken Knabb (London: Rebel Press, 2005), 70.

8. Ibid., 13. A spectacle self-sustains and self-promotes with a "non-stop discourse about itself, its never-ending monologue of self-praise." Its content is branding and the brand is the commodity, and every engagement within the spectacle "recreates its own presuppositions." See here also Ibid., 35.

9. As Debord notes, such a "manner of being concrete ... is precisely abstraction." Ibid., 15. Debord recognized, in his final film that "no vital periods ever began from a theory" but rather "a game, a struggle, a journey." Guy Debord, *In girum imus nocte et consumimur igni* (Paris: Gallimard, 1999), 26.

10. "It is a horrible sight to see life knocked over, walked on, crushed, flattened, and negated! But this negation of life is no different from what occurs each day with the gathering of millions of human beings in front of their screens. The horror of this negation is no different from the horror of the spectacle that was offered for their delight that night. That is the truth of the media world. For an instant, it is their own truth that appears before their hallucinating eyes." Michel Henry, *Barbarism* (London: Continuum, 2012), xiv, 16, 113.

11. Ibid., 10, 34.

12. Indeed "the more he [the individual] identifies with the dominant images of need, the less he understands his own life and his own desires" to the point that the individual's life is no longer identifiable as his own. Ibid., 16. Debord develops this work in a series of theses, the first of which is that "direct" encounters have been replaced with presentation/representation.

13. Georg Lukács, "Reification and the Consciousness of the Proletariat," in *History and Class Consciousness*, trans. Rodney Livingstone (Cambridge, MA: MIT Press, 1968), 87.

14. Debord, *Society of the Spectacle*, 17. Latour has continued in this trajectory today, emphasizing how technological systems modify the ends that we envision in the process of seeking what we originally intended. Means and ends are entangled, and not only are there means to ends, but ends to means. Bruno Latour, "Morality and Technology: The End of the Means," trans. Cousze Venn, *Theory, Culture, and Society* 19, no. 5–6 (2002): 247–60.

15. See also Debord's 1988 follow-up 2011. Guy Debord, *Comments on the Society of the Spectacle*, trans. Malcolm Imrie (London: Verso 2011), where he introduces "the integrated spectacle," which is the unity of concretized and diffused phenomena, ultimately becoming the means by which everything is transformed (via the spectacle's cunning deception and misdirection) into the structure of modern industrialization.

16. Maurice Merleau-Ponty, *Phenomenology of Perception*, trans. Donald A. Landis (London: Routledge, 2013).

17. Günther Anders, "Theses for an Atomic Age," in *The Life and Work of Günther Anders: Émigré, Iconoclast, Philosopher, Man of Letters*, ed. Günter Bischof, Jason Dawsey, and Bernhard Fetz (Innsbruck, Austria: Studienverlag, 2014), 12.

18. Debord, *Society of the Spectacle*, 61.

19. Walter Benjamin, in *Selected Writings, vol. 1. 1913–1926*, eds. W. Benjamin, Howard Eiland, and Gary Smith (Cambridge: Harvard University Press, 1996), 340.

20. For Benjamin, we are to "take common cause with whatever is unobtrusive and plain but relentless like water" because it uniquely can enact a dynamic veiling that is irreducible to an outward veneer or semblance. Walter Benjamin, *Selected Writings, vol. 4* (Cambridge: Harvard University Press, 1996), 248. For Weber, Benajamin's "abilities" are unique because they "involve an ongoing, ever-unfinished, and unpredictable process." Samuel Weber, *Benajamin's–abilities* (Cambridge, MA: Harvard University Press, 2008), 7.

21. Benjamin applies this notion in the context of Aesthetics: "Even if everywhere else semblance is deception, the beautiful semblance is the veil thrown over that which is necessarily most veiled. For the beautiful is neither the veil nor the veiled object but rather the object in its veil. Unveiled, however, it would prove to be infinitely inconspicuous." Benjamin, "Goethe's Elective Affinities," 351. See here Symons, who claims that *Unscheinbar* in the context of Benjamin's work denotes not "the impossibility of a moment, object, or image to shine forth as meaningful but precisely the *possibility* that something that seems unremarkable on its own account *does* present a surprising, unanticipated and even improbable . . . layer of significance." Stéphane Symons, "The Ability to Not-shine: The Word 'Unscheinbar' in the Writings of Walter Benjamin," *Angelaki: Journal of the Theoretical Humanities* 18, no. 4 (2013): 104.

22. Symons, "The Ability to Not-shine," 110.

Bibliography

Alston, William P. *Perceiving God*. Ithaca, NY: Cornell University Press, 1991.

______. "Religious Experience as Perception of God." In *Philosophy of Religion: Selected Readings*, edited by Michael Peterson, William Hasker, Bruce Reichenbach, and David Basinger. Oxford: Oxford University Press, 2009: 20–29.

Alvis, Jason. *Marion and Derrida on the Gift and Desire: Debating the Generosity of Things*. Dordrecht: Springer Press, 2016.

Anders, Günther. *Die Antiquiertheit des Menschen, Ausgabe in einem Band*. Munich: Beck Verlag, 1980.

______. "Theses for an Atomic Age." In *The Life and Work of Günther Anders: Émigré, Iconoclast, Philosopher, Man of Letters*, edited by Günter Bischof, Jason Dawsey, and Bernhard Fetz. Innsbruck, Austria: Studienverlag, 2014: 185–200.

Balthasar, Hans Urs von. *Glory of the Lord: Seeing the Form*, vol. 1. Translated by Erasmo Leiva-Merikakis. Edinburgh: T & T Clark, 1982.

Barbieri, William A., Jr. "The Post-secular Problematic." In *At the Limits of the Secular: Reflections on Faith and Public Life*, edited by William Barbieri Jr. Grand Rapids, MI: Eerdmans Publishing, 2014: 129–161.

Bataille, Georges. *Visions of Excess: Selected Writings 1927–39*. Minneapolis: University of Minnesota Press, 1985.

Beistegui, Miguel de. *Truth and Genesis: Philosophy as Differential Ontology*. Bloomington: Indiana University Press, 2004.

Benjamin, Walter. "Goethe's Elective Affinities." In *Selected Writings*, vol. 1, *1913–26*, edited by Marcus Bullock and Michael W. Jennings, 297–354. Cambridge, MA: Belknap, Harvard University Press, 1996.

______. *Selected Writings*, vol. 4. Cambridge, MA: Belknap, Harvard University Press, 1996.

Benson, Bruce Ellis, and Norman Wirzba. *Words of Life: New Theological Turns in French Phenomenology*. New York: Fordham University Press, 2010.

Benveniste, Emile. *Indo-European Language and Society*. Translated by Elizabeth Palmer. London: Faber and Faber, 1973.

Bernet, Rudolf. "Das Phenomenon und das Unsichtbare. Zur Phenomenologie des Blicks und des Subjekts." *Internationale Zeitschrift für Philosophie* 1 (1998): 15–30.

______. "The Secret According to Heidegger and 'The Purloined Letter' by Poe." *Continental Philosophy Review* 47, no. 3–4 (2014): 353–71.

______. "Voir ettre vu. Le phénoméne invisible du regard et la peinture." *Revue d'Esthétique* 36 (1999): 37–47.

Bernet, Rudolf, and Antje Kapust, eds. *Die Sichtbarkeit des Unsichtbaren*. Munich: W. Fink, 2009.

Bloechl, Jeffrey. *The Face of the Other and the Trace of God: Essays on the Philosophy of Emmanuel Levinas*. New York: Fordham University Press, 2000.

______. "The Twilight of the Idols and the Night of the Senses." In *The Experience of God*, edited by Kevin Hart and Barbara Wall. New York: Fordham University Press, 2005: 156-172.

Bonsor, Jack Arthur. *Rahner, Heidegger, and Truth: Karl Rahner's Notion of Christian Truth, the Influence of Heidegger.* Lanham, MD: University Press of America, 1987.

Bornemark, Jonna, and Hans Ruin. *Phenomenology and Religion: New Frontiers.* Södertörn, SE: Södertörn University Library, 2010.

Calhoun, Craig. "Rethinking Secularism." *The Hedgehog Review* 12 no. 3 (2010): 3.

Caputo, John D. *Demythologizing Heidegger.* Bloomington: Indiana University Press, 1993.

______. *Religion with/out Religion: The Prayers and Tears of John D. Caputo.* Edited by James H. Olthuis. London: Routledge Press, 2002.

______. *The Weakness of God: A Theology of the Event.* Bloomington: Indiana University Press, 2006.

Chretien, Jean-Louis. *The Call and the Response.* Translated by Anne A. Davenport. New York: Fordham University Press, 2004.

______. *Hand to Hand: Listening to the Work of Art.* Translated by Stephen Lewis. New York: Fordham University Press, 2003.

______. *L'Inoubliable et l'inespéré.* Paris: Desclée de Brouwer, 1991.

______. *The Unforgettable and the Unhoped For.* New York: Fordham University Press, 2002.

______. *Under the Gaze of the Bible.* Translated by John Marson Dunaway. New York: Fordham University Press, 2015.

______. "The Wounded Word." In *Phenomenology and the "Theological Turn": The French Debate,* edited by Dominique Janicaud, Jean-François Courtine, Jean-Louis Chrétien, Jean-Luc Marion, Michel Henry, and Paul Ricoeur and translated by Jeffrey Kosky and Thomas Carlson, 147–75. New York: Fordham University Press, 2000.

Courtine, Jean-François. *Heidegger et la phénoménologie.* Paris: Vrin, 1990.

______, ed. *Phénoménologie et théologie.* Paris: Vrin, 1992.

Dahlstrom, Daniel. *Heidegger's Concept of Truth.* Cambridge: Cambridge University Press, 2001.

Dastur, Françoise. "La pensée à venir: une pheénoménologie de l'inapparent?" In *L'avenir de la philosophie est-il grec?,* edited by Catherine Collobert, 135–49. Saint-Laurent, QC: Fides, 2002.

Davis, Joshua. "The Call of Grace: Henri de Lubac, Jean-Louis Chrétien, and the Theological Conditions of Christian Radical Phenomenology." In *Words of Life: New Theological Turns in French Phenomenology,* edited by Bruce Ellis Benson and Norman Wirzba. New York: Fordham University Press, 2010: 181–195.

Debord, Guy. *Comments on the Society of the Spectacle.* Translated by Malcolm Imrie. London: Verso, 2011.

______. *In girum imus nocte et consumimur igni.* Paris: Éditions Gallimard, 1999.

______. *Society of the Spectacle.* Translated by Ken Knabb. London: Rebel Press, 2005.

Descartes, Rene. "Principles of Philosophy." In *The Passions of the Soul and Other Late Philosophical Writings,* edited by Michael Moriarty. Oxford: Oxford University Press, 2015: 119–190.

Devisch, Ignaas, Laurens ten Kate, Aukje van Rooden, and Alena Alexandrova. *Retreating Religion: Deconstructing Christianity with Jean-Luc Nancy.* New York: Fordham University Press, 2012.

Douglass, Frederick. *My Bondage and My Freedom.* New York: Miller, Orton & Mulligan, 1855.

Dreyfus, Hubert. "Heidegger on the Connection between Nihilism, Art, Technology, and Politics." In *Cambridge Companion to Heidegger,* edited by Charles Guignon. Cambridge: Cambridge University Press, 1993: 345–372.

Dufrenne, Mikel. *Le poétique: Précédé de Pour une philosophie non théologique*. Paris: Presses Universitaires de France, 1973.

Dupont, Christian. *Phenomenology in French Philosophy: Early Encounters*. Dordrecht: Springer, 2013.

Dupuy, Jean-Pierre. *On the Origins of Cognitive Science: The Mechanization of Mind*. Translated by M. B. DeBoise. Cambridge: MIT Press, 2009.

Feuerbach, Ludwig. *The Essence of Christianity*. Translated by George Eliot. New York: Harper Row, 1957.

Figal, Günter. *Unscheinbarkeit. Der Raum der Phänomenologie*. Tübingen: Mohr Siebeck, 2015.

Fink, Eugen. *Play as Symbols of the World: And Other Writings*. Translated by Ian Alexander Moore and Christopher Turner. Bloomington: Indiana University Press, 2016.

______. *Sein, Wahrheit, Welt: Vor-Fragen zum Problem des Phänomen-Begriffs*. Den Haag: Martinus Nijhoff, 1958.

______. *Spiel als Weltsymbol*. Stuttgart: Kohlhammer Verlag, 1960.

Foucault, Michel. "Introduction." In *On the Normal and the Pathological*, edited by George Canguilhem and translated by Carolyn R. Fawcett, ix–xx. Dordrecht: Reidel, 1978.

Fritz, Peter Joseph. "Black Holes and Revelations: Michel Henry and Jean-Luc Marion on the Aesthetics of the Invisible." *Modern Theology* 25, no. 3 (2009): 415–40.

Gadamer, H. G. *Truth and Method*. Translated by Joel Weinsheimer and Donald G. Marshall. London: Bloomsbury, 2013.

Gonzalez, Francisco J. *Plato and Heidegger: A Question of Dialogue*. College Station: Penn State Press, 2011.

Grego, Peter. *The Collected Works of St. Teresa of Avila*, vol. 3. Translated by Kieran Kavanaugh and Otilio Rodriguez. Washington: ICS Publications, 1985.

Grumett, David. "Nouvelle Théologie." In *The Cambridge Dictionary of Christian Theology*, edited by Ian A. McFarland, David A. S. Fergusson, Karen Kilby, and Iain R. Torrance. Cambridge: Cambridge University Press, 2011.

Gschwandtner, Christina. *Degrees of Givenness: On Saturation in Jean-Luc Marion*. Bloomington: Indiana University Press, 2014.

______. *Postmodern Apologetics: Arguments for God in Contemporary Philosophy*. New York: Fordham University Press, 2012.

______. "Revealing the Invisible: Henry and Marion on Aesthetic Experience." *The Journal of Speculative Philosophy* 28, no. 3 (2014): 305–14.

______. "The Truth of Christianity? Michel Henry's Words of Christ." *The Journal of Scriptural Reasoning* 13, no. 1 (2014). Available at: http://jsr.shanti.virginia.edu/back-issues/vol-13-no-1-june-2014-phenomenology-and-scripture/the-truth-of-christianity-michel-henrys-words-of-christ/.

______. "The Vigil as Exemplary Liturgical Experience: On Jean-Yves Lacoste's Phenomenology of Liturgy." *Modern Theology* 31, no. 4 (2015): 648–57.

Guest, Gérard. "Aux confins de l'inapparent: l'extrême phénomenénologie de Heidegger," *Existentia* 12 (2002): 123.

Gurvitch, Georges. *Les tendances actuelles de la philosophie allemande, E. Husserl, M. Scheler, E. Lask, M. Hartmann, M. Heidegger*. Paris: Vrin, 1930.

Hackett, William Chris. "What Is Called Theological Thinking." *Modern Theology* 31, no. 4 (2015): 658–65.

Hart, Kevin. *Kingdoms of God*. Bloomington: Indiana University Press, 2014.

_____. "Poverty's Speech: On Liturgical Reduction." *Modern Theology* 31, no. 4 (2015): 641–47.

St. Augustine. *Confessions.* Translated by Rex Warner. New York: Signet Press, 2001.

German Editions:

Heidegger, Martin, GA 2. *Sein und Zeit.* Edited by Friedrich-Wilhelm von Herrmann. Frankfurt am Main: Vittorio Klostermann, 1977.

_____, GA 3. *Kant und das Problem der Metaphysik.* Frankfurt am Main: Vittorio Klostermann, 1929.

_____, GA 4. *Erläuterungen zu Hölderlins Dichtung.* Frankfurt am Main: Vittorio Klostermann, 1996 (1936).

_____, GA 5. *Holzwege* (1935–46). 2nd ed. Frankfurt am Main: Vittorio Klostermann, 2003.

_____, GA 7. *Vörträge und Aufsätz.* Pfullingen: Verlag Günther Neske, 1998.

_____, GA 8. *Was Heißt Denken?* Frankfurt am Main: Vittorio Klostermann, 1952.

_____, GA 9. *Wegmarken* (1919–58). 2nd ed. Frankfurt am Main: Vittorio Klostermann, 2004.

_____, GA 12. *Unterwegs zur Sprache.* Frankfurt am Main: Vittorio Klostermann, 1985.

_____, GA 13. "Aufzeichnung aus Der Werkstatt." In *Aus der Erfahrung des Denkens.* Frankfurt am Main: Vittorio Klostermann, 1983: 151–54.

_____, GA 15. "Seminar in Zähringen 1973." In *Vier Seminare*, edited by Curd Ochwadt. Frankfurt am Main: Vittorio Klostermann, 1986: 110–38.

_____, GA 18. *Grundbegriffe der Aristotelischen Philosophie.* Frankfurt am Main: Vittorio Klostermann, 1924.

_____, GA 26. *Metaphysische Anfangsgründe der Logik im Ausgang von Leibniz.* Edited by Klaus Held. Franfurt am Main: Vittorio Klostermann, 1978.

_____, GA 32. *Hegels Phänomenologie des Geistes.* Frankfurt am Main: Vittorio Klostermann, 1930.

_____, GA 39. *Hölderlins Hymnen "Germanien" und "Der Rhein."* Frankfurt am Main: Vittorio Klostermann, 1934.

_____, GA 40. *Einführung in die Metaphysik.* Frankfurt am Main: Vittorio Klostermann, 1935.

_____, GA 54. *Parmenides.* 2nd ed. Frankfurt am Main: Vittorio Klostermann, 1992.

_____, GA 55. *Heraklit. 1. Der Anfang des abendländischen Denkens (Heraklit).* Frankfurt am Main: Vittorio Klosterman, 1944.

_____. 2. *Logik. Heraklits Lehre vom Logos.* Frankfurt am Main: Vittorio Klostermann, 1943.

_____, GA 56/57. *Zur Bestimmung der Philosophie.* Frankfurt am Main: Vittorio Klostermann, 1919.

_____, GA 61. *Phänomenologische Interpretationen zu Aristoteles: Einführung in die phänomenologische Forschung.* Frankfurt am Main: Vittorio Klostermann, 1921.

_____, GA 65. *Beiträge zur Philosophie (Vom Ereignis).* Edited by Friedrich Wilhelm von Hermann. Frankfurt am Main: Vittorio Klostermann, 1989.

_____, GA 66. *Besinnung* (esp. "Mein bisheriger Weg"). Frankfurt am Main: Vittorio Klostermann, 1939.

_____. GA 83, *Zollikoner Seminare. Protokolle—Gespräche—Briefe.* Edited by Merdard Boss. Frankfurt am Main: Vittorio Klostermann, 1987.

English Editions:

Heidegger, Martin. "Aletheia: Heraclitus Fragment B 16." In *Early Greek Thinking*, translated by D. F. Krell and F. A. Capuzzi. San Francisco: Harper Collins, 1984: 102–24.

______. *The Beginning of Western Philosophy: Interpretation of Anaximander and Parmenides*. Translated by Richard Rojcewicz. Bloomington: Indiana University Press, 2015.

______. *Being and Time*. Translated by John Macquarrie and Edward Robinson. New York: Harper & Row, 1962.

______. *Contributions to Philosophy: (From Enowning)*. Translated by Emad and Maly. Bloomington: Indiana University Press, 1999.

______. *The Event*. Translated by Richard Rojcewicz. Bloomington: Indiana University Press, 2013.

______. *Hegel's Phenomenology of Spirit*. Translated by Parvis Emad and Kenneth Maly. Bloomington: Indiana University Press, 1988.

______. *Hölderlin's Hymns "Germania" and "The Rhine."* Translated by William McNeill and Julia Ireland. Bloomington: Indiana University Press, 2014.

______. *Identity and Difference*. Translated by Joan Stambaugh. Chicago: University of Chicago Press, 2002.

______. *Introduction to Metaphysics*. 2nd ed. Translated by Gregory Fried and Richard Polt. New Haven, CT: Yale University Press, 2014.

______. "The Language of Johan Peter Hebel." In *The Heidegger Reader*, edited by Günter Figal and translated by Jerome Veith. Bloomington: Indiana University Press, 2009: 295–97.

______. Martin Heidegger, "Letter on Humanism." In *Basic Writings*, edited by David Farrell Krell. New York: Harper & Row, 1977: 141–82.

______. "Letter on Humanism." In *Pathmarks*, translated by Frank A. Capuzzi and edited by William McNeill. Cambridge: Cambridge University Press, 1998: 239–75.

______. "Letters to Roger Munier (dated Feb 22, 1974)." In *Martin Heidegger*, edited by Michel Haar. Paris: Editions de l'Herne, 1983: 106–15.

______. "Lettre à Monsieur Beaufret (23 novembre 1945)." In *Lettre sur l'humanisme*, edited and translated by Roger Munier. Paris: Aubier, Éditions Montaigne, 1964: 129–30.

______. *The Metaphysical Foundations of Logic*. Translated by Michael Heim. Bloomington: Indiana University Press, 1984.

______. *Off the Beaten Track*. Edited and translated by Julian Young and Kenneth Haynes. Cambridge: Cambridge University Press, 2002.

______. "'Only a God Can Save Us Now': An Interview with Martin Heidegger." Translated by David Schendler. *Graduate Faculty Philosophy Journal* 6, no. 1 (1977): 5–27.

______. *On the Way to Language*. Translated by P. Hertz. New York: Harper & Row, 1971.

______. *Parmenides*. Translated by André Schuwer and Richard Rojcewicz. Bloomington: Indiana University Press, 1992.

______. *Pathmarks*. Translated by William McNeill. Cambridge: Cambridge University Press, 1998.

______. *Poetry, Language, Thought*. Translated by Albert Hofstadter. New York: Harper & Row, 1971.

______. *Phenomenological Interpretations of Aristotle: Initiation into Phenomenological Research*. Translated by Richard Rojcewicz. Bloomington: Indiana University Press, 2001.

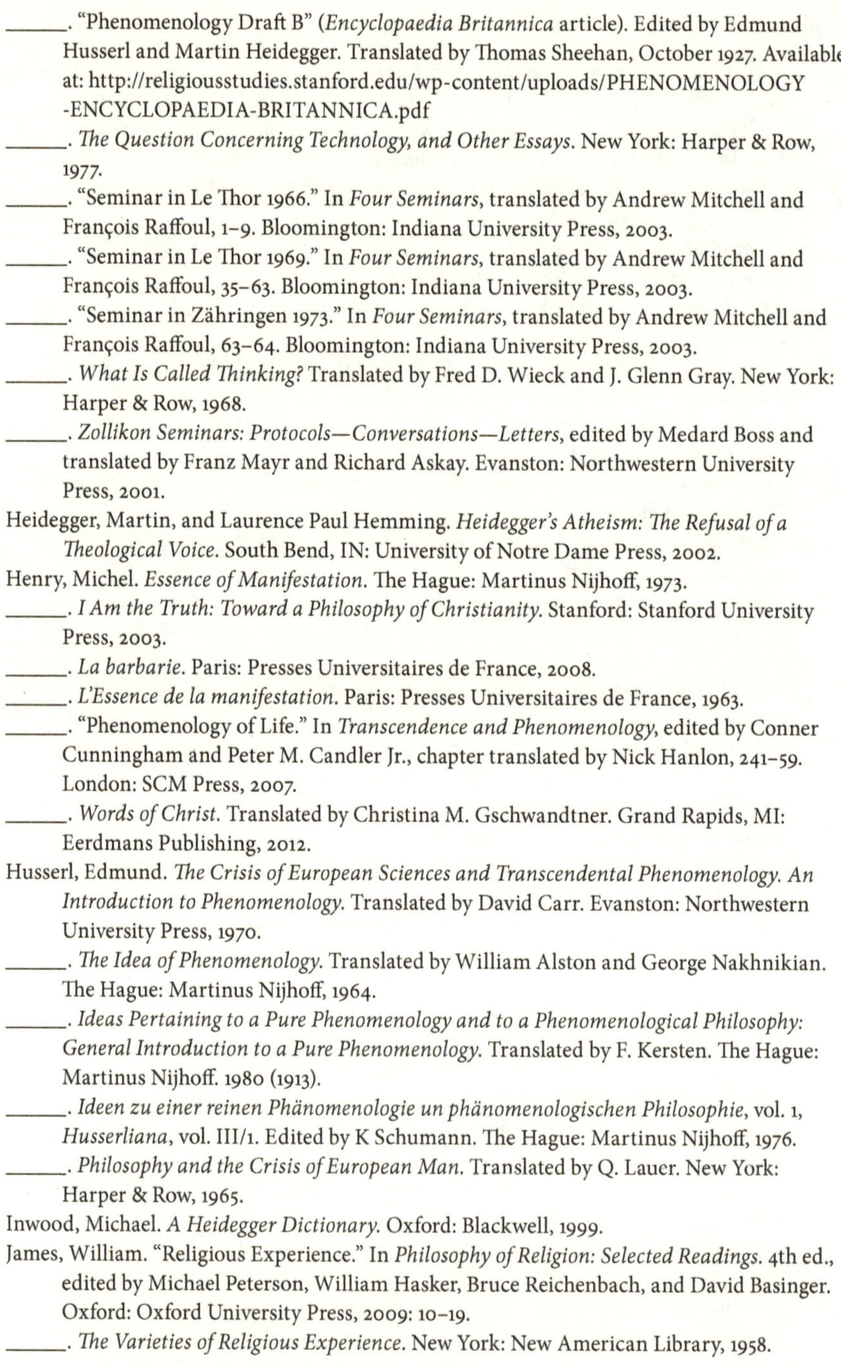

______. "Phenomenology Draft B" (*Encyclopaedia Britannica* article). Edited by Edmund Husserl and Martin Heidegger. Translated by Thomas Sheehan, October 1927. Available at: http://religiousstudies.stanford.edu/wp-content/uploads/PHENOMENOLOGY-ENCYCLOPAEDIA-BRITANNICA.pdf

______. *The Question Concerning Technology, and Other Essays*. New York: Harper & Row, 1977.

______. "Seminar in Le Thor 1966." In *Four Seminars*, translated by Andrew Mitchell and François Raffoul, 1–9. Bloomington: Indiana University Press, 2003.

______. "Seminar in Le Thor 1969." In *Four Seminars*, translated by Andrew Mitchell and François Raffoul, 35–63. Bloomington: Indiana University Press, 2003.

______. "Seminar in Zähringen 1973." In *Four Seminars*, translated by Andrew Mitchell and François Raffoul, 63–64. Bloomington: Indiana University Press, 2003.

______. *What Is Called Thinking?* Translated by Fred D. Wieck and J. Glenn Gray. New York: Harper & Row, 1968.

______. *Zollikon Seminars: Protocols—Conversations—Letters*, edited by Medard Boss and translated by Franz Mayr and Richard Askay. Evanston: Northwestern University Press, 2001.

Heidegger, Martin, and Laurence Paul Hemming. *Heidegger's Atheism: The Refusal of a Theological Voice*. South Bend, IN: University of Notre Dame Press, 2002.

Henry, Michel. *Essence of Manifestation*. The Hague: Martinus Nijhoff, 1973.

______. *I Am the Truth: Toward a Philosophy of Christianity*. Stanford: Stanford University Press, 2003.

______. *La barbarie*. Paris: Presses Universitaires de France, 2008.

______. *L'Essence de la manifestation*. Paris: Presses Universitaires de France, 1963.

______. "Phenomenology of Life." In *Transcendence and Phenomenology*, edited by Conner Cunningham and Peter M. Candler Jr., chapter translated by Nick Hanlon, 241–59. London: SCM Press, 2007.

______. *Words of Christ*. Translated by Christina M. Gschwandtner. Grand Rapids, MI: Eerdmans Publishing, 2012.

Husserl, Edmund. *The Crisis of European Sciences and Transcendental Phenomenology. An Introduction to Phenomenology*. Translated by David Carr. Evanston: Northwestern University Press, 1970.

______. *The Idea of Phenomenology*. Translated by William Alston and George Nakhnikian. The Hague: Martinus Nijhoff, 1964.

______. *Ideas Pertaining to a Pure Phenomenology and to a Phenomenological Philosophy: General Introduction to a Pure Phenomenology*. Translated by F. Kersten. The Hague: Martinus Nijhoff. 1980 (1913).

______. *Ideen zu einer reinen Phänomenologie un phänomenologischen Philosophie*, vol. 1, *Husserliana*, vol. III/1. Edited by K Schumann. The Hague: Martinus Nijhoff, 1976.

______. *Philosophy and the Crisis of European Man*. Translated by Q. Lauer. New York: Harper & Row, 1965.

Inwood, Michael. *A Heidegger Dictionary*. Oxford: Blackwell, 1999.

James, William. "Religious Experience." In *Philosophy of Religion: Selected Readings*. 4th ed., edited by Michael Peterson, William Hasker, Bruce Reichenbach, and David Basinger. Oxford: Oxford University Press, 2009: 10–19.

______. *The Varieties of Religious Experience*. New York: New American Library, 1958.

Jameson, Fredric. *Postmodernism, or, the Cultural Logic of Late Capitalism*. London: Verso, 2008.

Janicaud, Dominique. *Chronos: Pour l'intelligence du partage temporel*. Paris: Bernard Grasset, 1997.

______. *Heidegger en France*, vol. 1. Paris: Hachette, 2001.

______. *Heidegger en France*, vol. 2. Paris: Hachette, 2005.

______. *Heidegger in France*. Translated by François Raffoul and David Pettigrew. Bloomington: Indiana University Press, 2015.

______. *La phénoménologie éclatée*. Paris: Editions de l'Eclat, 1998.

______. *La puissance du rationnel*. Paris: Éditions Gallimard, 1985.

______. *Le tournant théologique de la phénoménologie française*. Combas: L'Eclat, 1991.

______. *Phenomenology and the "Theological Turn": The French Debate*. New York: Fordham University Press, 2000.

______. *Phenomenology "Wide Open": After the French Debate*. New York: Fordham University Press, 2005.

______. *Powers of the Rational: Science, Technology, and the Future of Thought*. Translated by Peg Birmingham and Elizabeth Birmingham. Bloomington: Indiana University Press, 1994.

Kandel, Eric R. *The Age of Insight: The Quest to Understand the Unconscious in Art, Mind, and Brain, from Vienna 1900 to the Present*. New York: Random House, 2012.

Kierkegaard, Søren. *Works of Love: Some Christian Reflections in the Form of Discourses*. Translated by Howard and Edna Long. New York: Harper & Row, 1964.

Krummel, J. W. M. "The Originary *Wherein*: Heidegger and Nishida on 'the Sacred' and 'the Religious.'" *Research in Phenomenology* 40, no. 3 (2010): 378–407.

Kühn, Rolf, and Michael Staudigl, eds. *Epoch und Reduktion: Formen und Praxis der Reduktion in der Phenomenologie*. Würzburg: Königshausen & Neumann, 2003.

Kunkel-Razum, Kathrin, ed. *Duden: Das Bedeutungswörterbuch, Band 10*. Mannheim: Duden Verlag, 2002.

Lacoste, Jean-Yves. "The Appearing and the Irreducible." In *Words of Life: New Theological Turns in French Phenomenology*, edited by Bruce Ellis Benson and Norman Wirzba, translated by Christina M. Gschwandtner, 42–67. New York: Fordham University Press, 2010.

______. "Continental Philosophy." In *The Routledge Companion to Philosophy of Religion*, edited by Chad Meister and Paul Copan, 651–60. London: Routledge Press, 2007.

______. *Expérience et absolu: questions disputées sur l'humanité de l'homme*. Paris: Presses Universitaires de France, 1994.

______. *Experience and the Absolute: Disputed Questions on the Humanity of Man*. New York: Fordham University Press, 2004.

______. *From Theology to Theological Thinking*. Translated by William Chris Hackett. Charlottesville, VA: University of Virginia Press, 2014.

______. *Le monde et l'absence d'œuvre et autres etudes*. Paris: Presses Universitaires de France, 2000.

______. "More Haste, Less Speed in Theology." Translated by Oliver O'Donovan. *International Journal of Systematic Theology* 9 (2007): 263–82.

______. "Perception, Transcendence and the Experience of God." In *Transcendence and Phenomenology*, edited by Conner Cunningham and Peter M. Candler Jr., 1–20. London: SCM Press, 2007.

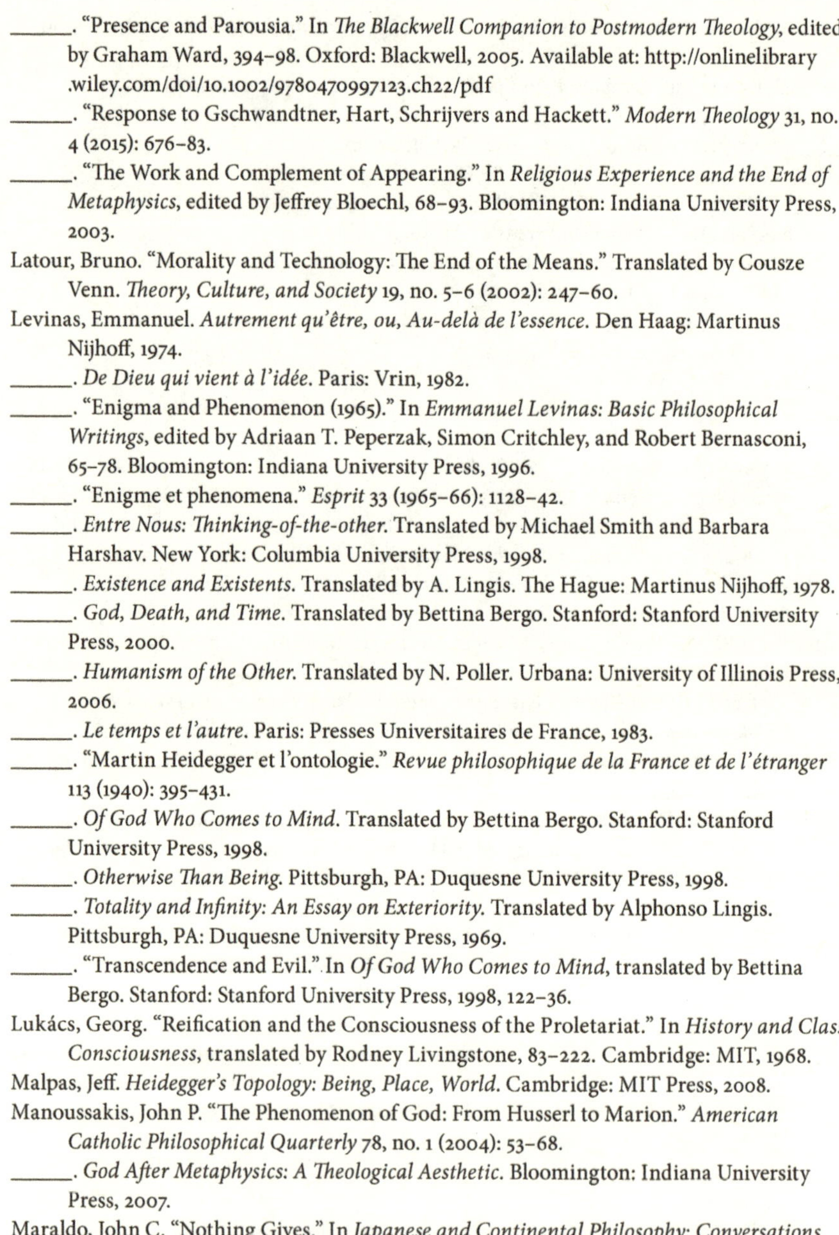

______. "Presence and Parousia." In *The Blackwell Companion to Postmodern Theology*, edited by Graham Ward, 394–98. Oxford: Blackwell, 2005. Available at: http://onlinelibrary.wiley.com/doi/10.1002/9780470997123.ch22/pdf

______. "Response to Gschwandtner, Hart, Schrijvers and Hackett." *Modern Theology* 31, no. 4 (2015): 676–83.

______. "The Work and Complement of Appearing." In *Religious Experience and the End of Metaphysics*, edited by Jeffrey Bloechl, 68–93. Bloomington: Indiana University Press, 2003.

Latour, Bruno. "Morality and Technology: The End of the Means." Translated by Cousze Venn. *Theory, Culture, and Society* 19, no. 5–6 (2002): 247–60.

Levinas, Emmanuel. *Autrement qu'être, ou, Au-delà de l'essence*. Den Haag: Martinus Nijhoff, 1974.

______. *De Dieu qui vient à l'idée*. Paris: Vrin, 1982.

______. "Enigma and Phenomenon (1965)." In *Emmanuel Levinas: Basic Philosophical Writings*, edited by Adriaan T. Peperzak, Simon Critchley, and Robert Bernasconi, 65–78. Bloomington: Indiana University Press, 1996.

______. "Enigme et phenomena." *Esprit* 33 (1965–66): 1128–42.

______. *Entre Nous: Thinking-of-the-other*. Translated by Michael Smith and Barbara Harshav. New York: Columbia University Press, 1998.

______. *Existence and Existents*. Translated by A. Lingis. The Hague: Martinus Nijhoff, 1978.

______. *God, Death, and Time*. Translated by Bettina Bergo. Stanford: Stanford University Press, 2000.

______. *Humanism of the Other*. Translated by N. Poller. Urbana: University of Illinois Press, 2006.

______. *Le temps et l'autre*. Paris: Presses Universitaires de France, 1983.

______. "Martin Heidegger et l'ontologie." *Revue philosophique de la France et de l'étranger* 113 (1940): 395–431.

______. *Of God Who Comes to Mind*. Translated by Bettina Bergo. Stanford: Stanford University Press, 1998.

______. *Otherwise Than Being*. Pittsburgh, PA: Duquesne University Press, 1998.

______. *Totality and Infinity: An Essay on Exteriority*. Translated by Alphonso Lingis. Pittsburgh, PA: Duquesne University Press, 1969.

______. "Transcendence and Evil." In *Of God Who Comes to Mind*, translated by Bettina Bergo. Stanford: Stanford University Press, 1998, 122–36.

Lukács, Georg. "Reification and the Consciousness of the Proletariat." In *History and Class Consciousness*, translated by Rodney Livingstone, 83–222. Cambridge: MIT, 1968.

Malpas, Jeff. *Heidegger's Topology: Being, Place, World*. Cambridge: MIT Press, 2008.

Manoussakis, John P. "The Phenomenon of God: From Husserl to Marion." *American Catholic Philosophical Quarterly* 78, no. 1 (2004): 53–68.

______. *God After Metaphysics: A Theological Aesthetic*. Bloomington: Indiana University Press, 2007.

Maraldo, John C. "Nothing Gives." In *Japanese and Continental Philosophy: Conversations with the Kyoto School*, edited by Bret W. Davis, Brian Schroeder, and Jason M. Wirth, 141–59. Bloomington: Indiana University Press, 2011.

Marion, Jean-Luc. "Aspecte der Religionsphänomenologie: Grund, Horizont und Offenbarung." In *Religionsphilosophie heute*, edited by Alois Halder, Klaus Kinzler, and Joseph Möller, 84–103. Düsseldorf: Patmos Press, 1988.

______. *Being Given: Toward a Phenomenology of Givenness.* Stanford: Stanford University Press, 2002.

______. *Étant donné.* Paris: Presses Universitaires de France, 1997.

______. *In Excess: Studies of Saturated Phenomena.* Translated by Robyn Horner and Vincent Berraud. New York: Fordham University Press, 2002.

______. "The Invisible and the Phenomenon." In *Michel Henry: The Affects of Thought,* edited by Jeffrey Hanson and Michael R. Kelly, chapter translated by Christina M. Gschwandtner, 19–39. New York: Continuum, 2012.

______. "The Irreducible." In *The Journal for Cultural and Religious Theory,* translated by Jason W. Alvis, 2018.

______. "Lacoste ou la correction de l'analytique existentiale." *Transversalités* 2, no. 110 (2009): 169–75.

______. "The Other First Philosophy and the Question of Givenness." Translated by Jeffrey L. Kosky. *Critical Inquiry* 25, no. 4 (1999): 784–800.

______. *Reduction and Givenness: Investigations of Husserl, Heidegger, and Phenomenology.* Translated by Carlson. Evanston: Northwestern University Press, 1998.

______. *Réduction et donation. Recherches sur Husserl, Heidegger et la phénoménologie.* Paris: Presses Universitaires de France, 1989.

______. "Sketch of a Phenomenological Concept of Gift." In *Postmodern Philosophy and Christian Thought,* edited by Merold Westphal, 127–28. Bloomington: Indiana University Press, 1999.

______. *The Visible and the Revealed.* Translated by Christina Gschwandtner. New York: Fordham University Press, 2008.

______. "What We See and What Appears." In *Idol Anxiety,* edited by Josh Ellenbogen and Aaron Tugendhaft, 161–62. Stanford: Stanford University Press, 2011.

Martin, Michael. "Critique of Religious Experience." In *Philosophy of Religion: Selected Readings,* edited by Michael Peterson, William Hasker, Bruce Reichenbach, and David Basinger. Oxford: Oxford University Press, 2009: 41–55.

McNeill, William. *The Glance of the Eye: Heidegger, Aristotle, and the Ends of Theory.* Albany: State University of New York Press, 1999.

Merleau-Ponty, Maurice. *Phénoménologie de la perception.* Paris: Éditions Gallimard, 1945.

______. *Phenomenology of Perception.* Translated by Donald A. Landes. New York: Routledge, 2013.

______. *Notes de cours, 1959–61.* Paris: Éditions Gallimard, 1996.

Miller, Adam S. *The Gospel According to David Foster Wallace: Boredom and Addiction in an Age of Distraction.* London: Bloomsbury, 2016.

Moltmann, Jürgen. *God in Creation: A New Theology of Creation and the Spirit of God.* Translated by Margaret Kohl. San Francisco: Harper & Row, 1985.

______. *The Spirit of Life: A Universal Affirmation.* Philadelphia, PA: Fortress Press, 2001.

Moore, Ian Alexander. "*Gelassenheit,* the Middle Voice, and the Unity of Heidegger's Thought." In *Perspektiven mit Heidegger,* edited by Gerhard Thonhauser, 25–39. Freiburg: Karl Aber, 2017.

Moran, Dermot. *Husserl's Crisis of the European Sciences and Transcendental Phenomenology: An Introduction.* Cambridge: Cambridge University Press, 2012.

Müller, Max. "Ein Gespräch mit Max Müller." Edited by Bernd Martin and Gottfried Schramm. *Freiburger Universitätsblätter* 92 (June 1986): 13–31.

Nancy, Jean-Luc. *Adoration: The Deconstruction of Christianity II.* New York: Fordham University Press 2012.

______. *The Creation of the World, or Globalization*. Translated by François Raffoul and David Pettigrew. Albany: State University of New York Press, 2007.

______. *Disenclosure: The Deconstruction of Christianity*. New York: Fordham University Press, 2008.

______. *God, Justice, Love, Beauty: Four Little Dialogues*. New York: Fordham University Press, 2011.

______. *L'Adoration: Déconstruction du christianisme 2*. Paris: Editions Galilée, 2010.

______. *La creation du monde ou la mondialisation*. Paris: Editions Galilée, 2002.

______. "La Déconstruction du christianisme." *Etudes philosophiques* 4 (1998): 503–19.

______. *Noli Me Tangere: On the Raising of the Body*. New York: Fordham University Press, 2008.

______. "Of Divine Places." In *The Inoperative Community*, translated by Peter Connor, Lisa Garbus, M. Holland, and S. Sawhney. Minneapolis: University of Minnesota Press, 1991: 110–50.

______. *The Pleasure in Drawing*. Translated by Philip Armstrong. New York: Fordham University Press, 2013.

Niebuhr, Richard H. *Radical Monotheism and Western Culture: With Supplementary Essays*. Louisville, KY: Westminster/John Knox Press, 1993.

Nietzsche, Friedrich. *Beyond Good and Evil: Prelude to a Philosophy of the Future*. Edited by Rolf-Peter Horstmann and Judith Norman. Cambridge: Cambridge University Press, 2003.

______. *Unfashionable Observations*. Vol. 2 of *The Complete Works of Friedrich Nietzsche*. Edited by Ernst Behler and translated by Richard T. Gray. Stanford: Stanford University Press, 1995.

______. "Unpublished Notes." In *Beyond Good and Evil*. Edited by Marion Faber. Oxford: Oxford University Press, 1998: 181–92.

Ó Murchadha, Felix. *Phenomenology of Christian Life: Glory and Night*. Bloomington: Indiana University Press, 2013.

Otto, Rudolph. *The Idea of the Holy: An Inquiry into the Non-rational Factor in the Idea of the Divine and Its Relation to the Rational*. Translated by John W. Harvey. Oxford: Oxford University Press, 1958.

Plato. *The Republic*. Book 10 in *The Dialogues of Plato*. Translated by B Jowett. Oxford: Clarendon Press, 1990.

Pöggeler, Otto. *Martin Heidegger's Path of Thinking*. Amherst, NY: Humanity Books, 1991.

Pollock, John L. *Contemporary Theories of Knowledge*. Totowa, NJ: Rowman & Littlefield, 1986.

Polt, Richard F. H. *The Emergency of Being: On Heidegger's Contributions to Philosophy*. Ithaca, NY: Cornell University Press, 2006.

Prevot, Andrew L. "Responsorial Thought: Jean-Louis Chrétien's Distinctive Approach to Theology and Phenomenology." *The Heythrop Journal* 56, no. 6 (2015): 975–87.

Proudfoot, Wayne. *Religious Experience*. Berkeley: University of California Press, 1985.

Raschke, Carl. *Force of God: Political Theology and the Crisis of Liberal Democracy*. New York: Columbia University Press, 2015.

Rhodius Apollonius. *The Voyage of Argo: The Argonautica*. Translated by E. V. Rieu. Harmondsworth, Middlesex: Penguin Books, 1971.

Ricoeur, Paul. *Essays on Biblical Interpretation*. Translated by Lewis Seymour Mudge. Philadelphia: Fortress Press, 1980.

Rockmore, Tom. *Heidegger and French Philosophy: Humanism, Antihumanism, and Being.* New York: Routledge, 1995.

Scheler, Max. Gesammelte Werke: *Der Formalismus der Ethik und die materiale Wertethik.* Edited by Maria Scheler. Bern: Francke, 1966.

Schenk-Mair, Katarina. *Die Kosmologie Eugen Finks.* Würzburg: Königshausen & Neumann, 1997.

Schleiermacher, Friedrich. *On Religion: Addresses in Response to its Cultured Critics.* Translated by Terrence N. Tice. Louisville, KY: Westminster John Knox, 1969.

Schrijvers, Joeri. "God and/in Phenomenology: Jean-Yves Lacoste's *Phenomenality of God.*" *Bijdragen, International Journal in Philosophy and Theology* 71, no. 1 (2010): 85–93.

______. "Jean-Yves Lacoste: A Phenomenology of Liturgy." *Heythrop Journal* 46, no. 3 (2005): 314–33.

______. *Ontotheological Turnings? The Decentering of the Modern Subject in Recent French Phenomenology.* Albany: State University of New York Press, 2011.

Schweitzer, Albert. *The Quest for the Historical Jesus.* Translated by W. Montgomery. Minola, NY: Dover, 2012.

Sheehan, Thomas. *Making Sense of Heidegger: A Paradigm Shift.* London: Rowman & Littlefield International, 2014.

______. "Reading a Life: Heidegger in Hard Times." In *The Cambridge Companion to Heidegger*, edited by Charles Guignon, 70–93. Cambridge: Cambridge University Press, 1993.

______. "Translator's introduction to 'Phenomenology,' Draft B (of the Encyclopaedia Britannica Article) with Heidegger's Letter to Husserl" in *Becoming Heidegger: On the Trail of His Early Occasional Writings*, 1910–1927. Edited by Theodore Kisiel and Thomas Sheehan. Chicago: Northwestern University Press, 2007: 304–6.

______. "What, after All, Was Heidegger About?." *Continental Philosophy Review* 47, no. 3 (2014): 249–74.

Simmons, J. Aaron, and Bruce Ellis Benson. *The New Phenomenology.* London: Bloomsbury, 2013.

Spiegelberg, Herbert. *The Phenomenological Movement: A Historical Introduction.* The Hague: Martinus Nijhoff, 1960.

Spinoza, Baruch. "Ethics." In Vol. 1 of *The Collected Works of Spinoza*, edited and translated by Edwin Curley, 408–620. Princeton: Princeton University Press, 1985.

Staudigl, Michael. *Die Grenzen der Intentionalität.* Würzburg: Königshausen & Neumann, 2003.

______. "From the 'Metaphysics of the Individual' to the Critique of Society: On the Practical Significance of Michel Henry's Phenomenology of Life." *Continental Philosophy Review* 45, no. 3 (2012): 339–61.

Steinbock, Anthony J. *Home and Beyond: Generative Phenomenology after Husserl.* Evanston: Northwestern University Press, 1995.

______. *Phenomenology and Mysticism: The Verticality of Religious Experience.* Bloomington: Indiana University Press, 2007.

______. "The Problem of Forgetfulness in Michel Henry." *Continental Philosophy Review* 32, no. 3 (1999): 271–302.

______. "Saturated Intentionality," In *The Body: Classic and Contemporary Readings*, edited by Donn Welton, 178–99. Malden, MA: Blackwell Publishers, 1999.

Sweeney, Conor. *Sacramental Presence After Heidegger: Onto-theology, Sacraments, and the Mother's Smile*. Eugene, OR: Cascade Books, 2015.

Symons, Stéphane. "The Ability to Not-shine: The Word 'Unscheinbar' in the Writings of Walter Benjamin." *Angelaki: Journal of the Theoretical Humanities* 18, no. 4 (2013): 101–23.

Taminiaux, Jacques. "Heidegger and Husserl's *Logical Investigations:* In Remembrance of Heidegger's Last Seminar." *Research in Phenomenology* 7, no. 1 (1977): 58–83.

Tengelyi, László. "New Phenomenology in France." *Southern Journal of Philosophy* 50, no. 2 (2012): 295–303.

______. "Selfhood, Passivity and Affectivity in Henry and Lévinas." *International Journal of Philosophical Studies* 17, no. 3 (2009): 401–14.

Tengelyi, László, and Hans-Dieter Gondek. *Neue Phänomenologie in Frankreich*. Frankfurt: Suhrkamp, 2011.

Tillich, Paul. *Dynamics of Faith*. New York: Harper One, 2009.

Trawny, Peter. "Die unscheinbare Differenz. Heideggers Grundlegung einer Ethik der Sprache." In *Phénoménologie française et phénoménologie allemande*, edited by Eliane Escoubas and Bernhard Waldenfels, 65–102. Paris: Harmattan, 2000.

Volf, Miroslav. *The End of Memory: Remembering Rightly in a Violent World*. Grand Rapids, MI: Eerdmans Publishing, 2006.

Waldenfels, Bernhard. "Antwort auf das Fremde. GrundzüAge einer responsiven Phänomenologier." In *Der Anspruch des Anderen. Perspektiven phänomenologischer Ethik*, edited by Bernhard Waldenfels and Iris Därmann, 7–14. Munich: Wilhelm Fink, 1998.

______. *Hyperphänomene. Modi hyperbolischer Erfahrung*. Frankfurt: Suhrkamp, 2012.

______. *Phänomenologie in Frankreich*. Frankfurt: Suhrkamp, 1983.

Weber, Samuel. *Benajamin's-abilities*. Cambridge: Harvard University Press, 2008.

Westphal, Merold. "A Phenomenological Account of Religious Experience." In *Philosophy of Religion: Selected Readings*. 4th ed., edited by Michael Peterson, William Hasker, Bruce Reichenbach, and David Basinger, 56–63. Oxford: Oxford University Press, 2009.

______. *Overcoming Onto-theology: Toward a Postmodern Christian Faith*. New York: Fordham University Press, 2001.

Withy, Katherine. *Heidegger on Being Uncanny*. Cambridge: Harvard University Press, 2015.

Wittgenstein, Ludwig. *Philosophical Investigations*. Edited by G. E. M. Anscombe. Oxford: Basil Blackwell, 1953.

______. *Tractatus Logico-Philosophicus*. London: Kegan Paul, 1922.

Wolfe, Judith. *Heidegger and Theology*. London: Bloomsbury, 2014.

Yandell, Keith. *The Epistemology of Religious Experience*. Cambridge: Cambridge University Press, 1993.

Yates, Christopher. "Checking Janicaud's Arithmetic: How Phenomenology and Theology 'Make Two.'" In *Analecta Hermeneutica* 1, no. 1 (2009): 73–92 online here: http://journals.library.mun.ca/ojs/index.php/analecta/article/view/7.

Zahavi, Dan. "Michel Henry and the Phenomenology of the Invisible." *Continental Philosophy Review* 32 (1999): 223–40.

Index

JASON W. ALVIS is Research Fellow and Lecturer in the Institute for Philosophy at the University of Vienna. He is author of *Marion and Derrida on the Gift and Desire: Debating the Generosity of Things* (Springer Press 2016) and European Editor for *The Journal for Cultural and Religious Theory.*

www.ingramcontent.com/pod-product-compliance
Lightning Source LLC
LaVergne TN
LVHW041111090826
844660LV00056B/154

* 9 7 8 0 2 5 3 0 3 3 3 2 1 *